DOWN RAMP!

DOWN RAMP!

The Story of the
Army Amphibian Engineers

BRIGADIER GENERAL
WILLIAM F. HEAVEY

COACHWHIP PUBLICATIONS

Landisville, Pennsylvania

Down Ramp!, by Brigadier General William F. Heavey
Copyright © 2010 Coachwhip Publications
First published 1947.
No claims made on public domain material.

ISBN 1-61646-057-1
ISBN-13 978-1-61646-057-0

  Front Cover: Preparing for Normandy, U. S. National Archives
  Back Cover: Omaha Beach, U. S. National Archives
  Front & Back Cover: Badges, Army Amphibian Engineers

CoachwhipBooks.com

CONTENTS

FOREWORD

Landing an army on a hostile shore has long been regarded as one of the most difficult of all tactical operations. Even if the expanse of water to be crossed is only a river and not an ocean, history has proved the danger and costliness of such operations. After tremendous preparations Alexander the Great crossed the Hellespont successfully, but no enemy opposed him on the far shore. Weather alone defeated the Spanish Armada's attempt to invade England. The cost in blood of an unsuccessful river crossing was demonstrated all too vividly at Fredericksburg in 1863. The British experienced the sting of defeat in the failure of the Dardanelles campaign in World War I.

Yet we entered World War II with stretches of water varying from the 50-mile turbulent English Channel to the 5,000-mile expanse of the Pacific separating us from our mortal enemies. We must cross these waters and make successful landings on enemy-held shores to get at our enemies. To all military students except a few extremists it was obvious that we would never win until our infantry crossed those waters to crush the enemy's heart. Air attacks without an atomic bomb or a naval blockade, no matter how stringent, could never do that alone.

As has always been its tradition in new developments, the Corps of Engineers made vital contributions to this amphibious part of World War II. This book strives to present the accomplishments and operations of the Amphibian Engineers in World War II. It is the story of the six brigades and the two separate battalions the Corps of Engineers launched to help win the Victory.

Grateful acknowledgment is made to the following Amphibians without whose help this account could not have been written: 1st Brigade: Brigadier General Henry Wolfe, Colonel E. M. Caffey, and Lieutenant Colonel Earl Houston; 2d Brigade: Major Barron Collier, Jr., and First Lieutenant L. S. Moore; 3d Brigade: Brigadier General D. A. D. Ogden; 4th Brigade: Brigadier General Henry Hutchings; 5th Brigade: Colonel W. D. Bridges; 6th Brigade: Colonel Howard Ker.

W. F. H.

1
Birth and Origin

Shortly after the Japs struck at Pearl Harbor, thoughts of all military commanders turned to how to get at the enemy both in the Atlantic and the Pacific. We could never win the war on the defensive. We must take up the offensive. In both the major theaters it would be necessary to cross extensive stretches of water to get at the enemy. Of course it would be the mission of the Navy to carry the Army safely through submarine-infested waters to near the enemy shore. But what about getting from *ship* to *shore?* How could this be best done and who should control it? Also what about *shore-to-shore* movements after the initial hold on the enemy shore was won? The Japs in their rapid campaign in the Malay Peninsula which resulted in the surprisingly quick fall of Singapore had only too effectively demonstrated early in 1942 the advantages of using the water for shore-to-shore movements rather than the land through its roadless jungles and in the face of a defender's hot fire. It was much better to bypass such obstacles by water than to force one's way through them, to go around a defensive position rather than through it; to land waterborne troops on beach after beach to outflank the enemy instead of making a costly overland attack.

It was obvious that World War II would not only be an *air* war and a *mechanized* War but also an *amphibious* War. The Army, the Navy, and the Marines had all given some thought to an amphibious war. Small-scale maneuvers with very limited equipment had been held in Puerto Rico and off the Carolina coasts. Thought had

been given to converting boats so they could be used for beach landings, but we all had to admit that in January 1942 the Japs were
far ahead of us not only in amphibious equipment but also in the
tactics of amphibious warfare. As a matter of fact they were far
ahead of the Germans, too. Had the Nazis been as far advanced in
the field of amphibious warfare in 1940 as the Japs were in 1941,
Britain might well have been invaded after France fell. Instead,
the German High Command admitted after the armistice that they
had no amphibious equipment ready for the invasion of Britain,
when Belgium and France crumbled sooner than expected.

With characteristic ingenuity the U.S. Navy quickly pushed the
development of special craft for landings. Some types of British
craft were copied but greatly improved. In early 1942, though, the
Navy felt it could not train a sufficient number of boatmen to meet
the demands of a channel invasion in Europe and the unknown
but extensive amphibious operations bound to come in the Pacific.
When it was suggested that the Army train and man some of the
landing craft to carry soldiers from ship to shore, the plan fell upon
fertile ground.

Colonel (later Major General) Daniel Noce was the pioneer who
foresaw the need for Army amphibian troops, not only operating
small landing craft, but also doing the essential shore engineering
on the beaches. Lieutenant General Lesley J. McNair, head of the
Ground Forces, and his Chief of Staff, Colonel (later General) Mark
W. Clark, first had to be won over to the important need for these
new specialized types of troops. Some thought combat engineers
could become specialists in this new type of operations by simply
taking some extra training. Colonel Noce pointed out that combat
engineers would always have their hands full with their own duties,
that highly trained amphibian specialists, knitted into well oiled
teams, would be needed to make successful landings.

Then came the problem of developing correct technique. What
craft and what navigation and signal equipment would be needed?
Beach markers? How about infra-red and ultra-violet for night
operations? What shore equipment? Wire mesh or steel plank for

roads? Cranes, fork-lifts, beach sleds? How to overcome obstacles on the beaches and under water? A thousand other problems. And where should the lines of demarcation be drawn between the Navy and the Army Amphibian Engineers and the Combat Engineers of the assault divisions?

Lieutenant General (later General) Brehon Somervell as Commanding General, Services of Supply (later Army Service Forces) was directed on May 9, 1942, to establish a boat training center at Camp Edwards, Massachusetts, and to be prepared to initiate combined training with an infantry division by July 15, 1942. The Chief of Engineers was charged with this mission. It was a tremendous task in a new field of operations and called for prompt and vigorous action. Colonel Noce, assisted by his imaginative Chief of Staff, Colonel Arthur G. Trudeau, established the Engineer Amphibian Command to carry out the War Department directive. Originally it was planned to organize 18 Engineer regiments (boat operating) and 7 Engineer Boat Maintenance battalions. Before these units were started, it was realized that in addition to engineers operating boats to get the troops ashore, special engineers would be needed to prepare the shore and to unload the heavy artillery, tanks, etc., which would be necessary to support the landing troops. Accordingly the type of organization shifted to a brigade made up basically of a regiment of boat engineers, a regiment of shore engineers, a boat maintenance battalion, and miscellaneous special troops. The soundness of integrating boat with shore engineers, signal, maintenance, ordnance and supply units into a team to be paired off with an infantry division or regimental combat team proved itself throughout the war. On June 5, 1942, the organization of 8 such brigades was authorized but later this was reduced to 3, only later to be expanded to 6.

The first training memorandum of the Engineer Amphibian Command dated July 27, 1942, stated the mission of the Command as follows:

> To organize, equip, train, operate, and administer such engineer amphibian units as may be needed

from time to time in the various theaters of operations, for shore-to-shore operations. Each such amphibian unit will normally be charged with the function of transporting troops of the combat unit to
which it is attached, or of which it is in direct support, together with equipment and supplies required
for these operations. These units are further charged
with control and improvement of the far shore, debarkation and movement of supplies to troops beyond the beach proper and evacuation and control
of landing craft, casualties, and prisoners of war
from the far shore.

It is interesting to note that the mission was restricted to shore-
to-shore operations. This was in deference to the Navy but it was
realized that in actual practice the Army Amphibian Engineers
would be employed along with the Navy in ship-to-shore operations as well as shore-to-shore. Their doctrine was worked up with
that in view. Both in the Atlantic and the Pacific, but to a much
greater degree in the Pacific, later operations confirmed the accuracy of this conclusion. By that time the Navy's opinion of the
Army's Amphibian Engineers had gone up so much they were glad
to have us reinforce them. In the early days, though, there was
considerable distrust and lack of confidence on the part of the Navy.
It was no easy job to win them over.

To carry out its mission the Engineer Amphibian Command had
to develop an entirely new doctrine of shore-to-shore operations.
All amphibious training undertaken previously by the Navy, the
Coast Guard and the Marines and by the few ground units which
had participated in amphibious operations was reviewed and much
of it utilized or adopted. The experiences of the British Navy and
Army were studied. The methods and equipment used by the Japs
in their successful amphibious operations in Malaya were carefully
scrutinized. In the field of navigation and control of landing craft,
the U.S. Coast and Geodetic Survey was particularly helpful. The
staff at Camp Edwards included not only Army officers of all

branches but also Navy, Coast Guard, Coast and Geodetic Survey, and British Army and Navy officers. The records of 200,000 officers and 3,000,000 enlisted men were reviewed in order to obtain personnel with aptitude or experience along the lines needed. To develop the best methods of boat maintenance and operation, civilian boat operators, both professional and amateur, were sought direct from civil life. Between June 1, 1942, and August 15, 1942, through the medium of yacht clubs, boating organizations, maritime publications, etc., four hundred officers were obtained by direct commission. The U.S. Power Squadrons were particularly helpful.

How the Engineer Amphibian Command sought boat officers is exemplified by this article which appeared in *Motor Boating* for July 1942:

> At last men operating small motor boats may contribute their services to the national war effort. The Army of the United States, recognizing the valuable work that small boat operators can perform, has organized the Engineer Amphibian Command for small boat, shallow draft, and off-shore operations. This Command has been ordered to train men in the five points of boat handling; boat handlers will be instructed in the military uses of small craft. The instructors of the military personnel should be men who have had at least ten years experience in small boat operation and maintenance. Men who are not afraid of going out in fog or heavy seas, who are willing and anxious to take chances for the national security, are the type desired.
>
> The Engineer Amphibian Command in its contribution to outpunch the Axis cannot use the following:
>
> 1. "Alibi-Ikes." Men who always can give a reason why their boat is not ready for sail or cruise, why they always are late at the starting line or seldom

finish a race. Action, not talk, is the language of the EAC.

2. Full-dress Admirals. They will continue to be needed at home to command the rocking-chair and fair-weather sailors.

3. Moonlight romanticists. The EAC is not organized to make love to the Axis!

4. Timid souls. Rough weather is ahead.

5. Canoe and rowboat sailors. The boys who sail 70-foot lakes.

6. Down-the-hatch sailors. The boys who rough it with "John Barleycorn."

7. Home-made maintenance sailors. These boys try to fix it and have to be towed to port, or never leave the dock.

8. The "Sloppy Joe Sailors." The boys who never clean their boats down, or put it off until tomorrow.

The EAC expects to commission a limited number of qualified civilians during the next three months. These men will be hand-picked by the personnel officer in conformance with the usual War Department standards and with the additional special qualifications listed below.

SPECIFIC QUALIFICATIONS FOR OFFICERS

1. Motor and sail boat operators. Owners or crew officers that can pilot or navigate small motor or sail boats.

2. Marine engineers, inboard or outboard. Those who have run a shop employing at least five marine mechanics.

3. Boat builders. Yard superintendents who have run boat yards employing over six men.

4. Marine and diesel engine men. Owners or superintendents of shops employing better than ten marine or diesel engine men.

The men with the above qualifications in addition to approximately four years experience must be skilled in the handling of men and be able to assume command and administrative responsibilities.

The age requirements are as follows:

Second Lieutenant, 24 to 30 (approximate pay, $190 per mo.) First Lieutenant, 31 to 34 (approximate pay, $260 per mo.) Captain, 34 to 41 (approximate pay, $300 per mo.)

A few field officers with previous military experience between the ages of 42 and 52 and possessing unusually high qualifications will be commissioned.

What to Do

Men of qualified experience who are interested in a commission in the Engineer Amphibian Command should supply the following information to the Engineer Amphibian Command, Office of the Chief of Engineers, Room 3112, New War Department Building, 21st and Virginia Avenue, Washington, D. C.:

Name, age, education, degree, major field, civilian occupation, salary, civilian hobbies, motor boat experience, lowest rank acceptable, limitation on availability.

On the whole, this group commissioned directly from civilian life after a short course in military training at Camp Edwards did exceptionally well in their specialties, especially in boat maintenance and procurement. What they lacked in military background was far outweighed by their technical value in their specialties. In early 1943 seventy-five more officers were commissioned directly from civilian life for assignment to the newly organized 4th Engineer Special Brigade and to the 692d Engineer Base Shop Battalion.

While the brigades were termed *Engineer* Amphibian (later Special) Brigades and all officers in the regiments either commissioned in or detailed to the Corps of Engineers, actually the officers and men came from all branches of the Army and from nearly all walks of civilian life. This proved to be fortunate for later on no matter what job the Engineer Special Brigades were called upon to do, there were always on hand men with special qualifications for it. When the 2d Engineer Special Brigade needed experts to handle the new 4.5-inch rockets it introduced in the Southwest Pacific, the Artillery and Ordnance men in that brigade proved invaluable. When the 6th Engineer Special Brigade was handed the unusual job, for Amphibian Engineers, of putting enemy coal mines in Europe back into operation, it had the specialists to do the job quickly and thoroughly.

For the primary activation of the Engineer Amphibian Command, personnel came from the 37th Engineer Combat Regiment, the 87th Engineer Battalion (Heavy Ponton), and six Quartermaster and Ordnance units, all of which were absorbed in the new amphibian units. Some five hundred officers were transferred from other organizations, 825 were ordered to the Engineer Amphibian Command from reserve status, and to December 31, 1943, a thousand more came as graduates of Officer Candidate Schools.

The 37,650 enlisted men up to the end of 1943 came from replacement training centers (20,250), reception centers (11,900) and transfers from other organizations of the Army. The War Department helped by ordering in from other organizations specialists such as able seamen, motor boat operators, and former sailors. About 1,300 men were recruited directly by the Engineer Amphibian Command, nearly all of whom were specialists on boats. However, the Command itself and its brigades were the real training schools for the mass of the officers and men. Reliance upon "claimed" skills proved unreliable and military methods were naturally different in some respects than civilian or yacht club procedures. It was in the excellent and varied schools of the Engineer Amphibian Command on Cape Cod and later at Carrabelle that the men were really made specialists. Too much credit cannot be given to the instructors of these schools for their thorough training and their original research.

The outstanding innovation of the Engineer Amphibian Command was the combination of boat engineers and shore engineers with supporting boat maintenance, signal, ordnance and quartermaster troops into an integrated and balanced team, the only one of its kind in any of the Allied armies. That this team paid dividends is exemplified by the fact that army commanders wanted nine such brigades for the invasions of Japan when only three were available and by General MacArthur's letter to the Chief of Staff quoted below:

GENERAL HEADQUARTERS
SOUTHWEST PACIFIC AREA
APO 500
19 March 1945
AG 370.2 (19 Mar 45) E

SUBJECT: Engineer Special Brigades.
To: The Chief of Staff, War Department, Washington 25, D. C.

1. In the succession of amphibious operations up the coast of New Guinea to Morotai, thence to the Philippines, the performance of the 2d, 3d and 4th Engineer Special Brigades has been outstanding. The soundness of the decision in 1942 to form organizations of this type has been borne out in all action in which they have participated. These units have contributed much to the rapid and successful prosecution of the Southwest Pacific Area. I recommend that careful consideration be given to the perpetuation and expansion of such units in the future Army set-up.

2. I pass on to you an item extracted from a report to me from Headquarters, Administrative Command, Seventh Amphibious Force, file A16-3, Serial

No. 0078, dated 15 February 1945, subject: "Reports
of the Lingayen Operation–San Fabian Attack
Forces."

"It is believed that the Engineer Special Brigade
as organized in the Southwest Pacific Area is the
most efficient shore party organization now functioning in amphibious warfare and that the permanent organizations of these regiments have contributed in a large measure to the success of amphibious operation in this theater."

DOUGLAS MACARTHUR
General of the Army,
United States Army
Commander-in-Chief.

It is true that in the European Theater the boat elements of the
brigades did not man landing craft except on a limited scale in the
North Africa landing. However, many think a boat-shore brigade
type of organization would have obtained better results than the
separate and distinct Navy small boat units and Army shore elements used in the Mediterranean and in the Normandy invasion.
Certainly the tonnages handled by the Engineer Special Brigades
in their operations in the western Pacific with their permanently
organized boat-shore teams exceeded the *pro rata* results obtained
in amphibious operations in the European Theater. It must be re-
membered, however, that no two beach operations are ever the
same. Tide, surf, enemy opposition, and obstacles vary in every
case so that accurate comparisons of any two operations are im-
practicable.

After an exhaustive but rapid study of all available sites, Camp
Edwards, Massachusetts, was chosen as the initial site for the headquarters of the Engineer Amphibian Command. It was realized that
winter would curtail training in that vicinity but the immediate
availability of an established army camp with existing housing,
supply and communication facilities only eight miles from Vineyard Sound with its varied beaches, bays, and islands outweighed

the disadvantages of a cold winter. It was necessary to get started without a minute's delay. By winter another site requiring more time for development could be obtained but now there was no time to wait. It is a historical coincidence that a "boat" regiment, Colonel John Glover's Amphibians, had been trained in Massachusetts 167 years before—to make the Delaware River crossing under General George Washington.

Headquarters of the Engineer Amphibian Command opened at Camp Edwards, Massachusetts, on June 10, 1942. The waters and varied beaches of Nantucket and Martha's Vineyard were ideal for training for shore-to-shore operations. Camp Edwards provided suitable camp facilities for the divisional troops to participate with the Amphibians in the combined operations. However, providing docks, mooring areas and fuel facilities for the large number of landing craft was a difficult problem.

In late May 1942 at a conference in London of General Somervell, Lord Louis Mountbatten (then Chief of Combined Operations), and General Sir John Dill, it was decided that the Amphibian Engineers for that theater would receive their initial training in the U.S. and their final in England. It was further decided that the U.S. Amphibian Engineers would wear the Combined Operations shoulder patch—gold tommy gun, anchor and eagle on a blue field, signifying combined operations on land, sea and air. The same patch in a different color combination was worn by the British Commandos and later, in red and gold, by the U.S. Navy Amphibious Forces. In addition, to denote the engineer amphibians, the War Department authorized wearing a pocket patch, a small sea horse in scarlet and white, the Engineer colors. It is interesting to note that Lord Mountbatten himself designed the Combined Operations patch and showed it to President Roosevelt.

It must be recalled that, in May 1942, the British idea of the cross-Channel invasion was a shore-to-shore operation. It was not until months later that the ship-to-shore plan actually used in the Normandy invasion was adopted.

Washburn Island on Waquoit Bay was the first area developed for boats. By June 28, with the assistance of the Boston Army

Engineer District, a system of docks and piers had been constructed, roads built, utilities constructed, allowing the 591st Engineer Boat Regiment of the 1st Engineer Special Brigade to occupy the island as its regimental area. Much to the dismay of some of the summer visitors, work went ahead full speed with great emphasis on night training. The boat regiments of all the brigades from the 1st to the 4th, as well as the 692d Engineer Base Shop Battalion, conducted some of their training from this area. Additional areas along Cotuit Bay were leased in late July 1942 and developed as Camp Candoit by the 592d Engineer Boat Regiment of the 2d Engineer Special Brigade. The 562d Engineer Boat Maintenance Company (later Battalion) of the same brigade developed the boat maintenance yards at Falmouth. The 692d Engineer Base Shop Battalion was the last unit to train in this area, closing it out in December 1943.

The Crosby Yacht Yard at Osterville was acquired on July 15, 1942. The marine maintenance detachment of the Engineer Amphibian Command first occupied this area, followed in rapid succession by the boat maintenance units of the 2d, 3d and 4th Brigades and by the power plant repair and hull repair companies of the 411th and 692d Base Shop Battalions. Not until January 1944 was this area returned to its owners. Within the Command this area was known as Camp Havdonit.

Provincetown Bay, near the tip of Cape Cod, was the site of tests to determine the extent to which DUKWs[1] could carry out in rough water the mission for which they were designed. These tests were conducted under the direct supervision of the Office of Scientific Research and Development, assisted by the National Defense Research Committee and fifteen civilian specialists. The Engineer Amphibian Command furnished equipment and a special detachment of 5 officers and 60 enlisted men. The 36th Infantry Division then taking amphibious training at Cotuit also furnished personnel. These special tests were conducted in November and December 1942 and had much to do with the successful development of this outstanding contribution to amphibious warfare.

When the 4th Brigade was activated in early 1943, the Camp Edwards area was so crowded it was necessary to utilize Fort Devens, northwest of Boston, for the basic training of that brigade until it could be moved to Camp Edwards about the middle of March 1943.

But when the Engineer Amphibian Command opened its Headquarters at Camp Edwards on June 10, 1942, the immediate job was to develop the proper organization, equipment, and technique and to whip the first units into shape as operating units capable of successfully landing troops on enemy shores and then unloading supplies and reinforcements to keep them there. The officers and men arriving there day by day wasted no time in becoming imbued with their jobs. The enthusiasm and spirit of the Command was really beyond description. No one reporting for duty could fail to feel it.

NOTES

[1] A DUKW is a 2½-ton amphibian truck, the workhorse of amphibious warfare.

2
EARLY DAYS AT CAPE COD

One of the major problems confronting the Engineer Amphibian Command as soon as it was formed was where the line should be drawn between the Army and the Navy, not only in the size of the craft the Army Amphibians would be allowed to operate but also on the question of the line of demarcation on the beachheads. It was fairly obvious that the Army Amphibians to accomplish their shore-to-shore missions would have to have both LCVP[1] (36-foot) to carry personnel and the LCM (50-foot) to carry trucks, artillery and tanks, all too large for the LCVP. But the question of whether the next larger craft, the LCT (105-foot) should be operated by either Army or Navy or only by the Navy led to many discussions. The speed of LCTs and their type of engines fell in the class of the LCM and the LCVP but the Navy wanted to retain control of all *ships*, admitting that the Army would need small boats. Finally it was decided to restrict the Army Amphibians to 36-foot and 50-foot landing craft. Later the Army Amphibians in the Pacific operated the LCM6 which was fifty-six feet long but, although the question of assigning LCTs to the Engineer Special Brigades kept recurring in the Pacific, they were never *assigned* to the brigades although frequently attached. The LCTs in the western Pacific did more work directly for the Army than they ever did for the Navy. They worked in close conjunction with the Shore Engineers and with the LCMs of the Engineer Special Brigades.

It was decided the Navy would handle the construction of all landing craft, allotting LCVPs and LCMs to the Engineer Amphibian

Command and supplying the spare parts. The Engineer Amphibian Command was authorized to study the design of these and similar craft and recommend improvements. More will be said later of the progress in these respects.

Another major problem was schools for specialists. Arrangements were made to train men as ship carpenters and mechanics at special schools at the Gray Marine Motor Company in Michigan; at Higgins Industries in Louisiana; and at Evinrude Motors and Manitowoc Shipbuilding Company, both in Wisconsin. In addition, schools for specialists were set up at Cape Cod so that those returning from the schools could serve as instructors for the larger classes to follow. By June 30, 1942, there were over a thousand officers in the Engineer Amphibian Command—28 from the Regular Army, 825 from the Officers Reserve Corps, 163 newly commissioned second lieutenants from Officer Candidate Schools, and the first contingent of 138 directly commissioned from civilian life. Six months later there were 2,899 officers and 37,651 enlisted men in the Engineer Amphibian Command.

Schools on Cape Cod were of all kinds from the advanced school for Amphibian officers to a welding and propeller school which instructed twenty-four students every four weeks. These schools were in addition to those established at civilian industrial companies, but utilized their graduates as instructors. Other students were sent to Army Ordnance School at Aberdeen, Maryland, to Naval Operating Base, Toledo, Ohio, and to the Army Motor School at Holabird, Maryland. Tractor operators and mechanics attended a school at Dunedin, Florida. To give some idea of the extent of this schooling, the summary of enlisted men trained is tabulated:

Where Trained	Number
At service schools outside the Engineer Amphibian Command	1,481
At civilian schools outside the Engineer Amphibian Command	3,368
In schools conducted by the Engineer Amphibian Command	33,627

New training manuals had to be prepared, frequently on subjects never before covered. Major Ralph Ingersoll (late Editor of *PM*) edited these manuals in a particularly interesting and descriptive manner. These manuals translated the language of the military and the sea into simple terms new men could understand. Experience in firing weapons was a major goal which paid off in lives saved later on. It was necessary to build new ranges at Camp Edwards and at Poponesset Bay on the Sound. The waterfront there was used as the firing line for antiaircraft firing out to sea.

A development board was formed under Colonel W. D. Luplow to carry out experimental projects on landing craft, amphibian tractors and trucks, pipelines, beach road materials and markers, and many other related types of equipment. The development efforts of the Engineer Amphibian Command were later transferred but not before many successful developments were accomplished. Among these were the beach tractor (later with armored cab), improvements in both LCVPs and LCMs, and their conversion into fuel-salvage and firefighting equipment units. Tests on the DUKW at Cape Cod and later with the 2d Engineer Special Brigade at Fort Ord resulted in modifications which perfected this outstanding innovation in amphibious warfare. As a matter of fact it was stated the DUKW was a "dead duck" until the improvements worked out with the Engineer Amphibian Command at Provincetown and later with the 2d Engineer Special Brigade in Monterey Bay, California, were incorporated in the improved models. It is well known how much the famous DUKW contributed to amphibious warfare both in the Atlantic and the Pacific. The Engineer Amphibian Command is proud of the part it took in improving the DUKW and in taking the first DUKWs both to the North African theater and to the Pacific. Its troop units trained thousands of DUKW operators.

The Engineer Amphibian Command development board worked in close conjunction with the Engineer Board at Fort Belvoir, Virginia, with the Research and Development Branch of the Office of the Quartermaster General, and with the Navy. Before its activities were transferred to other agencies, the Engineer Amphibian Command development board completed ninety-five projects of a major nature. Among these were the development of the Magnesyn Compass which allowed our small landing craft to navigate accurately and the use of radio direction finders on these small craft, much different from those on a large ship. Much research was carried out on the infra-red and ultraviolet light for night control of our small craft. It was also necessary to keep in close touch with the Navy on the latest improvements on fathometers and underwater locator equipment, and on radar.

With respect to the 36-foot craft (LCVP) the Engineer Amphibian Command had much to do with relocating the machine guns for better fields of fire, armor plating, underwater exhausts to kill the noise of the engines, standardization on the Gray diesel engine, and better location of the coxswain for control of his craft.

One of the outstanding contributions to small landing craft by the Engineer Amphibian Command was the change in the LCM3 (50-foot) to the LCM6 (56-foot). Marine architects of the Command at Cape Cod noted the poor speed obtained by two 225-horsepower engines in the LCM3. Despite the large power driving the craft a cruising speed of less than eight knots, when fully loaded, was being obtained. After considerable study it was discovered that by lengthening the craft six feet to get a better balance between length and beam we gained over one knot in speed as well as an increase of twenty per cent in cargo capacity. This remarkable increase in the value of the LCM was obtained with no change in the engines and no increase in fuel consumption.

To cover the wide field of this new type of warfare the Engineer Amphibian Command, in addition to the usual personnel, operations and supply sections, formed the following:

Piloting and Navigation Section under a senior officer of the Coast and Geodetic Survey.
Communications Section under a Signal Corps officer.
Shore Unit Section under a lieutenant colonel of Marines.
The Weapons Section headed by a Coast Artillery officer who had specialized in antiaircraft fire.
The Boat Unit Section under a Coast Guard officer.

The Surgeon of the Command, Lieutenant Colonel Barrow, after many experiments developed an antiseasick pill which was used in the invasion of Normandy and later was adopted as standard for the Army. There was no use carrying a combat soldier to the far shore in a small landing craft if, before you could land him, he became incapacitated by seasickness. A squeamish coxswain would never make a perfect landing in rough water. Lieutenant Colonel Barrow's pills solved this problem by preventing seasickness in all but a few. His pills were a boon to air travelers as well as to those going by sea. He also developed a jeep ambulance which, with some changes, was adopted as standard by the Army and improvised methods of carrying litter patients in landing craft.

Of course the purpose of all this individual schooling was to train officers and men for the units, as the real mission of the Engineer Amphibian Command was to get amphibian units ready for combined training with infantry divisions and to go overseas to their combat assignments. Accordingly the 1st Engineer Special Brigade was activated on June 15, 1942, with a tentative T/O (Table of Organization) strength of 349 officers, 20 warrant officers and 6,814 enlisted men. Only five days later the 2d Engineer Special Brigade was activated. By the end of June the 1st Brigade had been filled to strength of 6,266, the 2d Brigade to 2,507. During July these brigades were strengthened and on the 24th the 411th Engineer Base Shop Battalion was activated; also the Engineer Amphibian Command Band.

In early July the Army Ground Forces formed the Amphibious Training Center to supervise the combined training at Cape Cod and sent the 45th Infantry Division to Fort Edwards. Originally the 1st Brigade was scheduled to train with this division but when that brigade was suddenly ordered overseas (see Chapter 3) the only partly organized 2d Brigade had to take over this job. Training was so rushed that, despite the efforts of all concerned, the first amphibious exercises did not turn out too well. It was no simple maneuver to load thousands of troops with all their battle equipment in a hundred small landing craft and proceed under cover of darkness through choppy seas to land them on a strange beach at dawn. Higher staff officers began to realize that the problem was not simple, that particularly well trained amphibian boatmen and shore engineers would be required to make a successful landing. Thus while many were disappointed at the results obtained in these initial exercises, two useful purposes were served. First, higher headquarters realized that highly specialized and well trained Amphibian Engineers would be required, that Combat Engineers or infantry could not do the job with just ten or twelve days' extra training. Secondly, the Amphibians themselves realized more than ever the difficulty of their job and redoubled their effort to accomplish it.

Early August saw the Engineer Amphibian Command going ahead full steam. The 1st Brigade under General Wolfe was in the throes of suddenly shipping out overseas even before it had completed its initial organization and with only a part of its equipment ready. The 2d Brigade under General Heavey had expanded to 6,000 but lost 1,500 of these men to form the 540th Regiment, which like the 1st Brigade, was to be shipped overseas at once as Shore Engineers. Also the 2d Brigade was initiating training with a second division, the 36th Infantry Division, which had arrived from Texas for its combined training. On August 18 the 3d Brigade was activated under Brigadier General (then Colonel) D. A. D. Ogden. Over a thousand members of the Command were away attending civilian schools and other Army service schools. The specialist schools of the Command were getting lined up. A flotilla of nine Navy LCTs was coming to participate in the combined training exercises. The Engineer Amphibian Command development board was in the midst of many tests on shore and boat equipment. One group was testing waterproof clothing for boatmen; another, life preservers of all types for crew and for passengers; a third group was living on a new Quartermaster ration, the forerunner of the famous K ration. The medicos were fighting seasickness.

Maintenance of landing craft was a terrific problem. In addition to the fact that some damage was naturally done by green operators learning to run their boats, there was a definite lack of spare parts. The Navy had not yet gotten its flow of spare parts

under way. Their problem was also handicapped by the lack of standardization. There were at least five different types of engines in
the landing craft used at Engineer Amphibian Command, with
many non-interchangeable parts. Some craft were gasoline operated; others ran on diesel fuel. Even the batteries in the craft varied. Equipment was hodge-podge. An operator learning one LCP,
LCR, or LCPR (forerunners of the LCVP) would be transferred to
another and find a different engine and an entirely different set of
controls to learn. It was obvious that the boats would have to be
standardized. Every one agreed diesel was the best fuel so the Gray
diesel engine easily won out for motive power. Especially in combat when incendiary bullets would be encountered no one wanted
a gasoline-operated craft.

Solving these and many other similar headaches in the early
days at Cape Cod was what eventually, with much hard work on
the part of all concerned, resulted in the smooth-running, quick-
acting Engineer Amphibian Brigade organization which caused
Admiral Barbey of the Seventh Amphibious Fleet to report later as
"the most efficient type of shore organization for amphibious warfare."

[1] LC = Landing Craft; the next letter(s) indicate
what type. LCVP = Landing Craft, Vehicle and Personnel; LCMs can carry mechanized vehicles, to include
the 28-ton medium tank.

3
1st Brigade to England

The first call for the services of the Engineer Amphibian Command came quickly. During conferences of the Joint Chiefs of Staff held in London in June and July, an urgent need had developed for amphibian troops in England for use in proposed cross-Channel operations and for the amphibious training of our combat forces which had already begun to move into the recently organized European Theater. On July 23, 1942, orders were received at Headquarters Engineer Amphibian Command directing that one brigade be prepared at once for immediate overseas movement in highest operational priority. The newly constituted 1st Brigade, at that time the only brigade on an operational status, was at once designated and alerted for its new mission. Movement orders followed immediately, directing the brigade to the New York Port of Embarkation in time for sailing on the August 6 convoy to Great Britain.

Carrying out this order in the very limited time remaining presented a problem of considerable magnitude. The 1st Brigade, activated only since June 10, was still far below strength in both personnel and equipment. Many of its officers and men had just come into the service. Brigade Headquarters had functioned as such only since July 7 when Colonel (later Brigadier General) Henry C. Wolfe had assumed command. Its units had only just completed a short period of essential self-training on July 15 and had barely begun a program of joint amphibious training with the 45th Infantry Division. The organization of the brigade had not yet been definitely

29

determined; tables of equipment and organization were still under consideration. Much of the brigade's equipment was not available at Camp Edwards. Under these circumstances extraordinary measures were required to enable it to meet its sailing date and carry out its mission. The brigade was promptly brought to its full strength by transfer from other units of the command and by assignment of new personnel as they arrived. On July 24, a list of its requirements in supplies and equipment was sent to Washington for General Somervell (CG, ASF) who immediately held a personal meeting with the heads of the supply branches concerned and directed that all shortages in the brigade's equipment be placed at the New York Port of Embarkation within the next three days, irrespective of any existing priorities. Working day and night and assisted by all units of the Engineer Amphibian Command, the brigade devoted all its efforts to making ready for its movement. On August 1 the brigade commander with a small advance party proceeded to the port to make final arrangements. On the night of August 4 the brigade, less its motor transport, which had already proceeded overland to the port of Boston, entrained at Camp Edwards and proceeded to New York, embarking the following morning on the Army transports *Wakefield* and *Barry*. Its equipment, fully complete except for landing craft, which were to be provided by the Navy upon arrival in Great Britain, was now awaiting it on the Brooklyn docks, and was set up to follow it in separate convoy.

The brigade at that time consisted of Brigade Headquarters, Colonel H. C. Wolfe, commanding; 591st Engineer Boat Regiment, Colonel M. M. Boatner, commanding, which had been formed from the greatly expanded 37th Engineer Combat Regiment; the 531st Engineer Shore Regiment, Colonel R. L. Brown, commanding, similarly formed from the 87th Engineer Heavy Ponton Battalion; the 261st Medical Battalion, Major M. E. Smith, commanding; the 361st Quartermaster Battalion, Major F. D. H. Smith, commanding; the 561st Boat Maintenance Company, Major E. R. Huston, commanding; the 286th Signal Company, Captain R. P. Zebley, commanding; and the 161st Ordnance Platoon, First Lieutenant Berger, commanding.

On the morning of August 6 the convoy sailed and the 1st Brigade, 335 officers and 7,500 enlisted men strong, was on its way. Moving out on such short notice was a fine accomplishment. After an overnight stopover in Halifax where it was joined by additional ships, the convoy set forth across the Atlantic. Following the northern route past the shores of Newfoundland, south of Iceland, and around the northern tip of Ireland it dropped anchors in the Firth of Clyde near Glasgow, Scotland, on August 17. Aside from the usual shipboard rumors and submarine alarms, the entire voyage was uneventful and without incident. The brigade enjoyed a much needed period in which it could shake down its records and organization and commence plans for its probable task. There was every expectation that it might be called upon for immediate use in an amphibious operation shortly after its arrival and the time aboard ship was devoted to preparation for such a contingency. The Army Amphibians had started the first of their many journeys to come, journeys to Africa, Sicily, Italy, Normandy, Australia, New Guinea, New Britain, the Philippines, Borneo, Okinawa, Korea and Japan.

Immediately upon reaching the anchorage in the Clyde the brigade commander was met by Colonel R. R. Arnold of Headquarters, Engineer Amphibian Command, who with a small officer detachment had preceded the brigade to the UK by air to represent the Engineer Amphibian Command and make preliminary arrangements for all Engineer Amphibian Command activities. Colonel Arnold (later killed in North Africa) brought with him orders for disposition of the brigade. It was to be very much dispersed. Brigade Headquarters Company, the Medical Battalion, and two battalions of the 591st Boat Regiment were to be stationed in the vicinity of Belfast, Ireland; the 531st Shore Regiment in Naval camps near Londonderry, Ireland; and one battalion of the 591st Boat Regiment and the Boat Maintenance Company were to go to Roseneath, north of Glasgow.

Colonel Arnold also brought the rather startling information that the status of the brigade had changed materially while it was on the water and that there was now much uncertainty as to its future mission and duties. As a result he and the brigade commander proceeded immediately to ETO Headquarters in London, leaving the supervision of the disembarkation to Colonel Boatner, next in command. Several days were spent in consultations and conferences at ETO Headquarters, during which it developed that decision had been made that operation of all landing craft in the theater was to be taken over by the Navy and that the 1st Brigade was to be made available to the Navy for this purpose. Subsequent requirements for boat operating personnel were to be provided by the Navy and no additional Engineer Amphibian boat operators would be needed.

On August 11 the theater had established a Maritime Command under the command of Admiral A. C. Bennett, USN. The 1st Brigade was assigned to it on its arrival. Accordingly, the brigade commander reported immediately to Admiral Bennett, whose headquarters at that time were in London and spent some days with his staff planning for future activities. Plans of the Navy contemplated early establishment of Maritime Command Headquarters at Roseneath, Scotland, where the Navy would operate one amphibious training center, with another center near Londonderry, Ireland. It was agreed that Colonel Wolfe would serve as a member of Admiral Bennett's staff with particular responsibility for shore-party operations for which the Navy had made no provision in their plans. After a short visit to the units in Ireland, Colonel Wolfe proceeded to Roseneath and joined the Maritime Command staff, which by that time had been established there.

The next few weeks were a rather trying time for the brigade. The Maritime Command of the Navy was completely inexperienced in amphibious operations and had neither the trained personnel nor the equipment available to carry on amphibious training. A proposal by its training staff that the brigade furnish several highly qualified Army boat officers to teach landing craft operation to groups of junior naval officers, who would then conduct similar training for the brigade, was obviously unacceptable. All attempts to obtain landing craft to carry on the training of the boat regiment were without avail since all those being sent from the United States to England were being turned over to the British Navy as fast as they arrived. Suitable terrain and training facilities for general military training were almost non-existent and the beaches very restricted. The scattering of the brigade in several localities in Scotland and Ireland with little regard to its tactical organization made supervision of its training extremely difficult. An opportunity, however, was afforded to brigade units during this period to shake themselves down and to concentrate upon basic training for the many new men who had joined it immediately before its departure.

One unit—the Brigade Boat Maintenance Company—found its services sorely needed. The British Combined Operations Training Center at Inverary, a short distance north of Roseneath, where American combat teams were undergoing amphibious training, had accumulated a large backlog of unserviceable landing craft because of lack of maintenance and repair facilities, and operation of the center was being seriously interfered with. The Boat Maintenance Company, with its highly skilled personnel and ample stock of tools and spare parts from the States, at once set to work and in the space of a few weeks succeeded in relieving the situation. Major repairs were effected to over a hundred British landing craft including a number which had been returned in damaged condition from the Dieppe raid. The work of this unit was an invaluable contribution to the training program at the Combined Training Center and to the success of the operation which followed. This 561st Engineer Boat Maintenance Company was destined to pay for itself many times over during World War II.

A major problem confronting the brigade at this time was the assembly of the extremely large amount of equipment, much of it highly special, which had been assembled for its use at New York and which was now beginning to arrive piecemeal. A staff officer was placed in the Office of Chief of Transportation in London to examine the manifests of all cargo ships arriving. Detachments were placed at various ports with the mission of claiming and forwarding to Roseneath all equipment of the brigade as it was unloaded. Its complete equipment eventually arrived at six separate ports in fifty-five ships and, after several weeks of hard work, was concentrated at Roseneath and issued out to the units as needed.

This large stock of readily available equipment and supplies later turned out to be invaluable, even though much of it was not used by the brigade itself due to its changed mission. The 1st Infantry Division, badly in need of communication equipment because of the non-arrival of its own, was promptly furnished with its complete complement. Over 1,100 machine guns intended for armament of landing craft were taken to Africa and were made available to our combat forces at a time when these weapons were in very great demand. The entire stock was eventually put to very good use either by the Army or Navy.

Early in September 1942 the fortunes of the brigade underwent a sudden change for the better. In response to an urgent call from theater headquarters the brigade commander proceeded to London on September 10 where he was informed that Operation Torch—the invasion of North Africa—was "on" and that the brigade would participate as a part of the Center Task Force with the mission of assisting in the landing operation. The brigade was to be relieved from further duty with the Naval Maritime Command and to be assigned to the U.S. II Corps. Planning for the use of the brigade commenced immediately. As finally agreed upon, the plan was as follows: the 531st Engineer Shore Regiment with detachments from the 286th Signal Company was attached to the 1st Infantry Division for employment as shore parties in the assault landing. The 2d Battalion, 591st Engineer Boat Regiment, reorganized as a shore party, was similarly attached to Combat Command B, 1st Armored Division. The 1st Battalion, 591st Engineer Boat Regiment, was organized into ten 75-man hatch crews for manning cargo ships of the assault convoy. The remainder of the 591st Engineer Boat Regiment was to accompany the first follow-up to operate as docks operating personnel. The brigade commander with a small staff was placed on the staff of the Center Task Force commander under the British designation of "Principal Military Landing Officer" with the responsibility of operation of the Port of Arzew and adjacent beaches and, in conjunction with the British Navy, to unload the assault convoy. At the specific request of Admiral Bennett the 561st Boat Maintenance Company which had already so well demonstrated its capabilities was to remain with the Navy for assistance in execution of the naval mission of port clearance and operation. A 50-man detachment of the 591st Regimental Boat Maintenance Company was to be lent to the Eastern Task Force for assistance to the British Navy in boat maintenance on their beaches. The remainder of the brigade including the Medical Battalion and Quartermaster Battalion, for which spaces could not be provided on the assault convoy, were to follow later.

Upon the return of the brigade commander to Roseneath the brigade units were at once oriented and intensive training for the accomplishment of their new mission was begun. The 531st Engineer Shore Regiment and detachments from the 286th Signal Company were brought over from Ireland and attached to the 1st Division, the combat teams of which at that time were undergoing amphibious training at Roseneath, Toward, and Inverary. The 2d Battalion, 591st Engineers, reorganized as a shore battalion, joined Combat Command B of the 1st Armored Division south of Belfast. The remainder of the 591st Boat Regiment was moved from Ireland to Liverpool and Immingham, England, where it received training in the use of ships' winches and gear and dock operation. The 561st Boat Maintenance Company, remaining at Roseneath, engaged in an intensive training program with the Navy. Intensive efforts were made throughout the brigade to complete its equipment and obtain the additional items such as bulldozers and beach landing mats that would be required. On September 28 General Wolfe with a small planning staff returned to London to participate in the detailed planning activities of the Headquarters Center Task Force, remaining there until the middle of October by which time the planning for the operation had been concluded and movement of units of the task force to the ports for loading on the convoy had begun.

Loading of the assault convoy, carried out under the direction of the British Army Movements Control, presented many difficult problems due to unfamiliarity of our army with their methods and procedures. However, by October 17 the convoy loading was accomplished and the entire expedition was assembled in its ships in the Firth of Clyde where it was joined by the convoy of the Eastern Task Force. On October 18 the assault ships of the convoys proceeded north to the vicinity of Loch Linnhe, Scotland, where a final rehearsal of the assault was conducted just before daylight on the morning of the 19th. Following this the convoy returned to the Clyde area on October 20 to await its time to sail. During this period, except for the conduct of service command post exercises (CPXs) on shore, all personnel were required to remain on shipboard. On October 26, escorted by the British Navy, the assault forces of both the Eastern and Center Task Forces sailed for Africa and Operation Torch was under way. The Army Amphibians were beginning to pay their way, something they did many fold before the war was over.

4
ON WITH THE TRAINING

With the 1st Brigade well on its way overseas in early August 1942, all efforts on Cape Cod turned to training the new units and developing the correct procedure for amphibious operations. The 2d Brigade was next. As soon as organization and basic training were completed, the program was stepped up. Simulated combat operations were planned and executed. Working at first with small amphibian units and later, as more craft became available, with battalions and regiments of the 45th Infantry Division, the landing barges ploughed through the rough waters off Cape Cod to land these infantry troops on Martha's Vineyard—a beach presumed to be enemy territory. Transporting battle-equipped infantry soldiers, supplies, equipment, field pieces, motor vehicles, dozers and tanks, they strove to achieve the split-second accuracy in timing which is of primary importance in amphibious operations. The boatmen first had to learn how to operate their boats, how to land them in surf, keep them from being broached and then retract from the beach through the surf to bring in more troops and supplies. It was a job that could be learned only through bitter experience. They had to learn how to move in wave formation of eight to twelve boats with various maneuvers for approach at night or under fire in the daytime and how to deploy when attacked from the air. Then followed training in larger formations finally concluding with an entire boat battalion of 120 craft in one operation.

The shore units, at first divided into "near shore" and "far shore" companies, participated in these practice landings by loading and loading boats and setting up shore installations on the presumed enemy territory. The original idea was to have a near-shore company, trained in the proper methods of loading boats to capacity and still not destroy their equilibrium, remain on the friendly shore and load ships embarking on an operation. The far-shore company would establish the beachhead in enemy territory. Its mission included building landing ramps for the amphibious vehicles, clearing the beach of obstacles and mines, constructing exits from the beach proper, and many similar jobs. In addition to unloading ships, the far-shore companies would protect the newly won beachhead from enemy counterattack, either by land and sea, or air. They had to make preparations to facilitate the handling of the expanding amounts of supplies and the increased number of men that would arrive in subsequent waves. It was later learned through actual operations that the work on both the near and far shores could best be handled by the same company, so the shore company that loaded a ship was also placed on the enemy shore in time to unload that ship when it arrived. These shore engineers also had to be efficient combat soldiers and trained to fight. More than once the men of the shore companies, and the boat companies too, later demonstrated their ability to fight as infantrymen to hold and establish their newly won beachhead.

Initially the majority of the landing craft used by the brigade were LCP(R)s and LCVs. Some were gasoline operated and some used diesel fuel. The LCP(R) was used for the transportation of personnel and the LCV for small vehicles.

Throughout this story the type of landing craft used for particular operations will be indicated by initials. The prefix LC means Landing Craft. Thus, LCP(R) means Landing Craft, Personnel (Ramp) and LCV stands for Landing Craft, Vehicle. At this time the brigade had only a few of the larger craft called the LCM (Landing Craft, Mechanized), which was later to become the standard craft of the brigade. Much larger than the LCV, and diesel operated, it could weather rougher seas, travel longer distances and carry more cargo and personnel. Occasionally LCTs (Landing Craft, Tank), crewed by the Navy, participated in the problems.

To look back now at those early days and to compare those efforts with the large-scale operations in the Philippines, one is inclined to classify the early maneuvers on Cape Cod as small-time stuff, but they laid the groundwork upon which the success of later operations was based. Here the decision was made to adopt diesel-operated LCMs and LCVPs as the basic craft for the Amphibian Engineers.

One event that is always called to mind when relating the experiences of the 2d Brigade on Cape Cod is "that parade." By 10 September the 2d Brigade had been fully formed and at least fairly well equipped. With the band playing and flags unfurled, the boat and shore engineers of the brigade went through a complete parade carrying not only their weapons but also the anchors, tool kits, medical chests, rope, or various other odds and ends of equipment to designate the duty they performed. Wearing their heavy rubber parkas and paratroop boots, the men sweltered under the hot September sun. It was a unique and colorful spectacle giving all some idea of the variety and immensity of the unit. Brigadier General Noce, Commanding General of the Engineer Amphibian Command, joined General Heavey in taking this remarkable review. It was later repeated for a larger group of senior Army and Navy officers from Washington.

Brigadier General (later Major General) Noce left the U.S. on September 15, 1942, by air to inspect the 1st Brigade in Great Britain and to discuss amphibious training with the American and British headquarters. He returned to Cape Cod on October 3 pleased with the progress units of the 1st Brigade were making.

During the 2d Brigade's last few weeks on Cape Cod it lost nearly 3,000 men through group transfers as cadres for other amphibian units. It seemed as if those long hours of boat and shore training were almost in vain, because no sooner did a man get fairly well trained in his job than he was gone and a new man arrived to be trained from the bottom up. Despite all this exchange of personnel, the work of the brigade continued without much interruption. The training with the 45th Division ended with a problem which did not go off too well. Some waves of boats got lost at night in the murky waters off Martha's Vineyard and failed to land on schedule. All made it safely to the far shore but things did not click. Everyone was convinced the job of the Amphibian Engineer was no easy one and, with this in mind, they became more determined than ever to solve all problems, overcome all difficulties, and become an outfit that would always "Put 'em across" on time and at the right place.

While the 2d Brigade was being formed as a part of the Engineer Amphibian Command, another unit on Cape Cod—the Amphibious Training Command under Brigadier General Frank A. Keating—was busily engaged in training Rangers in commando tactics. During the last few days of September 1942 brigade boatmen worked with the Rangers and another arrival, the 36th Infantry Division. This work culminated in the only large-scale maneuver the 2d Brigade ever held in the United States. It was as realistic as actual combat except for the spilling of blood.

Extensive plans for the maneuver were made—the boats were put in tip-top shape, the men were carefully instructed in the duties they would perform, maps were checked and courses plotted, liaison contacts were made with the 36th Division and the Rangers. Arrangements were made to care for the large group of high-ranking Army and Navy officers who were coming from Washington and elsewhere to witness the maneuvers. Nothing was overlooked.

It was planned that on D-day at H-hour the main attacking force would land on Red Beach on Martha's Vineyard while supporting units landed on nearby Yellow and Green Beaches. Loading on the mainland was not started until dark fell. Troops and equipment of all kinds had to be loaded and the 25-mile trip made through choppy seas and murky darkness to hit the far shore exactly at first light.

Headquarters of Army Ground Forces at Washington, as well as the Navy and Marine Corps, sent observers to determine what the "Army Amphibs" could do. A failure on this maneuver might jeopardize their continuation. Lieutenant General McNair, Commanding General of Army Ground Forces, was the senior observer.

The seconds ticked away and H-hour rapidly approached. From shore there was still no sign of the first wave of boats. Suddenly dim shapes loomed through the murk. The offshore wind had drowned out the roar of the engines. The boats were coming! In perfect formation the first wave ploughed through the surf toward the beach. They landed at exactly H-hour. Our first real test had come out perfectly. It was a harbinger of success.

After the first wave landed, unloaded and retracted, the successive waves came in on schedule. Troops of the 36th Division and a battalion of Rangers clambered out of the boats and up the beach, simulating an attack on supposed enemy objectives. Planes overhead dropped a company of paratroopers to support the ground forces. Reports soon arrived by radio that the smaller landings on Yellow and Green Beaches, several miles away, had clicked perfectly. Observers willingly admitted that troops poured ashore so fast the defenders would have been overwhelmed.

Shore Engineers marked the beaches and set about establishing the beachhead by building supply, water, gas and oil, ration, and communication installations. The infantry was resupplied by the continuous waves of LCVs, LCMs, and nine LCTs manned by the Navy. Hundreds of tons of actual supplies and ammunition were unloaded by the shore engineers and placed in marked dumps. All three beaches were linked at once by radio and later by telephone.

One incident during this operation earned for the 2d Brigade its first War Department decoration. First Lieutenant (later Major) Ernest B. Huetter, 592d Engineer Boat & Shore Regiment, of San Francisco, California, was in command of a wave of boats as they made their way across Vineyard Sound. Suddenly one of the boats burst into dense smoke and flames. The heat was so intense that all hands immediately abandoned the boat, and it was left running crazily about at high speed, menacing the safety of other craft nearby. To further complicate the situation more smoke pots in the boat caught fire, enveloping the area in great clouds of opaque smoke. Lieutenant Huetter first directed the rescue of all men in the water, then boarding the burning boat, he brought it under control and subdued the flames with sea water. For his courage and quick thinking in preventing what might have been a tragic accident and holding the boat damage to a minimum, Lieutenant Huetter was awarded the Soldier's Medal. This sort of courage and aggressive action was exemplary of the many acts of heroism that later became almost commonplace when the Amphibians moved into action against the Japs and the Germans.

After two days the operation was called to a halt and pronounced a success. General McNair returned to Washington with the firm conviction that the Army had found the one link that was needed to carry the attack to the enemy—the fast, accurate, and hard-hitting Amphibian Engineers.

5
TRAINING SHIFTS TO CARRABELLE:
MISSION TO MACARTHUR

When the Engineer Amphibian Command occupied Camp Edwards as a training site it was realized that the winter would be so severe as to impede, and on occasion, actually stop all amphibious operations. Therefore studies for an all-year-around site were initiated soon after the headquarters was established on Cape Cod. Because of the urgent need for speed in training the first amphibian troops, there could be no waiting to develop a site. Camp Edwards, with its many existing facilities and buildings, had to be utilized for the initial establishment of the Amphibians.

In conjunction with Headquarters, Army Ground Forces, the search was on for a new amphibian base. It was surprising how few coastal areas had suitable beaches and sufficient ground area in sparsely populated country. Finally the War Department chose Carrabelle, Florida (later to be known as Camp Gordon Johnston). The reservation there is roughly triangular, extending twenty-one miles along the Gulf of Mexico. Working under veritable jungle conditions the 165,000 acres were surveyed by the Army Engineers of the Mobile District in twenty-one days and construction work started.

The contractors under the Corps of Engineers set a record preparing the reservation for soldier occupancy and building piers and fuel facilities for the many landing craft. Clearing the necessary parts of the island presented a real problem. The thick walls of *titi* encountered there required machetes just as much as the jungles to be encountered later in the Philippines and New Guinea. Snakes

43

were more numerous than they ever were in New Guinea. The work was well under way but far from completed when the 2d Brigade and the Army Ground Forces Amphibious Training Center started their moves by rail and truck from Edwards to Carrabelle in early October 1942.

A training program for combined operations of the newly arrived 38th Infantry Division and the 2d Brigade was promptly prepared. Reconnaissance of beaches was pushed. Much to the disgust of both boatmen and shore engineers the slope of the beaches was found to be very flat and bars were frequent. Landing craft would often ground a hundred or more yards from shore. Propellers were chewed up; propeller shafts bent. The boatmen longed for the ample waters and fine beaches of Cap Cod but the training under adverse conditions was what they needed to round out their experience.

After the successful completion of the maneuvers with the 36th Division on Martha's Vineyard, General Noce obtained authority to send a mission to General MacArthur to determine his needs for Amphibian Engineers. All deck space on west-bound cargo ships was vitally needed for planes to hold in check the strong Jap air power. No deck space could be spared for the bulky landing craft. The Engineer Amphibian Command, with approval of the Navy, had devised a unique plan to ship knocked-down LCVPs to Australia and to assemble the bulky craft there, thus saving a large percentage of their shipping space and doing away with the need for using deck space for them.

Headed by Colonel Trudeau, the Engineer Amphibian Command mission flew first to Brisbane where the plan was explained to General MacArthur in person. Then with the assistance of Brigadier General (later Major General) H. J. Casey, his Chief Engineer, the mission reconnoitered for a suitable site for the assembly plant and for the brigade's bivouac areas. At that time the Jap Air Force was too strong to permit locating the plant in New Guinea where it had been hoped to build it, so Cairns was selected for the plant with one regimental bivouac on the fine beaches twelve miles north of there. This fitted in with the plans to train Australian troops on the Atherton Tableland, a few miles from Cairns. However, plans had already been made for American troops to be trained in the Rockhampton area, five hundred miles to the south. Although beach areas here were not as suitable as in the vicinity of Cairns, the brigade, less one regiment, was accordingly required to set up in the Rockhampton area.

The mission returned to the states with the initial plans set for the assembly plant and for the two bivouac areas. General MacArthur asked the War Department for one brigade at once to be followed in due time by another brigade. The 411th Engineer Base Ship Battalion was to be dispatched first in order to get the plant in operation. However things were not to be as simple as that. With no Amphibians remaining in Australia to push construction of the plant and the bivouacs, practically nothing was accomplished. The shortage of labor and materials in Australia of course had much to do with this.

The Amphibious Training Center at Carrabelle had scarcely completed the directive for the first exercise of the 2d Brigade with the 38th Infantry Division when orders came for the 2d Brigade to move at once to Fort Ord, California, prepared to stage from there to Australia. Within a few days the 2d Brigade had left Carrabelle and the 3d was rushed from Camp Edwards to take over its craft and to carry on the combined training with the 38th Division. The 3d Brigade took over in an especially efficient way and moved some of its own craft from Cape Cod all the way to Carrabelle, using the protected waters of the Inland Waterway, parallel to the coast, for most of the trip.

Thus the 2d Brigade, instead of following the 1st Brigade to England as had been expected, moved in November 1942 to California en route to Australia. The 3d Brigade, just being organized at Edwards, found itself thrown quickly into combined training with an infantry division before it had completed its own basic training. It is interesting to fit the 1st Brigade into this picture too. As we shall see in the next chapter, it too, was under way right at this time for the famous landing in North Africa, the Allies' first real counterblow against the Axis.

6
North Africa, Sicily and Salerno

Operation Torch—code name for the North African Campaign—called for landings of troops staging both from the United Kingdom and from the United States. Its mission was to clear the northern portion of Africa of all Axis forces. The initial objectives called for landings in the Casablanca, Oran and Algiers areas. A total force of thirteen divisions, nine American and four British, was to land. For the movement to the far shore three naval task forces were formed: Western (Casablanca), Center (Oran), and Eastern (Algiers), the Western Task Force being U.S. Navy.

In this complex plan the 1st Engineer Special Brigade was assigned to support the 1st Infantry Division and Combat Command B of the 1st Armored Division. The brigade, as part of the Center Task Force, sailed from Glasgow, Scotland, on October 26, 1942. Back at Norfolk, Virginia, the 540th Regiment, which had been formed at Cape Cod, was joining the 36th Engineer Combat Regiment in forming the shore party for the Western Force under General Patton.

The plan of attack called for the bulk of the 1st Division and Combat Command B's tank force to land on the Arzew beaches some thirty miles northeast of Oran and envelop the city from the south and east. One combat team of the 1st Division was to land fifteen miles west of Oran and seize the high ground which dominated the city. Still farther to the west a small flying column, entirely tanks and armored cars, was to land at an isolated beach and make a dash for the vital airfields south of Oran.

46

The mission of the 1st Brigade, insofar as its shore units were concerned, was the normal one—to land the assaulting troops with their vehicles and equipment and to organize and operate the beaches for the reception of men, vehicles and supplies. The three battalions of the 531st Engineer Shore Regiment each supported a combat team of the 1st Division. Initially under division control, the Amphibian Engineers were to revert to the brigade commander who was also charged with operation of the port of Arzew and supervision of the unloading of the convoy. The 591st Boat Regiment was not needed for its normal task since all landing craft in the Center Task Force were to be manned by British naval crews. (Actually it turned out after the convoy was under way that the British were short twenty-five crews. The American Amphibians furnished the crews for these craft.) The 591st was accordingly made over into hatch crews and port operating units, types of supporting troops in which there was a sore deficiency. One of its battalions, however, was reorganized as a shore unit and assigned to the armored force for its assault landing. The Brigade Boat Maintenance Company, under naval control, also accompanied the expedition. A 50-man detachment of the Maintenance Company (591st) was attached to the British naval contingent of the Eastern (Algiers) Force to repair British landing craft. Remaining units of the brigade were to follow later.

After a practice landing in Scotland, the convoy on the night of October 26, 1942, headed far out into the Atlantic to escape enemy air observation. Its course lay westward almost to Iceland, thence southward to the Azores whence it would make its final dash eastward through the Strait of Gibraltar and into the Mediterranean. For those on board the voyage was full of interest. It was difficult to believe that the large-scale preparations required for the mounting and assembling of such a great convoy could have remained unknown to the enemy or that its movement could be unobserved. Submarine and air attacks seemed inevitable. As the days passed and D-day approached, tension naturally mounted. It was not until the evening of D minus 2 when the convoy slipped

SPAIN

Strait of Gibraltar

Gibraltar

Tangier

MEDIT

ALGII

Port Lyautey

Casablanca

RABAT

FEZ

Arzew   Mostaganem

Oran

A   F   R

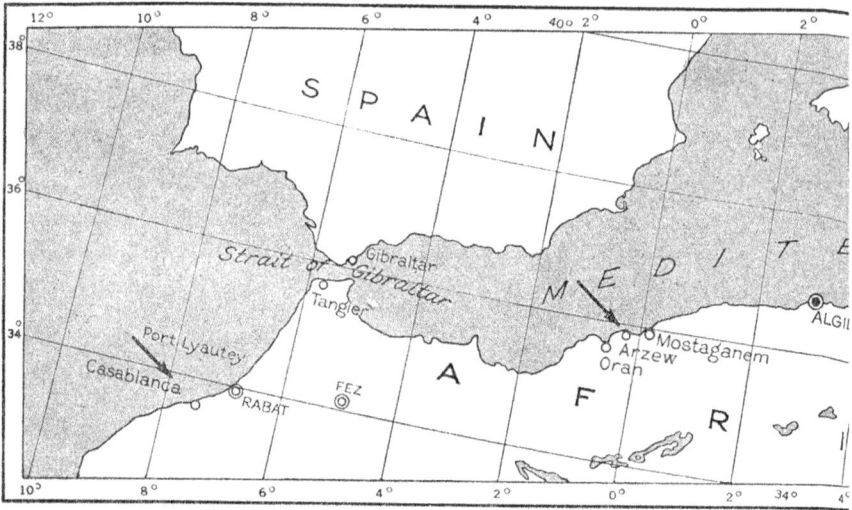

quietly through the Strait of Gibraltar with no sign of enemy interference that it began to be realized that secrecy had really been
preserved and that complete surprise might be achieved.

The evening of D minus 1 day found the Center Task Force due
north of Oran but not yet in sight of land. As darkness fell the
assault ships changed course to the south, took up landing formation, and proceeded cautiously into their initial anchorage areas
five miles off shore, where boats were lowered and disembarkation begun. So far all had gone well. By superb navigation the British Navy had brought the expedition to the appointed place at the
proper time. Weather conditions for the operation were perfect—a
pitch-black night, no wind, and a calm sea. Shortly before midnight the landing craft bearing the assault waves left the ships and,
led by guides from British submarines, headed in for their respective beaches.

Precisely at H-hour (1:00 A.M.,[1] November 8, 1942) the assault
wave landing craft grounded quietly and in good order on their
designated beaches. Initially the landing was entirely unopposed.
Finding the beaches deserted, the troops pushed rapidly inland
towards their objective, while the landing craft returned to their
ships to pick up the next wave. Some apparently got lost or returned
to the wrong vessel. As the night advanced, however, opposition

SARDINIA

Salerno
Naples

Palermo   Messina

Bizerte   SICILY

Canicatti
Porto-   Caltanissetta
Empedocle   Gela
Licata

Constantine   TUNIS

Strait of Messina

Sousse

MALTA

40

38

36

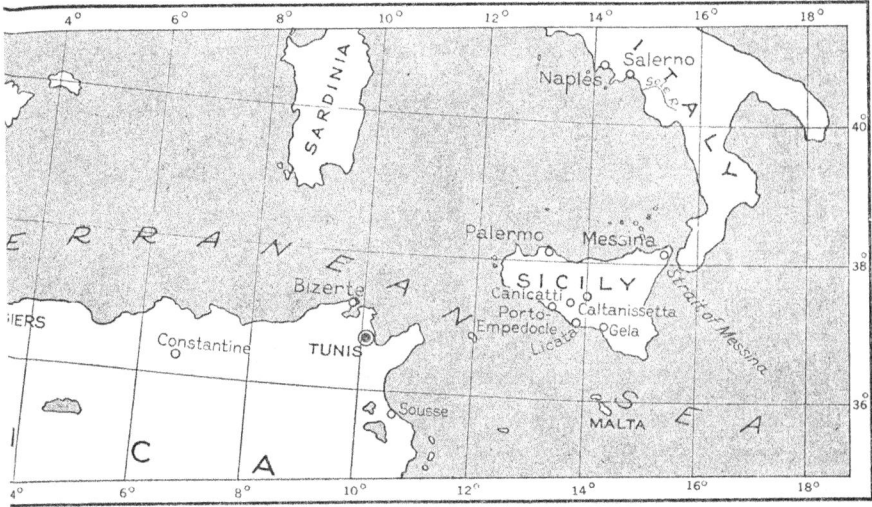

developed. A bold attempt by a small combined Army and Navy landing party to seize the mole and piers in the harbor of Oran proved abortive. The two small ships making the venture were taken under fire by the French naval garrison and sunk with heavy losses.

Shortly before dawn the 1st Ranger Battalion which had landed independently at H-hour successfully stormed the batteries dominating the Arzew harbor and captured their guns. The French garrisons were now thoroughly aroused and all landings began to encounter resistance. Brisk fighting broke out in Arzew. At daylight all craft coming in to the nearby beaches came under machine-gun fire from the harbor area while the transports, which upon the capture of the Arzew batteries had moved into an anchorage only a half mile off shore, were subjected to sporadic artillery fire from the hills and received several hits. Under cover of smoke screens the landing continued, though progress was materially slowed by inability to control and direct the landing craft, many of which had already become stalled upon the beaches. A flying column of light tanks from Combat Command B of the 1st Armored Division carried in British "Maracaibos," an improvised type of LST, was effectively unloaded under artillery fire by the use of treadway bridging.

By the middle of the morning enemy opposition in the town of
Arzew had been overcome and it became possible to bring ships
into the harbor. Throughout the day unloading proceeded both on
the beaches and in the harbor and by afternoon supplies had begun to flow in. The combat troops were all ashore and supporting
troops, vehicles and supplies had begun to follow. The shore parties had organized the beaches and were successfully operating
them in spite of a severe shortage in truck transportation. Throughout the late afternoon and evening as fighting inland became
heavier, numerous urgent calls for additional artillery and ammunition were received from the 1st Division creating difficult problems for those unloading the ships. During the night swells and
high surf forced the abandonment of beach operations for some
hours. Next morning the sea abated somewhat and beach operations were resumed.

On this morning a message was received from the task force
commander stating that an enemy attack on the Arzew beaches was
imminent and directing the brigade commander immediately to
organize the beaches for defense. This resulted in cessation of unloading operations for several hours during which the shore parties were subjected to misdirected strafing by several planes of our
own forces. In the evening sea conditions again worsened, beach
unloading was stopped and from then on until the end of the operation all unloading was carried on in the Arzew harbor.

Center Task Force assumed direct control of unloading operations on the morning of D plus 2. Thereafter, discharge of ships
continued in the Arzew harbor under the direction of the commander of the 1st Brigade. Shore battalions which had been operating the beaches and elements of the boat regiment moved into
Arzew for the purpose together with the 19th Combat Engineers
which now came under brigade control. With the fall of Oran on
November 10 and the surrender of all French forces in Africa on
the 11th, the pressure on the brigade diminished and thereafter
discharge of cargo progressed rapidly until the evening of November 13, when the convoy was completely unloaded, except for the

Zebulon B. Vance which had been delayed by the failure of one of her heavy booms.

The amphibious phase of Operation Torch had now come to a close. For the 1st Brigade it was an interesting and an enlightening experience. In spite of their own inexperience and handicapped by lack of unity in control of landing craft and serious shortages in transportation and beach unloading equipment they had nevertheless successfully accomplished their initial combat mission. In the first six days and nights they had assisted in the landing of the some 35,000 men, 3,200 vehicles, and 13,500 tons of supplies, and had completely unloaded the assault convoys in time for the return sailing. Working under great strain, for some men as long as sixty hours at a stretch, at times under fire, they had met all demands. At a cost of one officer killed in action, two men accidentally killed and several enlisted men slightly wounded, they had demonstrated the soundness of their organization and had learned much that was to stand them in good stead in future operations.

Termination of hostilities with the French brought no decrease in activities. Center Task Force, gravely deficient in support troops, and faced with the urgent necessity of developing the newly captured Oran base and of opening its partially blocked harbor for follow-up convoys that had already begun to arrive, leaned heavily upon the resources of skilled engineer troops available within the brigade. As fast as its units could be assembled from the beaches they were put to work. Brigade headquarters was established at Arzew and took over all troops and activities in that area. The boat regiment was moved to Oran where under control of the newly organized Mediterranean Base Section it participated in operation of the port: unloading ships, moving supplies and operating dumps. The shore regiment was particularly busy in the operation of Arzew port. Units of the regiment also engaged in building airfields, prisoner-of-war cages, and other construction projects. At the same time training was continued. Rifle ranges were constructed and weapons and other field training were carried on whenever men could be spared from work. During this period the remaining elements of the brigade, including the Quartermaster and Medical

Battalions, the Ordnance Company, and the remainder of the Signal Company were brought from England on subsequent convoys and rejoined the brigade at Arzew. The Quartermaster Battalion was assigned to operation of dumps, and hauling supplies, while the Medical Battalion took over the Arzew Station Hospital.

An important activity during this period was that of defense. Higher headquarters were concerned over the possibility of a hostile landing from Spain and the brigade, with some supporting artillery, was charged with defense of the coast from Arzew to Mostaganem. A defense plan was prepared, positions were selected and organized, and an observation system was established on critical beaches. Provision was made for antiaircraft defense of the Arzew port.

Throughout the weeks that followed, despite its current pressing activities, the brigade did not lose sight of its original amphibious mission. It was realized that more amphibious operations were to follow, either upon the successful conclusion of the Tunisian Campaign or even before. An immediate landing operation against the coast of Spanish Morocco was a possibility. The role of the brigade in such operations was still in doubt because of uncertainty as to whether operation of small landing craft would be an Army or Navy function. However, it was certain that the brigade would be used as shore engineers even if not permitted to operate small landing craft. Accordingly, immediate steps were taken to maintain the brigade in the best possible state of readiness and to further its normal training. Conditions in the vicinity of Arzew were almost ideal for amphibious training. Its harbor, beaches and weather conditions were extremely suitable and ample terrain existed for large-scale training. In late November 1942 General Wolfe recommended that Arzew be designated as the Theater Amphibious Training Center and be operated by the 1st Brigade.

The brigade initiated action immediately to prepare itself for such a mission. The Brigade Boat Maintenance Company which had been under naval control since the initial landing and was more or less marking time was, after considerable insistence, returned to brigade control. It went to work promptly at Arzew setting up its

shops and salvaging and placing in operating condition the numerous landing craft which had been abandoned by the British Navy
either in the harbor or stranded on the beaches. As a result of its
intensive efforts, which included sending salvage parties as far as
Algiers to obtain motors and spare parts from the large number of
craft left broached on those beaches, the brigade soon found itself
with a usable fleet of some forty assorted LCMs and British LCAs
(Landing Craft, Assault), enough for the initiation of small-scale
training. Training in boat Operation was immediately begun, using
initially personnel from the Boat Maintenance Company; and later
the Tank Lighter Company of the Boat Regiment which by then
had become available. During December as the training of its crews
progressed the brigade was able to carry out a number of day and
night landing exercises with the 1st Ranger Battalion and with its
own shore regiment (531st). These activities were a good start and,
while on a small scale, served to attract the attention of the higher
command to the capabilities of the brigade. Prospects appeared
bright for full-scale resumption of the brigade's boat operation
function and efforts were made to provide a flow of landing craft
and spare parts.

On January 11, 1943, the brigade was assigned to the Fifth
Army. A few days later the Fifth Army Invasion Training Center
for the conduct of divisional amphibious training was established
at Porte-aux-Poules, a few miles east of Arzew, under the command
of Brigadier General J. W. O'Daniel. The brigade was directed to
give the Center all possible assistance in the execution of its mission and from then on worked very closely with the Center. Staff
officers from brigade headquarters and its units collaborated with
the Training Center staff in preparation of amphibious doctrines and
the development of the special technique required for landing operations. Qualified transport quartermaster instructors, demolition
experts and other specialists were furnished to the Center. A battalion of the shore regiment was made available to the Center for
development of its installations and for shore-party demonstrations and exercises. Experiments in the breaching of beach and
underwater obstacles and in the use of various expedients for

unloading vehicles of supplies over the beach were conducted. Throughout January and February the trained boat crews of the brigade were able to meet all of the Center's requirements for landing craft and numerous landing exercises and demonstrations on a battalion scale were carried out very satisfactorily. The work of the brigade during this period contributed greatly to the early establishment and successful operation of the Invasion Training Center.

The 561st Engineer Boat Maintenance Company of the 1st Brigade, in addition to maintaining small landing craft for the Navy, designed and installed some of the first twin .50-caliber mounts for half-tracks for tank-destroyer units in North Africa. The unit ran into many unusual problems on the repair of ships as large as the *Queen Emma* class (2,500 tons) and British destroyers. When the *Ajax* was in a sinking condition, the company rendered valuable aid in the welding of side and deck plates. Several Liberty ship propellers were also repaired. These are only a few of the many varied tasks which befell the 561st. It was destined to continue its operations with the U.S. Navy and play an important part in all the Mediterranean campaigns to include the invasion of southern France.

By the middle of February it had become clear that the operation of landing craft was definitely lost to the brigade. This responsibility within the North African Theater was to be taken over by the Navy. In view of this decision the brigade withdrew from any further landing-craft activities and became a shore brigade.

The boat regiment (591st) had now become surplus to the brigade. One of its battalions had already been sent to Tunisia for emergency use as a truck battalion while the remainder was still engaged in operation of the port of Oran. In February the entire regiment was transferred to SOS with which it continued to be utilized as port troops almost until the end of the war. It is interesting to note that the regiment, reorganized in the fall of 1944 as a combat group, did excellent work with the Seventh Army and particularly in the assault crossing of the Rhine where its skilled boat operators were put to good use operating assault boats.

The shore regiment (531st) also sustained a serious reduction in its strength in February when one of its battalions was also sent to Tunisia for temporary duty as a truck unit. With the loss of these units and the uncertainty at this time as to any definite operational need for the brigade organization in the near future, the status of the brigade was at its lowest ebb. Serious consideration in higher headquarters was given to its inactivation in order that its headquarters personnel could be used elsewhere. On February 22 General Wolfe was transferred to duty as Engineer of SOS taking a number of the brigade staff with him while other key personnel were scattered on various assignments. Command of the brigade was assumed by Colonel Brown, the commander of the shore regiment, and training operations with the Invasion Training Center continued to the extent practicable.

The uncertainties concerning the future of the brigade suddenly disappeared late in March when word came that Operation Husky—the invasion of Sicily—was to be carried out and that the brigade was to participate. Due largely to the personal efforts of General Noce, Commanding General of EAC, who was then present in the theater, it was to be given responsibility for the operation and maintenance of the beaches in the operation against Sicily. For this purpose the brigade would be augmented by the 540th[2] and 36th Combat Engineers, both of which had had shore-party experience under General Patton in the Casablanca landing, and by other auxiliary units as required. The task that now confronted the brigade was one of great importance. The operational plan of the Seventh Army contemplated not only assault landings across difficult beaches against a skilled and alert enemy but its maintenance by beach supply for an indefinite period irrespective of the availability of any ports—an operation that had never before been successfully accomplished by any army in the face of enemy opposition. Moreover, the brigade in addition to its normal shore-party duties was to be charged with the additional function of operation of the beach dumps and any captured ports.

The brigade entered at once into a period of intensive preparation for its task. On March 22, 1943, General Wolfe, together with the brigade staff officers that had gone with him, rejoined the brigade. Arrangements were made for the early concentration in the Arzew area of the additional engineers and other type units that would be required and for the reorganization of these units to conform to the brigade's normal procedure. Operational planning for the operation started immediately in conjunction with Seventh Army headquarters. The brigade plan as finally established provided for several "beach groups." Each was built around a shore regiment as a nucleus and consisted in addition to that regiment of certain Quartermaster, Ordnance and other special type units, a DUKW battalion and a Navy beach battalion. Each beach group was designed to support the landing of one divisional sub-task force, with an estimated average capacity of 1,500 tons of supplies daily. Acting initially under divisional control, the beach groups would come under control of the Amphibian brigade when the beaches were consolidated. Provision was made for the expansion of the brigade staff by officers from the several technical services for the performance of its dump operation mission.

The 36th and 540th Combat Engineer Regiments arrived in the Arzew area early in April and shortly afterwards the battalion of the 531st Engineers that had been working in Tunisia also returned. The general plan for the amphibious training of the task force provided that the Fifth Army Invasion Training Center would provide training facilities and in conjunction with the Navy establish and coordinate divisional training programs. Upon the arrival of the 3d Infantry Division, the 36th Engineer Regiment which was to comprise its beach group, immediately joined up with it and its battalions engaged in a series of landing exercises and problems with the divisional combat teams. The first of the new Navy beach battalions, designed to work under the shore regiment as an integral part of the beach group, also arrived. Composed of new personnel, the Navy unit required much basic training. By arrangements with the Navy it was placed with the 531st Engineers and trained under their direction.

Many problems confronting the brigade remained yet to be solved, the most serious of which was assurance that the required unloading capacity could be met. With the advent of the DUKW into the theater and with fuller realization of its capabilities, confidence grew that this target would be achieved. The Organization and training of the necessary DUKW units, however, presented a heavy training load. A DUKW training program was instituted immediately and some 1,200 operators were trained for the operation by the 1st Brigade. The newly developed types of naval landing craft, now arriving in large numbers at Arzew, also presented difficult beaching and unloading problems, particularly the LST which, due to its deep stern draft grounded far off shore on a flat beach, rendering the unloading of vehicles, even though waterproofed, almost impossible. Several expedients were tried to bridge this gap but it was not until the arrival of the naval ponton cubicles which formed a causeway into the shore that the problem was solved. Many experiments were conducted in quick methods for breaching beach and underwater obstacles, a task for which the brigade together with the Navy and divisional engineers was held responsible. Methods of clearing the obstacles and mines on the beaches were readily developed but the problem of elimination of underwater obstacles was never satisfactorily solved.

Upon the completion of its training cycle early in May the 3d Division departed for Tunisia taking with it its beach group (36th Engineers) and there continued its preparations in the vicinity of Bizerte. The 1st Infantry Division took its place at the Training Center where, joined by the 531st Engineer Beach Group, it commenced its training cycle.

During this period the brigade experienced its only enemy air attack while in this area, resulting in the death of five of the brigade's men. The Brigade Boat Maintenance Company, which had been counted upon for DUKW maintenance, was lost to the brigade. In accordance with theater agreements of the previous winter, this fine unit was turned over to the Navy for use in repair of its landing craft, where it remained until the conclusion of all amphibious operations in the theater. Reverting to the Army in the late summer of 1944 it was returned to the United States for use in the Pacific. While under naval control it participated in all amphibious operations in the European Theater. Its record was a splendid one and completely justified the forethought and energy that had gone into its organization.

On May 25 a change in commanders occurred. General Wolfe left the brigade and went to Allied Force Headquarters as Deputy G-3. Colonel E. M. Caffey, formerly commander of the famous 20th Engineer Combat Regiment, assumed command.

At this time discussions at Force Headquarters indicated that the mission of the brigade in the Husky operation would be considerably enlarged. As finally decided, this enlargement turned over to the brigade, after the landing phase, responsibility for the execution of all supply plans within the theater of operations emanating from Force Headquarters, including the operation of ports. This was rather a large-sized order and required the reorganization and augmentation of the brigade headquarters to a strength of 100 officers and 400 men and an increase in troop strength to a total of 30,000. Eventually Colonel Caffey used about 23,000 of the brigade and attached troops and many thousands of prisoners and hired laborers.

For movement to the target, once in the assault convoys the brigade troops travelled with the sub-task forces to whom they were attached for the initial or landing phase of the operations. The expedition staged out from ports all along the North African coast from Oran to Tunis during the latter part of June and early July. By the afternoon of July 9 (D minus 1), the sea near Malta was swarming with thousands of ships and craft, all seemingly headed toward the Strait of Messina on a course to the northward. At dusk the course was changed to the westward and the expedition slid along the southwestern coast of Sicily. By midnight the Seventh Army was in the transport areas. During the afternoon the rising wind had made the sea so rough that a landing next morning seemed impossible. However, General Patton's weather man, who had picked the weather for the landing in Morocco a few months earlier, was on the job. He called the turn again. As the evening wore on, the wind died away and the seas abated so that conditions were good enough for the attack to proceed as planned.

The landings were scheduled over a front of about fifty miles. On the right the 45th Infantry Division was to land with the 40th

Engineer Beach Group and capture the Comiso airfield. In the center the 1st Infantry Division with the 531st Engineer Beach Group would land east of Gela and push in to the airfield at Ponte Olivo. On the left the 3d Infantry Division with the 36th Engineer Beach Group would capture Licata and push inland. Elements of the 82d Airborne Division were to be dropped near the Ponte Olivo Airport. The 2d Armored Division and other troops with the 540th Engineer Beach Group remained afloat initially as a reserve.

Out in the transport area there was a quiet bustle as the boats were hoisted out and the troops embarked. The chug-chug of the boat motors died away as the small craft moved toward the beaches, Ashore, except for fires started by an earlier bombing and the occasional sweep of a nervous searchlight, nothing could be seen. Thousands held their breath and wondered—what?

At 2:45 A.M. on July 10, as the first waves of the 1st Division hit the beach at Gela, at least one question was answered—Americans were definitely not welcome. The red glow of interlaced tracers hung a curtain along its beaches and there was heard the rattle and roar of a battle. The scene was repeated at Licata and elsewhere. At dawn enemy bombers and fighters arrived to add to the commotion and were never long absent during the next two days. The landings on the right and left progressed inshore rapidly but heavy infantry-supported German tank attacks in the center made the going rough in the 1st Division sector. German artillery firing over open sights from the heights back of Ponte Olivo also caused considerable annoyance. Through D-day and D plus 1 the 1st Division was repeatedly counterattacked but by the end of D plus 1 the Germans had had enough and began to withdraw and the situation all along the front was good.

During this first phase the shore engineers were engaged in their normal duties of clearing away obstacles and mines, improving beach exits and roads, arranging facilities on the beaches, and landing troops, vehicles, and supplies. At Licata and Gela they aided in clearing the enemy out of his beach fortifications and at Gela assisted in repelling the enemy's tanks. Following the excitement of the landing they settled down to the exhausting and never-ending task of feeding in supplies and reinforcements for an advancing army.

On D plus 4 brigade headquarters was divided to reassume control of its troops and take over the supply of the army. This presented a considerable problem because the greater part of the headquarters was still in Africa and did not arrive for several days. However, through the splendid work of the beach group commanders—Colonels Brown, Marvin, Mason and Gerdes—coordinated effort was attained and the ground work laid for a rapid consolidation of the unloading and supply effort.

Spread out as they were, the activities of the brigade could succeed only if adequate communications of all sorts could be arranged. Because of local conditions which impeded its proper functioning radio was used only occasionally and main reliance was placed on messengers and telephones. The messengers took a terrific beating on the narrow, dusty, traffic-jammed roads. The wire lines were frequently cut, sometimes for pure cussedness. Where the cutter seemed honest in his story of seeking wire for his hay he was given the benefit of the doubt and deported to Africa. Where the case was actual sabotage, the punishment was more severe.

The enemy had destroyed a considerable number of bridges as he withdrew, but since most of the streambeds were dry this was merely an annoyance in the brigade area. A few hours' work by the mine detector crews would clear a route around a bridge site and then the bulldozers would rough out a bypass that served all purposes. Fortunately none of the steel railway bridges in southern Sicily had been seriously damaged.

Study of available information in Africa indicated that the island of Sicily was well served by railroads. The big question was how many of them would be found intact or would remain undamaged. Immediately after the landing vigorous reconnaissance was undertaken by Seventh Army engineers and by the brigade to ascertain the condition of the trackage, terminals and other features and to locate engines and rolling stock. A few days' work served to get the line in operation along the south coast and inland toward Canicatti. Removal of bearings and critical parts by the enemy and general dilapidation necessitated extensive repairs to much of the equipment. One source of worry was the possible destruction of one or more of the numerous tunnels. Many had been extensively mined or filled with straw so that they could be burned out but luckily there was no tunnel damage. The most constant anxiety, once a start had been made on getting trains rolling, was water for the locomotives. These used huge quantities of water on account of the steep grades and heavy curves. The usual sources of water and of watering facilities had been destroyed or extensively damaged. This problem was eventually solved but in the process the railroad was wryly renamed "The Sicilian Southeastern Dehydrated." The 727th Railway Operating Battalion (from the Southern Railroad) took hold in excellent fashion and as much as any one other agency was responsible for keeping the campaign moving. Shortage of vehicles, long hauls over narrow, tortuous, steep roads, and driver exhaustion would have so slowed the delivery of supplies that without the railway the campaign would have gone very much more slowly.

As the troops advanced inland, the brigade inherited responsibility for a large part of southern and south central Sicily. The security of the area had to be undertaken with very scanty forces. The greatest emphasis was laid on guarding the railroad, especially tunnels and bridges. Outside of a few parachutists who dropped in and were promptly rounded up, the enemy made no attempt to disrupt the rear areas. There was some sabotage, especially against wire communications, but excellent work by the Counterintelligence Corps and the AMG quickly weeded out the disaffected local inhabitants. Actual or potential evildoers were confined or deported promptly. In the towns and countryside military and local police forces maintained a high degree of order. As a whole the population was glad to be out of the war and welcomed the opportunity to live quietly. Food was a cause of concern and steps were taken to facilitate the gathering of the wheat harvest, to provide power for flour mills, and to restore local traffic. To aid in combating disease constant effort was devoted to the water supplies of the towns and to getting them cleansed of the filth of ages and of the debris of war. To aid in the production of foodstuffs many of the populace were put to work clearing mines from the fields and getting them off the beaches used by the fishermen.

Until better facilities could be had, it had been planned to use the small ports at Gela, Licata, and Porto Empedocle for the bulk of the unloading. The port facilities at Gela were an open anchorage, well off shore, and a well constructed pier. Someone had blown out sixty feet of the pier but engineers soon repaired this. Within a few days after the landing it was decided to close out activities at Gela and to concentrate unloading at Licata and Porto Empedocle. At these two places there were small harbors inclosed by moles, and better rail and road nets. Considerable work had to be done to repair bomb damage but this was rapidly taken care of and the redistribution of the brigade's forces completed.

The 40th Engineer Beach Group was charged with taking over Porto Empedocle. The 36th Engineer Beach Group remained at Licata, aided by a battalion of the 540th Engineer Combat Regiment. The 531st Engineer Beach Group gradually passed to road and security missions.

The campaign moved along rapidly and soon outran the projected schedule. New tactical plans were put into operation. The combined speed-up and change of plans were reflected in the activities of the brigade. The axis of supply, which at first had been north and south, had to be split to provide an axis to the northwest to provide for the corps headed for Palermo. A minor axis reached out to the westward to the zone of the 82d Airborne Division. Then the main axis was bent off to the northeast. At this time the brigade was working in a fan-shaped area eighty miles deep with the handle of the fan at Licata. From the shore to the most advanced Army supply points the entire supply organization was manned by basic and attached troops of the 1st Brigade under Colonel E. M. Caffey. The old Army axiom that the impetus of supply must be from the rear was being followed every minute of the day. Besides the great job of pushing things forward to the troops, there was also the operation of evacuation facilities to bring back the sick and wounded and load them out for Africa.

The emphasis seemed always to be on more ammunition for the front. The brigade met the demand. Truck convoys loaded with explosives actually passed through areas where the shells of the enemy's isolated artillery criss-crossed overhead with American shells. Issue points were set up very close to the front. At Messina an Army ammunition dump was started alongside some 105s while they were still firing preparatory to moving forward. During one crisis every vehicle in the brigade except ambulances, DUKWs and jeeps, was hauling ammunition into Caltanissetta.

About July 20 it seemed certain that Palermo would soon be captured. The 540th Engineer Beach Group was shaken loose, re-organized, and readied to move into Palermo with port repair troops, DUKWs and the ever-necessary bulldozers to rehabilitate the port and to set up a system of supply eastward along the north shore. The plan was carried into execution about July 22, the com-mander of the 540th reporting upon arrival at Palermo to Seventh Army headquarters. Besides being very largely instrumental in starting supplies moving along the northeast coast, the 540th Beach Group furnished the troops and DUKWs to assist the infantry in several end runs around the Germans on the way to Messina.

As the port of Palermo was gradually brought back into opera-tion, the work of unloading through the small ports of Porto Empedocle and Licata gradually diminished although the forward-ing of supplies already in storage went on very much as before with little rest and no relief. The American Army was headed east and was soon in a friendly race with the British Eighth Army to see which one would be first to enter Messina. What kind of uniform was worn by the first man into that city is not a matter of record in headquarters of the 1st Brigade. All that mattered was that by August 17 (D plus 38) soldiers of the 15th Army Group, American and British, had taken Messina away from the enemy and the cam-paign was over.

Without including the assistance furnished by the 1st Brigade at Palermo, the beaches and minor parts in southern Sicily had contributed as follows to the campaign: personnel, 199,165; vehicles, 23,940; long tons of supplies, 161,726. Approximately 50,000 casualties and prisoners had been evacuated to the rear. The Seventh Army had been supplied in a fast-moving campaign in which the axes of supply changed and lengthened daily. The details would fill books. In a message of congratulation General Patton summed them up— "The supply and maintenance service performed a miracle." The brigade was content with this word from the man it regarded as America's grandest soldier.

As time went on officers and men of the beach area group designated to take over the island had been worked into the activities carried on by the brigade so that when the time came (August 20-21) they could assume direction of affairs and take over such of the base area troops as had become attached to the brigade. The brigade could then prepare for further undertakings. The change-over was made without incident and the shore troops sat back— but not for long.

By August 27 the 36th Engineers and the 531st Engineers were loading out for Africa to make the Salerno landing with the Fifth Army. A detachment from brigade headquarters was sent to Fifth Army headquarters at Mostaganem (forty miles east of Oran) to check plans. Other troops of the 1st Brigade joined Fifth Army elements in Africa and still others joined British X Corps. Such amphibious troops as remained in Sicily passed to Fifth Army control. For those moving in the assault convoys it was a time of rush and sweat. They had to load out of Sicily on August 27, go to Africa, rejoin, re-equip, plan, load out, travel to Italy, and land at Salerno on September 9.

The proposed battleground was a very uninviting spot for an amphibious landing. It lay on the floor of an amphitheater facing the sea with the Germans in force occupying the reserved seats and backed by their artillery in the high balconies. The beach itself was flat as was the country behind it for several miles. There were numerous canals and streams, with a sizable one, the Sele River, running into the sea straight through the position. A few miles back from the beach rose high, precipitous hills full of well dug-in German positions.

British X Corps was to land on the left toward Salerno; American VI Corps supported by the 531st Engineer Shore Regiment was to land on the right near the old Roman city of Paestum. The beaches were heavily mined, fortified and defended. The German Air Force was present in strength. German tanks roamed about in the hinterland to back up the defense. As regards the weather, landing conditions were admittedly good. However, this good weather gave the enemy excellent visibility on our beach operations and fine flying conditions for his bombers. For some days after the landing it was nip and tuck. As at Gela on the invasion of Sicily, only more so, enemy tanks and artillery kept the beaches and the area directly behind them smoking. The German Air Force was a continual bother and attacked the beaches and shipping as many as twenty-two times in the course of a single day. A 500-pound bomb landed with very tragic results in a shore battalion command post where an officers' meeting was being held. The bulldozers of the shore engineers were very appealing targets to the German artillery and drew their fire like bees to honey. By the time the beachhead was secure, practically every dozer operator of the first few days had been replaced.

It was nearly a month before Fifth Army broke through the encircling hills and seized Naples. After that they were supplied through that port. In the meanwhile the 540th Engineers had come in at Salerno to help on the beaches. The 36th Engineers were then serving as Corps engineer troops after having gone through the tank wringer on the Salerno plain.

The 40th Engineers came in to help tidy up Naples. With the establishment of unloading facilities here, the 540th was shifted from Salerno to the port and the other Amphibian Engineer troops moved up-country to perform miscellaneous, useful engineer work pending another landing. The 540th proved to be a Jack-of-all-trades.

In mid-November 1943 the headquarters of the 1st Brigade, the 531st Engineer Shore Regiment, the 201st Medical Battalion, the 286th Signal Company, the 262d DUKW Battalion, the Small Arms Platoon, and the 3497th MAM Company (specialists on DUKW repair) sailed for the United Kingdom by way of Africa to get ready for what turned out to be the biggest show of all, the invasion of

Normandy. Score to date for the 1st Brigade: Morocco, Algeria, Tunisia, Sicily, Italy; four hits, four runs, plenty of errors . . . but five battle stars and valuable experience which could be learned only in actual combat. The 1st Brigade was now truly a veteran outfit.

The heroism of the Amphibian Engineers was summed up in the following newspaper article widely read throughout the States:

ARMY'S HEROIC ENGINEERS WRITE
GLORIOUS PAGE IN ITALY
WITH THE AMERICAN FIFTH ARMY

Italy, Sept. 12, 1943. (U.P.) Many American amphibious engineers have died on the Italian beaches.

They have died not only with their boots on, but in the actual course of their work and they have established a record for courage which those who have watched them will never forget.

While other soldiers have been able to dive into convenient foxholes they have stayed right out there in the open, working tirelessly under threat of strafing attacks and submitting to repeated heavy attacks by heavy German bombers.

Despite this they have kept up their inexorable, unwholesome job of shifting thousands of tons of ammunition from landing craft to dumps, building roads and making it possible for our beachhead to become solidly established.

Theirs has been the greatest feat of collective heroism ever witnessed. While other troops have been able to concentrate on defending themselves and destroying the enemy, they have been unable to take cover for a minute. It was and is their courage which is making our fight possible.

NOTES

[1] It is interesting to note that the influence of British Commando raids caused this landing to be made under cover of darkness. Some of the confusion and lost boats in the North Africa landing helped the many advocates of daylight landings. Only one of MacArthur's landings (the first) was made at night.

[2] The 540th Engineer Combat Regiment was formed by the Engineer Amphibian Command in the fall of 1942 at Camp Edwards, Massachusetts, from personnel furnished by the 2d Engineer Special Brigade. See Appendix B.

7
2D BRIGADE TO AUSTRALIA

The 2d Brigade was scarcely established in its new camps at Carrabelle on the flat sandy shores of the Gulf of Mexico and busily engaged on reconnaissance of beaches and establishment of a boatyard when orders came to move at once to Fort Ord, California, for staging preparatory to shipping for Australia. Trudeau's mission to MacArthur (see Chapter 5) had resulted in an urgent request by General MacArthur to the War Department for Amphibian Engineer troops. There was quick action by the War Department in meeting his request. The 2d Brigade had fully expected to train with the 38th Infantry Division at Carrabelle before going overseas. With its sudden move to the Pacific, the 2d had to turn all its landing craft and training plans over to the 3d Brigade, which was rapidly transferred from Cape Cod to Carrabelle.

Fort Ord turned out to be a model garrison with fine barracks, paved roads, surfaced drillfield, etc. So different from Carrabelle! Instead of the "few days" the brigade expected to be at Ord, it was soon obvious that it would be weeks before transports could be made available. (The loss of the large transport *President Coolidge* by striking an American mine in the southwest Pacific was said to have disrupted the schedule). Training of boat and shore engineers, especially in combat firing and in communications, was renewed. There were only thirty old landing craft but maximum use was made of them. The surging swells of Monterey Bay proved more difficult than either Cape Cod or Carrabelle. The delay in departure also enabled the brigade to participate in the initial training in the new 2½-ton amphibious truck, the DUKW, soon to become famous, and in the 4.5-inch barrage rocket. The 2d Brigade took these two important innovations in amphibious warfare to the western Pacific with it and was the first unit to employ them in combat against the Japs.

In mid-January 1943 final embarkation orders arrived and on the 24th the Brigade started moving in echelons from San Francisco to Australia. The scattered transports landed over a period of weeks at various ports in Australia from Sydney in the south to Townsville 1,200 miles up the east coast. It took literally months to assemble all the troops and their gear in the two main areas assigned to the 2d Brigade, Cairns and Rockhampton, over six hundred miles apart. Brigade Headquarters was ten miles from Rockhampton, where Lieutenant General Eichelberger's I Corps headquarters had been established when he returned from New Guinea. As soon as Sixth Army headquarters arrived the 2d Brigade was assigned to that Army under Lieutenant General (later General) Walter Krueger. The Brigade was fortunate in drawing this assignment, for General Krueger immediately recognized the need for amphibian engineers and helped their development throughout the war. He was a most valuable friend and leader.

The 2d Brigade had been in Australia only a few days before the Tokyo radio was heard to announce, "Welcome to Australia, American Amphibian Engineers. We know you will assemble boats at Cairns. We'll be over to see you one of these days." But they never came! Instead the Amphibs went over to see them.

All keyed up to go immediately into combined training with Australian and American troops, the Amphibians got a rude awakening when they found no landing boats available. The fine assembly plant at Cairns where hundreds of landing boats were to have been ready just did not yet exist. The 411th Engineer Base Shop Battalion which was to operate the plant had arrived in late January 1943 to find the plant not even started and the site encumbered with an old sawmill whose owners were holding out for a high settlement. The 411th had to turn its machinists into carpenters and electricians. On top of this, the transports bringing the

Amphibian troops and equipment and knocked-down landing barges from the States seemed to vie with each other in arriving at widely separated ports. It was many weeks before the equipment was sorted out from the mass of materiel for other units and finally delivered over the rushed Australian railways (with their variable gauges) to its proper unit.

In the meantime the 2d Engineer Special Brigade, with the 411th Base Shop Battalion attached, had been working at top speed in the heaviest tropical rains and mud, building a 450-foot boat assembly plant with three production lines at Cairns. There was a battle for priorities to get this or that lumber, and of course the American electrical equipment did not fit into the Australian system until after much adjustment and reconstruction.

Finally on April 7, 1943, the first landing boat (LCVP) was turned out at Cairns. Once under way the plant operated with the efficiency of a mass production assembly line. Soon seven completed boats were being delivered each day. The brigade took on new life as the boatmen got back to the throttles of their well-loved boats and began to learn this improved type of LCVP which they had not seen in the United States. These craft were armor-plated; those used in the United States for training were not. Combined training with the Australian troops in the Cairns area, who were anxious to get their first amphibious instruction, was soon started. In the very waters in which Zane Grey had fished off Cairns, many Australians were seasick for the first time in their lives, but soon they were toughened to that.

After some preliminary training it was learned that one of the regiments of the 2d Brigade would be teamed with the famous 9th Australian Division (The Rats of Tobruk), for combined training near Cairns for an amphibious operation scheduled for New Guinea. All took hold with renewed vigor and determination. It was not long before the Australian and the Amphibian staffs were talking in the same terms, we Americans becoming familiar with their organization, abbreviations, and tactics, and they with ours.

In May 1943 a detachment of the 592d Engineer Boat and Shore Regiment moved with ten LCMs from Australia to Port Moresby,

New Guinea, the first Amphibian Engineer unit to land on that elongated island of mountains and jungles which was to keep the Amphibians busy for many months to come. This first detachment operated on a supply run to the Australians at Bulldog near the Lakekami River, two hundred miles west of Port Moresby, an area where no roads had ever existed. These waters were subject to Jap air attack. Coral reefs were extensive and treacherous. Later, part of this detachment moved to Milne Bay, where they were engaged in lighterage for this base which was soon to be so important, both to the Army and to the Navy.

In the early days of the war Milne Bay was a pestilential hole, saturated with malaria. The official rate was 4,000 per 1,000, which means each soldier could expect an average of four attacks of malaria per year. In 1942 the Japs had invaded this bay and made a successful amphibious landing on its north shore under cover of darkness and heavy rain. Advancing a few miles through the jungle, this Jap force attempted to capture the recently constructed airstrip. Here an American engineer general service regiment, the 43d, which had constructed the strip, made an undying name for itself by defeating the Banzai attacks of the Jap force. The airstrip became littered with Jap dead. The remnants were mopped up by the Australian infantry who pursued the dispersed Japs through the infested jungles. Meanwhile the American and Australian air forces had driven off the supporting Jap fleet, sinking some of their small landing craft.

Incidentally some of these Jap craft were later raised, repaired, and put into operation by the Allies. The 2d Brigade had a good opportunity to compare their craft with the latest Jap models. They found many good points in the Jap craft. Their marine design was so much better than the American blunt-nose flat-bottomed boats that the Jap diesel engines needed only a third as many horsepower as the American to make eight knots. On the other hand the ramps of the Jap small landing craft were narrow and unwieldy and restricted the types and sizes of vehicles which could be carried.

In the meantime Major General Horace Fuller of the U.S. 41st Division called for Amphibian Engineers and their landing craft to help him push from Buna on to Salamaua. Just as soon as the Cairns plant could turn out the craft, an ESB task group from the 532d Regiment under Major (later Lieutenant Colonel) Harry F. Rising was shipped to Milne Bay. This force moved by night from Milne Bay in their small craft around the north coast to Oro Bay. This was the first group of Allied landing craft to go around the north coast of New Guinea—but not the last. They were the vanguard of over two thousand boats the Amphibian Engineers were to navigate around that coast headed for the Japs. The 2d Brigade's first casualties were in this group when Jap bombs hit their bivouac a few nights after their arrival at Oro Bay.

On June 14, 1943, a third task group from the 2d Brigade, this group under Colonel A. L. Keyes, moved from Cairns to New Guinea. This group opened up a new station on the tiny island of Samarai, forty miles by water from Milne Bay. Samarai is a beautiful South Sea island, so different from dirty, muddy Milne Bay.

Thus in June 1943 the 2d Brigade had three groups in New Guinea, one at Port Moresby with part of it moving to Milne Bay; another at Samarai preparing a new base for the amphibians; and a third at Oro Bay getting ready to support U.S. troops in a drive from Buna to the northwest. General MacArthur had stopped the Japs at the Milne Bay airstrip and shoved them back from Port Moresby over the lofty Owen Stanley Range. General Eichelberger had captured Buna and thereby gotten a foothold on the north coast of New Guinea. But to continue this slow push by land through towering mountains and impenetrable jungle would take ages to defeat the Japs. General MacArthur knew that. Although his resources were limited he was ready now to fulfill his "I shall return" pledge and he intended to use amphibious attack as his main weapon in the campaigns to come. His amphibious "end runs" in the campaign from Nassau Bay to Corregidor will undoubtedly be studied as a classic military operation for years to come. In Chapter 9 we shall describe the opening operations and how the Amphibian Engineers assisted him in this most unusual type of military campaign.

8
3D AND 4TH BRIGADES GET READY

In any story of units as widely dispersed in the theaters of war as those of the Amphibian Engineers it is necessary to pause now and then in order to summarize where the various units were engaged. Let us take stock as of January 1, 1943. The headquarters of the Command together with the specialist schools and the development board was still at Camp Edwards, Massachusetts. The waters of Nantucket Sound and Vineyard Sound were whipped by wintry winds which cut amphibious training to tests by the Development Board. To date three brigades had been formed.

The 1st Brigade, veterans of the Oran landing, were on port work in North Africa. Its boat maintenance unit (561st) under Lieutenant Colonel Earl Houston was still attached to the United States Navy, having been split into six separate units when it embarked from Scotland for North Africa on October 16-18, 1942. These six detachments had done absolutely indispensable work in the maintenance of boats for the Navy. In addition, during the assault phase before its maintenance shops could be set up ashore, the American Amphibs operated 25 small landing craft (LCAs) for the British when our Allies found themselves short of boat crews. The 561st did remarkable salvage work after it was set up ashore. Of 63 craft stranded and abandoned by the Navy east of Arzew, the 561st salvaged 60 and, after much repair work, put all 60 back into operation. Spare parts for small craft being nearly non-existent at Oran, the 561st sent a salvage detachment to Se-Cuff, 12 miles east of Algiers, and salvaged 34 Gray diesel engines from craft the

73

British had abandoned there after the November 8 landing. Another detachment salvaged 500 feet of treadway bridge sunk in the initial Arzew landing. The 561st was probably the only engineer and maintenance company in the war to construct surgical equipment. When an Army hospital near Oran ran out of bone-setting equipment after D-day and none was to be found anywhere, four enlisted men of the 561st duplicated the complicated sets and furnished the hospital all the sets that were needed.

The 2d Brigade, after its urgent priority move from Carrabelle to Fort Ord en route to Australia, found itself stymied there by lack of shipping to MacArthur's theater. Its advance detachment was already in Australia as was the advance detachment of the 411th Base Shop Battalion.

The 3d Brigade was actively engaged in combined training with the 38th Infantry Division at Carrabelle, Florida, where it had taken the 2d Brigade's place. In addition to taking over all the craft left by the 2d at Carrabelle, the 3d Brigade brought down from Cape Cod thirty of its own LCMs in a convoy through the inland waterways down the Atlantic coast and up the west coast of Florida. This was by far the longest trip any group of small landing craft had made up to that time. Combined training with the 38th Infantry Division was completed on January 15, 1943, whereupon similar training was immediately initiated with the 28th Infantry Division. This second period lasted until March 8, 1943.

The 411th Engineer Base Shop Battalion had been activated at Camp Edwards on August 17, 1942, under Major (later Colonel) James A. Bender. A platoon of its depot company went to England with the 1st Brigade. The battalion's mission, originally higher echelon maintenance of boats, had been changed to operation of the assembly plant for knocked-down LCVPs in Australia as arranged by Trudeau's mission (Chapter 5). Half the battalion had been sent to New Orleans on November 1 to receive instruction in the operations of the assembly line for landing craft at Higgins. The other half moved to Fort Ord, California. In late December 1942 the entire battalion assembled at San Francisco for shipment to Cairns, Australia, to build and operate the LCVP assembly plant there.

The next Amphibian Engineer unit to be activated was the 4th Engineer Amphibian (later Special) Brigade at Fort Devens, Massachusetts, on February 1, 1943. The initial commander was Major General Noce, in addition to his duties as commander of the Engineer Amphibian Command. Then Colonel Trudeau, formerly his Chief of Staff, commanded the brigade for a short period. Colonel (later Brigadier General) Henry Hutchings was then assigned command. He held this command until early 1946 when he returned to the States, after having led his brigade through New Guinea and the Philippines to the occupation of Japan. The major portion of the officer and enlisted cadre for the 4th Brigade was carefully selected from the 3d Engineer Special Brigade. The enlisted fillers, all selected men from all sections of the United States, arrived soon after activation and began their basic training on the snow- and ice-covered ground at Fort Devens.

Prior to the formation of the 4th Brigade and during the period of basic training of the brigade, plans for the complete training of all specialists were carried out. The policies in this regard had been decided after very careful study as to the type of man to be selected and the course to be given him. There were three types of schools employed for the specialist training:

a. Those run by large corporations for benefit of the Army, such as the General Motors and Gray Engine School for the diesel engine; the Higgins Industries, Inc., School for boatmen in New Orleans, etc.

b. Schools run by the various services of the Army; examples: Ordnance schools for machinists, welders, battery repairmen, etc.; and similar schools by other services.

c. Schools run by the Engineer Amphibian Command where it was felt that the facilities and instructors available in the command were superior for the purpose to those available elsewhere; where the convenience was so important and the numbers so large that adequate facilities and instructors were arranged for (for example,

basic radiomen, cooks and bakers, mess sergeants, etc.);
or for specialists peculiar to the Engineer Special Brigades and for which we were compelled to run our own
schools.

Nearly 1,500 specialists were thus given preliminary training,
either prior to or during the period of basic training of the brigade, with the result that when the brigade was put together it had
the best balanced cadre and specialist group of any of the four brigades, and the preliminary training enabled it to develop very rapidly.

There was a further capitalization on the lessons learned over
a long period of time by the Classification Section of the Command's Director of Personnel Office. Some of these lessons had
been learned by members of this Section during the early days of
the Replacement Training Center at Fort Leonard Wood. They had
been improved upon and applied with increasing effectiveness
during the period of activation and training of the first three brigades and were then reviewed and crystalized into the final set of
policies and procedures which were applied to the 4th Brigade. The
classification of the incoming men for this brigade was a very excellent piece of work and resulted overall in placing a round peg in
a round hole much better than any unit organized to date. It was
the subject of many commendations by visitors from outside the
Command.

The preparation of a complete set of manuals for the use of
special brigades was begun in 1942. The experienced staff officers
and commanders within the command prepared the basic data. The
amplification, illustration, arrangement, and final writing were
placed in the hands of a group of experts under then First Lieutenant Ralph Ingersoll. Several of these pamphlets were available for
use by the 4th Brigade and the material of other pamphlets while
not in final form was in such form as to be used beneficially by the
brigade. This set of manuals received very wide distribution
throughout the world by other services and other nations. They
were a very valuable aid in the training of this brigade.

The first review of the 4th Brigade was held March 26, 1943. The troops marched by with a precision and military bearing that belied the fact that they, for the most part, were recruits of only a few weeks' training. But, of course, they had not yet really gotten into their amphibian training. Shortly thereafter, as soon as space was available, the 4th Brigade moved to Camp Edwards, Massachusetts. Some of its units spent a short time in Camp Edwards proper while they were preparing the camps on the Sound. By the middle of April the camps at Washburn Island, Cotuit and Falmouth had been occupied and the Brigade had embarked upon its amphibious training program.

The immediate objective was to prepare the brigade by June 30 to perform its primary mission, that of transporting an infantry division from a friendly near shore to a hostile far shore and maintaining it there. By intensive specialist, individual, small-unit, and progressively larger-unit amphibious training, including a series of boat-shore company and regimental amphibious problems, the 4th Brigade was prepared for its test problem held June 28-30, 1943. This successful brigade maneuver proved that, within five months of its activation date, the 4th Brigade was able to perform its complicated primary mission in a creditable manner.

During July and August the 4th Brigade received combat and general engineer training in addition to perfecting its amphibious technique. This period culminated in August with another brigade maneuver, this time on the rougher waters of Nantucket Sound. Immediately after this exercise one of the shore battalions was sent to Camp Myles Standish, Massachusetts, where it carried out a vital post construction training. One shore company from each regiment was sent to the Boston Port of Embarkation for practical training in loading and unloading vessels and other allied port operations.

During this same period every man received expert instruction in swimming, diving and life saving under the auspices of the American Red Cross. Emphasis was placed upon instilling in each man confidence in his ability to sustain himself if thrown into the water without life-jacket or preserver. This period of water training and safety was climaxed by an exhibition of precision water

drills, daring dives into flaming oil-covered water, life-saving drills
and other types of aquatic maneuvers.

At the shore camps night problems were emphasized, both on
land and at sea. During these problems the men learned the lone-
liness of the night at sea. Having to rely upon their own good judg-
ment and upon whatever navigation equipment was provided them,
they learned how to reach their objective, the enemy beach, in the
dim mists of morning. In these night problems in rough seas, brigade men frequently distinguished themselves beyond the normal
call of duty. One soldier received the Soldier's Medal for extraordinary bravery and attention to duty, the first of many decorations
to follow for the members of the 4th Engineer Special Brigade.

An essential part of the training of the 4th Engineer Special
Brigade was the training of individual specialists. This was accomplished by continuing to send individuals to various civilian schools
throughout the United States and to centralized schools conducted
by the Engineer Amphibian Command and by the brigade at Camp
Edwards.

Major General Noce made a second trip to the European Theater in March 1943, Colonel Hutchings serving in his place until
his return. Finally on May 19, 1943, General Noce was permanently
transferred from the command he founded, going to an important
staff assignment in the European Theater. It had been decided that
no more special brigades would be formed by the Command. Again
Colonel Hutchings took his place. For his brilliant leadership of
the Engineer Amphibian Command, General Noce was awarded the
Distinguished Service Medal.

Headquarters, Engineer Amphibian Command, much reduced
in size, continued to function at Camp Edwards in support of the
amphibian troops it had formed until December 27, 1943, when it
was moved to Camp Gordon Johnston, Florida.

In the meantime, on May 20, 1943, the 692d Engineer Base
Shop Battalion was activated at Camp Edwards, Massachusetts.
Its mission was to furnish higher echelon maintenance support
for the large number of Engineer Special Brigade landing craft
scheduled for the Western Pacific. Lieutenant Colonel Paul E.

Gieselmann, who as an engineer from the Mobile Engineer District, had built Camp Carrabelle in 1942, was the commander of this battalion. Part of this 1,000-man battalion moved to Carrabelle (Camp Gordon Johnston) for two months to assist in boat maintenance there. Early in December 1943, the entire battalion was moved to New Orleans where it embarked for New Guinea via the Panama Canal.

In answer to General MacArthur's call for another amphibian brigade in the Western Pacific, the 3d Brigade moved during the period April 10-30, 1943, from Camp Gordon Johnston, Florida, to Fort Ord, California, to stage for shipment to Australia. As the 2d Brigade had had difficulty getting suitable replacements for its losses in the Western Pacific, Brigadier General Ogden arranged for the 3d Brigade to leave the United States with an authorized overstrength of twenty-five per cent in the grade of lieutenant and fifteen per cent as privates. This far-sighted policy was to pay dividends later after the brigade had been in action. However, much to the disgust of its officers and men, the 3d Brigade had to wait at Fort Ord for over six months before it could ship out for the Western Pacific. It was reported this delay was caused by the shortage of shipping and the change of priorities in troops being shipped overseas.

Early in September 1943 the 4th Brigade was separated from the Engineer Amphibian Command and moved to Camp Gordon Johnston. The immediate problem was to engage in combined training with the veteran 4th Infantry Division, which later distinguished itself in the European Theater of Operations. This training was carried on during October and November with several of the brigade's units winning commendations for their enthusiastic and thorough work.

The final divisional maneuver was run off in the Gulf of Mexico during a sudden tropical storm which whipped up 10-foot seas. Due to expert seamanship and boat handling all but five of the small landing craft reached the far shore. These five foundered and sank. At one time over a hundred men were struggling in the water, Amphibians as well as the infantry passengers. By intelligent rescue and life-saving methods not a single man lost his life. These operations served to complete the amphibious training of the brigade and weld it into a highly skilled organization, capable of performing any combined operation within the capabilities of its equipment.

The brigade's Boat Maintenance Battalion (564th) and the Boat Maintenance and Salvage Sections of the regiments performed expertly by keeping over seventy per cent of the Brigade boats in operating condition at all times despite marked shortage in critical spare parts and the hard usage given the boats. This was climaxed by having over ninety per cent of the boats operating for the final division maneuver even though the boats were old, had been used continually for two months, and many critical spare parts were scarce or lacking altogether. Many repairs had to be improvisations.

The 4th Division was alerted at Camp Gordon Johnston for overseas movement and departed for the European Theater. Almost simultaneously the Army Service Forces Training Center was established at Camp Gordon Johnston, the largest amphibious training center in the United States. The 4th Brigade contributed its overstrength in officers and men to this endeavor and assisted by providing cadre and instructors on special duty and by providing many other services. Simultaneously the brigade commander, Brigadier General Henry Hutchings, Jr., became commander of the Army Service Forces Training Center, Camp Gordon Johnston, but retained command of the Brigade as his principal assignment.

At the close of its first year of endeavor, the 4th Brigade was busily engaged on a high-priority construction program to rehabilitate and enlarge Camp Gordon Johnston to accommodate the new training center and in training 1,300 recruits to take the places of the trained men transferred from the brigade to the Army Service Forces Training Center.

Early in January 1944 it was learned that the brigade would soon head overseas. The task of equipping, packing and preparation for movement of the 4th Brigade to the port of embarkation was begun. From early March until June units of the brigade passed through the port of embarkation at San Francisco en route to the Pacific War Zone. After some of the units had already embarked it was learned that the 4th Brigade would be required to furnish a thousand men for a steel barge construction program upon arrival in Australia. The Boat Battalion of the 534th Engineer Boat and Shore Regiment was selected for this assignment. A brigade liaison officer in California contacted the Kaiser Ship Building Corporation and worked out a ten-day training program for this new type of work. The selected troops went direct to the Kaiser yards at Richmond, California, and engaged in intensive instruction in welding and riveting. The troops were billeted and fed at the shipyards. Before this training program was completed these brigade troops were working on the line with the regularly employed shipyard workmen. At the close of this intensive training program the Kaiser Ship Building Corporation praised highly the skill of these versatile boatmen and many commendations were received.

When the 4th Brigade shifted to Camp Gordon Johnston in September 1943 its commander, Brigadier General (then Colonel) Hutchings, relinquished command of the Engineer Amphibian Command to Colonel T. M. Mulligan, who had been with the Command from its earliest days. On December 27 the Command was moved to Camp Gordon Johnston, finally having closed out at Camp Edwards. There it was attached to the Army Service Forces Training Center. It had been decided that no more Engineer Special Brigades would be activated in the U.S. On April 1, 1944, Lieutenant Colonel M. V. Pothier, its last commander, officially terminated the Engineer Amphibian Command. He had been with the Command from its earliest days.

It must be recalled that the Command was originally organized because of the inability at that time of the United States Navy to furnish enough trained small-boat crews to carry out operations for crossing the English Channel as then being planned. It was inevitable that, sooner or later, this "inability" would be considered terminated.

In the European Theater the Amphibian Engineers, although restricted to shore work, had fully justified their organization and had paid off many fold. In the Western Pacific, where amphibious operations were more extensive, the Amphibians had proved themselves indispensable as boat-shore teams linking the Army and the Navy. Their value in that theater was emphasized by General MacArthur in his recommendation that the Engineer Special Brigade organization be retained in the postwar Army and by Vice Admiral Barbey, commander of the Seventh Amphibious Fleet, who stated that in his opinion the Engineer Special Brigade was the most efficient type of shore organization for amphibious warfare.

The Engineer Amphibian Command closed with the realization that its duty had been well done, that in an entirely new field of warfare it had made the vital contributions of an efficient shore engineer organization in the European Theater and of the excellent boat-shore teams ideal for amphibious warfare in the Western Pacific. In addition, it had pioneered many new developments discussed elsewhere in this book. It was unfortunate that not one of the brigades ever went into action with the division with which it had trained in the United States. The 2d Brigade trained with the 45th and 36th Infantry Divisions; the 3d Brigade with the 38th and 28th; the 4th Brigade with the 4th Infantry Division; yet all five infantry divisions went to Europe while all three amphibian brigades went to the Western Pacific. *C'est la guerre!*

9
MacArthur Starts His Return:
Nassau Bay–Lae–Finschhafen

At the close of Chapter 7 it was pointed out that amphibious attack was to be one of MacArthur's main weapons in his "return" to the Philippines. The terrain of New Guinea prohibited extensive land operations. The abrupt and lofty mountain ranges and dense jungles would be harder to overcome than the Japs. The difficulty of the short advance from Port Moresby to Buna over the Kokoda Trail had demonstrated this. Roads did not exist at all; even trails were almost impassable for foot soldiers and totally so for even the jeep. Malaria was another enemy to be considered. In the initial operations it was more dangerous than the Japs.

MacArthur's first drive was two-pronged, the Navy to move Sixth Army troops to two islands, Kiriwina and Woodlark (north of Milne Bay), which Australian scouts had found were unoccupied by the enemy; and the 2d Engineer Special Brigade to move a task force of the 41st Division from Buna to Nassau Bay. This bay was well in rear of the Jap front line. There was every reason to expect strong enemy opposition but it was planned and hoped to land on a beach where the Japs would be weak. That is the big advantage to the attacker in an amphibious attack. He can pick the point of attack and concentrate heavily on it. The defender cannot be strong at all beaches. The attacker's problem is to pick a beach where the enemy will probably be weak, where the enemy would be surprised. This usually means picking a beach where the terrain and surf conditions are difficult but not too difficult to prevent a safe landing.

NASSAU BAY–SALAMAUA

On the north coast of New Guinea elements of the 41st Division had been pushing the Japs north of Buna, but progress had been very slow mainly because of the lack of landing craft. In early June the 532d Engineer Boat and Shore Regiment had deck-loaded some LCVPs to Milne Bay and then run them under their own power under cover of darkness to Oro Bay (205 miles), the brigade's first long run in coral-reefed waters with which it was to become very familiar. Despite warnings to machine-gun defenders of that base that American landing craft would arrive that night, one itchy-trigger machine gunner was sure these strange craft blinking recognition signals to shore were Japs trying to fool him. He was an accurate gunner, too, for his second burst pinged on the armor-plate of several boats. The fact that it deflected American bullets gave the men confidence that Jap bullets too would be turned, but, of course, this was not to apply to the .50s and the 20mms and the 40mms which were encountered later.

After only one incomplete rehearsal with the task force from the 41st Division, a convoy of all available landing boats (29 LCVPs and an LCM), and three captured Jap landing barges operated by the Americans, convoyed by two PT boats, took off from near Morobe on June 29 for a landing at Nassau Bay behind the Japs. Every mile of the trip meant heavier seas and winds and more blinding rain. However, orders gave no leeway; the landing had to be made that night. A few minutes behind schedule due to the storm, the leading wave of LCVPs hit the beach, encountering 10- to 12-foot surf but fortunately no Japs. The surf was too much for the 36-foot boats. Only a few were able to retract before being swamped by the crashing waves. However, the troops were landed without the loss of a single man, even though considerable equipment was lost. The captured Jap barges turned back without attempting to land. Twenty-one of the LCVPs were left turned every which way on the beach and soon pounded into distorted shapes by the heavy waves. The boatmen rescued what equipment they could from the boats and reported to the infantry commander, who assigned them a position on the southern flank of the beach. There

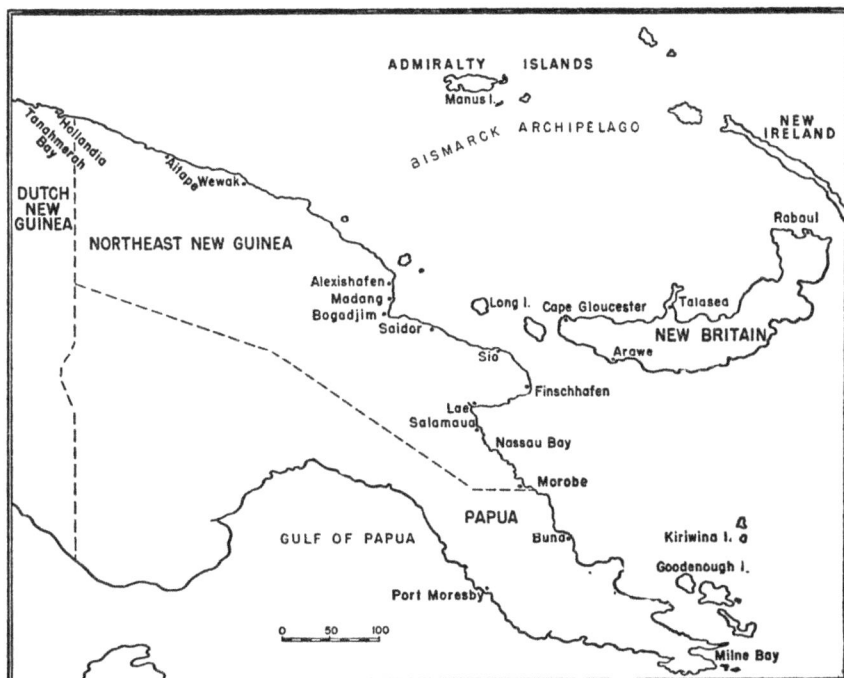

were plenty of Japs in the neighborhood, especially on Cape Dinga, just a mile south of Nassau Bay. A wounded Jap captain, captured later, said the roar of the American boats, trying desperately to get off the beach after unloading, had made them think tanks were being unloaded, so they held up their counterattack until they could verify this.

Finding there were no tanks and that the American force was small, the Japs counterattacked with great vigor the next evening, July 1. The boatmen on the south flank were hit at the same time that the infantry on the north flank had their hands full. One English-speaking Jap shouted out, "532d Engineers, we'll get you." How he knew the number was never found out. Well, they did "get" some Americans but when they closed to hand-to-hand fighting at night, the Japs found the boatmen skillful with knife and bayonet. It was necessary only to disembowel a few of them for the rest to flee, although later reports indicated there must have been 400 Japs in the attack against only 68 boatmen, and possibly as many as 700 Japs. Many of them were found dead the next morning. The

infantry commander later stated that all would have been lost had
the boatmen not repelled that attack on the south flank for all his
reserves had already been committed on the north flank where the
other Jap threat was made.[1]

This operation expanded day by day as more Japs were encountered and driven back on Salamaua. The land route was practically
impassable because of the jungles, steep mountains, and frequently
flooded streams. Every night the boats of the 2d Engineer Brigade
carried up more troops, artillery, ammunition, tractors, jeeps, and
the hundred other items an army must have. Every return trip
brought something back—casualties, sick, mail, relieved troops.
Often the boats had to cut down their motors and land quietly in
the dark, as close as 500 yards from Jap machine gunners. At other
times they reconnoitered along the coast in broad daylight to draw
enemy fire so hidden Allied artillery could knock out the Japs. If
Jap mortar fire on the beaches got too close at night, the boats
would retract and lay to quietly until the moon went down or until
the fire ceased, when they would go in again and complete unloading. Sometimes they made two or three landings in one night. At
this time the Jap air force was so strong that no Navy craft were
allowed to advance northwest of Milne Bay. It was not until late
August 1943 that a naval vessel as large as a destroyer or an LCT
ventured along the north coast of New Guinea. The advance up the
rugged coast from Buna to Salamaua would have been impossible
without that line of communications made up of 2d ESB craft.

The number of ESB landing boats required for the Salamaua
operation built up to over a hundred. Both Australian and American troops used them in the 74-day campaign which culminated in
the fall of Salamaua on September 12, 1943.

LAE CAMPAIGN

Having completed the combined training with the 9th Australian Division at Cairns, the task force of the 2d Brigade which was
to go in with that division in the Lae landing assembled at Morobe
about August 20. Very detailed plans were worked out for this
important operation. The enemy was reported to have as many as

20,000 troops at Lae. There was every reason to expect that the beaches would be heavily defended. Air photos disclosed coast defense guns emplaced near the Jap airstrip at Lae. Allied bombers encountered heavy antiaircraft fire every time they approached Lae.

The 532d Shore Engineer Battalion and some of the boatmen were rushed from Morobe to Milne Bay where a final rehearsal for the operation was held with the Navy and the Australians. Then, on the evening of September 3, their plan worked out to the last detail, the Amphibian Engineers with their tractors, mats, conveyors, signal lights, and everything else, took off from Morobe (in 44 LCVPs, 10 LCMs, 3 LCSs, and 9 LCTs) for the Lae landing on Red Beach, 75 miles away. This landing shortly after dawn came off with the precision of a well-oiled machine. Amphibian scouts dressed as Aussies landed in the first wave, shore engineers in the third and subsequent waves. The attacking Jap planes disabled two LCIs on the beach, but missed the small craft. The intensive previous training, the thorough rehearsal, and the careful staff work all paid dividends. True, the enemy resistance at the beach was insignificant at first except for the air attack at 7:05 AM.; but just to carry off one of these complicated movements at night, landing on a strange beach with reefs and coral, unloading rapidly, and getting the craft away promptly is no small accomplishment.

The Shore Engineers did an effective job in unloading supplies and getting them distributed to dumps over hastily constructed roads in virgin jungles. On the first night rain set in and for ten days the entire area was a quagmire. Every bit of road had to be corduroyed, as no rock was available in the wet jungles. Bombing and strafing by enemy planes occurred daily and on some days several times until antiaircraft defenses were increased. Life on Red Beach near Lae from September 4 to September 16 was very unpleasant. Death was frequent.

As the Australians advanced toward Lae, practically all supply had to be accomplished by the brigade boats. Not even a jeep could negotiate the soaked coastal terrain during part of this time. To meet these increased demands, it was necessary to increase the number of LCMs from 10 to 21 and to bring from Morobe as many as 60 LCVPs. Every night after September 6 a small boat convoy would feel its way through uncharted coral to find a small strange beach on which to land the troops, food and ammunition the Aussies had to have for their advance. These boatmen were often under artillery and mortar fire as Japs attempted to prevent this gradual encroachment on their coast.

A few days after the initial landing, a severe storm caught the Aussies in the midst of an attempt to cross the flooded Buso River. One infantry battalion, by a combination of swimming and using rubber boats, had managed to cross most of its personnel and get a foothold on the enemy side. However many had lost their rifles and no machine guns had been brought across the river. Here was a critical situation. Japs held the coast just west of the river mouth and soon realized that only a small and poorly armed force had succeeded in crossing the river which was still rising. The Aussies immediately rushed rifles, ammunition, machine guns and more troops to be loaded in the brigade boats. Assisted by the poor visibility caused by the continuous heavy rain, the boats went around the mouth of the river and began landing in rear of the Jap lines to reinforce the cut-off Aussies. These boats worked continuously for 60 hours, transporting over 1,500 troops and a great quantity of supplies and artillery. The boats were hit by mortar and 75mm fragments and by machine-gun bullets, but all kept on the job.[2] This crossing of the last serious obstacle sealed the fate of Lae, which fell two days later, on September 16, 1943.

During this 12-day campaign and the subsequent assembly of troops in and near Lae which lasted until September 30, the 2d Engineer Special Brigade's relatively small boat force transported over 12,000 passengers and 10,000 tons of cargo. Major General Wooten, the Australian commander, stated: "Not for one hour has my advance on Lae been held up by failure of the 2d Engineer Special Brigade to deliver troops, supplies or ammunition at the time and place needed."

This could never have been accomplished without the closest cooperation between the Australian staff officers and those of the brigade. This close comradeship between the Aussies and the American Amphibians was exemplified by this extract of an article in an Australian newspaper:

> The Lae and Finschhafen campaigns have pro-vided a fine example of the effectiveness of Austra-lian-American cooperation. In addition, the A.I.F. [Australian Imperial Force] has been supplied by its "Navy," a fleet of barges manned by the 2d Engineer Special Brigade. Cooperation in the air is an imper-sonal detached matter. In an entirely different cat-egory is the active and man-to-man cooperation of the U.S. boys who man the supply barges. These Yanks have fought and some have died alongside Australians, and have done both so gamely as to win the respect and affection of the Diggers.

During the Lae operation the Shore Engineers (532d) managed to shoot down two Jap planes. The Boat Engineers, not to be out-done, shot down two from their boats. Out of more than a hundred boats involved, boat losses to all the Jap bombing and strafing were only one LCM, one LCS, and three LCVPs. Considering the large number of attacks experienced, the Amphibians came off very lightly.

Finschhafen Campaign

Lae fell on September 16, 1943. With the thought that a quick amphibian strike at Finschhafen would catch the enemy by sur-prise, General MacArthur ordered an attack there for September 22. With only four days to reorganize and prepare for this assault, an Australian brigade of the 9th Division, reinforced by about 550 Shore and Boat Engineers of the 2d Engineer Special Brigade from Lae, landed successfully north of Finschhafen on Scarlet Beach. The brigade initially furnished 10 LCMs and 15 LCVPs for this operation, transporting all the American troops and equipment in

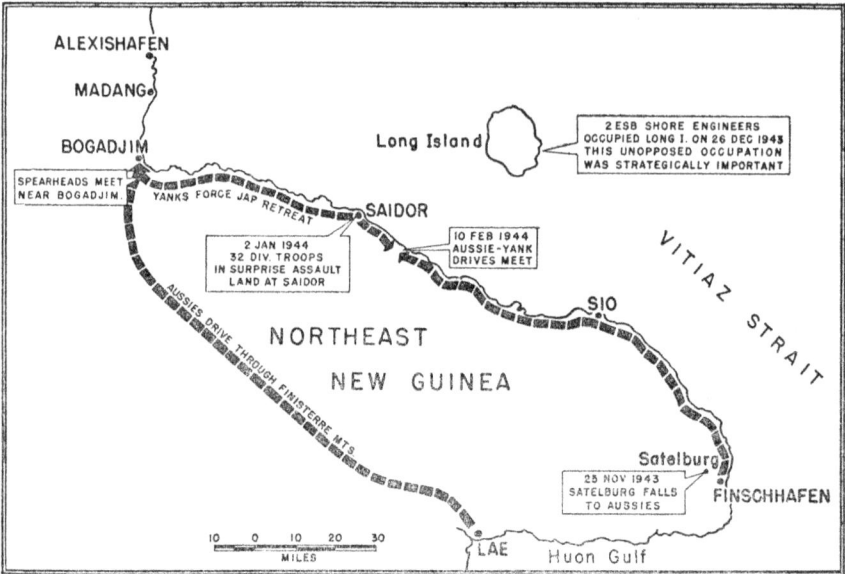

these craft from Red Beach while the Navy moved the Aussies in their larger craft for the initial landing. Amphibian scouts of the 2d Engineer Special Brigade again landed in the first wave, marked the beach for the subsequent waves, and started a search for coral heads, enemy mines, etc. The shore engineers with attached medical, beach control and signal detachments started landing in the third wave and were ready for the Navy's large LCTs and LSTs when they came in. The heavy Allied naval bombardment blotted out some of the enemy defenses, but the first two waves suffered casualties due to the fire from the hidden pillboxes. The surprised Japs soon recovered and were active in counterattacks from the direction of Finschhafen.

The boats had to anchor in the open seas off Scarlet Beach, riding out not only storms but also frequent enemy bombing, just as they had done off Lae. However, the Japs apparently thought the shore with its dumps a more attractive target than the dispersed boats, for again it was the Shore Engineers who had the greater casualties. Rain was not as heavy nor as frequent as at Red Beach, and initial difficulties ashore were not as serious as in the Lae landing. Later on, the heavy vehicular traffic plus heavy rains caused serious problems in ground traffic.

The Aussies met strong resistance as they pushed southward on Finschhafen, and it was necessary to reinforce both the boat and shore elements as more Australian troops and artillery were committed. The 2d Brigade's boats travelling only at night brought up another Australian brigade from Lae. The Jap air reaction was more severe than it had been at Lae. The men witnessed frequent aerial battles overhead as American fighters intercepted frequent Jap bombing attacks. Occasionally Japs would break through and attack the boats and shore installations, especially at dawn and at twilight.

Soon the Aussies had advanced so far to the south that the shore elements had to provide part of the perimeter defense landward as well as the seaward defense of Scarlet Beach. Naval LSTs and LCTs arrived on several of the following nights and were unloaded expeditiously in the short time they could remain on the beach and still get well on their return trip under cover of darkness. The brigade boats, just as in the Lae operation, ran frequent supply missions to Launch Jetty, halfway to Finschhafen. By October 2 they opened up a regular supply run from Lae to Scarlet Beach, bringing up more troops, supplies and ammunition. These trips involved round trips of over 140 miles. These convoys were vulnerable to enemy air attack, which the Japs continued both day and night. Our losses, though, were remarkably small. At night the boatmen cut their motors to hide the wake of their boats from the Jap planes. During the day General Kenney's planes kept away most of the Jap planes.

Early on the morning of October 11 a Jap force in the landing barges attempted a surprise landing on the Allies' own beach, Scarlet Beach. Later reports indicated that while ten Jap barges had started out for this attack, only four approached Scarlet Beach. Taking advantage of a very dark night and a quiet sea, the Jap boatmen (learned later from a prisoner) let their ramps almost down when 600 yards off the beach, cut their motors, and quietly paddled their boats in for the landing. Fortunately, the keen eyes of an Amphibian sergeant detected the strange craft when still 200 yards out. He immediately opened up with his 37mm gun, soon followed by an Aussie Bofors which, however, had difficulty depressing enough to hit the barges. One Jap barge foundered; the survivors jumped to the other barges.

However, the heroes of the occasion were two shore engineers manning a .50-caliber machine gun at the other end of the beach opposite the point which the Japs selected for their landing. Waiting in the dark until they could see that the ramps were lowered so that armor-plate would not deflect its fire, the gun opened a murderous fire at only 25 yards. Many Japs were killed in the boats, but others jumped overboard and closed on the gun with hand grenades. Orders were issued to abandon the exposed gun and withdraw to a line the Aussies and the shore engineers were forming a hundred yards back from the beach on a bluff. The gun crew did not heed these orders but continued the battle, two against more than a hundred. With grenades hitting around them, they managed to load a second belt, and, although both were wounded by this time, continued the struggle. More and more Japs fell before their gun, some only seven feet away. A grenade finally blew the gunner's leg off, and later he was found dead with his finger still on the trigger and the last round in the second belt fired. (This 19-year-old high-school boy, Private Junior N. Van Noy, was awarded the Medal of Honor posthumously.) His assistant, disabled by his wounds, managed to grab a rifle and fire it into the heart of a Jap coming over him with a bayonet. The dead Jap fell across him and was still there when help arrived and the shore engineer regained consciousness. This two-man gun crew had, almost alone, defeated the Jap landing. Even at that, things might not have been so good on Scarlet Beach that night if all ten barges had succeeded in landing instead of only four. The Allies never found out what happened to the other six barges.

TAMI ISLANDS

Twelve miles off Finschhafen lay the Tami Islands, suspected of harboring Japs. On October 3 a boat force of 14 LCVPs and 2 LCMs landed an Aussie company through the encircling coral reefs. Instead of the hot fire expected, natives in outrigger canoes joyfully greeted the white man once more. Japs had occupied their island for many, many moons, and had departed only a half moon ago. The well-constructed pillboxes covering the only landing beach clearly indicated that an earlier landing would have met hot resistance. Some may ask why the Jap abandonment of the islands could not have been determined from the natives on the mainland. Some natives did say the Japs had left but others were certain they were still there. The islands had so many caves that the only way to be certain was to capture the islands and inspect the caves.

SIO CAMPAIGN

With Finschhafen in Allied hands, the 532d Regiment assembled in Finsch Harbor and nearby Dreger Harbor, obtaining protected anchorages for their boats for the first time since the Scarlet Beach landing over two months ago. Some boatmen sleeping ashore for the first time in many days complained of the ground being too steady for good sleeping. As the mission of the Australian division was now to push northward in the direction of Sio, all of the 532d was brought up, under the regimental commander, Colonel Steiner, to the Finsch area to support this operation.

The coast from Finschhafen to Sio was much different from that previously encountered. Here there were very few beaches, and they were always small and often rocky. Between these few beaches were shores as rocky and rough as the coast of our rock-bound Maine. Also, as it was the season of the northwest monsoon, once around Huon Peninsula the seas were always much rougher. At times they were just too rough for any small landing craft. However, the boatmen, always eager to meet new difficulties, tackled the new situation with determination.

After a lull in work for the Amphibians while the Aussies were overcoming stubborn Jap marines on the heights of Sattelberg, the nightly resupply missions started to keep troops, ammunition, and supplies rolling to the Aussies as they pushed northward along the coast. There was not the glory nor the excitement of an initial landing to keep everyone keyed up. Rather it was stubborn determination to get the goods through that kept the men going. The shore engineers were themselves out developing new beach areas, one after another, as the advance progressed. These beach reconnaissance parties and the initial openings of new beaches were so close to the retreating Japs that the boats were frequently under fire. Fortunately, the Japs' fire had shown no increase in accuracy, and these boatmen got off as lightly as in the earlier Nassau Bay–Salamaua operation. The losses to storm and surf were heavier, but these risks had to be run. The Aussies must be, and were, supplied their tea and bully beef, their artillery and ammunition, their tanks and their mail.

At Sattelberg the rocket support battery of the 2d Brigade assisted the Aussies by firing barrages of the new American 4.5-inch rocket for the first time in the Southwest Pacific. The Japs indicated little love for these rockets. Startled by this new type of weapon, their artillery opened up for the first time in wild firing against this new enemy, but, as they could not tell where the rockets were coming from, their fire had no effect except to disclose their positions to the eager and accurate Aussie 25-pounders. After the rocket barrage, Aussie infantry rushed the shelled area but found no live Japs left to oppose them.

With the Huon Peninsula firmly in his hands and with new troops arriving, MacArthur was now ready to extend the sphere of his attack. The 1st Cavalry Division, an old Regular Army unit, and the 1st Marine Division of Guadalcanal fame but now reconstituted, after a good rest at Melbourne, were both ready to hit the Japs. Where would MacArthur hit next? Should he invade New Britain and take the Jap stronghold of Rabaul? Or would he merely contain Rabaul with his growing air force and continue up the New Guinea coast and capture the Jap stronghold of Wewak?

NOTES

[1] Among the Amphibians killed that night was Lieutenant Arthur C. Ely, of New York City.

[2] It was here that Lieutenant McPherson won the Distinguished Service Cross and several boatmen the Silver Star.

10
THE NORMANDY INVASION

To understand the role played by the Engineer Special Brigades in the Normandy invasion it is necessary to have a general picture of the over-all plan of operations and the commanders involved in its execution. With General Eisenhower as Allied Supreme Commander, the U.S. Ground Forces participating in the initial phase were consolidated into the U.S. First Army under General Bradley, and the British–Canadian component into the British Second Army. The U.S. Navy Task Force (122) under Admiral Kirk was charged with the cross-Channel transport of the U.S. forces; the British Navy was to land the British Second Army.

The Allied plan called for simultaneous landings on D-day by both U.S. and British forces following a brief naval and air bombardment of the beaches. The British on the left were to grab an anchor position behind the Orne River. The reinforced U.S. First Army on the right was to establish two beachheads west of Port-en-Bessin, then rapidly swing to the northwest to gain control of Cotentin Peninsula and seize the port of Cherbourg. Thereafter the combined plan called for a general wheeling movement to the left, still pivoted on the British, with the U.S. forces forming the hammerhead.

On the U.S. left, V Corps was to land on Omaha Beach; VII Corps on the U.S. right on Utah Beach. Between these two beaches was an obstacle formed by the river deltas and the low marshy ground between. To join the two zones of action required the seizing of the canal and river crossings in the vicinity of Carentan. Until this was accomplished the two U.S. corps were separate forces. Two U.S. airborne divisions were to be dropped ahead of the beach assault to facilitate the difficult landing of VII Corps and to permit its early junction with V Corps.

During the initial landing and for an unknown period thereafter it would be necessary to supplement the First Army with special units trained and equipped to carry on the functions normally performed by the communications zone. These units were attached to the Engineer Special Brigades. These brigades within specific limits embracing beach maintenance areas would be given full responsibility for such functions as traffic control, road construction and maintenance, security from ground and air attack, discipline and police.

Brigades were allocated beaches as follows:

Omaha Beach: 5th and 6th Engineer Special Brigades and 11th Port Headquarters. (Coordinated by Headquarters, Provisional Engineer Special Brigade Group)

Utah Beach: 1st Engineer Special Brigade.

Initially the Brigades would be under the direct control of the Corps responsible for the assault phase but subsequently the beaches and adjacent hinterland to a depth of four miles were to be designated as beach maintenance areas and placed under Army control.

In late April 1944 Brigadier General D. G. Shingler was ordered overseas to U.S. First Army to set up and head the Amphibious Section of that headquarters. General Shingler remained on this assignment through The final phases of the training, participated in the actual landings on D-day and represented the Army commander in all U.S. beach operations until he was injured by a truck on July 8, 1944, and evacuated to the U.S.

The magnitude of the operations on Omaha beach requiring the employment of the 5th and 6th Engineer Special Brigades, as well as the 11th Port, necessitated the formation of Headquarters Provisional Engineer Special Brigade Group to exercise over-all control and coordination. The headquarters was to be an operational unit but later it took over certain administrative functions.

The first officers reported to the Group headquarters on March 1, 1944, and on March 8 Brigadier General W. M. Hoge assumed command. By the end of April Group headquarters comprised 52 officers and 221 enlisted men.

Close cooperation between the Amphibian Engineers and the Navy would be very essential. The U.S. naval organization conformed to the ground force plan. Task Force O (Admiral Hall) was to land VII Corps and Task Force U (Admiral Moon) was to land V Corps. A naval beach battalion was attached to each of the three Engineer Special Brigades for the duration of the operations. They handled ship-to-shore communications (radio, flag and blinker), repair of small landing craft, and hydrographic survey work as well as assisting in the evacuation of battle casualties.

With this short summary of the plan and organization of the Engineer Special Brigades for this hazardous operation let us look briefly at the terrain. The tides along the beaches selected for the landings varied from 9.4 to 24 feet and uncovered an average of 300 yards of hard-packed sand. The extremely flat slope of the beaches in many places was disadvantageous to landing craft. Deep and shifting runnels frequently caused craft to ground by the stern while there was still as much as six feet of water at the ramp. Behind the beaches rose bluffs and hills 100 to 125 feet high cut by occasional small valleys and by minor defilades. While June weather in Normandy is temperate, day-to-day conditions vary greatly. June is a "dry" month but rain falls on an average of eleven days and normal precipitation for the month is over 2.0 inches. The beaches are exposed to winds from the northwest, north, and northeast, but usually June is a calm month with winds greater than thirteen miles an hour occurring only five days in the month and winds of gale proportions very infrequent. The surf is usually moderate averaging less than a foot more than half the time although a surf of three to five feet occurs on five to seven days a month.

As far back as December 1943, the decision had been reached to launch the attack against the continent of Europe in daylight rather than at night. The advantage of directed air and naval support during hours of daylight far outweighed any possible gain in the element of surprise from a night landing. The next problem was to decide on the hour of the attack.

Both the Ground Forces and the Navy were particularly interested in the height and flow of the tide as this would have much to do with fixing the time of the landing. Obstacles along the beaches chosen for the assault further complicated the timing of the assault in relation to the height of the tide. Would it be better to have the obstacles exposed at low tide, land far out, and work through the obstacles? Would it be better to trust to underwater demolition teams to neutralize the obstacles and then land at high tide as close in as possible?

The flow of the tide beginning about three hours after high water along the Normandy coast was so fast that landing craft would not be able to discharge personnel and still pull away from the shore. At low water, craft would ground so far out that personnel would have to advance across a wide strip of exposed beaches. Also the slope of the beach, even though very gentle, was so irregular that troops advancing from the low-water mark would have been forced to cross stretches of the beach where the water was over their heads in depth. A landing at high water had many advantages but all these were offset by the fact that the underwater obstacles had been emplaced by the enemy so as to offer maximum interference at high water. These obstacles could, of course, have been more easily eliminated had troops been able to land at low tide. The best compromise solution was finally determined to be at a time three hours before high tide and one hour after first light. The first date when these conditions held was May 2 but when the decision was made in January to enlarge the operation by an assault on Utah Beach, the operation was postponed until June 5 when the desired conditions would again take place. A month's delay, rather than two weeks, was decided on in order to take advantage of a spring tide rather than a neap tide. The former was also desirable from the point of view of the airborne effort which required moonlight conditions to insure the accuracy of the paratroop drop.

Many considerations thus had to be coordinated to enable General Eisenhower to select the proper hour for this hazardous landing.

The Germans, long negligent of beach obstacles, started work vigorously along the Normandy beaches in April 1944. By D-day the beaches were well protected by a combination of all kinds of hedgehogs, gates, stakes and ramps well sprinkled with Teller mines, but gaps did exist and could be spotted on the air photos.

Back of the beach proper were located the first enemy defense lines. Most of the summer residences had been torn down by the Germans to clear the field of fire for the major emplacements on the slopes and atop the hills. A few houses were left standing for use as command posts and machine-gun emplacements. Barbed-wire entanglements were present but minefields were a more serious obstacle. Gun emplacements were set into the sides of the hills. Enfilade fire was the rule, making it difficult to locate the emplacements. On top of the hills were pillboxes, dugouts, and interlocking trenches. Although the installation of remote-control flame-throwers was under way, fortunately the Germans did not have any ready by D-day. Well behind the bluffs the enemy had artillery and mortar positions covering nearly all parts of the beach.

When to the above is added the danger of submarine and air attack en route to and while on the far shore, it is obvious that the invasion of Normandy was a most hazardous operation. Let us now see in more detail how each brigade prepared for its part in the stupendous operation and how it fared in the actual landing.

The public press and military journals have featured the exploits of the tactical units and their outstanding achievements in the Normandy invasion. On the other hand, little has been said, even within military circles, of the problems faced and the achievements recorded by the thousands of officers and men who hit the beach on D-day and quietly worked there through enemy fire and storm to support this major amphibious operation—and to support it in the face of even possible reversal.

Each adverse development served only to increase the load on the Engineer Special Brigades: (1) the rough sea on D-day swamped many a craft needed for use later; (2) the unexpectedly heavy enemy resistance on Omaha Beach disrupted the timetable at the very start; (3) the storm of June 19-22 wrecked the artificial harbor and much of the floating plant; (4) the opening of the various ports was delayed beyond expectation; (5) revised tactical requirements demanded a rate of discharge across the beaches far exceeding that for which beach operating facilities had been designed; (6) the open beaches had to continue operations long after experts had indicated that rough seas would preclude such operations.

There is no doubt but that the success of the invasion of Normandy depended more than is generally recognized on the skillful, courageous, and determined effort of the shore parties—the Engineer Special Brigades with attached troops—on Omaha and Utah beaches. Without this wonderful support in the early days of the landing, all the heroic efforts of the Queen of Battles, the Infantry, would have gone for naught.

THE STORY OF THE 5TH BRIGADE

Early in November 1943 the 1119th Engineer Combat Group under Colonel W. D. Bridges, fresh from amphibious training in the United States, arrived at three camps in the vicinity of Swansea, South Wales. The Group at this time consisted of Headquarters and Headquarters Company and the 37th, 336th and 348th Engineer Combat Battalions. On November 11, 1943, the 5th Engineer Special Brigade was activated absorbing all troops of the 1119th Group. The following day Major General (then Brigadier General) W. M. Hoge assumed command and established his command post at Penllergaer, South Wales. Almost immediately, quartermaster, ordnance, medical, transportation, chemical warfare, and signal units began arriving for incorporation in the new brigade.

The 5th Brigade (and the 6th) were organized especially to support the assault landings on the coast of Europe. The brigades which operated in the European Theater of Operations differed from those of the Pacific Area in that they did not operate their own small landing craft, the Navy being assigned this function. In place of the boat units the European Theater of Operations brigades were assigned additional service units to make possible the enormous capacity for handling cargo, which was necessary to support the large-scale operation involved in the invasion of the Continent.

As a basis for organization during the assault phase of the operation, when it was anticipated that communication would be difficult, the brigade was divided into three engineer combat battalion beach groups. Each beach group had as its nucleus an engineer combat battalion to which was attached service troops necessary to support the landing of a regimental combat team of an infantry division. The three beach groups immediately began combined exercises on the Gower Peninsula to develop the team-work which would be so essential for a successful amphibious operation.

Meanwhile, the brigade staff was preparing lists of the special equipment which would be needed. These lists were based upon the training experiences of the various units in meeting their quotas of tonnage and upon the experiences of personnel in previous operations. A few items of the equipment in addition to the standard equipment of the units that comprised the brigade were as follows: 27 D-7 or D-8 angle dozers, 27 power cranes, 4 motorized road graders, 10 tractors and 15 six-ton Athey trailers. Procurement of items on the special list was a gigantic task which continued until the troops actually embarked for the landing in June.

About February 1, 1944, First Army Operation Plan "Neptune" was received by brigade headquarters and key personnel were briefed on the brigade mission, tactical plan and aspects of the target area.

On February 17, 1944, Headquarters Provisional Engineer Special Brigade Group was activated, General Hoge becoming its Commanding General on March 8. This headquarters was to command the 5th and 6th Brigades as well as certain units scheduled to land after the assault. Initially personnel for the group headquarters was drawn from the 5th Brigade. Colonel Bridges resumed command of the 5th ESB.

On March 11 and 12 brigade headquarters and the 37th Battalion Beach Group participated in Exercise Fox with the 1st Infantry

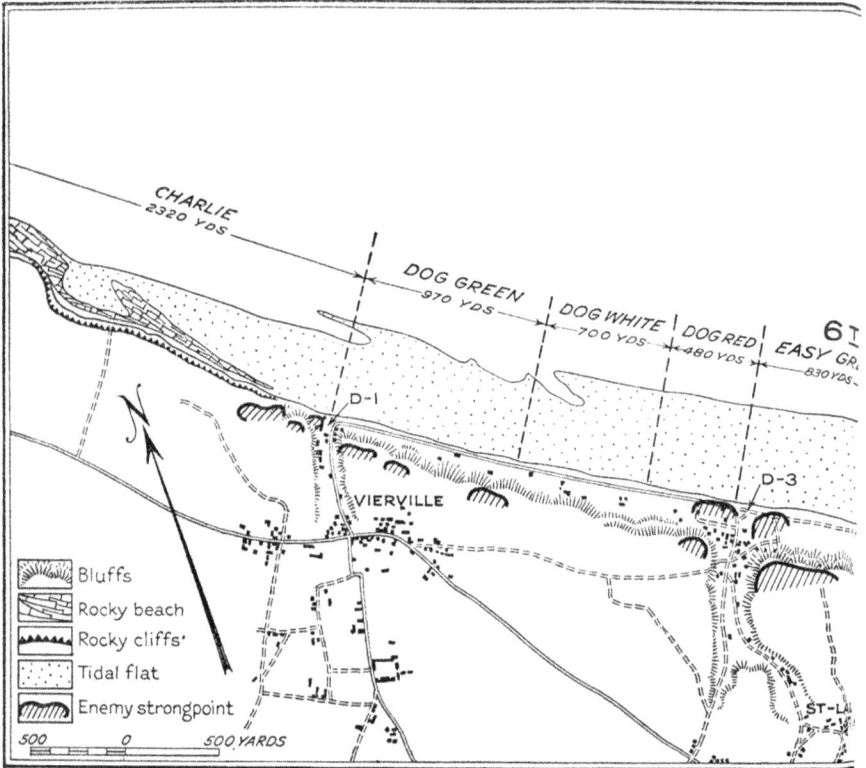

Division, under control of V Corps. The exercise was held at Slapton Sands in Cornwall on the southern coast of England with the 37th Battalion Beach Group (5th ESB) supporting the 16th Infantry Regimental Combat Team. Full-scale naval gunfire support was provided, and the units performed their missions under conditions very closely simulating actual combat. Even had this exercise failed completely from a tactical point of view, it could not have failed to impress upon the units the immense volume of reports required for such an operation and the difficulties of preparing them in the field.

Upon its return from Slapton Sands, brigade headquarters immediately began work on its operation plan for the invasion. A planning group was established at Plymouth under supervision of V Corps. This group consisted of representatives from the Navy, the assault units, the brigade group and from both the 5th and 6th

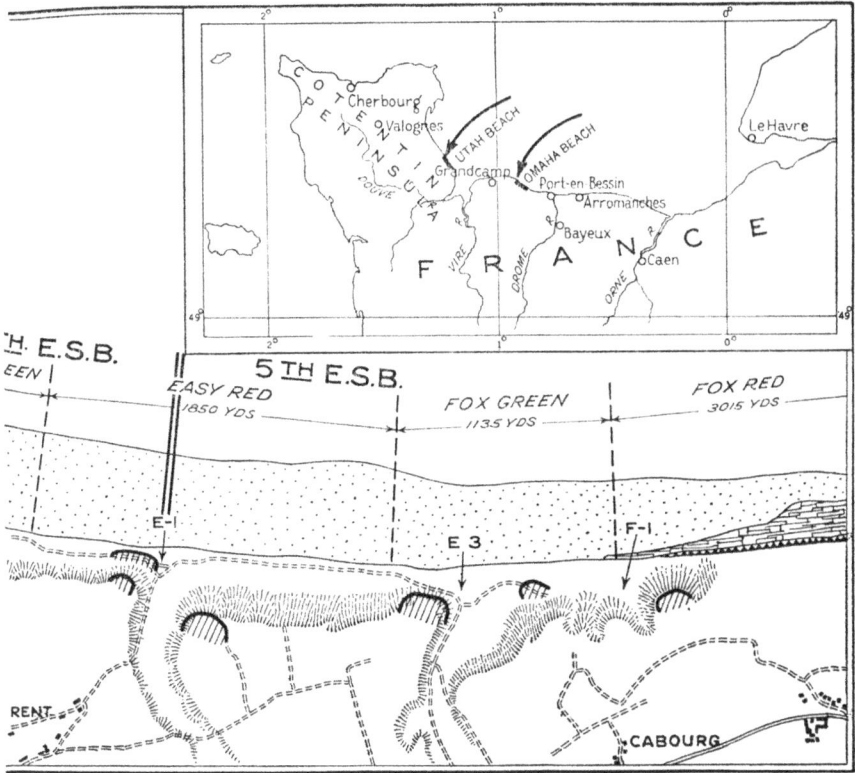

Brigades. Preparation of the plan with its short deadline and many changes severely taxed the physical endurance as well as the mental capacities of all staffs concerned.

During the planning period the battalion beach groups kept undergoing intensive training in their planned role. This training culminated in Exercise Lion at Oxwich Bay on the Gower Peninsula of South Wales. The entire 5th Brigade participated in the exercise, which was held on April 4-6. On April 16 Colonel Doswell Gullatt reported to the brigade and assumed command.

The climax of the pre-invasion training occurred during the period May 3-7 in Exercise Fabius I, the dress rehearsal for the assault phase of Operation Neptune. The exercise began with the assembly and marshalling of all assault force troops in secret areas along the Channel coast. After the units had been divided into craft loads, they boarded the transports and landing craft at embarkation points dispersed along the coast. These operations could not have failed to impress even an uninformed observer as the real thing. No doubt the night May 2-3 was a wakeful one for the German garrisons along the Channel coast as the convoys steamed into the darkness, bound they knew not where. At dawn on May 3 the brigade troops stormed ashore with the assault infantry but again it was at Slapton Sands, another practice maneuver. They immediately began breaching obstacles, clearing mines and laying roadways of chespaling (a British road material) and of Sommerfeld track to enable the supporting artillery and armor to get off the beach. Beach markers were erected and the beachmasters from the brigade's attached 5th Naval Beach Battalion began guiding the craft in to the debarkation points.

By the afternoon DUKWs of the 453d, 458th and 459th Amphibian Truck Companies, which had landed initially carrying howitzers and ammunition for the artillery, were plying back and forth from the beach unloading cargo from coasters anchored offshore. Dumps and transit area for the assembly of troops and vehicles were in full operation in areas as soon as they had been cleared of mines. On May 4 the troops of the 1st Division terminated their phase of the problem and began moving out of the area. Brigade troops, however, continued unloading cargo and consolidated the beach maintenance area. On May 7 the brigade troops ceased operations and returned to the assembly areas where they were to remain incommunicado until the landings.

The remainder of the time in England was one of frenzied activity. Deficiencies noted during the dress rehearsal had to be corrected; additional equipment had to be distributed. Motor vehicles and bulldozers had to be waterproofed. Every man had to be briefed as to his individual mission and as to how it fitted into the master plan. Solution of these problems was made more difficult by the fact that troops of any one unit were usually separated in two or more widely dispersed assembly areas. Some of the last-minute changes had to be distributed to the commanders after they were aboard ship.

At last on June 1 the long awaited embarkation began. Day and night troops poured into the ports and boarded their vessels—men with assault packs, carrying pole charges and bangalore torpedoes, trucks overloaded with explosives and ammunition, and tanks with extra tracks and sand bags lashed on for additional protection. On June 3 the embarkation was complete and D-day was announced as June 5.

The morning of June 4 the LCTs weighed anchor and moved to sea in convoy. The transports were to leave in the late afternoon but about noon word was passed that D-day had been postponed until June 6. To preserve radio silence the LCT convoys had to be called back by dispatch boat. Some of the LCTs had almost reached sight of the Normandy coast before they received the word. "What the hell! Another dry run!"

On June 5 the convoys departed again—first the slow LCTs, then the LSTs and LCIs. Finally, late in the afternoon the transports weighed anchor and put to sea with gun crews at battle stations. The troops settled down to a restless night of waiting. It was still rough and prospects of a quiet landing were not good. Practically every one wondered how much surf there would be on the beaches as well as how much enemy fire.

Grey shapes filled the twilight of the summer evening in the English Channel. All of a sudden the public address systems of the convoy signaled "Attention," and a clear confident voice sounded above the roar of the flying spray:

"Men, I have a message for you from the Supreme Commander:

> Soldiers, Sailors and Airmen of the Allied Expeditionary Forces! You are about to embark on the Great Crusade toward which we have striven these many months. The eyes of the world are upon you. In company with our brave Allies and brothers-in-arms on other fronts, you will bring about the destruction of the German war machine, the elimination of Nazi tyranny over the oppressed peoples of Europe, and security for ourselves in a free world.

Your task will not be an easy one. Your enemy is well trained, well equipped, and battle-hardened. He will fight savagely.

But this is the year 1944. Much has happened since the Nazi triumphs of 1940-41. The United Nations have inflicted upon the Germans great defeats, in open battle, man to man. Our air offensive has seriously reduced their strength in the air and their capacity to wage war on the ground. Our home fronts have given us overwhelming superiority in weapons and munitions of war, and placed at our disposal great reserves of trained fighting men. The tide has turned. The free men of the world are marching together to Victory!

I have full confidence in your courage, devotion to duty, and skill in battle. We will accept nothing less than full Victory!

Good luck! And let us all beseech the blessing of Almighty God upon this great and noble undertaking!"

The 5th Engineer Special Brigade was on the way; this time for keeps.

By 2:00 A.M. the larger vessels were anchored in the transport area 15,000 yards off the landing beach. Soon our bombers began droning overhead as they came in for their bomb runs. Chandelier flares provided a glow in the sky over the beach punctuated by the bright flashes of exploding ack-ack and bombs. The battle was on. With the approach of dawn, the naval bombardment began and the initial waves of landing craft left the rendezvous areas seven miles off shore and headed for the beach. H-hour for Omaha Beach was 6:45 A.M.

Omaha Beach upon which the 5th Brigade landed was a five-mile beach bounded on both ends by high cliffs at the water's edge. It was located on the Normandy coast about ten miles to the east of the mouth of the Vire River. The ten-foot tidal range uncovered

300 yards of hard-packed sand. The slope of the tidal flat was bro-ken by runnels, some of which were six feet deep, and by small outcroppings of peat on parts of the beach. Immediately inshore of the high-water mark was a pile of shingle consisting of well rounded stones from one to six inches in diameter backed by a low dune line. These stones were to prove an effective barrier against the passage of vehicles.

In shore there was a flat expanse of sand about 200 yards wide which gave way to a steep slope rising 100 to 120 feet. Behind the slope was a level plateau of farmland broken by hedgerows of sod-covered earth. Behind the 5th Brigade beaches three valleys ran from the beach inland providing access to the high ground.

The assault beaches were designated from west to east, Dog Green, Dog White, Dog Red, Easy Green, Easy Red, Fox Green and Fox Red. The three eastern beaches, Easy Red, and the Fox beaches, were assigned to the 5th Brigade.

The Germans had prepared a thorough defense of the Omaha area since it was one of very few suitable landing beaches on the coast. Well emplaced artillery and weapons enfiladed the entire beach. Several bands of antitank and antipersonnel minefields were located behind the dune line and to seaward the beach was cov-ered by overlapping bands of obstacles. Many of these obstacles had mines attached and were provided with anti-removal devices.

As the craft bearing men of the 1st Division and the 5th Brigade approached the beach, the impregnability of the defense became more and more apparent. As soon as they beached the craft were met by withering fire from 88s and machine guns. Those able to do so took cover among the obstacles, some of which were above the water. The rising tide, however, soon forced them to leave this meager cover and dash across the hundred yards of fiat sand that separated them from the relative safety of the dune line. Leaving many dead and wounded to be engulfed by the rising water, the troops built up a thin firing line just above the high-water mark. Salt water and sand interfered with the operation of many weapons.

Meanwhile craft continued to land more troops although many of the men had to swim and wade through neck-deep water after their craft had struck the obstacles. The plans for clearance of the obstacles had failed because the intense enemy fire decimated the demolition teams and the incoming troops prevented the blowing of charges on obstacles around which they had taken desperate and scanty cover.

In spite of the heavy losses the firing line gradually built up and officers began organizing groups to push inland. These groups had to cross minefields and unbreached wire entanglements before they were able to find cover along the steep slopes behind the beach. By 9:00 several penetrations had been made by small groups, but these initial penetrations did little to lessen the fire on the beach.

The first landings by Brigade troops were made at 7:00 A.M., H plus fifteen minutes, by members of the 37th Engineer Combat Battalion. These men had been briefed that they would find the beach practically clear of small-arms fire and the assault infantry progressing inland in an orderly manner. They were to erect beach markers and begin organizing the beach for the landing of support troops and artillery. Seeing that their assigned mission was impossible, they quickly added their weight to the firing line and blew gaps through the wire entanglements with bangalore torpedoes. Later members of the 348th Engineer Combat Battalion landed and joined the fight.

At 9:00 the situation on the beach was indeed critical. The beach was clogged by wrecked vehicles and landing craft. With no roadways opened vehicles that did land were forced to remain in the field of fire of the defenses. Communications along the beach and to the ships were practically nonexistent. Casualties lined the beach. In order to prevent further confusion all landing of vehicles was suspended.

The period between 9:00 A.M. and noon was one in which all members of the Brigade ashore distinguished themselves. Two bulldozers operated by Pvts. Vinton W. Dove and William J. Shoemaker, of the 37th Engineer Combat Battalion, lurched up and down the beach throughout the day. Defying constant artillery and mortar fire, they cleared beach obstacles, made paths for vehicles through the shingle strip, removed roadblocks, filled in antitank ditches, and helped to prepare road exits. Although these two men were recommended by their commanding officer for the Silver Star, their conduct was deemed by higher headquarters as worthy of even greater recognition, and they each received the Distinguished Service Cross.

Elements of the 348th Battalion beach group arrived next, and with what seemed to be agonizing slowness, made truly remarkable progress in clearing the beaches before the exits, thus permitting additional craft to land. Moreover, an access road was built through to the beach exit, and the antitank ditch blocking the road was successfully filled by Engineer Special Brigade dozer operators. Abandoned vehicles that blocked passage through a minefield gap were removed into an adjacent field.

While awaiting the arrival of the main body of the road construction detail, men from both the 37th and the 348th Battalion Beach Groups combined for further offensive operations. Enemy positions firing at the main exit were effectively silenced. Some groups penetrated inland, eventually establishing a bivouac area where troops could regroup. Others intensified their efforts in the hazardous task of mine clearing.

Men and officers of the 61st Medical Battalion (5th ESB) with members in every beach group, went swiftly and efficiently about their tasks. Aid stations were set up. They administered first aid on the open beach under a hail of enemy fire of all calibers. Blood plasma was given when necessary and over 600 of the wounded were evacuated to outgoing ships. When wounded men lying exposed on the tidal fiats were endangered by the rising water, the medics disregarded danger to transfer the men to safer positions. Flaming gasoline trucks and exploding vehicles loaded with ammunition were a deadly menace, but the medics worked courageously in the face of all hazards. Necessary supplies were so short that time and again the men whose sole protection was a white band with a red cross were compelled to expose themselves to devastating fire while rummaging through wrecked craft, burning vehicles, abandoned packs, and even the bodies of deceased men to get the needed items.

At about 10:30 AM. an LCI and a lone LCT drove their way through the obstacles and opened fire with their weapons on enemy shore positions. At about the same time a destroyer approached shore, swung broadside and opened fire at point-blank range on the emplacements and moved along the beach. These actions not only eliminated some of the emplacements, but provided fire support for assault parties ashore to destroy others.

By 12:30 P.M. observed enemy artillery fire on the beach had lessened and the small-arms fire had substantially abated. One exit from the beach had been cleared and troops were moving inland in an orderly fashion. Artillery fire was still taking a heavy toll of the men on the beach, but once inland, there was opportunity to reorganize units, Meanwhile, organization of the beach had reached the point where CPs were established, mines were being cleared, matting was being laid on the sand to facilitate the passage of vehicles, and the wounded were being cared for.

The afternoon of D-day showed a continuing slow progress in the development of the beach. However, enemy artillery fire apparently adjusted by observers in concealed positions along the bluff continued to have devastating effect on beach installations. Landing craft discharging their loads and any small groups of personnel drew accurate fire. Mortar fire was placed on evacuation stations with such effect that wounded awaiting evacuation had to be widely dispersed.

At about 3:00 P.M. the main body of the 336th Battalion Beach Group, after several attempts at landing on the beach it had been ordered to develop, was forced to land on Dog Green some 400 yards to the west. The landing of one craft load of this unit was typical of the difficulties encountered by units throughout the day. This craft upon being hit by shell fire was forced to beach on a sandbar. The personnel, in the face of intense artillery fire, waded through thirty yards of waist-deep water, swam a 50-yard runnel and dashed across the open to the protection of wrecked vehicles and landing craft along the high-water mark. Once assembled it was necessary for the beach group to make its way over 4,000 yards of exposed beach to Fox Green Beach.

Upon arrival at their beach the men of the 336th salvaged two mine detectors from the debris on the beach, cannibalized parts from three disabled dozers to make two workable ones and began pushing an exit road through a draw in the face of heavy sniper fire. Two tanks followed the mine-clearance teams and the dozers. At the same time areas on the beach were cleared of mines and the antitank ditch was filled to make it passable for wheeled vehicles. In anticipation of the opening of this exit, craft waiting offshore were ordered to beach and discharge their vehicles. At 8:00 P.M. two tanks moved over the new road, and by 10:30 fifteen tanks had utilized the exit to move inland where they provided much-needed fire support for the infantry.

Darkness on D-day (11:00 P.M.) found the situation on the beach progressing nicely. However, some thousand yards inland the beachhead was thinly held by units of a fraction of their original strength. Support troops and reinforcements were all very late in landing. In order to help defend the beachhead, some of the brigade units were moved into the line as infantry. One platoon of the 336th Engineer Combat Battalion on moving up to help secure the left flank of the beachhead found six lone infantrymen armed with five rifles and a BAR holding the exposed flank.

As soon as darkness forced the fighter cover to withdraw to England the Jerries came in from the south to attack the transports and beach installations. Every gun, afloat and ashore, opened up on each plane causing shell fragments and .50-caliber slugs to rain on the troops dug in along the beach. Fortunately the bombing and strafing by the planes had little effect.

There was little rest and practically no sleep that first night. Shortly after 1:00 A.M. the next morning the third exit road in the brigade sector was opened by the 348th Battalion Beach Group, and the way was now clear for full-scale landings of troops and vehicles.

The morning of D plus 1 found a bedraggled body of troops looking out of their foxholes. There were stragglers from all units, some intentional and some who just didn't know where to go. Staff officers were looking in vain for units scheduled to have landed. Stalled vehicles and splintered landing craft added to the invasion litter of lifebelts, sodden cartons of cigarettes, ruined radio sets and mine detectors. To seaward the horizon was obscured by hundreds of ships awaiting unloading by landing craft which lay in splinters on the beach. Fortunately, the sea had abated and there was less artillery fire on the beach.

The beach groups took stock of the situation and continued their work in improving the beach. They repaired vehicles and separated usable supplies from those washed ashore. Landing points along the beach were cleared of obstacles and wreckage. The exit roads were improved and a few areas inland were cleared of mines for use as transit areas and dumps.

Comparatively quiet though the day was, the work was not done without enemy intervention. Shortly after noon the enemy rained heavy mortar fire on the beach. One round landed directly in the command post of the 37th Engineer Combat Battalion, killing two men and wounding several others. In mid-afternoon Company B of the 348th routed a dozen stunned Germans out of a dugout situated in the midst of the battalion area.

By the morning of D plus 2 only sporadic artillery was falling on the beach and the men of the brigade could look back on the assault phase of the operation as completed. The operation when viewed in the light of the plan had not been highly successful. The beach exits which were to be cleared of fire by H plus 30 minutes and opened for wheeled traffic by H plus 3 hours had not all been opened until the morning of D plus 1. Little if any of the 4,900 tons of cargo scheduled to be unloaded during the first two days had reached the beach, and unloading of troops and vehicles was far behind schedule. But when viewed in the light of the actuality, the miracle is that the invasion was able to succeed at all. The American organization of the beach during the assault had been so successful that soon after the cessation of accurate enemy fire, full-scale unloading operations could be initiated.

For its heroism in the assault operation the entire 37th Battalion Beach Group was awarded the Distinguished Unit Citation. The entire brigade including all assigned and attached units was awarded the Croix de Guerre with Palm by the French Government, and many individuals received awards ranging from the Distinguished Service Cross to the Bronze Star. Twenty-five individuals of the brigade were awarded the Croix de Guerre for their heroic actions.

The casualties during the assault phase especially among key personnel had been heavy. Hardest hit of all brigade units was the 37th Engineer Combat Battalion which lost its Commanding Officer, Lieutenant Colonel Lionel F. Smith, its S-2, S-3, and two of its four company commanders. Its officers were certainly real *leaders!*

For planning purposes the development of the beach area was divided into four phases: the assault phase, during which cargo was stacked along the beach; the initial dump phase, when cargo was stacked in areas a short distance inland; the beach maintenance area phase, during which cargo was moved to large dump areas as much as five miles inland; and the port phase, in which a large portion of the unloading was to be carried out in the shelter of artificial breakwaters and over floating piers. Actually the first three phases overlapped, and the fourth or port phase never really occurred.

The brigade's beach maintenance area dumps opened on June 12 and 13 by which time the beach operations were progressing ahead of plan, and the backlog of shipping from the assault phase was rapidly dwindling. Huge breakwaters were being constructed of sunken ships and concrete caissons by the Navy; long floating piers, which had been towed across the Channel, were being assembled and anchored in place. A few optimists of the brigade were beginning to think of returning to England and leaving to port troops the operations within the artificial harbor. The optimism was short-lived, however, for on June 19 a northeaster raised seas which made cessation of unloading necessary. The storm continued for three days, dashing landing craft and barges into the beach and pounding the breakwaters with huge seas. On June 22 when the weather cleared the concrete caissons which made up the outer breakwater showed only jagged edges above the water. Many of the ships which made up the inner breakwater had broken their backs. Of the floating piers, nothing remained but twisted wreckage, and crushed landing craft lined the high-water mark several deep, effectively blocking the entire beach. Ashore the supply situation was so critical that artillery ammunition had to be carefully rationed, and there was imminent danger of a shortage of food. The three days, during which unloading was suspended, built up a large backlog of ships to be unloaded.

The 5th Brigade immediately set about clearing beaching points of wrecked craft and unloading ships carrying priority ammunition. Inasmuch as manifests for the ships had not been received, locating the ships and ordering them in to berth proved to be a task requiring constant activity on the part of the beach groups. On June 23 in spite of all obstacles the 5th Brigade exceeded its tonnage quota by unloading 5,226 tons. Improved methods and better equipment raised this quota until on August 25 (D plus 80) the brigade unloaded 9,056 tons across the open beach in a single day's operations, a record which surprised higher headquarters very pleasantly.

As the unloading progressed the development of the beach also progressed. The entire area was graded to provide temporary storage space for supplies. Abandoned pillboxes were converted to command posts and the roads along the beach were paved with gravel. Dumps were carefully organized so that supplies could be easily located and dispatched upon call. Immediately upon their arrival, incoming vessels were called in for unloading.

Unloading during the later period was greatly complicated by the arrival of cargoes which were destined originally for Cherbourg, where it was contemplated that full port facilities would be available. Such items as crated tanks and tractors severely taxed the ingenuity of the shore engineers on the beach in unloading them from landing craft. While the delay in the opening of large-scale operations at Cherbourg and other Channel ports placed a heavy load on the troops on the beach, it did serve to show just what the 5th Brigade was able to do under the adverse conditions encountered.

On July 30 Colonel Gullatt was taken ill and had to be evacuated to the United Kingdom. Colonel Bridges assumed command of the Brigade, a position he was to continue to hold until the inactivation of the Brigade in the United States.

By D plus 100 the 5th Brigade had handled 480,000 tons of cargo and had unloaded 57,000 vehicles, more than any other organization on Omaha Beach. This record was attained only by all personnel working in shifts, twelve hours per day, seven days per week. Attained in the face of all kinds of weather and over an open beach this record cannot be minimized. Undoubtedly it played a large part in the success of the operations of the tactical troops in driving to the borders of Hitler's Germany.

The 348th Beach Group

The eastern flank of the Omaha Beach sector was operated by the 348th Engineer Battalion Beach Group under Lieutenant Colonel Earl P. Houston. Its mission was to land and supply the 16th, 18th and 26th Regimental Combat Teams of the 1st Infantry Division. Due to the heavy enemy reaction in this area the efforts of the 348th Beach Group were greatly obstructed. Minefields were even more numerous than expected and consisted of many different types of mines, making their removal extremely difficult and dangerous. But the main deterrent to progress in setting up the beach organization was the heavy and continuous artillery and small-arms fire. Prior to landing, the shore engineers had been told that all small-arms fire would be cleared from the immediate beach area by H plus 2 hours. Actually it was many hours before all fire in the beach area ceased. However, in the night and early morning of D plus 1 the necessary personnel and equipment finally got ashore and some semblance of organization began to appear.

The section of the Omaha beach area operated by the 348th Engineer Battalion Beach Group of the 5th Brigade was not protected by blockships or breakwaters of any kind. However, it was found that these blockships, where used to protect other areas, did not afford any great amount of protection nor result in much, if any, increased tonnage over the beaches they did protect. Moreover, the blockships had the disadvantage of requiring the cargo ships to anchor farther out at sea in order to stay clear of them. The openings between the blockships were a hazard during night operations for both ferry craft and DUKWs, considerable currents being set up by the tide in these restricted passages. Hours of operation per day in areas having this protection were not materially lengthened during stormy weather over areas without any protection. The best record for daily, monthly and total tonnages moved over a given beach was obtained by the 348th Beach Group over Fox White, Red and Green Beaches, which had no protection whatever.

On October 2 the 348th Engineer Combat Battalion, the 487th Port Battalion and the 4141st Quartermaster Service Company with two truck companies, were ordered to Arromanches, the site of the British artificial harbor about thirty miles east of Omaha Beach. The weather conditions at Omaha Beach having finally reached the point where it could not be operated efficiently, higher authority decided to transfer this port from British to U. S. Army control. The mission of operating this port was assigned to the 348th Engineer Combat Battalion under Lieutenant Colonel Earl Houston. Ammunition having a high priority was handled direct from the artificial harbor to nearby railroad trains. For several weeks six ammunition trains a day were loaded out from this artificial harbor. This operation kept up until bad weather shut the port down in mid-November.

The 348th was then ordered into Cherbourg to operate the port area known as the Terra Plain. The operation of this area had not been well handled and the trickle of supplies moving through the area had been far from satisfactory. An average of 1,800 tons per day had been handled prior to the arrival of the 348th. A short time later this same area using identical equipment was handling an average of 4,300 tons per day. The 348th Engineer Beach Group had worked through the initial assault landings at Omaha Beach, moved to the artificial harbor at Arromanches and then on to Cherbourg. During these operations they had gained experience and adeptness, second to no other unit in the European Theater of Operations at handling supplies over an open beach, through an artificial harbor and through an organized port.

After D plus 100 there was a steady decline in the beach activities, due partly to the fact that the ports of Cherbourg, Le Havre and Rouen began operations and also to the increasingly bad weather in the Channel which curtailed unloading operations over open beaches. The dumps in the beach maintenance area, however, still contained thousands of tons which had to be shipped by rail to forward areas. Movement of this cargo to the railhead was made difficult by continual rain which turned dump areas into morasses. Even tractors and tracked trailers became bogged.

On November 19, 1944, the beach was officially closed and unloading operations ceased. Thus the 5th Brigade completed the principal mission for which it had been activated. Notwithstanding this fact, there remained much to be done in the beach area. Huge piles of steel rails, telephone poles and pipe were stacked about the beach, where they had been left because of lack of transportation. Many supplies in dump areas were inaccessible due to the deep mud. Living conditions were not suitable for sub-freezing weather. The fast tempo of operations on the beach had left little time for winterization of billets and the wet weather made duckboards necessary for all paths. The entire efforts of the brigade were immediately committed to rearrangement of supplies, repair of roads and provision of adequate winterized quarters.

Soon after the closing of the beach, units of the brigade began leaving for new assignments, leaving brigade headquarters with fewer and fewer troops. The dissolution reached its climax on December 22 when the 37th, 336th, and 348th Engineer Combat Battalions departed for assignment to forward units. By December 31 the brigade consisted only of Brigade Headquarters and Headquarters Company, one Quartermaster Battalion headquarters and one Quartermaster Service Company. On this date Headquarters and Headquarters Company received orders to move to Paris.

Brigade Headquarters and Headquarters Company arrived in Paris on January 4, 1945, and established themselves in St. Cloud, a fashionable suburb. After six months of living in foxholes and shacks made of old crates, houses with beds and carpets on the floors looked too good to be true.

In Paris brigade headquarters was assigned the primary mission of supervising construction activities in the area and training newly arrived engineer units. It was then contemplated that the 5th Brigade headquarters would move forward and take control of general and special service regiments operating in the Advance Section Zone about February 28. This movement, however, never materialized.

On January 12, 1945, the first units were attached to brigade headquarters. They were the 1251st and the 1252d Engineer Combat Battalions which were to arrive from the United Kingdom. The 1252d arrived about January 13 and departed almost immediately on January 25 for other duties. The 1251st arrived about January 15 and commenced a training program and limited construction activities.

The first construction task assigned the Brigade while operating under Seine Section was to construct defensive barriers around supply and communications installations in the Paris area, which were thought to be endangered by the German breakthrough in Belgium. This task was divided between the 1251st and the 1252d Engineer Combat Battalions.

Soon after the departure of the 1251st Engineer Combat Battalion about January 25, the 151st Engineer Combat Battalion, an organization with considerable construction experience in the Aleutian Islands, arrived in Paris. Subsequent to the arrival of the 151st Engineer Combat Battalion, all construction projects assigned to the brigade were in turn assigned to that organization. These projects consisted of hospital expansions, improvement of depots and construction of staging camps for airborne forces to participate in the Rhine crossing.

On February 8 Colonel Bridges was appointed Engineer Supply Officer of the Seine Section and the brigade was assigned the additional mission of operating all engineer depots in the Paris area. To accomplish this mission all depot operating engineer organizations in the area were assigned to the brigade. The headquarters necessary to supervise the activities was set up at Depot E-508-A at Gennevilliers, to the north of Paris proper.

A few days after the 5th Brigade assumed control of the depots the Seine River began rising toward flood levels, threatening to inundate the greater part of the depots. Aggressive control measures were immediately instituted; supplies which might be damaged by water were raised; boats were provided; warehouse doors were sealed; some supplies were loaded into railroad cars for storage in the marshalling yards; and earthen levees were constructed and reinforced. An interesting historical fact in this connection was that at Depots 508A and 508B, the new dikes were erected on the base of ancient French structures of similar nature. Although the river rose above the predicted crest, and the depots were inundated to such a degree as to prevent receipt of supplies, issues were not suspended and damage to supplies was negligible. As soon as the waters subsided, depots resumed full-scale operations and within a week the backlog of supplies in the railroad yards was reduced to normal.

During the period the 5th Engineer Special Brigade controlled the depots, constant study was being made to determine how the limited personnel and equipment might be used more efficiently. Many changes were made and by March 10 the depots were handling over 3,000 tons per day with an elastic organization that could readily have handled more had the occasion arisen.

On February 26 the newly activated Headquarters and Headquarters Company, 1409th Engineer Base Depot, was attached to the brigade to provide a single organic headquarters to supervise the operation of all E-508 depots. This unit gradually assumed control of the depots and was in complete command of the situation by March 27, when the brigade was relieved of responsibility for depot operation.

On April 1, 1945, the main body of the 5th Brigade Headquarters and Headquarters Company moved from Paris to Le Havre and established headquarters at an ancient French harbor defense installation, Fort de Tourneville, overlooking the city. On April 7 Brigade Headquarters and Headquarters Company took over the task of supervising all engineer work in the northern district of Normandy Base Section.

The Staff organization as developed in Paris proved to be admirably suited for the execution of the new mission in spite of its complicated nature. The magnitude of the task confronting the staff can best be appreciated by considering that during the period April 7 to May 25 the brigade was assigned a total of ten engineer general service regiments.

The most important work of the Brigade during this period was the development of redeployment camps in the Le Havre–Rouen area, for 170,000 men. Redeployment camps upon which the brigade engaged in work were, Lucky Strike, Philip Morris, Twenty Grand, Herbert Tareyton, Old Gold, Pall Mall, and Wings. In addition to these camps the brigade engaged in developing necessary facilities in the area for the maintenance of the transient personnel.

VE-day (May 7) was a happy one for the members of the brigade, but it provided no decrease in the tempo of the operations. Indeed the pace became even faster due to advances in the completion dates and increases in capacities of the redeployment camps. On May 25 in anticipation of its own redeployment, the 5th Brigade was relieved of its construction missions and all units were relieved from assignment.

On June 1, 1945, Brigade Headquarters and Headquarters Company moved to Fort Ste. Addresse at Le Havre for the mission of operating the camp as a staging area. This area was appropriately named Camp Home Run. Staging of the troops consisted of inspection and certification of baggage, adjustment of individual equipment, changing of foreign money and movement of troops to shipside. The staging area operated under direct command of the Commanding Officer, Le Havre Port of Embarkation. For the purpose of operating this area the brigade staff was completely reorganized to provide necessary sections to carry out the new mission.

On June 9 the first troops, about 300 officers and enlisted men having critical scores for discharge, arrived at Camp Home Run. Within three days all of these had been loaded aboard ships and the camp was again empty. This lull gave all sections an opportunity to revise their operating procedures on the basis of lessons learned by practical experience.

The proximity of Camp Home Run to the dock area, its good accommodations and the ease of control of troops in the area made it an ideal plan for the staging of small units and casuals. Consequently the advance parties of most small units were sent to the camp. During the month in which the brigade operated the area advance parties of six infantry divisions, one armored division, one corps headquarters and numerous separate battalions were staged. Those troops lucky enough to pass through that staging area were amazed to find within the walls of the old fort soft beds, running water, and good chow to say nothing of movies twice a day, Coca Cola, and manicures, all free of charge. In spite of all these luxuries, it can hardly be said that a single man was sorry to leave the area and board a ship for the United States.

An interesting sidelight of the brigade's stay in Le Havre was the dedication of a monument to the brigade dead which took place at Omaha Beach on June 6, 1945, just one year after the landing. Representatives of nearly all of the units assigned to the brigade for the landing, were present. The monument, a cement obelisk decorated with marble plaques, now stands overlooking the beach atop the German pillbox. After the ceremony at Omaha Beach, Colonel Bridges and several members of his staff went to Utah Beach. At Utah Beach they took part in a ceremony at which the French government presented the Croix de Guerre with Palm to the 5th Engineer Special Brigade consisting of all units assigned and attached as of June 6, 1944. The award was presented for the outstanding services of the brigade in the assault landings and in the subsequent buildup of troops and supplies over Omaha Beach.

On June 28, 1945, Brigade Headquarters and Headquarters Company received alert orders for redeployment via the United States after July 1. On June 30 a provisional detachment took over the operation of Camp Home Run and staged as one of its first units, Headquarters and Headquarters Company, 5th Engineer Special Brigade.

On the evening of July 4, 1945, Brigade Headquarters and Headquarters Company boarded the USS *West Point* at Le Havre. The following morning the vessel sailed on her first voyage to return troops for redeployment. Also aboard the ship were members of the 87th Infantry Division and Headquarters V Corps.

Pleasant weather prevailed throughout the crossing. On the morning of July 11 the *West Point* sailed into New York Harbor to a tremendous ovation of boat whistles, public-address systems on blimps and waterborne WAC bands. That afternoon the troops debarked and moved to the staging area at Camp Kilmer, New Jersey, for dispatch to their homes for recuperation.

On August 17, 1945, after a period of recuperation marked by the arrival of VJ-day, members of Headquarters and Headquarters Company began arriving at Camp Gordon Johnston, old home of the 2d, 3d and 4th Engineer Special Brigades. By August 25 the unit was assembled with the exception of some enlisted men who had critical scores and were held at their reception stations for discharge.

Although Japan had surrendered, Brigade Headquarters and Headquarters Company were still scheduled for redeployment to Japan about October 10. Consequently a schedule was set up for a three-week period of refresher military training to consist of a review of basic subjects and firing of weapons. This program was started September 5, 1946.

Soon the high-point men began leaving the brigade for discharge and reassignment. By September 7, when the unit was relieved from its alert for redeployment, there remained hardly sufficient men to do the necessary housekeeping.

On October 20, 1945, the 5th Engineer Special Brigade was inactivated, leaving as mementos only a simple concrete monument atop a Normandy pillbox, many white crosses in a beach cemetery, and a record of jobs well done.

The 6th Brigade on Omaha

The 6th Brigade was formed much as the 5th Brigade and was originally attached to it. On May 7, 1944, the U. S. First Army relieved the 6th from the 5th and placed it under the Provisional Engineer Special Brigade Group. During the early part of the planning phase it was realized that the 5th and 6th Brigades could not carry out all the missions assigned them. As a consequence, the 11th Port Group with a final strength of over 8,600 officers and men was attached to the ESB Group. This did not prove too satisfactory, though, as the 11th Port troops had been trained in the operation of ports and not in unloading over beaches, a much different and more difficult job.

From its arrival in the United Kingdom on January 20 the 6th Brigade was kept busy training at Torquay and Paignton. After several small exercises the Brigade participated in both Exercise Fox and Exercise Fabius which was the dress rehearsal for the invasion of Normandy. The 6th Brigade's experience on D-day was similar to that of the 5th already described. The 6th Brigade lost its commander on the way into the beach on D-day when Colonel Paul W. Thompson was seriously wounded and evacuated. Colonel Timothy L. Mulligan took his place.

Group Command Lands

The command party of the Provisional Brigade Group left the USS *Ancon* in an LCVP about 2:00 P.M. on D-day. Grounding a hundred yards off-shore, the party disembarked in waist-deep water and proceeded to shore under fire. The party then set up its command post at a concrete pillbox which had been the command post of the U. S. 1st Division. It remained there for six days when the command post was moved to St. Laurent. When darkness fell on D-day the infantry, artillery and tanks had not reached any of their objectives. The beaches were so crowded that engineer troops had to stop their work at midnight. At midnight General Hoge took over responsibility for Omaha Beach, coordinating 5th ESB and 6th ESB.

German documents captured later revealed that at 4:55 P.M. on D-day Field Marshal Von Rundstedt transmitted to the German Troops Hitler's order to liquidate the beachhead by evening. However, the night passed without attack other than a few planes whose bombs did no damage.

Although D-day operations were thus far behind schedule for the Amphibian Engineers due to the enemy opposition, early on D plus 1 operations began to improve and from then on the work hummed, except during the unprecedented storm of D plus 13 to D plus 16. With this brief look at the operations on Omaha Beach let us now review those of the 1st Brigade which had landed at Utah Beach. During the first hundred days over a million tons of supplies, a hundred thousand vehicles from the lowly but powerful jeep to the massive 32-ton tank, and six hundred thousand men had poured over Omaha Beach. During the same period the Amphibians outloaded some 24,000 prisoners of war and 43,000 casualties. Truly a wonderful accomplishment!

THE 1ST BRIGADE IN NORMANDY

Upon withdrawal from the campaign in Italy, what remained of the 1st Brigade after losses in Sicily and at Salerno and the transfer of many units to the Fifth Army, sailed from Naples on November 18, 1943. Barring submarine troubles and some brushes with the Germans' new-fangled radio-controlled glide bomb and a few old-fashioned air attacks, the voyage was uneventful.

Upon arrival in the waters of the United Kingdom some units were installed in Ireland, some in Scotland, but by December 12 all had assembled in the country around Truro, well down in Cornwall. The quiet, serene countryside was restful after the brigade's year in the smashed-up regions of North Africa, Sicily, and Italy. It was pleasant to be in a place where many things were so much like those at home and where the local inhabitants even spoke our language, after a fashion.

The brigade arrived with no equipment, tired from a year in the field and five campaigns, under strength, and with many sick from delayed malaria. An inexperienced division of V Corps was shortly to try its hand at an amphibious exercise but the show would not be complete without shore troops. The corps commander appreciated the situation and said the brigade did not have to take part but that it would be of great help if it could possibly be arranged. As always, the 1st Brigade responded. By means that will never be understood and efforts that can never be fully appreciated, by Christmas Day the brigade had scoured England for equipment and had assembled and serviced it, had planned its part in the exercise, which was full-scale; had borrowed officers to round out a scratch headquarters and the units needed to complete its organizations; and was soon loading out for the exercise under Colonel Caffey's able leadership.

The loading was made on Slapton Sands on the south coast of England. The beach was of shingle that sloped at an angle of about twenty per cent. There was a 20-foot tide. The only vehicles that could cross the beach unaided were bulldozers and even they mired at times. Two hundred yards back of the shore was a deep lagoon that ran the full length of the landing area. Behind that were steep hills with a few narrow, tortuous roads. While the amphibs did not know it then, they were seeing country something like their destination on the "pay run" a short time later.

It was about as difficult a situation as one's worst enemy could select. However, in spite of natural obstacles and the handicap imposed by working with strange borrowed units and new associates, the experience and spirit of the old faithfuls from the Mediterranean turned out a greater production per capita than the brigade ever attained before or since. Even though only an exercise, Operation Duck One stands as a monument to the 1st Brigade.

From January through April 1944 the brigade, still under Colonel E. M. Caffey, built itself up to a strength of some 16,000, including attached troops, and perfected its organization and training. There was an endless succession of exercises, some with the 29th Division and some with the 4th Division, fresh from training with the 4th ESB at Carrabelle, Florida. Finally toward the last of April came Tiger, the grand rehearsal. There was bitter reality in Tiger. German E-boats got through to attack three LSTs carrying units of the brigade and there were tragic losses, many of them Amphibians. Valuable engineer equipment, much of it irreplaceable at the time, went down.

The end of the first week in May saw the brigade moving into the mounting areas. Enemy air activity was slight but sufficient to cause further losses in the brigade almost up to the day of sailing. At long last on June 5, 1944, the brigade sailed—destination Utah Beach. The weather was clear and the sea smooth as the thousands of vessels stood up the Channel under a canopy of fighter aircraft.

Shortly after midnight the anchors splashed down in the transport area fifteen miles off the Cotentin Peninsula. Not a shot had been fired nor a bomb dropped during the crossing from England. Now at anchor a few miles from the enemy and still, except for an occasional burst of antiaircraft fire away over on the coast, nothing happened. It seemed impossible but there it was.

With the approach of daylight, at the line of departure it was possible to make out the expected low-lying coast and the wooded hills behind it. At H minus 30 minutes the shoreline began to jump under the impact of American bombs and there was a comforting sustained rumble as the sticks landed. The silvery bombers were a beautiful sight as the sun's rays glanced off them. A little later a deep rumble from the sea announced the opening of the naval gunfire. Hundreds of shells swooshed over to do the Germans no good. Finally the rockets cut loose by the thousands and then there was a rush. In just a moment the machine guns and light cannon of the landing craft opened against the dunes and in went the boats.

At low tide Utah Beach is a broad, flat, firm expanse of sand resembling Daytona Beach in Florida. Back of the high-water line is a concrete or stone seawall backed by dunes running up to twenty-five feet. Behind the dunes there is a rolling strip of meadow a few hundred yards wide. In rear of this strip there is a depression ordinarily drained by ditches. With usual thoughtfulness, the Germans had blocked off the drainage months before so that the depression formed a lake several miles long, from 200 to 2,800 yards wide, and deep enough in many places to be over a man's head. Rising from the lake, tree-covered hills reach a height of several hundred feet. They were covered also with guns ranging from old French 75s to 150mm rifles.

Returning to the beach, there was a considerable variety of obstacles between the low- and high-water marks but they caused no difficulty The first wave of boats landed to seaward of them and the men walked through them. Navy and Engineer units cleared them off fairly well before the tide rose.

At frequent intervals along the water front the enemy had strong-points with heavy concrete works hidden in the dunes. They were armed with flamethrowers, machine guns, and small cannon all well wired in and mined. There was brisk fighting across the beach but luckily the main landing was nearly a mile off course and struck between two strong-points instead of smack on one as planned. This fortunate error was due to the sinking of the two leading control vessels on the way in and the effect of a set of an offshore current to the southward. Left largely to their own devices and without landmarks, the boat waves simply headed for the shore. An additional benefit from the off-course landing was that it put the attack outside of the only road across the lake that was out of water.

The infantry of the 4th Division pushed inland smartly. By the end of the day they were on the hills and had linked up with the 82d and 101st Airborne Divisions which had dropped elements several miles inshore just before daylight. Parts of the 1st Brigade had landed in the first and following waves. As soon as the necessary reconnaissance could be made and plans altered to meet the landing on the wrong beaches, the appropriate parts of the brigade were called in and the long, hard grind was on for the Amphibians. It lasted for five months.

Trouble on the beaches lasted all D-day. D-day was a long day because darkness did not come until 11:00 P.M. The enemy had excellent observation and plenty of artillery. The German salvos straddled the beaches. The hostile guns were repeatedly dive-bombed, plentifully shot at by the Navy, and attacked by the infantry and the engineers but no sooner quieted than they opened again. Finally the nearer ones were overrun and, although there was shellfire on the brigade's workshop for over two weeks, it was all long range and not very disturbing. Enemy aircraft put in brief appearances but it was only a nuisance and not a problem.

The brigade operated Utah Beach until the winter storms of November brought operations to a close. A few weeks after the landing it took over the Utah Beach Command with 25,000 troops, then the Utah District with 40,000, and finally an enlarged Utah District which included all of the Cotentin Peninsula with 70,000 troops. Its activities resulted in the landing on the beaches of 836,000 men, 725,000 long tons of supplies, and 220,000 vehicles. It evacuated 37,000 casualties, 65,000 prisoners of war, and two U.S. airborne divisions. It back-loaded across the beach over 325,000 tons of supplies.

Having accomplished its task in Normandy in December, as was usual after every major amphibious operation, the brigade was practically disbanded. The headquarters left for the Pacific, leaving behind only a waste of desolate beach and a monument to its heroic dead.

In planning for the invasion of Normandy, both British and American staffs agreed that the troops could not be sustained for long over open beaches. It was a definite requisite that a port be captured soon and its docks and channels opened up for Allied shipping. Cherbourg was captured but the Germans had done such a thorough job of destruction and used such ingenious mines that it took weeks instead of days for the Navy to open up the channels of that port. Only the unending and superhuman efforts of the shore engineers on Omaha and Utah Beaches kept the battle rolling during those critical days.

ARTIFICIAL PORTS AND HARBORS

No history of the Amphibians would be complete without reference to the artificial ports and harbors of the Normandy operation, not that the Amphibians constructed the harbors but because their work was affected by these harbors. Operation plans for the invasion of France called for the construction of two complete artificial harbors (Mulberries), one at Omaha Beach (U.S.) and one at Arromanches (British), and a harbor for small craft only (Goose-berry) at Utah Beach (U.S.). In addition "port" facilities of float-ing piers and sunken ponton causeways were to be constructed. The latter were to be used for the direct discharge to shore of per-sonnel and light vehicles, the former for unloading from ships moored alongside. The harbors were to create quiet water anchor-ages for unloading operations and for protection of small landing craft in storms which were bound to occur.

The Mulberry off Dog and Easy Beaches in the Omaha Area was started on D-day when the first blockships were sunk. On D plus 6 the floating breakwater was completed; on D plus 9 the first pierhead and floating pier was completed. By that time 53 Phoe-nixes (concrete caissons each 200 feet long and 60 feet wide) had been sunk in place. The design, towing and placing of the compo-nents of this harbor represent a magnificent achievement with particular credit to the Navy and its construction battalions. The execution of the work involved numerous problems and difficul-ties. On the first day charges fired on one blockship failed to sink it. Only a few seconds later the German artillery registered a direct hit and obligingly sunk the blockship although slightly out of position. On June 19 (D plus 13) a particularly severe storm struck, raging for three days. Sections of the floating breakwater were bro-ken up and sunk or washed ashore. Floating piers were destroyed along with a number of LCTs and smaller craft which pounded against the piers and were sunk. The beaches were soon jammed with the wrecks of small landing craft, barges, Rhino ferries and at least two LSTs. Construction of the Mulberry had to be aban-doned. Any contributions it could have made to operations, had it been completed, would be largely conjectural. As it was, little pro-tection was afforded by the Phoenixes. The Gooseberry did offer some protection to the small craft during all storms except the June gale and provided sheltered water for unloading operations. The floating piers and pierhead discharged no cargo and handled less than one per cent of the vehicles and personnel.

Without a complete harbor and in spite of the severe three-day June storm which not only stopped unloading operations but littered the beach with wrecks, the Provisional Engineer Special Brigade Group (5th and 6th Engineer Special Brigades and the 11th Port for forty days only) discharged 926,689 long tons of cargo during the first ninety days of Operation Neptune, an average of over 10,000 tons per day during this critical period. At least for Omaha Beach the artificial harbors did not pay their way and were not worth the tremendous effort and cost involved in their construction.

At Utah Beach the Gooseberry was made of sunken blockships to provide refuge only for small landing craft. Two sunken ponton causeways were placed by the Seabees. The latter proved quite successful but the Gooseberry did not serve its purpose. Small craft had to seek protection in natural inlets. A report of the 1st Engineer Special Brigade states that not only did the Gooseberry "not begin to justify the time, effort, or materials put into its construction but that it prevented the full use of about 600 yards of good beach." Despite the failure of the Utah Gooseberry and the time lost by storms, the 1st Engineer Special Brigade exceeded the planned capacity. For the first seventy days the brigade averaged 5,700 long tons per day against a planned capacity of 5,500 but as at Omaha the artificial harbor, it is reported, did not pay its way in any respect. However, the Mulberry at Arromanches was reported to be a success, due in part to less exposure to storms. Although a greater tonnage was discharged by DUKWs than over the piers, the artificial harbor made easier the operation of the DUKWs and the small landing craft.

LATER OPERATIONS OF THE 6TH BRIGADE

The 6th Brigade continued to operate Omaha Beach throughout the summer and fall of 1944, unloading cargo and troops, operating dumps, improving roads, and performing other miscellaneous missions, until the Beach was closed in late October 1944. The tremendous success of the Engineer Special Brigade in moving supplies, equipment, and personnel across open beaches so surprised the enemy and so ably supported our own field forces that our campaigns across France were able to progress with amazing rapidity and to crush the German field armies in France and drive them back to their homeland defenses. This success has been so often recounted that its brief mention here is made only for background purposes.

After the close of Omaha Beach there was a period of almost a month during which the elements of the brigade relaxed, regrouped, performed essential tasks of self maintenance and clean-up of equipment, improvement of billet areas, improvement of roads, and reconstruction of temporary bridges. The brigade at this time operated under the command of Omaha District, of Normandy Base Section. Its troop list remained essentially unchanged, with engineer combat battalions, quartermaster battalions, ordnance battalions, DUKW companies, the MP company, and other miscellaneous troops still assigned to the brigade. During the period of this breathing spell one after another of its units were detached and assigned to other missions, until by the first part of December 1944 only the engineer and quartermaster battalions remained. Rumors as to the future mission of the brigade ran high—it was going to make another landing in southern Europe—it was going to the Pacific—it was going to be broken up.

Defense of Western Coast

On December 1, 1944, the 6th Engineer Special Brigade was made responsible for the security of the western coast of the Cotentin Peninsula, from its northern tip, near Cherbourg to a point west of Mont-St-Michel, where the Normandy Base Section joined the Brittany Base Section. The danger lay in the possibility of a raid in force which might be mounted by the desperate German force of some 20,000 who held the Channel Islands just off the coast. The strength of their defense was attested by the survivors of many vessels which unfortunately came within the range of the islands' coastal guns. Intelligence reports predicted that the severe shortage of food on the islands might induce this strong force to attempt to break out, land in force on the Cotentin Peninsula, and disrupt the rear area supply installations. The enemy was known to possess sufficient small craft to effect this desperate plan.

After reconnaissance the brigade commander established a command headquarters at Barneville-sur-Mer, and distributed three engineer combat battalions along this extensive beach line. The 149th Engineer Combat Battalion,[1] with headquarters at Carteret, held the northern third. The 203d Engineer Combat Battalion, with headquarters at Coutances, held the center. And the 147th Engineer Combat Battalion,[1] with headquarters at Granville held the southern third. A tank-destroyer company rendered mobile support by performing a constant road patrol with radio-equipped scout cars and half-tracks. An engineer special service regiment and two general service regiments were in nominal support, and the 156th Infantry Regiment based on Paris represented the reserve.

This very small force with no additional supporting weapons constituted at best a watchman service. Prior warning of any attack was considered essential and to that end a special signal section was formed, connecting all outposts and CPs with an effective wire and radio net. A 24-hour signal center in brigade headquarters received and coordinated reports from all localities. Three radar installations, one in each battalion sector, kept a constant plot on all craft moving between the islands, and guaranteed at least a 70-minute alert on any movement toward the mainland. This radar, radio, and wire system was probably the most effective element of the entire defense. This defensive mission lasted only four weeks, the brigade being relieved just after Christmas by the 156th Infantry.

When the Germans attacked the "Bulge" on the day before Christmas, all three engineer combat battalions were detached from the brigade and rushed to the front to support our forces desperately defending the Ardennes. Forward headquarters was closed on Christmas Day and brigade headquarters was re-established in its original location at Gincohy on Omaha Beach.

GENERAL CONSTRUCTION

On December 29, 1944, Headquarters and Headquarters Company were relieved from assignment to Normandy Base Section and assigned to Advance Section, Communications Zone. The command moved by organic motor transportation to Dun-sur-Meuse, twenty-six miles north of Verdun, arriving after a two-day motor march on January 2, 1945.

The brigade immediately assumed responsibility for all engineer work, except railway repair, in approximately half of the area of Advance Section. The large area for which the brigade became responsible was bounded roughly by Sedan–Verdun–Bar-le-Duc on the west; Toul–Nancy on the south; Metz–Luxembourg on the east; and Arlon–Sedan on the north. Principal missions included the construction of ten general hospitals; the construction of hard-standings, provision of lighting facilities, and maintenance of interior roads in a quartermaster depot and an ordnance ammunition depot; and the maintenance of all principal roads within the sector. Attached general service regiments, construction battalions, dump-truck companies, and utilities detachments performed all work with brigade headquarters responsible for planning, assignment of projects, general supply, assignment of equipment, and supervision.

During the three-month period of this assignment, the principal units attached to the Brigade were the 365th, 372d, 390th, 1314th, 1323d, 1325th, and 1326th Engineer General Service Regiments, and the 371st Engineer Construction Battalion. The major troop effort was devoted to the maintenance of roads, with an average of two general service regiments always working on general construction projects, especially the many needed general hospitals.

The general hospitals constructed under 6th Brigade supervision were located in Verdun, Bar-le-Duc, Toul, Commercy, and Nancy in France, and in Hilon, Belgium. In all, a total of 14,000 bed capacity was provided the Medical Department. Due to the extremely high casualty rate in our breaching of the Siegfried Line defenses during this period, it was necessary for the Medical Department to take beneficial occupancy of these hospitals prior to their completion. Thus, it was necessary for engineer troops to work around patients, and this fact caused many additional difficulties which ordinarily would not have been encountered.

Road maintenance and snow control were a constant and major problem. During January 1945 snow fell in the area on twenty-six of the thirty-one days in the month. Brigade maintenance gangs spread many tons of sand and grit on these roads to permit the safe passage of military vehicles. In addition to military personnel, the French Département des Pouts et Chausses kept some 2,000 civilians spreading grit from brigade stockpiles. All available dump trucks worked twenty-four hours a day during this period.

In February came the much-dreaded thaws, and the notably poor French roads were severely damaged. Where possible traffic was restricted as to speed and load limit. But General Patton's Third Army had to have food from the Verdun Quartermaster Depot and ammunition from the enormous Étain Ordnance Depot. So our engineers were faced with a reconstruction program as well as a maintenance program. To supply its operating units, elements of the brigade operated four quarries and three central premix asphalt plants.

During this period brigade headquarters moved from Dun-sur-Meuse to Verdun, where it remained throughout this phase. Living for the first time in a city, with central heated billets, hot-water baths, and civilian laundry facilities, the *esprit* of the brigade moved still another notch higher. All hands were proud of the obvious accomplishments of the brigade, and it was with reluctance that, on Easter Sunday, April 1, 1945, the personnel of headquarters mounted its transportation and moved forward again to perform another totally different mission.

COAL MINING

On March 28 the brigade was assigned the mission of establishing a management organization for the reactivation and operation of the German coal-mining industry. After a preliminary reconnaissance a headquarters was established on April 1, 1945, at Homberg on the Rhine. The great Ruhr pocket was still holding out, and this was as close to the center of the coalfields as the headquarters could go. Rheinpreussen House, selected for headquarters, was within 800 yards of the German lines and was eight miles forward of the CP of the 94th Division, which was holding in that sector. For many nights the headquarters of the 6th Brigade was treated to accurate mortar fire, and twice the 368th Engineer General Service Regiment was required to move its CP as a result of German artillery bombardments.

The organization thus formed was titled Advance Section Engineer Rhine Coal Control. The Commanding Officer, 6th Engineer Special Brigade, was Commanding Officer, Rhine Coal Control. The brigade formed the framework on which the entire management organization was hung. In addition to its T/O personnel, the Brigade Headquarters and Headquarters Company was authorized an excess of 100 officers and 400 enlisted men. The organization absorbed also the former Allied organization, which had managed coal distribution in Belgium. This organization added some hundred British and American officers and approximately 200 enlisted clerks and statisticians to the new organization. Also some 150 French, Belgian, and Dutch officers joined, together with their orderlies and chauffeurs.

Again a hasty reorganization was necessary. An active Headquarters Commandant Section was established, which, assisted by Headquarters Company, operated all billets, enlisted messes for British and for American personnel, a combined officers' mess for over 250 officers, and a motor pool containing over 300 jeeps and commandeered private cars. The operation of messes alone posed a big problem, which was nicely solved by the employment of a large number of Polish displaced persons as cooks, KPs, waitresses, etc. Eventually the Headquarters Commandant took over, for the use of Rhine Coal Control personnel, the complete business offices of a large coal syndicate, together with three blocks of officials' residences.

The most important early accomplishment was the fashioning of an organization to manage this vast industry, and the selection of personnel for key positions. Fortunately, many competent coal-mining technicians were made available from both American and British sources. A system of deputies was established, and every key position from the commander down was occupied by an American officer with a British deputy, or the reverse.

It was expected that many attempts to sabotage mine properties would be made, and that many mines would be flooded. To prevent this, spearhead detachments consisting of security troops accompanied by technical experts for both surface and underground installations closely followed the advance of our forces as the Ruhr pocket was compressed. These detachments took physical possession of mines as soon as they were captured. Power plants, pumps, ventilating fans, chemical laboratories, and records were quickly checked and thereafter carefully guarded. Surprisingly, *no* effort to sabotage mine workings was discovered throughout the entire occupation. On the contrary, the German management was found to be exceedingly anxious to protect the properties and to keep them working. Also, this management set about the work of rehabilitation with great alacrity. Troops used for occupying mines consisted of the U.S. 368th Engineer General Service Regiment and the British 44th Pioneer Group.

Many mines were inoperative for lack of power. To expedite resumption of service, a Power Planning group borrowed from SHAEF and coordination with U.S. Ninth and Fifteenth Army staffs planned and executed repairs to plants and transmission lines which quickly restored minimum power service to mines as required.

Distribution and transportation were of major importance. Prior to the war most coal not used locally in the great blast furnaces of the Ruhr was transported by barge over a great river-canal system. All waterways were blocked by war action, wharves and coal quays damaged, and barges sunk. In addition, railyards and rail lines had suffered extensive damage. The Engineering and Transportation Divisions combined forces to effect repairs to main lines and rail spurs, build needed bridges, locate empty rail wagons, and devise means of transporting coal out of the fields. This work progressed steadily and rapidly. The great Rhine River rail bridge at Duisburg was constructed and work of clearing the Rhine for barge traffic was in progress.

To facilitate supervision and direction, Rhine Coal Control was subdivided into seven districts—five located in the Ruhr, one at Aachen, and one in the great brown coalfields near Cologne. Each district was fully responsible for production, shipment, and management, with over-all policy and management emanating from Rhine Coal Control.

On June 25, 1945, with the withdrawal of all U.S. forces into the new American Zone, Rhine Coal Control in its entirety was turned over to the British. During the three months of its management 6th Engineer Special Brigade acting as Rhine Coal Control had occupied and placed in operation over 200 mines; had uncovered approximately 6,000,000 tons of coal in stockpiles; and had stepped up actual coal production from zero to more than 2,000,000 tons per month. Again the brigade was able to feel pride in the accomplishment of a very special mission.

On June 25, 1945, again with no assigned or attached troops, Headquarters and Headquarters Company started on the long road home. It moved first to La Maison Roarge near Vouziers, France. On July 5 it proceeded to Camp Home Run at Le Havre where personnel and equipment were processed for redeployment through the U.S. While awaiting shipment, officers and men who had participated in the invasion of France just a year before were able to revisit the scene of their heroic exploits on Omaha Beach. Finally on July 14, 1945, the brigade departed from the continent of Europe by water transportation for the U.S., landing home on July 23.

All personnel were authorized 30-day recuperation leaves and furloughs, and the brigade reassembled at Camp Gordon Johnston, during the early part of September 1945. As a result of the end of the Japanese war redeployment training was suspended, shipping orders were revoked, and finally the brigade was inactivated in October 1945.

These later operations of the 6th Engineer Special Brigade emphasize the value of an organization of this type in special operations as opposed to its primary mission in amphibious operations.

Although organized and trained especially for the one major amphibious assault, this unit adapted itself to and performed superior service in three totally different types of unusual missions. Its aggressive reorganization to fit specific tasks, the high spirit of its personnel, and the will to get the job done proved it to be truly an engineer *Special* Brigade.

NOTES

[1] Both the 147th and 149th were awarded the Distinguished Unit Citation for their work on Omaha Beach on D-day.

11
ISLAND HOPPING IN THE SOUTHWEST PACIFIC

To resume the story of operations in the Southwest Pacific, it should be recalled that with the Huon Peninsula firmly in Allied hands (Chapter 7) and with the arrival in New Guinea of both the 1st Cavalry Division from the U.S. and the 1st Marine Division from Melbourne, MacArthur was ready either to invade New Britain or to continue to drive up the coast of New Guinea and take Wewak. Allied air photos showed that both Rabaul and Wewak were strongly fortified. Would MacArthur merely block them off and by-pass them in his drive on the Philippines? It did not take him long to show his decision.

ARAWE

On December 15, 1943, the amphibians participated again with American troops in a landing at Arawe, the first on New Britain. As reefs were particularly bad here, only Alligators and Buffaloes (seagoing tanks) comprised the first four waves. By the time the 2d ESB landing boats came in the fifth wave, the scouts ashore had found openings through the fringing reef to get to the narrow beach. However, one LCVP did get hung up on coral, and, before the boat could be refloated, Jap strafers came in and filled it full of holes. After the initial landing, more LCMs of the 2d Brigade arrived with the Navy LCTs and remained on the far shore when the Navy large craft returned to the near shore.

Jap air attacks at Arawe were particularly savage for the first few days. On the second day a Navy APC was sunk by a direct hit

139

and went down in four minutes. The brigade's small landing craft put off to the rescue while more bombs and strafing were hitting all around them. Every man on the APC was saved, even though many were wounded. Lieutenant Colonel White, the Amphibians' commander, was seriously wounded and had to be evacuated.

Here at Arawe the rockets were used for the first time in a combat landing. After the naval bombardment ceased, the rockets opened fire from two Amphibian Engineer DUKWs and a Navy LCI and effectively covered the landing beach and its flanks until the leading wave was only 150 yards from the shore. As a result only a few wild rifle shots were received from the shore, although the Japs had three 75mm guns emplaced in that area.

With many Jap barges known to be in the vicinity, one of the most important jobs was patrolling by water, especially at night, to prevent a Jap surprise landing. The Navy's PT boats were kept busy but they drew too much water to penetrate into the small bays where Jap landing craft could hide. The Amphibs' small boats drew this job. Encounters with Jap planes were frequent. Outside of one occasion when a Jap dive bomber, its pilot killed by the boat's aerial gunners, continued on his dive right into the stern of one of the LCMs and exploded, the Amphibians came off well. At least five Jap planes were shot down by the boat gunners in the various strafing and bombing attacks which occurred up to December 31, 1943.

CAPE GLOUCESTER

On December 26, 1943, the Marines of the 1st Marine Division landed at both Yellow and Green Beaches on Cape Gloucester in New Britain. The 2d Brigade furnished boat detachments for both beaches but the Marines had their own shore parties, having used them at Guadalcanal. At Green Beach rocket craft of the 2d ESB covered the waves of landing boats in the initial landing after the naval bombardment had ceased. The beach was fairly free of coral, so the landing boats were able to land on time and in proper formation. Again enemy opposition on the beach was light but intensified after the Marines went ashore.

At Yellow Beach the brigade boats were in reserve on the initial landing but had the usual resupply and similar missions thereafter as in previous operations. A new mission assigned to them was to patrol at night off all possible landing beaches where Japs could strike the Marines in rear. This was essential, for intelligence reports showed that the Japs had as many as three hundred barges within striking distance.

Maintenance of boats on Yellow Beach was a most difficult problem. The beaches were rocky and the waters full of coral. Propellers were continually being chewed up, shafts bent, and bottoms damaged as the heavy surf pounded the boats being loaded or unloaded on the beaches. Several times Japs put bullet holes or mortar fragments into the boats. Improvisation was the rule in repairing these barges. Shortage of shipping space had prevented bringing over the usual heavy equipment for boat maintenance. Instead, divers had to work under water in pounding surf, changing propellers and making other repairs.

The Green Beach force, having accomplished its mission, was evacuated in LCMs from that exposed beach after many delays due to the heavy surf. Here the brigade lost one LCM and one LCVP, which had to be abandoned the last day when Japs pressed closely on the heels of the Marines being moved around to Yellow Beach. As the northwest monsoon season was on in full blast, very heavy surf and seas were experienced in all these operations. They were the most difficult the boatmen had been called upon to face. Confidence in the small landing craft rose when they weathered 20-foot seas which had turned back the Navy's larger PT boats. But the boatmen and their passengers frequently took terrific beatings, tossed about by the high waves and soaked with sheets of driving spray and heavy rains. After all, these small landing boats were neither designed nor intended to be oceangoing steamers. But they had a job to do and they did it.

The rocket detachments went into action several times during the first week. On one occasion they definitely put out of action four Jap pillboxes which had been holding up the Marine advance. On another occasion they shelled a deep ravine through which Japs

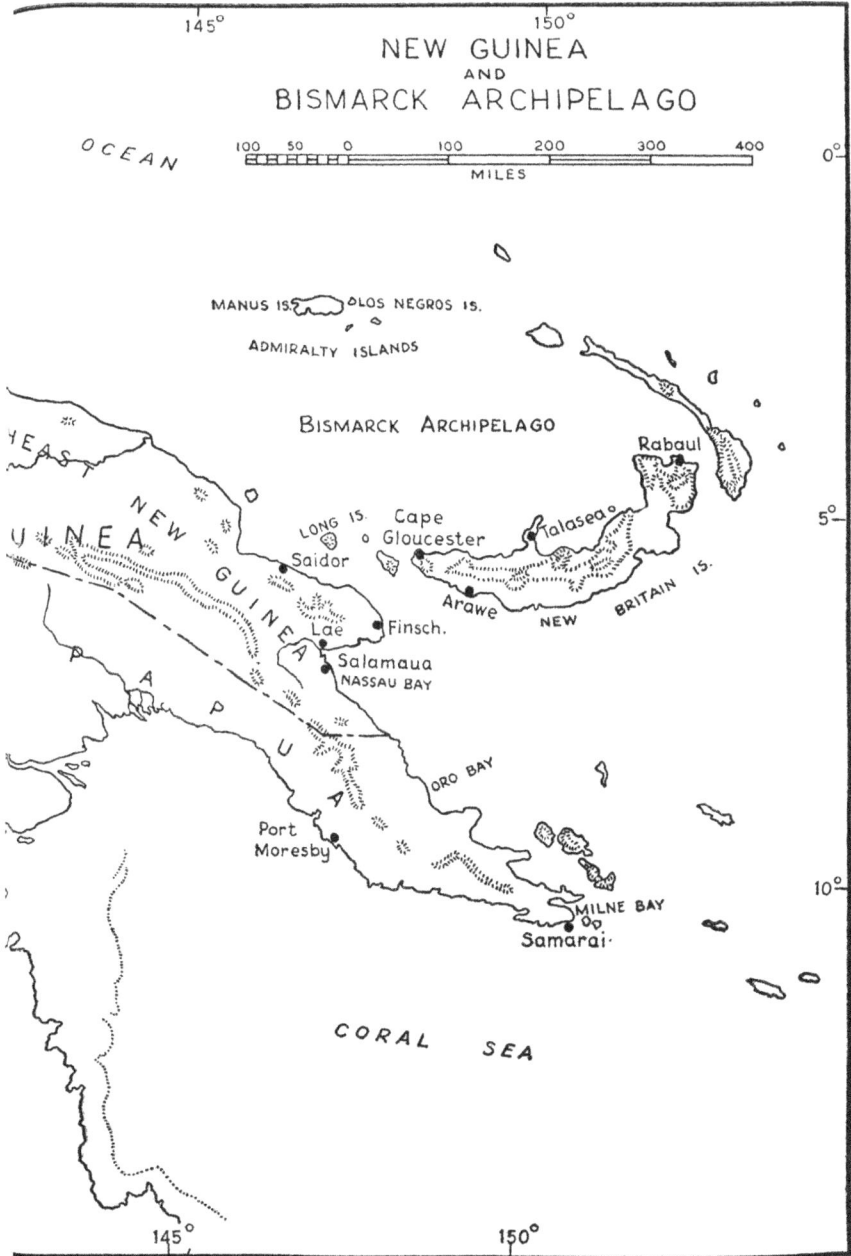

NEW GUINEA
AND
BISMARCK ARCHIPELAGO

OCEAN

100 50 0 100 200 300 400
MILES

145°   150°   0°

MANUS IS.   LOS NEGROS IS.
ADMIRALTY ISLANDS

BISMARCK ARCHIPELAGO

Rabaul

HEAST
NEW
GUINEA
GUINEA

LONG IS.   Cape
Saidor   Gloucester   Talasea
Lae   Finsch.   Arawe   NEW   BRITAIN IS.
Salamaua
NASSAU BAY
PAPUA

5°

ORO BAY

Port
Moresby

MILNE BAY
Samarai·

10°

CORAL   SEA

145°   150°

were passing, thinking they were masked from our fire. Here many casualties were inflicted.

LONG ISLAND

On the same day the Marines landed at Gloucester, an Engineer Special Brigade task force (Company D, 592d) proceeded a hundred miles from Finschhafen to Long Island via PT boat and effected a successful landing by rubber boat. The first two rubber boats capsized in the surf on the strange beach, but no men or equipment were lost. Later boats succeeded in getting ashore without capsizing. The combat force was followed later that morning by an LCM and LCVP convoy which made the 100-mile trip in exposed seas from Finschhafen without untoward incident. This convoy brought an Aussie radar detachment and twenty days' rations and supplies for both United States and Australian troops as well as a bulldozer and other equipment. This force under Lieutenant Colonel Kaplan lived on this advanced isolated island for three months but not once did the Japs attack it.

SAIDOR LANDING

With the Gloucester landing so successful, the Sixth Army followed up with another landing, this time at Saidor, between Sio and Madang, to cut off the Japs retreating from the Huon Peninsula. New Year's Day was the take-off day for this 32d Division task force with a long jump from its staging area on Goodenough Island. There the 542d Shore Battalion, with attached medical company and the usual communications detail, had had time for one brief rehearsal with the task force. Off Finschhafen the Navy convoy bound for Saidor paused only long enough that afternoon to pick up the brigade's landing boats. The formidable convoy with several Navy destroyers and cruisers in the offing continued on and effected a landing shortly after daybreak with no opposition from the enemy. Fortunately, seas were calm and the small boats experienced no trouble.

At Saidor the 542d Shore Engineers, reinforced by well organized manpower from the 32d Division, established a record in unloading the LSTs. Despite poor beaches and difficult terrain directly in rear of the beaches, six LSTs were unloaded within three hours and able to leave on their return trip before any enemy air reaction. In February, the 533d (3d ESB) relieved the 2d Brigade's troops at Saidor.

In the first five months of operations, MacArthur's advance had covered only a couple of hundred miles. The Americans and Australians had little to work with at the beginning but the foundations were being laid by General MacArthur for harder blows against the fanatical Jap and for deeper thrusts into his territory.

The Arawe (December 15) and Gloucester (December 25) landings on New Britain had made the Japs think the Allies were headed for Rabaul. This fortress was considered the key to the Jap defense system in the Solomons and Bismarck Sea areas. On October 12, 1943, our Air Forces had begun a full-scale and unremitting attack on the Rabaul bastion, punctuated now and then with naval bombardments. To strengthen the idea that Rabaul was our next objective, the Marines from Gloucester made a subsidiary landing at Talasea, a 120-mile jump towards Rabaul. Elements of both the 2d and 3d Engineer Special Brigades combined to furnish the necessary small landing craft. This was the first combat action for the 3d Brigade. This landing brought forth one innovation when Marine pilots in low-flying Cub planes bombed the beach with light bombs and gasoline cans just before the leading wave hit the beach. Another innovation was partly lowering an LCM ramp while at sea to allow a Sherman tank loaded on the LCM to engage an enemy tank on shore. After firing only a few rounds a direct hit was scored, thus establishing the first known instance of a tank firing from an LCM at sea to destroy a tank on shore.

THE ADMIRALTIES

Captured diaries later revealed the Japs took the Rabaul bait and expected the next blow to fall there. Much to their surprise, it fell on the Admiralty Islands. The 2d Brigade furnished a regimental task group to the 1st Cavalry Division for this operation. The

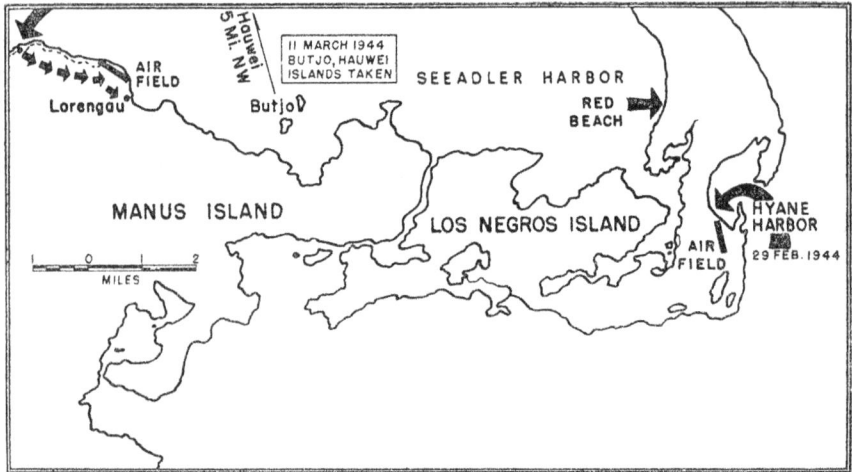

initial landing in Hyane Harbor, thanks to the heavy air and naval bombardment, met little opposition but it did not take long for the Japs to react. Soon both our boat and shore engineers became hotly involved in fighting Jap counterattacks. The original beachhead on Los Negros Island was shallow in depth and unloading was frequently interrupted by mortar and artillery fire and by Jap infiltrations. The shore engineers at one time were fighting with their backs literally at the sea and suffered several casualties, mostly in the confused fighting at night. The landing craft which remained in Hyane Harbor engaged in machine-gun battles with the Japs on the flanks of the small beachhead; the craft also threw rocket fire on them. Rocket LCMs were in operation on at least six different occasions in the first few days. The support battery of the 2d Brigade also manned a considerable number of Buffaloes (LVTs) which were used to cross the numerous coral reefs and swamps.

As soon as the airfield on Los Negros Island was secure, small Butjo Island was occupied and artillery was set up there. Then a full-fledged landing with supporting naval and air bombardment was launched west of Lorengau on large Manus Island with the mission of seizing the Lorengau airfield. In this operation the 2d Brigade manned some forty LCVPs, LCMs and Buffaloes, making two round trips from Red Beach.

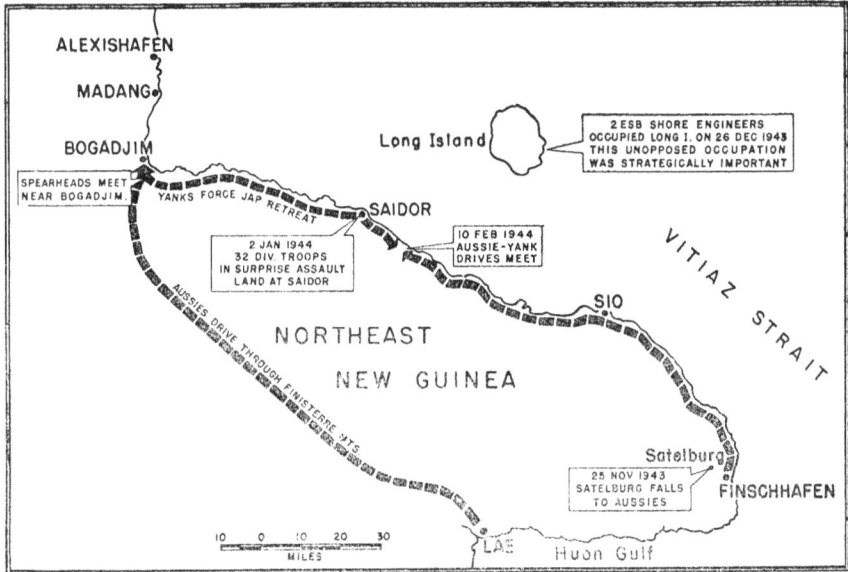

ALEXISHAFEN
MADANG
Long Island
2 ESB SHORE ENGINEERS OCCUPIED LONG I. ON 26 DEC 1943 THIS UNOPPOSED OCCUPATION WAS STRATEGICALLY IMPORTANT
BOGADJIM
SPEARHEADS MEET NEAR BOGADJIM.
YANKS FORCE JAP RETREAT
SAIDOR
2 JAN 1944 32 DIV. TROOPS IN SURPRISE ASSAULT LAND AT SAIDOR
10 FEB 1944 AUSSIE-YANK DRIVES MEET
VITIAZ STRAIT
SIO
AUSSIES DRIVE THROUGH FINISTERRE MTS.
NORTHEAST
NEW GUINEA
Satelburg
25 NOV 1943 SATELBURG FALLS TO AUSSIES
FINSCHHAFEN
10 0 10 20 30
MILES
LAE Huon Gulf

HAUWEI ISLAND

As far as the 2d Brigade was concerned, the outstanding exploit of these operations, however, was the first landing on little Hauwei Island, a few miles out in Seeadler Harbor, north of Manus. Here a lone LCVP, covered by a single PT boat, landed a reconnaissance patrol of some twenty-five cavalrymen on March 11. Aerial photographs of the island and information from friendly (?) natives indicated the island was unoccupied. However, the Japs were there in force and very cleverly concealed. They allowed the cavalry patrol to land and then ambushed them as they pushed inland. Other Japs opened up on the PT boat and the LCVP. The latter was armored and returned the enemy fire. The PT boat was hit and retired. The lone LCVP, seeing the patrol in trouble on shore, dashed back to the beach under continuous fire and at one point picked up eight of the survivors, five of whom were wounded. As the craft retracted from the beach, the coxswain spotted another point on the island where a few more isolated Americans were signalling for rescue. Again he pushed his craft in to the shore and despite more enemy fire, succeeded in picking up that group and retracting a second time from the beach.

By this time, Jap mortar fire was hitting all around the craft, which veered right and left trying to throw the Japs off their aim. Soon a shell hit close beside, penetrating the armor. The craft began to sink. The crew had previously put life preservers on all the men including the wounded. The coxswain kept driving the craft on but a minute later it went down under him. All personnel floated clear. After several hours in the water, the floating men were relieved to see a returning bomber fly low to investigate the bobbing men in the water. An hour later a rescuing craft was picking them up although in the last few minutes a hungry shark tried to interfere with the rescue. All of the crew and many of the cavalrymen were decorated for their part in this operation.

A few days later Hauwei Island was subjected to a new landing in force preceded by a heavy artillery bombardment. All the remaining Japs were quickly mopped up. For the next few weeks the brigade's craft were busy carrying cavalry details to outlying islands and as far as the western end of Manus, as the remaining Japs were being annihilated.

ON TO MADANG

In the meantime, boats from the 542d EBSR[1] were operating with the 32d Division both east and west of Saidor as the Japs were pushed back in both directions.

Working northwest with the Australians from Finschhafen as far as Sio was the 532d EBSR. The monsoon season had changed and the increased winds made life hard for our boatmen as they buffeted the rip tide waters of Vitiaz Strait. Finally, on 10 February, the Yanks from Saidor and the Aussies from Sio met at Yagomi. The Allies' hold on the New Guinea coast was solid as far as Bogadjim only a few miles from the Jap citadel at Madang and two hundred miles from his Wewak bastion.

HOLLANDIA NEXT

The next operation was by far the largest up to that time. General MacArthur decided to bypass the Wewak–Hansa Bay area, where the Japs were feverishly working to be ready to meet us,

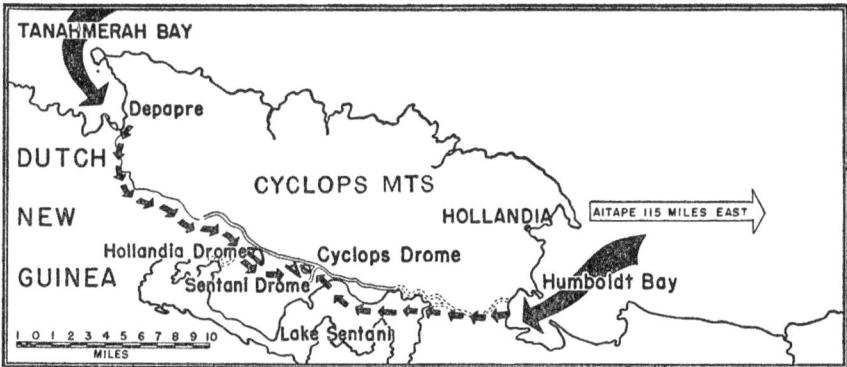

and to strike a three-pronged blow well behind the Jap lines. The 2d Brigade was assigned the mission of supporting the two main divisional landings at Hollandia and Tanahmerah while the 593d Regiment of the 3d Brigade supported the landing of a regimental combat team at Aitape. The Allies had to stage from two widely separated localities, from Goodenough Island with the 24th Infantry Division and from Finschhafen with the 41st Infantry Division.

The 532d Regiment had previously operated with part of the 41st Division in the Nassau Bay–Salamaua operation. That was in the days when the Jap strongly disputed our use of his waters and air. Strange to relate, the full-scale rehearsal with the 41st Division was held on the very same Red Beach east of Lae at which the 532d had landed with the Australians seven months previously.

The 542d Regimental Task Group (the boat and shore units with attached boat maintenance and medical companies from Brigade Special Troops) had its rehearsal with the 24th Division in a practice move from Goodenough to the New Guinea mainland. Both rehearsals showed a few spots where better coordination was necessary and helped a great deal in getting the essential teamwork necessary for a successful amphibious operation.

The 2d Brigade's support battery was divided into two detachments, one to go to Hollandia and the other to Tanahmerah. In addition to its rocket and flak LCMs, the battery manned 35 Buffaloes (LVTs), as coral reefs were known to be extensive at both landing areas. The Buffaloes, although slow in speed, had already proved themselves to be indispensable in the coral-studded waters of the Admiralties and at Arawe and Cape Gloucester on New Britain.

It was the largest movement of small landing craft of any Pacific operation to date. In addition to over 50 Buffaloes, the 2d and 3d Brigades furnished LCMs, LCVPs and 20 miscellaneous craft, such as rocket and flak LCMs. The more than 250 craft furnished for this operation compared with 30 for the Nassau Bay operation ten months previous. On that operation the naval escort consisted of two PT boats; now it consisted of battleships, cruisers, destroyers, rocket and personnel LCIs, subchasers, tugs and, for the first time in SVPA, escort carriers with their fighters and bombers ready to protect us beyond the reach of land-based planes. Every American on that convoy was inspired. The American Eagle was beginning to show his claws.

Off Manus Island the two task force convoys united, made a false start toward Palau to mislead any hidden coastal watchers, lurking Jap planes or subs trying to spot our movement. Then after dusk it turned westward for Hollandia. As far as the eye could see the ocean was covered with all the varied type of amphibious craft with their escorting screen of cruisers, destroyers, and flattops. This was Big Show stuff!

Dawn of April 22 found the attacking forces off their respective objective areas, busily engaged in launching the small landing craft and Buffaloes to take the attacking troops ashore. Seas were fairly calm with only a slight swell to hamper the small landing craft. The naval bombardment went off as scheduled with no reply from shore. Then the rocket craft closed in to their firing range of 1,100 yards and plastered the beaches as wave after wave of landing craft formed up for the assault. At Aitape, Tanahmerah and Hollandia every detail went off as scheduled. The enemy was so surprised that most of them fled from the beach area. This was attested to by teapots still boiling and bowls of rice only half-consumed when the leading wave landed on the beach at Hollandia. The few who remained to fight it out were soon obliterated by the devastating bombardment; only scattered sniper fire met the troops as they landed. On subsidiary landings in Depapre Bay and at Pim, the Buffaloes made landings on coral beaches where the LCMs and LCVPs could not land.

The landing had clicked better than any previous operation. Everything went as planned. However, the work on shore was a different story, for the landing craft poured troops and supplies onto the narrow beaches much faster than they could be removed. All the beaches at Hollandia and Tanahmerah proved more difficult than aerial photographs and intelligence had indicated. They were very shallow, backed up by a hinterland of almost impenetrable mangrove swamp, and with absolutely no existing exits. In one instance a stream identified from aerial photographs as "10 to 20 yards wide" actually proved to be a swamp, armpit-deep in most places, extending inland from 100 to 400 yards. The shore engineers had their busiest time in months. Although beaches were greatly congested, all naval transports were unloaded on D-day and got away before dark, with no enemy air attack.

On the night of D-plus 1 (April 23) a single Jap plane slipped through our antiaircraft defenses and dropped three bombs directly on congested White Beach at Hollandia. Despite valiant efforts by shore engineers and Navy fireboats to quell the flames, the exploding ammunition and burning gasoline were too much and the entire beach was swept by flames from one end to the other, burning for forty-eight hours before it could be extinguished. The contents of a dozen LSTs were lost. Casualties were not heavy as the small boats landed fearlessly in the face of recurring explosions to pick up groups isolated by the flames. Several individuals were decorated for their courageous action and the Collecting Platoon of the 2d Brigade Medical Battalion won the Distinguished Unit Citation for its heroic work.

For the next few weeks, the Amphibian Engineers were kept busy unloading the myriad supplies needed for a big base. The support battery moved its Buffaloes across Sentani Lake and landed the infantry which seized the Jap airfields several miles inland, thus saving expensive advances against the Japs through swamps and over mountains.

After the major landings at Hollandia and Tanahmerah, there were several subsidiary landings. Typical of these was the landing at Wan. Although natives had reported the beach protected by over a hundred Japs with several machine guns, resistance evaporated as the waves of landing boats approached. News of the terrific barrage of naval guns and rockets at Hollandia must have reached the Jap defenders. Our worst enemy here was the sharply breaking surf which pounded the boats on hidden boulders just below the water surface. Several boats were disabled but timely salvage saved them all. This mission returned that night with five Jap prisoners.

WAKDE–SARMI

Early in May, the 593d Regiment (3dESB) at Aitape, with a boat company of the 2d Brigade attached, was alerted to furnish a task group for a landing 120 miles up the coast at Sarmi on the mainland opposite Wakde Island, where the Japs had a good airfield. This landing came off without incident on May 17, 1944. (The 533d Regiment took over the job at Aitape. Its gunboats [LCMs] later had several clashes with the Japs.)

The next afternoon a landing was made on Wakde Island, three miles offshore, to take the airfield. The Air Forces and Navy had plastered the small island from one end to the other. Little if any resistance was expected. However, as a safety measure, the usual rocket barrage was laid on the beach just ahead of the boat waves.

Suddenly, when 300 yards from shore, the two leading waves of boats came under a hail of crossfire. The Japs had taken turrets from disabled planes and dug them into the sandy beach so that only the gun muzzles protruded. The passengers lay flat in the bottom of the boats and avoided the enemy fire but the coxswains had to stay up to keep formation and to control their craft. Also, the bow lookouts had to watch for submerged coral heads and signal the coxswains how to avoid them. Many of the crews were hit but as soon as a coxswain went down, the engineman or the seaman jumped up to take the controls. Not a boat faltered. On one craft every member of the crew was hit. A Red Cross worker, who had gone along as observer because of the expected easy landing, jumped to the controls and succeeded in beaching the boat. For this action he was awarded the Silver Star. Although many of the boatmen were hit, not a single passenger was wounded until the ramps were dropped. Their low positions in the boat plus armor-plate on the passengers' section of the craft protected them. After the landing, 68 slugs and fragments of 20mm shell were found in the bottom of one LCVP. All damaged boats were later repaired and put back into action.

For its magnificent work that afternoon, this boat company (Company A, 542d), with its 21 officers and 338 men, was later awarded the Distinguished Unit Citation.

THE BIAK LANDING

On the same day as the Wakde landing, orders were issued for one of the 2d Brigade's regiments and the brigade support battery to participate with the 41st Division in a major landing on Biak Island. This island was reported to be heavily fortified, several naval defense guns being sited to protect its beaches and important airfields back of the beaches. This large island was ringed with coral reefs, indicating a difficult unloading job and the need again for those invaluable Buffaloes. Its beaches were protected by coastal guns.

Four days later, shore, boat, and support battery personnel were being briefed for the Biak operation. The tempo had increased. No longer were weeks and at times as much as a month available to plan an operation. Now it was a matter of a few days at most and in the case of smaller landings only a few hours. But the Amphibians' Standing Operating Procedure had been clarified by now and was well understood throughout the brigades. They knew how to fit into the Navy's plans. Moreover, most of the troops had been in at least one previous amphibious operation and it was no novelty for them. The term "veteran" began to be heard.

When the convoy arrived off Biak, the beach was in a mist which was soon thickened by the smoke of the naval bombardment and of the bombs dropped by more than fifty B-24s. There was no wind and the humidity held the smoke down on the beach. All landmarks were blotted out. As a result, the first wave of Buffaloes manned by the support battery hit west of the proper beach. The error was discovered before the second wave landed (the smoke having lifted somewhat) and this wave managed to shift west to the proper beach. All subsequent waves landed correctly. Fortunately, the troops landed by the first wave managed to move west by land to join their unit so no damage was done. As expected, the fringed coral reefs prevented the LCVPs and LCMs from reaching the beach but the troops waded in a hundred yards over the reef to the beach. The larger landing craft, LCTs and LSTs, could not get in close enough to unload except at one break in the reef spotted by our reconnaissance party. Here the bulldozers made it ashore under their own power, the drivers being almost shoulder deep in the water; only the frame of the bulldozer and the elevated exhaust pipe appeared above the surface. Luckily the two corral jetties the Japs had constructed were found to need only minor repairs by our bulldozers before LCTs and LSTs could disgorge their vehicles on them. In addition the shore engineers installed two ponton causeways over the reef to deep water. These causeways had been brought forward in sections ingeniously carried on the outside of each LST. Only one LCT was able to unload there, so a shuttle was run from LSTs out in the stream which could not be accommodated at either of the two jetties. Buffaloes and DUKWs were also kept busy unloading the LSTs in the stream, assisting the LCTs in this big job.

The installation of ponton causeways at Biak was the first instance of their use in the Southwest Pacific. As expected they proved very valuable and were slated to be used in many of our subsequent operations. The only real difficulty in their use is holding them in place in storms and in cases where lateral currents are strong. Guy lines can hold only so long. Driving pile dolphins seems the best solution but that is difficult to do in the early stages of an operation.

The Japs, except a few in caves just behind the beach, had withdrawn, but two days later they struck back and effectively bottled up an infantry unit, which was cut off from its supplies on the beach, and was soon short of water and ammunition. Every available LCM. LCVP, and Buffalo was dispatched to evacuate by sea the troops cut off by the Japs. Unfortunately, the fringing reef was bad and only Buffaloes succeeded in negotiating it. They took ammunition and water in to the troops and began the evacuation by ferrying casualties to the LCVPs, LCMs and LCTs waiting off the reef. The Japs did not sit idly by and allow the evacuation to proceed uninterruptedly. One covering destroyer received a direct hit and had to retire. Several times all craft had to pull off because of the heavy mortar and machine-gun fire. However, by taking full advantage of the dark night, all the troops and most of their equipment were evacuated safely. The flak LCMs and Buffaloes did yeoman service in covering the evacuation but had to be very careful in their return fire as no one knew definitely the location of the flanks of our cut-off force. The flak LCMs definitely put out of action one or more enemy mortars which had been harassing the evacuation.

The beach and dump areas were frequently bombed as the Japs had many airfields within striking distance. They inflicted some damage and a considerable number of casualties, mainly at night, but the unloading proceeded ahead of schedule as the shore engineers expanded the jetties to land six LSTs simultaneously while the new Parai jetties were built to accommodate eight more LSTs. Another old stone jetty was improved to accommodate six LCTs or as many as twenty LCMs.

During the first ten days of the operation the support battery definitely shot down four planes. The shore engineers experienced some actual combat, reinforcing the infantry. On one occasion they established and held roadblocks to hold off counterattacking Japs. They also had to mop up in the many caves in the cliffs back from the beach where the Japs hid until the infantry passed on. In action at one cave, a shore engineer patrol of 2 officers and 4 men succeeded in rescuing 2 wounded infantrymen and killed over 60 Japs in the encounter, with only 1 wounded on the Amphibs' side.

After the airfields were secured, subsidiary landings were made along the coast and to the outlying islands. Three of these operations were large enough to be classed as regular landings. Operations extended as far as Soepiori Island, 80 miles from the original landing on Biak Island. This landing took place on September 7 in the face of light and ineffective opposition.

During these operations the brigade's craft were subjected to frequent air attack and succeeded in shooting down several planes. One day a lone LCM was pushing along the northern coast to take supplies to an outlying infantry patrol. On the way one of the crew saw a few hundred yards off shore an unusual island, massed with underbrush and low coconut trees. To be on the safe side against an enemy sniper, he gave it a burst of machine-gun fire and was surprised to receive machine-gun fire in return. Maneuvering to bring both their .50-caliber machine guns to bear on it, the gunners raked the small island for several minutes. All fire from the enemy having ceased, the LCM cautiously closed in and, to the crew's surprise, found that the island was a Jap landing craft very heavily camouflaged. It contained several dead Japs and some important documents which were promptly turned in to the Intelligence Section.

In the meantime the 3d Brigade, under Brigadier General Ogden, had completed its movement from Fort Ord, proceeding to New Guinea and to the Cairns area in Australia where the 2d Brigade had trained. The LCVP assembly plant at Cairns had completed most of its work by now, having assembled 901 landing craft (LCVP). Its operation saved deck space for the shipment of hundreds of planes and tanks. Many of its assembled craft had gone to the Navy and to the Australians as well as to the 2d and 3d Brigades and to the various base sections.

The big need now was LCMs instead of LCVPs. Liberty ships could bring out from the States only two or three LCMs per ship and then only if cargo of higher priority did not take up the available deck space. Accordingly a plan was worked out by the Engineer Amphibian Command and by General MacArthur's Chief Engineer, Major General H. J. Casey, to ship sectionalized LCMs for assembly in New Guinea, thus saving an enormous amount of deck space on the freighters bound for the western Pacific. Part of the 411th Base Shop Battalion which had been operating the LCVP assembly plant at Cairns moved from Australia to Milne Bay to start the new assembly plant. Lieutenant Colonel J. A. Bender, who had commanded the 411th up to this time, moved to Brisbane to take charge of the barge assembly plant there for the Transportation Corps. Major Rose took Colonel Bender's place as commander of the 411th Base Shop Battalion. The latter went to Brisbane to initiate a new program of assembling large knocked-down steel barges.

As the 411th, even when helped by the 5211th Battalion, did not have nearly enough personnel to operate and build the plant, the first mission of the 3d Brigade upon its arrival in New Guinea was to complete the plant and get it into efficient operation. Schools for welders and for shipfitters were opened up on a large scale so as to have trained personnel to operate the plant as it was finished.

The 563d Engineer Boat Maintenance Battalion joined in the job in October 1943 and was reinforced by the Shore Battalion of the 543d Regiment in December. Weather and other conditions at Milne Bay were very poor but 21 LCMs were assembled in December 1943 followed by 90 in January, 120 in February, and not less than 150 monthly thereafter. These units were relieved in June 1944 by the 4th Brigade and by the Boat Building Command. The assembled boats were issued not only to the brigades but also to the harbor craft companies of the Transportation Corps, to the U. S. Navy and to the Australians. Most of the craft shipped to this plant for assembly were the newly designed LCM#6 which was six feet longer than the LCM#3 previously used. The new LCM not only was a knot faster than the old type but also carried twenty per cent more cargo at the same fuel expenditure.

The hulls of the LCMs were fully assembled in the United States and then cut into four or five sections so that all the sections would fit into the holds of freighters, all engines and accessories being packed with the sections. The Milne Bay plant then welded the sections together on an assembly line and the engines and accessories were installed as the boats went down the assembly line to be launched in the waters of Milne Bay. Had not this plant worked out so well, the Amphibian brigades would undoubtedly have run short of LCMs at critical times. As it was, they were never short of craft once the plant got into operation.

However, the advance had been so rapid along the coast of New Guinea that the plant was soon too far to the rear. A run of over a thousand miles was necessary to get a craft from Milne Bay to Biak. The three brigades working together arranged a route with maintenance and fuel stations and harbors of refuge at stated intervals so that crews making the long trip could not only get their boats in shape but get food and rest themselves. Initially, naval escort was required when the boats were passing the cut-off Japs in the Wewak–Hansa Bay area. Later even this escort was omitted and the boats ran by at night, being careful to stand off a few miles out of range of the Jap coastal defense guns.

THE 3D BRIGADE GETS INTO THE FRAY

As 1943 drew to a close, the 3d Brigade was setting up its headquarters on Goodenough Island but with some elements widely scattered. One boat company of 533d Regiment was at Cairns in Australia working with Australian troops. The 533d Shore Battalion from Milne Bay arrived Christmas Day to take over the shore work at Finschhafen from the 2d Brigade. It had been through the 40-inch rain (in one week) at Milne Bay, so found Finschhafen attractive—for New Guinea. Part of 543d Regiment and all of the Boat Maintenance Battalion were busily engaged at the LCM assembly plant at Milne Bay.

It was not long before the 3d Brigade had detachments in combat. In February 1944 one boat company went under its own power to support the cavalry in their push towards Gasmata. A boat-shore team of the 533d Regiment moved around the western end of New Britain to support the 1st Marine Division, relieving a force of the 2d Brigade which had gone in on the initial landing on December 26, 1943.

All of the 593d Regiment except two boat companies participated in MacArthur's April drive on Aitape–Hollandia–Tanahmerah. The boats of the 593d remained in this area until August 1944. They engaged in almost daily patrol actions with the Japs attempting to break out of Wewak and move to the west. The 593d Headquarters and its Shore Battalion, however, left Aitape in May for a landing in Maffin Bay. Supported by a boat company of the 2d Brigade, this Amphibian group supported the 158th Infantry Combat Team in the initial landing on the mainland and in the landing the next afternoon on the tiny island of Wakde. Here the beachhead was defended by the shore engineers against several Jap counterattacks. However, it was on the mainland that the shore engineers had their hottest time. Several Jap breakthroughs had to be liquidated by the shore engineers near the beaches. One such action occurred on the evening of June 1. The shore engineers had just finished chow and some antiaircraft gunners had gone in swimming, when a Banzai attack by a group of Japs who had infiltrated through the defense perimeter pushed through right to the beach. The Japs' speed and the suddenness of attack caught the Americans off guard. Soon the men in swimming and the shore engineers were being sprayed by fire from their own guns manned by Japs. The shore engineers quickly rallied and an all-night fight ensued. It was fourteen hours before the Japs could be dislodged from their captured guns and the remnants driven back into the dense jungle. All the American antiaircraft guns were recovered by the shore engineers, none of them, strange to relate, any the worse for having been in the hands of the Japs for fourteen hours.

When the 5th and 6th Australian Brigades needed amphibious support in mopping up the Japs cut off between Wewak and Saidor, a company of the 593d Regiment was assigned to give them small-boat support along the shore. There were numerous patrol actions but no major landings. Of course for those involved in the patrol action, it was just as much a battle as a major action even if it was not mentioned in a GHQ communiqué.

NOEMFOOR

The next major landing for the Amphibians was on the island of Noemfoor, an island some 30 miles in diameter, between Biak and the New Guinea mainland. It was important because of two Jap airfields on it. The Amphibian group consisted of the 593d Regiment (less its boat battalion) but with a boat company of the 533d Regiment and the support battery of the 2d Brigade in support. Colonel van den Berg of the 3d Brigade commanded the Amphibian group from both brigades. The Buffaloes (LVTs) of the support battery were needed because of the known poor beach conditions. The entire island of Noemfoor was surrounded by a wide fringing reef which made unloading very difficult.

Company A of the 543d Regiment made a remarkable record by running under its own power the entire 900 miles from Finschhafen to Noemfoor. The last 300 miles of this long trip had to be made nonstop in order to reach the objective on time.

The assigned mission of the support battery was to protect the initial advance of the assaulting infantry with automatic-weapons fire. When the assault troops were landed, the battery divided into two parts. One group working under enemy artillery fire, used their tracked landing vehicles to pull wheeled vehicles or DUKWs over the coral reef. This salvage work made possible the rapid landing of needed supplies. The other group of the support battery advanced along the airstrip with the assaulting infantry. Fortified pillboxes dug into the limestone terraces on the far side of the airstrip threatened to hold up the advance. The support battery unhesitatingly used their light amphibious vehicles as land tanks, advancing to within several feet of the fortified entrances and blasting the positions with flamethrowers and automatic weapons. The use of amphibious vehicles as tanks against fortified positions armed with mountain guns and 37mm cannon, a use beyond the capabilities for which the vehicles were designed, was an exhibition of gallantry. The work of the battery that day was commended by Major General Edwin D. Patrick, the Task Force commander. (He was later killed in action in the Philippines.)

The flak LCMs were active in patrolling and shelling with rockets along the coast in waters generally too shallow for the Navy's PT boats. The LCMs expected encounters with Jap barges or patrol craft but none occurred. Instead the Jap craft were bottled up in Broe Bay where they were later found destroyed by the Japs to prevent the Americans from using them. We had previously captured several Jap barges and used them in our work, being careful to use large American flags to protect them from attack by friendly planes.

The shore engineers and boatmen of the 3d ESB participated in two other landings on the shores of Noemfoor after the support battery had returned to Wakde. Their boats ran many tons of supplies from Biak to Noemfoor where their shore engineers constructed jetties to unload over the outlying reefs.

Since Noemfoor Island was destined to be an important American airbase, the shore engineers, in addition to the usual dump and jetty construction and to the endless job of unloading, undertook much construction work. They grubbed, cleared and rough-graded a hundred acres for a new airstrip and built 1,500 feet of taxiway with hard standings for many planes. They cut, cleared and graded and then maintained over twelve miles of roads. One job required the construction of a waterpoint and over a mile of pipeline.

The 3d Brigade troops spent many days on Noemfoor and finally helped in evacuating it, moving thousands of tons of supplies to Biak, which was maintained as a base after Noemfoor was abandoned.

SANSAPOR

On July 30, 1944, the 543d Regiment drew the mission of supporting the 6th Infantry Division in a landing on New Guinea at Sansapor. This beach was very exposed and subject to high surf. This had the advantage of completely fooling the Japs as to the possibility of an Allied landing there but it was very hard on the boats of the Amphibian Engineers. Surf averaged five feet and occasionally all work had to be stopped as the small boats rode out seas which produced surf as high as 12 or 15 feet. No casualties from enemy action were experienced by the Amphibians as the Japs, short of ammunition and rations and much disorganized, had withdrawn before the Americans landed.

THE 4TH BRIGADE ARRIVES

In the meantime the well-trained 4th Engineer Special Brigade began to arrive from the States under the command of Brig. Gen. Henry Hutchings, via the usual Edwards–Carrabelle–Ord route.

The Boat Battalion, 534th Engineer Boat and Shore Regiment, was committed to fabricate steel barges at the Balimba Ship Yards, Brisbane, Australia, arriving in May 1944. While these men disliked being put on a base section job instead of the combat they expected, they went to the work with vigor.

Also, during the troop movements from the east coast to the staging area orders were received to organize a heavy shop company within the 564th Engineer Boat Maintenance Battalion, for the purpose of performing fifth echelon maintenance on boats and engineer equipment in the theater. Heavy shop equipment was purchased on the open market. In June 1944 when the 564th Engineer Boat Maintenance Battalion arrived at its first overseas base, Oro Bay, New Guinea, the Heavy Shop Company was activated and immediately established its facilities on the beach at Oro Bay.

The command post of the 4th Engineer Special Brigade was closed at Camp Gordon Johnston April 20, 1944, and opened again May 23, 1944, at Oro Bay, New Guinea, in a site initially used by elements of the 2d ESB. This site had been picked as a likely location by General Hutchings during a trip to the theater in March of the same year.

The 534th Engineer Boat and Shore Regiment (less Boat Battalion) arrived at their overseas destination, Milne Bay, New Guinea, May 15, 1944. They established their camp in the jungle mud during six days of heavy continuous rain. As soon as their equipment was discharged from the ship they commenced port operations.

Eight days later the 544th Engineer Boat and Shore Regiment arrived at their overseas destination, Oro Bay, New Guinea, and established their camp on the beach. Elements of the Boat Battalion were immediately assigned the task of ferrying new LCMs from Milne Bay to the various units at Oro Bay.

The Boat Battalion, 594th Engineer Boat and Shore Regiment, arrived at their overseas destination, Milne Bay, New Guinea, on May 1, 1944. Elements of this battalion relieved the 3d Engineer Special Brigade at the boat assembly plant, Milne Bay, and engaged in the construction of welded LCMs under the supervision of the Commanding Officer, 5211th Engineer Battalion.

The Shore Battalion of the 594th Regiment arrived overseas May 24, 1944, and engaged in port operation and cargo handling at Oro Bay. All units of the brigade were overseas and established at Oro Bay, Milne Bay, and Australia by the middle of June 1944.

The brigade units continued for several weeks their non-tactical operations of barge construction, LCM assembly, unloading and lighterage of cargo, dock, road and building construction, and the ferrying of LCMs from the assembly plant at Milne Bay to the various army installations along the coast of New Guinea.

Between late June and the end of July the three Boat Company–Shore Company teams of the 544th Engineer Boat and Shore Regiment, reinforced by regimental troops, supported battalion combat teams of the 31st Infantry Division in amphibious exercises in the vicinity of Oro Bay and Buna. All nine battalion combat teams of the 31st Infantry Division were thus trained.

Early in July 1944 the 534th Regiment (less Boat Battalion) moved from Milne Bay to Oro Bay and engaged in varied construction projects.

In July 1944 the Boat Battalion, 594th Engineer Boat and Shore Regiment, was relieved of its duties at the boat assembly plant, at Milne Bay, by the 1307th General Service Regiment. It then moved in its own boats to Oro Bay and engaged in cargo handling and lighterage.

Also late in July, Companies A, B, and C, 564th Engineer Boat Maintenance Battalion, were reorganized and redesignated 3015th,

3016th, and 3017th Engineer Maintenance Companies, respectively. However, they remained assigned to the 564th Engineer Boat Maintenance Battalion.

On August 8, 1944, the 534th Engineer Boat and Shore Regiment (less Boat Battalion) received telegraphic orders to move to Aitape, New Guinea, to stage for the Interlude Operation (Morotai, Halmahera group in the Netherlands East Indies). They were assigned to the Tradewind Task Force (XI Corps), supporting one regimental combat team from the 32d Infantry Division. This was the first combat landing for the 4th Brigade.

The Boat Battalion, 534th Regiment, was still at the Balimba Boat Yards, Brisbane, Australia. Through standardization of construction procedures and improvements of manufacturing techniques it effected a reduction of the man hours necessary to construct a barge to forty per cent of that required at the outset of the operations.

On August 3, 1944, the 544th Engineer Boat and Shore Regiment was alerted for movement from Oro Bay to Wakde to stage for the Interlude Operation. They were assigned to the Tradewind Task Force (XI Corps) supporting two regimental combat teams from the 31st Infantry Division. Movement of the Boat Battalion by organic craft was initiated on August 12, 1944, convoys departing from Buna in company echelons. The sea distance to Wakde was approximately 900 miles. Stopovers were made only for refueling and for water. This was probably the longest sea voyage for a combat operation ever undertaken in landing craft as small as LCMs and the officers and men proved that they were veteran soldiers of the sea. The voyage was made without untoward incident by the 185 craft.

Early in August 1944 the Boat Battalion, 594th Engineer Boat and Shore Regiment, moved by organic craft from Milne Bay to Oro Bay and Buna. By directive of Sixth Army, Company A, 594th Engineer Boat and Shore Regiment, then moved by organic water transportation from Oro Bay to Cape Gloucester and Arawe, New Britain, Bismarck Archipelago, to relieve Company A, 533d Engineer Boat and Shore Regiment (3d ESB). By the same directive

Company B, 594th Engineer Boat and Shore Regiment, moved by organic water transportation from Oro Bay to Finschhafen to relieve Company C, 543d Engineer Boat and Shore Regiment. Company C, 594th Engineer and Shore Regiment, remained at Buna to prepare for a concentrated four weeks program of amphibious training with the 11th Airborne Division, recently arrived from the States with no amphibious training.

Early in September 1944 Company A, 594th Engineer Boat and Shore Regiment, went forward to relieve elements of the 3d Engineer Special Brigade in the Madang, Finschhafen and New Britain sectors. Their mission was to operate refueling points, lighter cargo, do patrol activity and land small assault groups along the coasts of New Britain in support of the 40th Infantry Division. Company B, 594th Regiment, operated a weekly convoy schedule from Finschhafen to Madang with stops en route at Sio, at Saidor and at Long Island.

THE 4TH BRIGADE AT MOROTAI

The object of the Interlude Operation was the seizure of the southern end of Morotai Island and the establishment of air and naval facilities to support further operations to the north. The task groups from the 4th Brigade for the Interlude Operation were the 534th Engineer Boat and Shore Regiment (less Boat Battalion) plus attached 3015th Engineer Maintenance Company and Detachment 1, 164th Ordnance Company, and the 544th Engineer Boat and Shore Regiment (less Company C) plus attached 3017th Engineer Maintenance Company and Detachment 2, 164th Ordnance Company.

The landings were made on the worst beaches ever used in an amphibious assault. What appeared to be a white sand beach or a white coral shelf on the aerial photographs, actually was gray mud about three feet deep, spotted with coral heads beneath the water. No equipment from LCMs was lost in unloading, but much required towing and winching ashore. Many pieces of equipment from LSTs, including bulldozers and tractors, could not reach shore. On D-day only three of the eight shore battalion bulldozers were able to reach the beach from LSTs on Red Beach. Until earth ramps and piers were constructed all shipping was diverted to White Beach where the footing was more solid. It was indeed fortunate that security had not failed and permitted the Japs to oppose this landing in force. The Japs had apparently expected a landing on Halmahera, a hundred miles to the southwest.

On White Beach unloading went quite smoothly, much of the credit for this efficiency going to the 534th Regiment for their excellent loading plan. Their equipment was loaded in such a way that Cats and DUKWs were the first vehicles to debark from each LST. Whenever vehicles and equipment bogged down, the Cats and DUKWs were on the job. Due to the large number of small tactical groups, including radar and antiaircraft artillery, outloaded to adjacent islands, the LCMs could do little lighterage until D plus 3.

The 3017th Engineer Maintenance Company, attached to the 544th Engineer Boat and Shore Regiment, moved two platoons forward to provide boat maintenance for the forward boat elements. Through their efforts the boat battalion commander was able to keep ninety-five per cent of all small craft in operating condition.

The 534th Engineer Boat and Shore Regiment (less Boat Battalion) and the 544th Engineer Boat and Shore Regiment continued their logistical support and construction projects at Morotai Island until they were alerted for the Luzon Campaign.

All other units of the brigades were busy on lighterage work at the various bases in New Guinea, New Britain, and the Admiralties and on the movement and resupply of infantry units mopping up the scattered Japs. The shore engineers furnished many hatch crews and deck details in unloading the many ships now pouring from the States to the Southwest Pacific. It was obvious that preparations were being made for major operations, undoubtedly to the Philippines.

As the Amphibs closed their New Guinea campaign the credit entries in their work against the Japs were as follows:

Jap planes definitely shot down	22[2]
Casualties definitely inflicted	1088
Prisoners taken (all Japs)	126
Enemy barges sunk or captured	120

The large ratio of prisoners taken (much larger than in the case of the infantry) was due in the main to capture of exhausted Japs in the water. Rarely did men find Japs in the water who preferred drowning to being rescued but a few did commit suicide by drowning.

NOTES

[1] Engineer Boat and Shore Regiment. (All regiments whose numerals ended in 2 were from 2d ESB; in 3 from 3d ESB, etc.)

[2] The Amphibians never claimed an enemy plane if there was any other unit firing at it at the time it was hit. Fortunately, the Army Amphibians never lost a single person as a prisoner to the Japs.

12
Back to Bataan and Corregidor

General Macarthur's entire plan of operations in the Western Pacific had been based on carrying out his motto "I Shall Return." His eyes were continually on the Philippines. New Guinea, New Britain, the Admiralties, and Morotai were merely stepping-stones from which to launch the attack to recover the Philippines, to put Corregidor back into American hands.

The initial plan was to strike first in Southern Mindanao on October 15, 1944, and then a few weeks later, with a foothold firmly established there, to strike at Leyte on December 20 and finally at Lingayen on February 20, 1945. It was felt that Jap air power in the Philippines would be too strong to risk a landing in the Central Philippines on the first blow. However, Halsey's naval strike in August met much less resistance than expected and moreover the naval fliers put out of action a surprisingly large number of enemy planes, well over three hundred. When Admiral Halsey recommended that the initial landing in Southern Mindanao be skipped and that the tempo be stepped up with a landing on Leyte, MacArthur quickly acquiesced.

The original troop list had called for the 3d Brigade to go in on the Mindanao landing. When the point of attack was shifted to Leyte, it was at first thought they would be similarly employed in the Leyte landing but near the end of September, GHQ suddenly changed the troop list to throw in the 2d Brigade. The reason for the change was never fully explained but it is thought it was due mainly to the fact that the 3d Brigade was widely dispersed on jobs

168

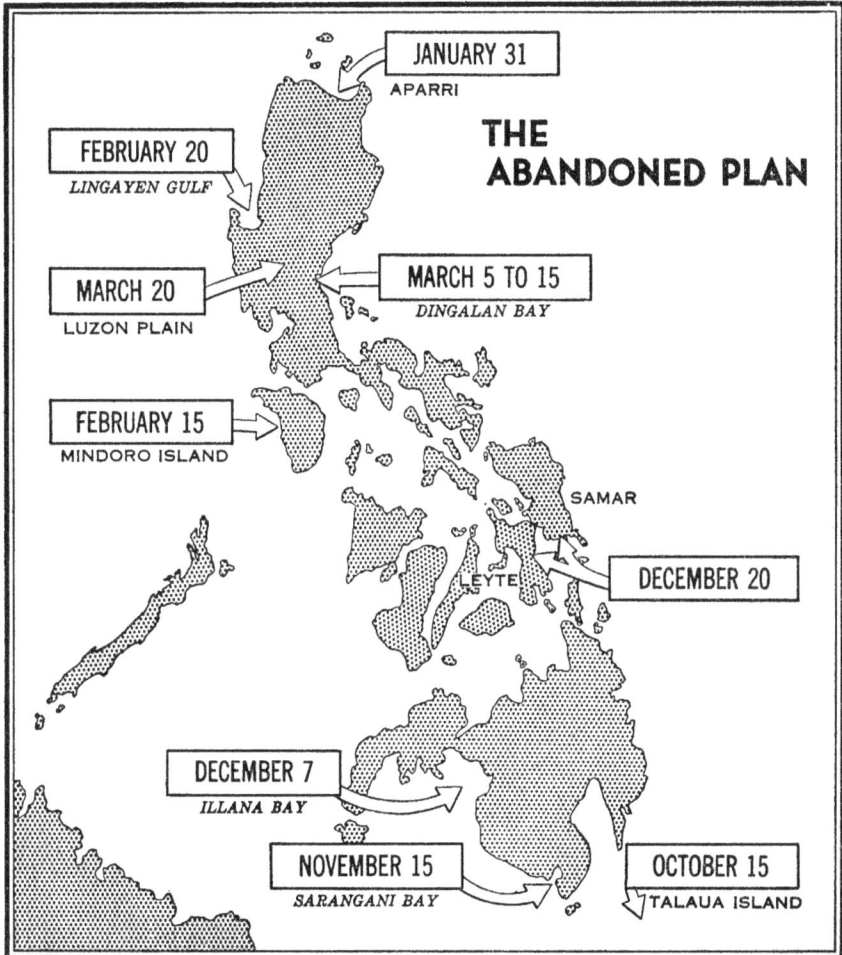

JANUARY 31
APARRI

THE
ABANDONED PLAN

FEBRUARY 20
LINGAYEN GULF

MARCH 20
LUZON PLAIN

MARCH 5 TO 15
DINGALAN BAY

FEBRUARY 15
MINDORO ISLAND

SAMAR

LEYTE

DECEMBER 20

DECEMBER 7
ILLANA BAY

NOVEMBER 15
SARANGANI BAY

OCTOBER 15
TALAUA ISLAND

(Reproduced by courtesy of LIFE.*)*

in New Britain and New Guinea while the 2d Brigade was fairly
well concentrated not far from Hollandia and Manus which were
to be the near-shore staging areas for the invasion of the Philippines. The personnel of the 3d Brigade were disappointed. They
were eager to go in on the Big Show. The 2d Brigade men were
tired from their many months in New Guinea with numerous combat landings, but they took on new life when told it was now to be
the Philippines.

The Leyte landing had many points of difference from the
Normandy landing. The latter was across only a relatively short

expanse of water; the former was a 1,200-mile jump. The Normandy landing could get air cover from thousands of land-based planes. Dependence here would have to be placed on carrier-based planes. Good as they were, there was always the danger of enemy attack on the American carriers and a small floating airfield is never as safe as a land field. The naval bombardment at Leyte with the last-minute plastering by the 4.5-inch rockets was more powerful than at Normandy and much more effective. On the other hand, the Jap beach defenses and obstacles at Leyte were nowhere as effective as the Germans' on Omaha and Utah beaches. Few realize that the Leyte landing was actually a larger one than Normandy. More soldiers were put ashore on Leyte on D-day than landed on both Omaha and Utah beaches on D-day. However, supporting echelons reached Normandy much sooner than at Leyte due to the much shorter distance back to the staging area.

When the decision was reached that the 2d Brigade would be the one to support Sixth Army in the Leyte landing and the time for D-day was selected, it was found that the 2d Brigade had less than three weeks to get ready. Both 3d and 4th Brigades pitched in to help, transferring a hundred of their newer LCMs to the 2d Brigade and accepting the 2d Brigade's battered craft. They also helped out in building up the 2d Brigade's stock of spare parts for the invasion. Such cooperation was common between the brigades. They always helped each other out, billeting one another's men, swapping parts as needed, and fueling each other's craft.

The Leyte operation required more ESB craft than the Aitape–Hollandia–Tanahmerah operation. Due to the distance involved and the fact that intervening waters might be infested with enemy submarines, the brigade's small craft were not allowed to make the long trip under their own power. It was necessary to work out with the Navy a detailed plan to lift all the brigade's more than 400 landing craft to the far shore. The possibility of typhoon prevented any consideration of towing the small craft behind the Navy's larger craft. All the small boats had to be lifted. This was finally worked out by substituting the brigade's small craft for the Navy's, thus requiring the Navy to leave their organic boats in New

Guinea or the Admiralties until they could return to pick them up on subsequent trips. In addition, the 2d Brigade put its 2 small tugs, 4 fuel barges, 4 crash boats, and 2 small freighters in a slow tow to make the long trip under their own power, arriving D plus seven days.

The trip from Hollandia to Leyte via Palau was uneventful. Not a Jap submarine nor plane, nor even stormy seas interfered. Three days out of Leyte the big convoy heard that a typhoon had hit the advance force whose mission was to land on two islands at the entrance to Leyte Gulf. However, seas had calmed by the time the main convoy reached the gulf early on the morning of October 20, 1944.

Just before the naval bombardment started that morning, a fast Jap reconnaissance plane of a new type flew low over the entire convoy and, although every gun opened up on it, it escaped with the news of the invasion. What it brought back to the Jap head-quarters must have astonished them. The gulf was full of Ameri-can ships from mighty battleships with 16-inch guns to the small LCIs, with hundreds of transports and large landing craft, many of which were already disgorging the smaller LCVPs and LCMs for the initial assault on the beaches. No Buffaloes (LVT5) were in these waves, for, finally, we had gotten out of the coral-infested waters of eastern Australia and New Guinea to clearer waters and sandy beaches. In landing boats a faster run from the transport areas to the beaches was possible than in the slow Buffaloes. Speed, of course, was important as the waves of boats approached the shore and our supporting bombardment had to lift.

On the northernmost beach, White Beach, there was almost no opposition, only stray machine-gun and sniper fire. On the next beach, Red Beach, opposition was stiffer. Not only did consider-able mortar and machine-gun fire sweep the approaches but some 75mm guns on the left flank opened up from hidden positions. Fortunately, these guns were in fixed emplacements and sited so that they could sweep only a narrow zone to sea and could not fire on the beaches proper. The three LSTs on the flank closest to these guns all received six or more direct hits. Casualties were fairly

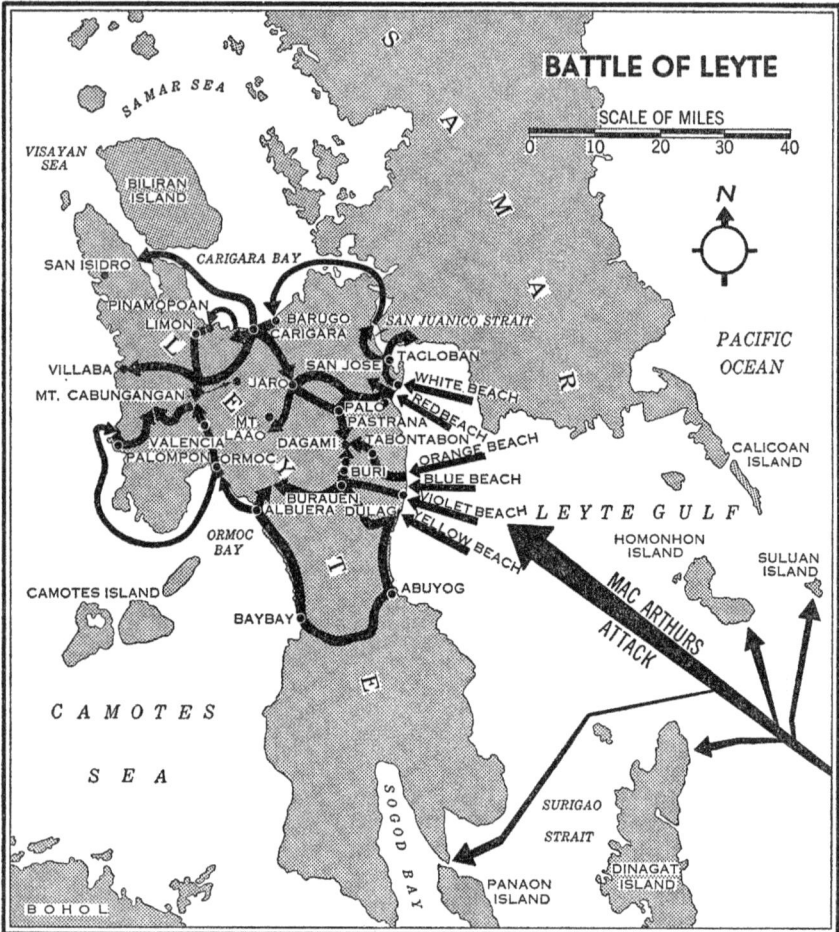

(Reproduced by courtesy of LIFE.)

heavy on these LSTs. Only by heroic and prompt action did the
Navy fire crews succeed in quelling the fires on two of them. Four
of the 2d Brigade's LCMs were hit by mortar fire but none was lost.
One rocket LCM taken in tow by the salvage LCM barely made the
haven of an LSD[1] where it sank inside the ship on the well deck. It
was repaired on the LSD as it returned to Hollandia for a second
trip. A few of the Navy's LCVPs were sunk by enemy fire. A few
were lost in the surf.

As anticipated from study of maps and aerial photographs,
White Beach proved to be the most suitable beach. At Red Beach
only one LST was able to approach close enough to the beach to

unload. A second LST lowered its ramp and a bulldozer attempted
to get to shore but slid into eight feet of water and jammed the
ramp so it could not be lifted. All the other LSTs grounded by the
stern with bow in such deep water and so far out from shore that
landing was impossible. Although this contingency had been
expected and this brigade had urged that ponton causeways be
brought in with the LSTs to land on Red Beach, none was made
available until they could be towed from the Dulag area, arriving
late on the night of D-day. No underwater obstacles or mines were
encountered on the beaches. However, on D plus 2, during an LST
landing on Cataisan Point, three vehicles were damaged by booby
bombs as they hit the beaches.

Aside from the difficulties encountered on Red Beach due to
only one LST being able to unload directly on shore by ramp, unloading on both Red and White Beaches was hampered by a very
difficult swamp parallel to the beach and only 100 to 300 yards
back from the high-water line, and also by numerous antitank
ditches which had been constructed by the Japs. However, all the
LSTs on White Beach and the one LST which was able to reach
Red Beach were unloaded and able to retract by early morning D
plus 1. The eleven LSTs which were unable to beach on Red Beach
were unloaded in the stream by LSMs and LCMs until three ponton
causeways could be brought from Dulag and installed on Red
Beach. On the morning of D plus 1, unloading on these ponton
causeways was initiated. They proved satisfactory except for the
difficulty which the LST commanders had in grounding their LSTs
near the causeways. Considerable time was lost in fitting the causeways to the points at which the LSTs grounded.

On the night of D plus 1, one ponton causeway was put out of
action for several hours due to being hit by an LST coming in at
almost full speed. While two or three sections of causeways were
sufficient for the initial landings, later it was necessary to use as
many as five sections to reach the grounded LSTs. This change was
believed due only in part to a lower tide, the other reason being
that the ships' propellers apparently built up a sandbar which was
not there when the first LSTs came in for their landings. By 6:00

P.M. on D plus 1, six of the Red Beach LSTs had been unloaded, and all at the White Beach, plus two AKAs. The next day the remaining eight LSTs, two AKAs and one AK completed unloading and were able to leave by 5:00 P.M. completely unloaded.

Although shore work was interrupted by numerous air raids and air alerts, Navy craft were able to return to the near shore on the schedule set, and in the case of one echelon, a day ahead of schedule. Naval beach parties furnished by Cyclone Task Force operated in conjunction with each shore party. The Navy transport groups furnished transport beach parties to assist the shore party in unloading boats from the respective transports. These transport beach parties were a great help to the shore party and operated most efficiently and with great energy. The result was that LCMs and LCVPs used in unloading these transports were able to return to the APAs for subsequent unloading so promptly that the average unloading time for the APAs was held to 4.5 hours. As the APAs carried an average of 1,300 troops and 450 tons of bulk stores and equipment, this meant that the average tonnage handled per hour was about 100 tons, which, it is believed, is a record for SWPA. The fact that this brigade had been associated with the Seventh Amphibious Force in numerous preceding operations and knew its methods, and many of its beach personnel, had much to do with the successful results. Almost 100,000 tons of supplies poured across the two beaches in the first six days. Only two shore engineer battalions performed this work, but of course they were reinforced by many attached units.

On the same day of the landings at White and Red Beaches, a third task group from the 2d Brigade supported the 21st Infantry Regimental Combat Team in a landing on Green Beach, sixty miles to the south. The Japs had fled prior to our landing so no opposition was received. During the next twenty days, the small boats there carried 72 different patrols landing on 48 separate beaches in tropical, reef-infested south Leyte. Contacts were made with guerrillas and supplies delivered to them. The Japs who did succeed in escaping headed north for Ormoc.

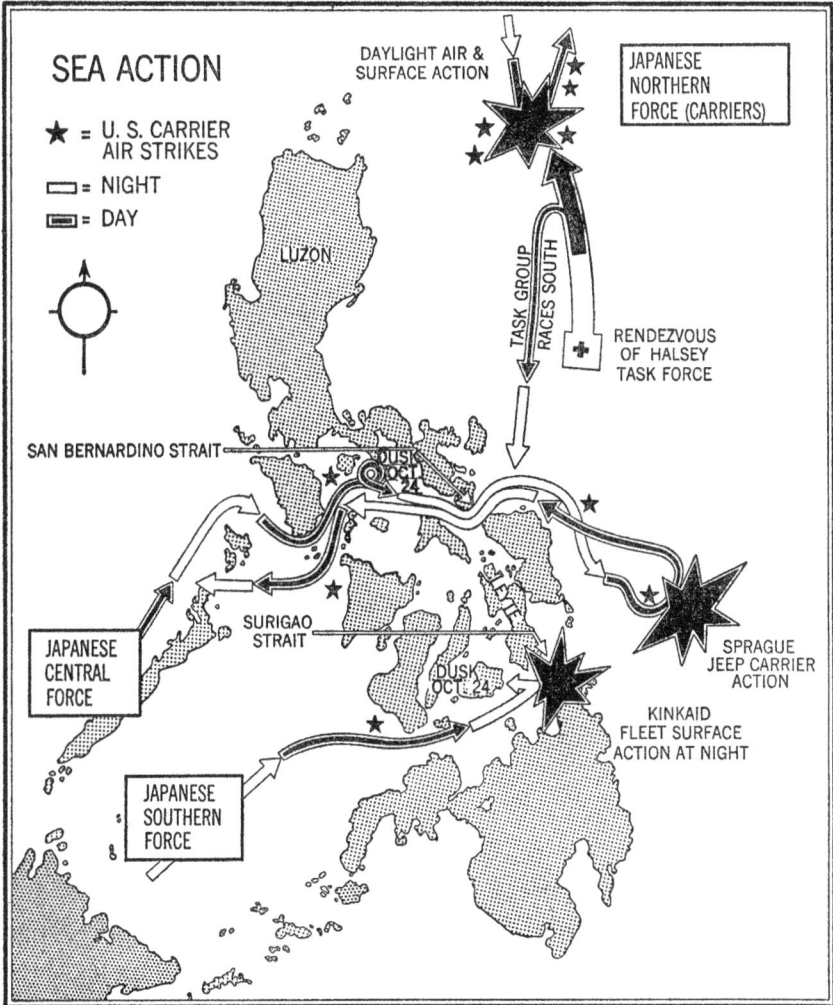

SEA ACTION

★ = U. S. CARRIER AIR STRIKES

▭ = NIGHT

▭ = DAY

DAYLIGHT AIR & SURFACE ACTION

JAPANESE NORTHERN FORCE (CARRIERS)

LUZON

TASK GROUP RACES SOUTH

RENDEZVOUS OF HALSEY TASK FORCE

SAN BERNARDINO STRAIT

DUSK OCT. 24

JAPANESE CENTRAL FORCE

SURIGAO STRAIT

DUSK OCT. 24

SPRAGUE JEEP CARRIER ACTION

KINKAID FLEET SURFACE ACTION AT NIGHT

JAPANESE SOUTHERN FORCE

(Reproduced by courtesy of LIFE.)

During all these operations the troops were undergoing the miseries of a wet season and, of course, 1944 would be a much wetter year than usual at Leyte. One 80-knot typhoon hit early in November and another one later in the month. The boatmen had to keep their craft headed into the wind with anchors down and engines full speed ahead to keep from being driven ashore. A number of the larger naval craft, with larger surfaces exposed to the terrific wind, were unable to hold and were beached. One PT boat was washed inland so far it had to be abandoned. The beaches were strewn with abandoned craft.

The light Leyte roads were soon churned to a morass by the heavy Army trucks and twenty inches of rain a week. Almost everything had to be moved by boat. Troops, ammunition, and supplies were carried on the forward trips, with sick and wounded on the return trips. Only one landing strip, that at Tacloban, could be kept in operation due to the heavy rains. Work was rushed on new strips and lighterage gave priority to unloading pierced-steel planking for these urgently needed airfields. There were always more demands for the brigade's craft and for the LCTs furnished by the Navy than could be met. There was a daily battle to determine who would get priority for the available craft.

In the Leyte–Samar operations was found the exact situation for which the Amphibian Brigade had been formed. Its facilities were utilized to the maximum. The shore engineers with attached port, DUKW, truck, and service companies and Filipino civilian labor, were extremely busy unloading ships over Red and White Beaches. Every available means of lighterage was used, from the Navy LSTs, LSMs, LCTs and decked barges propelled by outboard motor units (known as Elephants), to our small LCMs and LCVPs and DUKWs. The brigade established sub-beaches to reach outlying detachments and the boats were kept busy in the movement of troops and in re-supplying echelons throughout the islands. Radar units were moved to isolated areas. Guerrillas were picked up and moved from point to point, all by small landing craft.

The first boats to navigate the narrow strait between Samar and Leyte was a convoy of ten LCMs loaded with troops of the 1st Cavalry Division, on October 23. The convoy was headed by two flak LCMs, each of which was armed with fourteen .50-caliber machine guns, a 37mm automatic gun, and two 20mm antiaircraft guns. Fire from the banks of the narrow strait was expected and there was always the chance of air attack, so the Amphibs were kept on the alert. The fire from the shores did not eventuate but the air attack did. It was a bright sunny day. Suddenly eight fast-flying Japs came down the strait and, spotting the apparently helpless landing craft, peeled off to attack them. The gunners were ready. When about six hundred yards away, the leading Jap plane crashed into a barrage fired by over forty guns. It burst into a ball of flame and disintegrated, followed in a few seconds by a second one. The other Jap planes veered off and let the LCMs proceed. Soon the Navy PT boats followed us through the strait and began operations on the west coast of Leyte.

The 2d ESB Hydro Survey party, commanded by Lt. Col. Robert Tucker, who was detailed to the 2d Brigade in 1942 from the Coast and Geodetic Survey, rendered valuable service in finding suitable beaches for naval landing craft on both Leyte and Samar and in locating and buoying a channel to the dock in Tacloban. He worked close behind the advancing infantry. It was feared the channel would be too shallow to allow fully-loaded Liberty ships to proceed to the dock but a suitable channel was found. Strange to relate, it was free of mines. The Japs had several hundred horn-pronged mines ashore but none had been installed. Colonel Tucker also found the dock in perfect shape except for one small Jap ship sunk at one end of the dock. This ship had been sunk by an American air attack. No booby traps were found on this dock. The 1st Cavalry Division having secured the land areas around the dock, Colonel Tucker guided the first two Liberty ships to the dock on the afternoon of the fifth day. Over one thousand tons of cargo were unloaded the next day, gradually increasing to three thousand tons a day as unloading facilities and warehouses were obtained. By this time the Japs awakened to the value of the dock and bombed it heavily inflicting casualties and damage to both ships and dock, but never stopping the work for more than a few minutes at a time. The shipping and landing beaches received their share of bombing too. Outside of the crude coral jetties at Biak, this Tacloban dock was the first dock the Amphibs had found intact in any of their operations in the Western Pacific. It made them think they were getting back to civilization.

ORMOC LANDING

Ormoc was the only important port on the west coast of Leyte. Realizing that the Japs were concentrating on Ormoc both from southern and eastern Leyte, the Sixth Army decided to land a strong force just south of Ormoc on December 7 to cut off these forces and their supply and reinforcement by sea. The rocket LCMs threw over 300 rounds into Ipil to reinforce the naval bombardment and then strafed the beach. The landing was a success but the Jap air force reacted violently. Several naval vessels were hit and the brigade's LCMs did yeoman service picking up survivors from two LSMs and an APD which sank. The boatmen suffered several casualties in doing this and several of the LCMs were hit but none was sunk.

The next day a convoy of LCMs evacuating casualties from the Ormoc area came under intense Jap air attack three times. With nothing but their own machine guns and the 20mm guns on the flak LCM to protect them, the gunners succeeded in shooting down five planes without the loss of an LCM, but they suffered a number of casualties that day. The hastily installed boat maintenance shops at Baybay were kept busy patching the many holes in the boats.

On Christmas Day another amphibious landing was made at Palompon, north of Ormoc, cutting off the enemy's last supply and escape route from Leyte. A barrage of rocket and gun fire from the support LCMs preceded that landing. With the closure at Palompon, the Leyte–Samar operation was officially over but there was still much mopping up with heavy fighting in the jungles and mountains for several weeks.

CAMOTES ISLANDS

In January 1945 the 2d Brigade participated in two small combat landings on two islands of the Camotes group west of Leyte. These operations were performed without assistance from the Navy. Rocket and flak LCMs furnished the fire support for the 30 landing craft and the 48 Buffaloes used in these landings. At Ormoc the Amphibs had captured a supply of special U. S. 75mm ammunition which the Japs had captured at Bataan and brought to Leyte to fire at us. Instead, the 75mm gun on the flak LCM fired this ammunition at the Japs with effective results.

Mindoro Landing

General MacArthur did not wait for the Leyte–Samar area to be entirely cleared up but struck on December 15 at Mindoro. The 532d Regiment, veterans of the first landing at Nassau Bay, participated in this operation which put Americans close to southern Luzon. The landing itself was easy—weather, beaches, and lack of enemy opposition being ideal. However, Jap air reaction en route to Mindoro was very heavy. We lost several LCMs on the way to Mindoro due to enemy air attack but none after arrival there. Jap "*Kamikaze*" pilots were active. At Mindoro the shore engineers encountered some civilized areas and put the local railroad and ice plant back into operation a few days after their arrival. The boat maintenance engineers showed great ingenuity in improvising spare parts for the engines to repair them after the many months of disuse. Their shift from the boatyards to railroad roundhouse was only a matter of minutes.

Just as the Jap Navy had been forced to react after the Leyte landing, again the Mindoro landing forced its hand. Fortunately, an American submarine torpedoed and sank the large carrier of the Jap naval task force off Formosa before it came within range of Mindoro. The Mindoro beaches and airfields came in for two hours of long-range naval bombardment at night from some Jap cruisers but our air force made it too hot for the Japs to stay on the job. Very little damage resulted to the shore installations. Nearly all of the Jap shelling was wasted.[2]

At Mindoro there was the usual resupplying of outlying radar stations and patrols. On one of these runs shortly after dawn two LCMs encountered five American PT boats which had run aground on reefs, close to Luzon during a night sweep. After considerable maneuvering, the LCMs pulled all five off the reefs. This action probably saved the PT boats from destruction as they would have been fair prey for the Jap planes attacking them had they been still aground later that day.

Returning to the Philippines meant much to the Amphibians just as it must have to all the American soldiers. Here they felt they were liberating a people. They had all read of the tumultuous

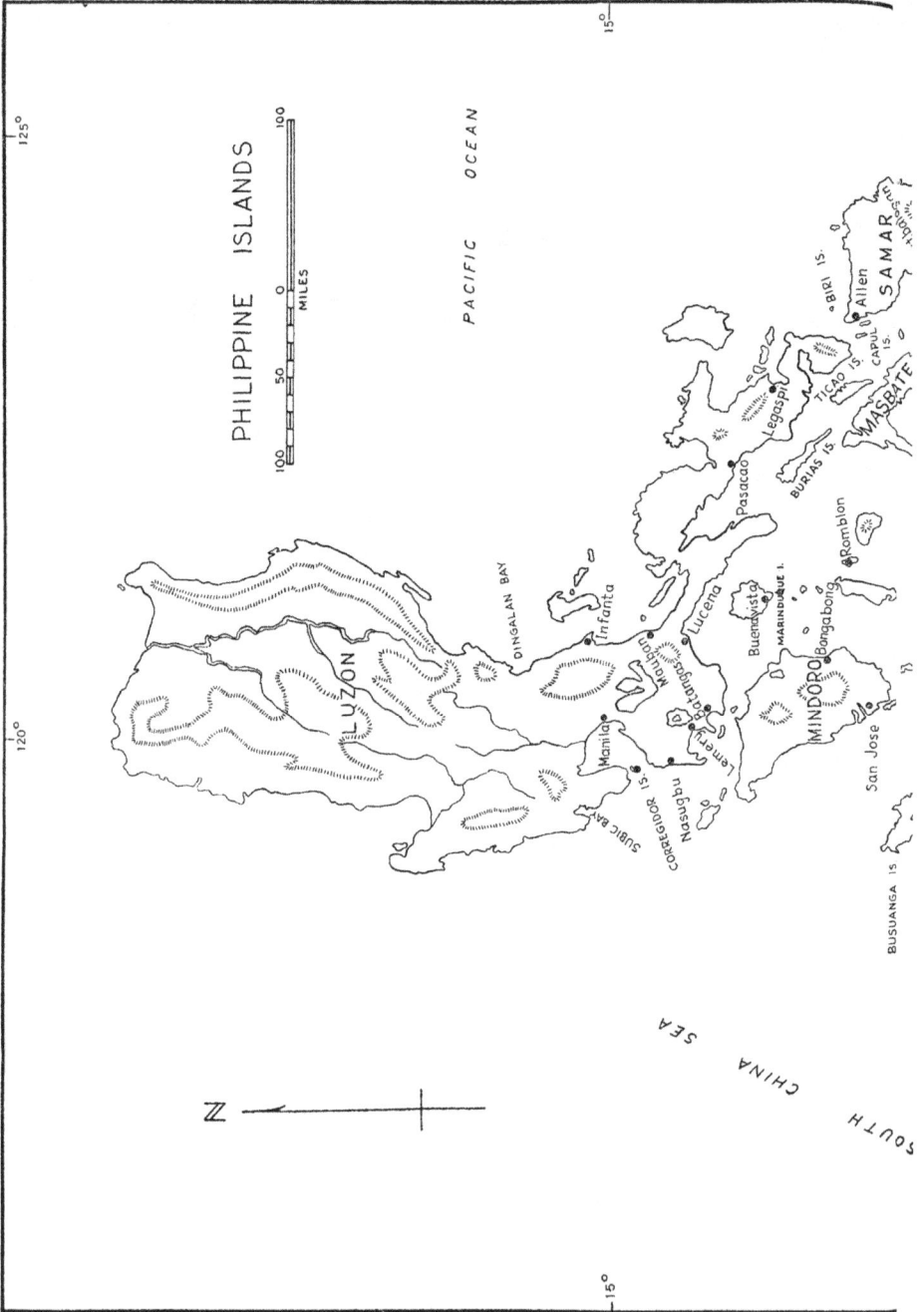

PHILIPPINE ISLANDS

MILES

PACIFIC OCEAN

welcomes given the Allies by liberated peoples in Europe. No welcomes greeted the Amphibians in New Guinea and the Bismarcks, perhaps the least developed corner of the world. Only a new series of mangrove swamps, coral reefs, and forest-clad mountains greeted the Amphibians in that country.

In the Philippines it was different. It is true the Filipinos had little of material value to offer us. The Japanese had reduced them to utter poverty. But they were certainly glad to see the Americans. The Filipinos are a neat, sturdy little people. The children quickly learned the "Veectoree" sign and to say "Joe" to every GI. The girls were cute and clean. The men, though small of stature, were well built and good looking, their skins a warm brown. They went to work willingly on the beaches but the Americans soon found out it would take two or three Filipinos to lift the weights one American could handle. Yes, the Amphibians really got a lift in morale from the Filipino people. All were glad to leave New Guinea.

THE LINGAYEN OPERATION

The development of Leyte and Mindoro, with the December 15 landing on Mindoro serving to focus Jap attention on the south of Luzon, was the prelude to MacArthur's next big blow, the landing on Luzon itself. The concept of this operation visualized a major amphibious assault mounted from New Guinea and Leyte to destroy the hostile forces in Central Luzon and to reoccupy Manila. The landing forces were comprised of the I and XIV Corps, the 25th Infantry Division and the 158th Infantry RCT, all under Sixth Army. The 4th Engineer Special Brigade with two regiments (533d and 543d) of the 3d Brigade provided Amphibian Engineer support. The mission was to seize a beachhead in Lingayen Gulf, push down through the central plains to recapture Manila and then to complete the conquest of Luzon.

Lingayen Gulf, an indentation in the west central coast of Luzon, roughly a hundred miles north of Manila, was the area selected for the landing. It was on these very same shores, three years before, that the Japs had invaded the Philippines. At the southern end of the gulf there are shallow sandy beaches with flat and in part marshy land extending southward. This flat continues into the central plain of Luzon thus affording the easiest approach to Manila. On the east and west sides of the gulf there are ranges of hills and mountains, rising abruptly on the west. Fortunately, there is little rise or fall of tide in the gulf and January, the month selected for the landing, offers the driest conditions of the year in the low ground.

Like the Leyte operation, the Lingayen operation required a large number of small landing craft. The only means to get these craft forward was on naval assault shipping. ESB craft were staged at the various mounting points sufficiently in advance of the operation so that they could be picked up by the large naval ships. Initially 69 ESB boats were to be made available to I Corps, 84 to XIV Corps, and 29 to the reinforcement group. All Army LCMs would be under the control of the Navy attack force during the assault and revert to the control of the 4th Brigade upon completion of the assault unloading. In addition, the Navy was to establish a lighterage pool of 24 LCTs and 44 self-propelled barges which were to work in close liaison with the LCMs of the Amphibians.

Four beaches on the southeastern side of Lingayen Gulf were selected for I Corps. These beaches were designated White I, White II, White III, and Blue Beaches. The 533d and 534th Regiments of 3d ESB were to support the two assault divisions landing on these beaches. The 544th and 594th Regiments of 4th ESB were to support the landings by XIV Corps on Yellow and Orange Beaches. Two days after the initial landings the 534th Regiment (less its Boat Battalion) was to support the 158th Regimental Combat Team on Red Beach on the extreme left flank of the landing beaches. Thus the plan seemed simple. Its execution though was not to be so simple.

Offshore slopes of the beaches were known to be very flat, indicating that landing craft would ground well out from the beaches. Ponton causeways would be necessary for LSTs. Surf was known to be fairly heavy, especially if a storm whipped up the China seas.

The staging of the Amphibian troops for this operation was a major problem due to their wide dispersal. Fortunately, more time was available than in the hurried Leyte operation. Subordinate units did get their orders in time to effect orderly assembly.

The 533d at Aitape not only had to make plans for its staging but had to unload the Australian 6th Division which was replacing the U. S. 43d Division at Aitape. The 533d started loading out its 99 LCMs and its shore engineer equipment on December 1. A delay in D-day from December 20 until January 9 was a stroke of luck, for otherwise the 43d Division and the 533d could never have made the "show." The convoy got under way on December 28, everyone glad to leave New Guinea.

The 544th was ordered to leave one boat company at Wakde Island to continue lighterage duties there. The remainder of the regiment was alerted on October 20, 1944, to stage from Bougainville.

The 534th was to go in without its boat battalion, which was still engaged at the barge assembly plant in Australia. Morotai was ordered as the staging point for the 534th. The 4th Brigade Headquarters and Special Troops were alerted for a December 1 loading at Oro Bay, New Guinea. This meant the Brigade staff had to operate for over a month from a Navy ship, an LSD. This had its advantage as well as its disadvantages. Food and living conditions on the LSD were fine but communications with the various dispersed units of the Brigade were difficult.

The 594th Regiment of 4th ESB had a particularly difficult job to assemble for its part in the invasion of Luzon. The regiment had to assemble at Cape Gloucester on New Britain to stage with the 40th Division. All during early November 1944 units of the regiment came in their own boats from Oro Bay and Buna on New Guinea and from Talasea and Arawe on New Britain where they had been in support of 40th Division units since September. The Gloucester area was very poor for mounting out a reinforced division so the shore engineers built an embarking point complete with jetties and approach roads. On December 18, 1944, the entire force held a practice landing near Lae on the very beach where the 2d Brigade had made its combat landing with the 9th Australian

Division on September 4, 1943. Then the convoy proceeded to Manus and weighed anchor there December 31 for the invasion of Luzon. Company B (594th) was left behind at Arawe, New Britain, where it was attached to the 3d Brigade and operated for the Australian First Army.

The big convoy pushed up the western coast of Mindoro, brazenly exposed to Jap air and submarine attack. In their first day in the Gulf 17 warships suffered serious damage, mainly from Kamikaze planes. A couple of midget submarines made a daring attack on the cruiser division. A Jap light cruiser made a spectacular exit from Manila Bay and headed for the convoy, only to go down in a matter of seconds as a result of American torpedoes.

Shortly after midnight January 8, 1945, the attack force of many hundred ships arrived off the entrance of Lingayen Gulf. Suicidal attacks by Jap Kamikaze planes had not been as dangerous as expected by many. Launching, loading and assembly of the small boats into waves went off without a hitch but, as at Biak, smoke and haze that covered the entire area hampered movement of the craft to the line of departure. The first assault waves landed in LVTs in order better to operate in the water courses and wet terrain immediately behind the beaches. Then came the waves of LCVPs and LCMs. No boats got lost but some waves were three to ten minutes late and hit the beach out of prescribed position. On White I and II the boats made "dry" landings. Mortar fire fell close to the LCMs but only one boatman was a casualty. A few boats had hits above the water line. Three 533d LCSs[3] of 3d ESB manned by Amphibians under Major E. H. Laughton entered the Bued River at H plus 15 minutes and went into action on the flank of the 103d Infantry. Although hit several times, the armor of the small craft turned the Jap fire and they quickly silenced several enemy guns. One Amphib on these valiant little craft was later wounded at the head of navigation, a half mile up the river.

On White III landing conditions, as expected, proved very poor. After futile attempts to get LSMs and LSTs into this beach, it was finally decided to abandon it altogether and to shift its traffic to White I and II where conditions were better.

The ESB Shore Party (533d EBSR) reconnaissance teams landed at H plus 35 minutes and proceeded immediately to locate installations and place signs. Luckily no clearing was necessary so the dozers, as soon as landed, proceeded to improve roads and construct dumps, bunkers and ditches. MPs had traffic under control as soon as the vehicles began to come ashore.

The ESB defense force quickly established a perimeter 5,000 yards long to free the tactical commanders from defense of the newly won beaches. Due to the diversion of traffic from White III there was some confusion in priorities on unloading on White I and II. Repeated efforts by the shore party's commanders through both Army and Navy channels failed to obtain explicit instructions and there was some delay in getting critical cargoes unloaded.

No enemy air bombardment was received on either White I or II beaches, the Jap's air power being much less than at Leyte. However, both White I and II received intermittent mortar and 75mm fire the first five days and on two nights received about twenty rounds of inaccurate 240mm artillery fire. Total casualties in this Shore Party (3d ESB) amounted to 2 killed in action, 21 wounded, and 1 missing. During this period the 533d did not lose a single boat, in contrast to the 13 LCVPs and 2 LCMs abandoned by the Navy on the surf-swept beach.

The 543d Regiment (3d ESB) staged some of its boats from Sansapor and others from Biak. These boatmen had been kept busy for weeks on lighterage and running supplies to outlying islands, the old story of Amphibian Engineer activities in New Guinea. It was a terrific job for both the maintenance personnel and the boatmen to whip their boats back into shape for the Luzon operation but all were so tired of New Guinea they took new life at the prospect of going to the Philippines. All craft were ready on time and loaded on naval assault craft for the long trip to Lingayen.

The 544th Regiment, with many attached troops, landed on Yellow Beach in the vicinity of Lupis on D-day at H plus 10 minutes. The advance elements arrived on the beach without encountering any enemy resistance. Fair weather prevailed throughout the landing but the surf was fairly heavy and poor beach conditions

existed. A dune line ranging from 4 to 10 feet in height ran along
the entire beach area, making the construction of good access roads
very difficult. This dune line was approximately 35 feet from the
low-water line and parallel to it, thus initially confining the unloading activities to that small space. Mobile loads coming off light-
ers had to be routed laterally along the beach further crowding the
limited area. On D-day the surf was moderate and allowed a comparatively easy landing. The surf became worse on D plus one,
reaching a maximum of ten feet, and at 4:30 P.M. it became necessary for the Navy to stop unloading operations. The next day the
surf was still heavy but it was necessary to resupply the combat
troops who had moved some distance inland. Accordingly, landing craft were called in and cargo was moved across the beach, although quite slowly. LCVPs were unmanageable in the pounding
surf and many broached. Some were completely destroyed. One
Navy control boat sank without warning and self-propelled barges,
loaded with cargo, broached and remained high and dry on the
beach. It was then decided that this was the normal condition of
the surf in that area and that it would be best to abandon it. A
hydrographic survey was made of the Dagupan River and transport cargo unloading was shifted to the protected beaches up the
river on D plus three.

Every possible way of handling cargo was employed. Anything
that could be man-handled was unloaded by human chains and
roller conveyers. LVTs were used to move POL[4] directly from the
ramp of LSTs to dumps. When LVTs were not available, drums of
oil and gasoline were floated ashore. The LST beach continued to
operate until all scheduled LSTs were completely unloaded.
Dagupan was developed to accept cargo from LCMs, LCTs and
LSMs and soon logistical support was ahead of the demands of the
combat units.

The 594th Regiment landed in the first assault waves on Orange
Beach in the vicinity of Lingayen without opposition. Several
snipers harassed the first assault troops ashore but they were soon
cleared out. The enemy garrison, fearful of our naval bombardment, had withdrawn before the landing. There were several air

alerts the first few nights but only a few bombs were dropped on the beach. Some Japs tried to infiltrate on the right flank of the perimeter but they were dispersed by the LVTs.

Extremely difficult surf conditions were also encountered on Orange Beach, forcing the small landing craft to proceed up the Calmay River and use its banks for discharging points. One LCM went well up the river and for 120 continuous hours acted as a ferry for the tactical troops. A service unit consisting of a detachment from the Ordnance Company of 4th ESB and one of its Engineer Maintenance Companies established their respective maintenance facilities on the beach and worked on a 24-hour schedule restoring to service the vehicles, heavy equipment and landing craft which had been put out of commission by the heavy surf.

The 543d Engineer Boat and Shore Regiment landed on Blue Beach, in the vicinity of Dagupan, on D-day at 9:30 A.M. It had been considered probable that the enemy would defend the beach so an intense barrage of naval gunfire was laid down, culminating with rocket fire from LCIs. However, no resistance was encountered on the beach except for three Japanese who fired on a shore battalion reconnaissance party. There was no evidence of prepared positions or obstacles on this beach. The Japs apparently did not expect a landing here. The assault force moved inland rapidly.

The beach was wide enough to permit lateral traffic and temporary parking as well as temporary dumps for supplies. The sand packed so firm under traffic that no matting or corduroying was necessary. The gradient of the beach was too slight to allow dry landings by any type of small craft. Quite a few vehicles drowned out in deep water while attempting to reach shore from their grounded craft. Most of the LCMs grounded a hundred yards offshore and were forced to dig their way to the beach, retracting in the same manner. This saved much equipment and probably many lives but it also taxed the boat maintenance facilities. Until D plus 3, when an area was located where maintenance could be performed, repairs on LCMs of both the 3d and 4th ESB were effected by the Navy repair ships.

Blue Beach was strafed by enemy aircraft soon after the initial landing but casualties were few. In the evening of D plus 2 and again on the morning of the next day, enemy aircraft got through to drop several bombs on the beach. Unfortunately one of these made a direct hit on the command post of the naval beachmaster and caused many casualties. Damage to shore installations was light. American antiaircraft fire brought down two of the enemy planes. Due to blackout and security orders and to continued air alerts, night lighterage dropped to a negligible amount.

There was only a medium surf the first day on Blue Beach but a heavy surf averaging six feet developed the next two days. Many boats broached and some were damaged beyond repair. The third day the surf lessened and soon a steady flow of supplies and equipment was crossing Blue Beach and the dumps were well stocked and operating efficiently.

The advance command echelon of Headquarters of 4th Brigade landed on Blue Beach on D-day, established its bivouac area a half mile inland, and began functioning as a Special Staff section of Sixth Army Headquarters. General Hutchings as brigade commander represented the commander of Sixth Army in observing unloading operations on all beaches, in distributing available equipment among the various beaches, in surveys of new beaches, and in preparing the necessary data and reports.

On January 19 (D plus 10) responsibility for logistical support in the Lingayen area passed to the Sixth Army Service Command under Major General H. J. Casey. Under this new headquarters, the 4th Brigade was regrouped for more effective control. The engineer boat and shore regiments were relieved from Corps and Division and reverted to the 4th ESB under its commander, Brigadier General Hutchings. Colonel Wayne S. Moore of 533d EBSR of the 3d ESB was assigned command of the San Fabian group; the 544th ran the Dagupan group; the 594th the Lingayen group. The 534th, having no boat battalion with it, worked under the Base Commander on the rehabilitation of Dagupan. The 564th Boat Maintenance Battalion (4th ESB), just up from Oro Bay, set up its yards on the west side of the Dagupan River. In addition to its usual function of maintenance of the Brigade's boats, the 564th Engineer Boat Maintenance Battalion, which had landed on D-day, established a boat pool to provide craft for ferries, for special tactical missions and for reconnaissance. At its peak 30 LCVPs and 20 LCMs were available for these special missions. Tonnage rolled in quickly to support the rapid advance of the Sixth Army on Manila. Operations continued full steam ahead until the Amphibian troops of the 4th ESB moved around to Manila and those of the 3d to other operations. Numerous ESB units drew commendations for their work during the Lingayen operations.

The 534th Engineer Boat and Shore Regiment (less Boat Battalion) had been ordered to support the 158th Regimental Combat Team in a, simultaneous assault landing in the vicinity of San Fernando (north of the main landings in Lingayen Gulf), seize San Fernando, and hold it until relieved by the 43d Infantry Division which was proceeding northward. However, prior to the main landings, guerrilla reports indicated that the main enemy defenses in the objective area were concentrated in the hills in the rear of San Fernando. While still at sea the battle orders for this landing were rescinded and the troops were recommitted to support the Lingayen Gulf assault.

On D plus 2 the 158th Regimental Combat Team with the 534th Engineer Boat and Shore Regiment (less Boat Battalion) in support, landed on Red Beach, the extreme left flank of the D-day landing beaches. Continuous heavy artillery fire, from dusk to dawn, seriously limited beach operations. Several LSTs received direct hits causing many casualties. Another hazard which caused some damage, and had a somewhat demoralizing effect, was the enemy's use of small, fast, explosive-laden suicide boats. These small boats would appear out of the dark, without warning, and crash into ships and boats at anchor. They caused some damage but their hiding places were soon hunted down and they were eliminated.

Company D of the 534th supplied three mine and demolition sections, one section being attached to each infantry battalion. Upon debarkation, these sections proceeded north with the 158th Regimental Combat Team, to Rabon. They were employed in removing

enemy mines and performing miscellaneous combat engineer
assignments for the force. One section was given a mission to pass
through the enemy lines, locate and destroy an ammunition dump.
This mission was carried out successfully. Several men were
wounded, one was killed, but all later received decorations for
heroism in the face of the enemy.

On January 13 the 534th was detached from the 158th Regimental Combat Team and attached to I Corps. One shore company
remained to maintain the road net from the beachhead to Damortis.
The remainder of the regiment then worked in support of Blue
Beach unloading operations.

At the close of the Luzon assault phase, the 4th Brigade supported the logistical effort in the Lingayen Gulf area, concerned
principally with the development of port handling facilities and
their operation at White Beach near San Fabian, on the Pantel River
at Dagupan, and in the Calmay River near Lingayen. It also engaged
in building construction projects, road building, and general engineer work.

The 533d and 543d Engineer Boat and Shore Regiments
supported the effort at Sub-base 1 at San Fabian until the 543d
was alerted for movement to Mindoro and was relieved of beach
operations February 9, 1945.

The 534th Engineer Boat and Shore Regiment (less Boat Battalion), after completing its mission on Red Beach, was assigned
the construction and repair of base utilities and communications
in the Dagupan area. When the 543d was alerted to go for the
Mindanao operation, the 534th Engineer Boat and Shore Regiment
(less Boat Battalion) assumed control of White Beach under operational control of the 533d.

The 544th Engineer Boat and Shore Regiment supported the
logistical effort on the Pantel River at Dagupan, working under
the supervision of Sub-base 2. The 594th operated Sub-base 3 in
the Lingayen sector, furnishing all sub-base and port overhead and
reporting directly to Base M.

The American troops made remarkable progress in their drive
on Manila, entering its suburbs by February 1. The ESB units were

anxious to shift operations from Lingayen Bay around to Manila Bay as soon as safe. However, in addition to driving the Japs out of that area, it would be necessary to clear the channel of mines and obstructing sunken ships and to search all the docks for booby mines.

Finally, on February 19 the 594th Regiment was ordered to discontinue its operations in the Lingayen sector and to prepare to move to Manila. Prior to this both the 533d and the 543d Regiments of the 3d ESB had been informed they would be relieved to participate in the coming invasion of Mindanao, far to the south.

Moving all its Boat Battalion in its own boats and the rest of the regiment by truck, the 594th established itself on Balut Island, North Harbor, in Manila Bay, less than two weeks after the first combat unit had entered Manila. The bay was still obstructed by hundreds of sunken ships. The dock areas were littered with the debris of Jap demolitions. The main pier was so badly damaged by the Jap engineers that it was necessary to clear it of tons of debris and then to build an entire new floor of Bailey bridges before ships could be unloaded. The city of Manila too was a shambles and required much work before its streets could be made passable.

The 544th Engineer Boat and Shore Regiment was relieved of its logistical effort in the Lingayen sector on March 5 and moved to Manila; the Boat Battalion went by water on its organic craft; the balance of the regiment travelled by land convoy.

Upon departure of the 544th, the 534th Engineer Boat and Shore Regiment (less its Boat Battalion) with two boat companies from the 543d attached to it, took over all lighterage in the Lingayen Gulf area. On 23 March this group, less boat elements, together with other major elements of Base M, moved from San Fabian to San Fernando and began the construction and development of that port as the primary base in the Lingayen area.

The 4th Brigade Headquarters moved from Dagupan to Manila on March 5, taking over the operation of the Port of Manila. The mission of the brigade in Manila was to initiate the rehabilitation of port facilities and begin lighterage operations to furnish logistical support for tactical forces in Southern and Central Luzon.

These efforts were concerned mainly with the development of suitable beaches in North and South Harbors, the development of North Harbor piers and beaches to permit both mechanical cargo handling and manual ramp cargo handling and the selection and development of maintenance, refuge and anchorage areas for landing craft.

In all their operations in the Philippines the brigades employed native labor, both skilled and unskilled. During the Manila Port Operation over 8,000 laborers were employed daily for port and beach operations. The major labor problems experienced were turnover and absenteeism. This resulted in many difficult operating, personnel, and payroll problems.

At Lingayen and Manila the 264th Medical Battalion, under the operational control of Philippine Base Section, operated three holding stations for the evacuation of casualties. Company A maintained an air holding station at Lingayen, Company B operated a holding station for water evacuation in Pasay, Manila, and Company C operated an air holding station at Nielson Field, Manila.

In May the 534th Engineer Boat and Shore Regiment (less Boat Battalion), still at San Fernando, undertook the largest project assigned to them to date. It called for the construction of a 2,000-bed general hospital, complete with access roads, and the installation of all facilities.

On June 10 the Brigade headquarters was relieved of direct port operation to get ready for the next major invasion, that of Japan. The organization of the Port of Manila had reached a point where organic base troops were organized and equipped to assume operation of pier and ship facilities formerly controlled by the brigade. The boat and shore regiments continued lighterage but on a greatly decreased scale as they initiated preparations for the projected invasion of Japan.

One detachment of the 4th Brigade consisting of Company B of the 594th and a platoon of the 3016th Engineer Maintenance Company was still far to the rear in New Britain in amphibious support of the 5th Australian Division, which was containing Rabaul. General Hutchings made many efforts to move forward this "lost" force but the Australians were firm in declaring it "indispensable." Finally orders were issued for the company to move in its own boats eight hundred miles to Hollandia whence it would be shipped to Manila by heavy shipping.

The 533d (3d ESB) continued its operations at San Fabian until March 25 when it too was relieved to get ready for a landing under Eighth Army far to the south on Mindanao.

The 4th Brigade and the two regiments of the 3d ESB which assisted it in the Lingayen sector had done such creditable work as to merit the many commendations received. The 4th Brigade had gone through a complete cycle of making amphibious assaults on an enemy shore, operating the beaches in support of an invading army, and then shifting to a devastated port and developing it into a 10,000-ton per day port in support of all the troops in Luzon.

SOUTHERN LUZON

While the 4th Brigade, with two regiments of the 3d attached, was supporting the Lingayen landing, the 592d Regiment (2d ESB) was staging for the landing on January 11, 1945, north of Subic Bay with the XI Corps. This landing was effected without even a preliminary naval bombardment. The Japs fled just before our arrival, allowing the Filipino guerrillas and civilians to welcome the Americans to the beach. Soon the base for the XI Corps was moved around to Subic Bay and the shore party set up on a good beach there. Their bivouac area was the old target range camp used by the U.S. Marines in the days before Pearl Harbor and Bataan.

In the meantime, another landing was made by the 11th Airborne Division at Nasugbu south of the entrance to Manila Bay. For this operation forty of the 2d Brigade's landing craft had to proceed from Leyte to Mindoro where they joined the naval task force and proceeded on to Luzon. Winds off the China Sea had a long fetch to blow surf up on the poor beaches at Nasugbu. The next few days were hard ones for the boatmen. When the 11th Airborne Division pushed farther inland, the boatmen were able to use the Wawa River, thus gaining protected anchorages for their craft. The flak and rocket LCMs were busy every night patrolling against Jap suicide boats loaded with heavy charges of explosives. Although one freighter was sunk and others damaged, none of the brigade's craft was damaged and the Amphibs destroyed or captured several of these fast Q-boats.

Then followed amphibious patrol action along the west coast of Bataan from Subic Bay, culminating in a full fledged landing at Mariveles at the foot of the Bataan Peninsula. Some light opposition was encountered here but surf and bad beaches hampered the small landing craft more than the Japs. However, one dark night several of their fast Q-boats sneaked into a Navy anchorage and sank four large Navy landing craft. The smaller craft of the Amphibian Engineers escaped attack. Four Army LCMs were near a large Navy landing craft which struck a mine and sank. One of the LCMs went alongside the flaming ship and took off personnel while the others rescued the survivors who had jumped into the sea.

The Mariveles force spread out over southern Bataan, forcing the Japs north and emplacing artillery so it could fire on Corregidor. A separate force known as the Rock Force had accompanied the Mariveles Force. Its mission was to capture Corregidor, thus opening up Manila Bay. The very morning after the Mariveles landing, the flotilla of small ESB landing craft escorted by the larger naval craft formed up and headed for Corregidor. All knew that opposition would be heavy for this time there were no mountains to which the Japs could withdraw. They also knew that despite the heavy air strikes and naval bombardment, many Japs and guns would survive and fire at them.

Terming Corregidor "the Rock" has given many who were never on the island a false impression of its size. Actually Corregidor is not a small island but stretches out five miles, and is shaped like a polliwog. Nearly all its coast line is a series of rocky cliffs dropping as much as 500 feet perpendicular to the sea. On only a few narrow beaches could amphibious landings be made at all. The one selected for the 2d Brigade's boats to hit was on the south shore of Bottomside.

The plan of attack called for a terrific air blasting of "the Rock" and a naval bombardment, then a sudden dropping topside of

B A T A A N

Mariveles

MANILA BAY

North Channel

Corregidor I.

La Monja

N

Caballo I.

South Channel

El Fraile I.
(FORT DRUM)

Ternate

Carabao I.

C A V I T E

0　　　　　　　5 Mi.

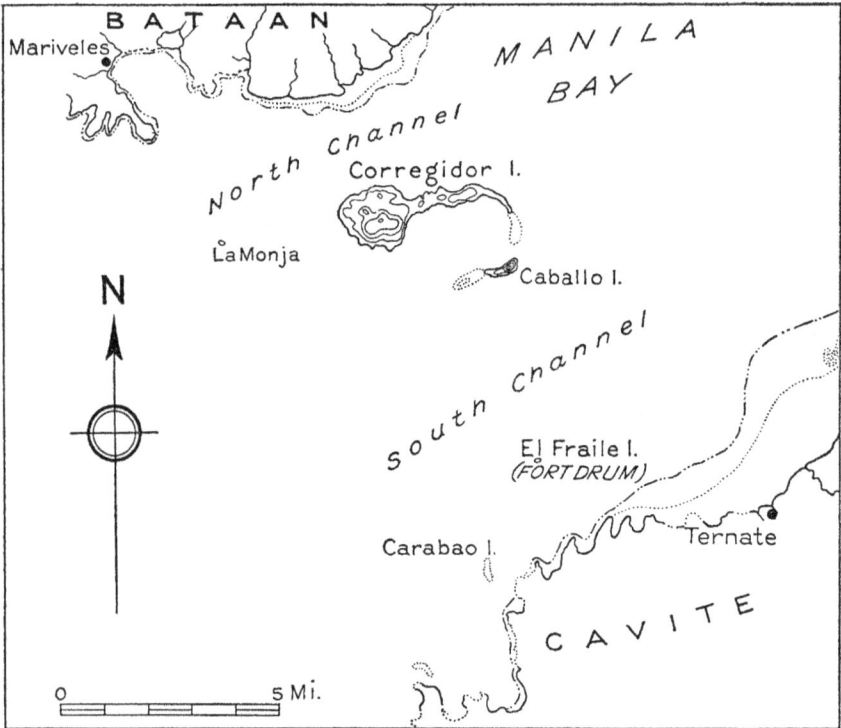

parachute troops to attract the defenders at which time the amphibious attack was to be launched.

Paratroopers started dropping on the Rock at 8:30, shortly after the small craft had started from Mariveles. For eighty minutes they kept dropping in small groups. As the leading wave of boats approached 300 yards from the island, heavy crossfire opened up, as expected. The coxswains drove their craft forward full speed, hoping they would not strike mines, while the boat gunners kept firing to hold down the Jap fire. The first wave hit the beach amidst exploding mortar shells. Down went ramps and out poured the doughboys, up from flat on their bellies on the bottom of the boats. A tank rumbled out of one of the LCMs on the first wave; a shore engineer bulldozer out of another. Both hit mines and were disabled but others kept coming. A cargo truck received a direct hit as it was crossing the ramp of its LCM. A bulldozer jerked the truck off and miraculously the ramp raised and the LCM retracted from the beach. Many men were hit but others sprang up

ROCK PT. JAMES RAVINE

CHENEY RAVINE

COLD STORAGE & POWER PLANT
PUMPING STATION

BOTTOMSIDE
DOCK AREA
MALINTA HILL
INFANTRY PT.

(TOP SIDE)

MALINTA TUNNEL

CAVALRY PT.

NORTH PT.

KINDLEY FIELD

BLACK BEACH

GEARY PT.

C A B A L L O B A Y

ORDNANCE PT.

MONKEY POINT

N

CORREGIDOR ISLAND

SCALE IN MILES
0   1/4   1/2

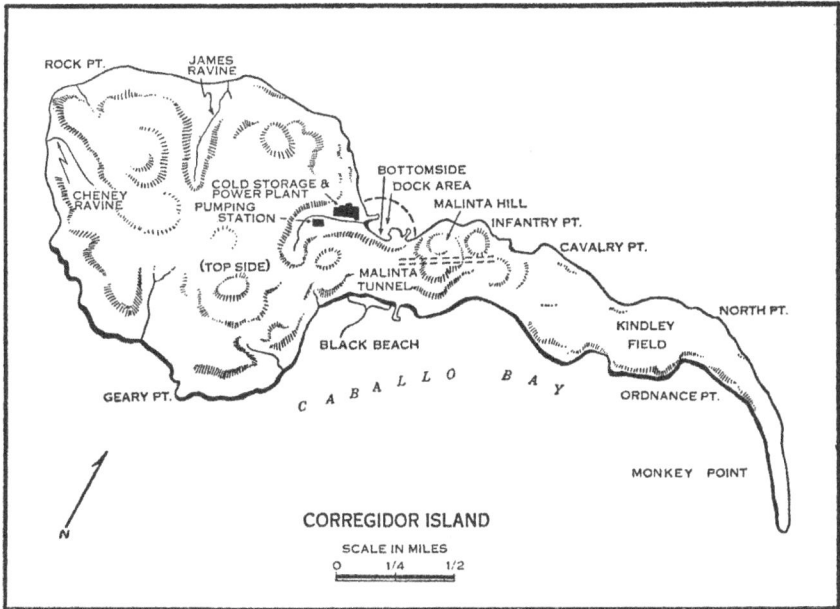

to take their places. Corregidor was soon in American hands but every boat in the initial landing had been hit. LCM 712 in the third wave had the record, forty separate hits. A few days later the maintenance men had it patched up and back in operation.

For their heroic work that day the entire "Rock Force," as the attackers were named, received the Distinguished Unit Citation. Companies A and F of the 592d Regiment won here their first Distinguished Unit Citation. These troops were to receive a second one for their heroic work in another operation. The coordination between the Army, Navy, and Air Forces in the attack at Corregidor will long go down as a magnificent example. It was later determined that the Jap garrison of over 6,000 actually far outnumbered the initial attacking force.

There were many heroic incidents in the Corregidor landing. Several of the small craft got off the beach only by the heroism and quick action of crew members under heavy fire. A platoon of paratroopers cut off on a rocky cape were rescued by two LCMs which pushed in under heavy fire to pick them up, but not without casualties.

After the initial landing some Japs decided that Corregidor was too hot a place for them and attempted to escape to the mainland on the Bataan Peninsula. Navy patrol and the 2d Brigade's picket boats were on the job; the latter captured over forty exhausted Japs swimming in the water and had to kill others who would not surrender. One LCVP decided the simplest way to handle Japs who would not surrender was to ram them. This particular LCVP accounted for over twenty Japs in *bancas* or on rafts by this effective method of attack which was so economical of ammunition. As far as known, it was the only LCVP in the war which adopted the Navy's tactics of ramming the enemy.

Capturing Corregidor did not fully open up Manila Bay. Two other small islands at the entrance to the Bay remained in enemy hands, Caballo and Carabao, as well as Fort Drum (El Fraile Island).

CABALLO ISLAND

Caballo Island, a short distance from Corregidor, was very rocky and honeycombed with enemy caves. An initial landing was made on March 27 but six days later the situation was stalemated with Japs still in many caves. It was decided to construct a super flamethrower. On LCM 503 were installed tanks with 3,400 gallons capacity and a pump powerful enough to throw five hundred gallons a minute. With tanks filled with a mixture of three-fourths diesel fuel and one-fourth gasoline, the flamethrower LCM landed on April 5 on rocky George Beach, directly under the cliff on Caballo Island. The engineers in a few hours laid 800 feet of four-inch pipe up the 175-foot cliff. The Japs kept up intermittent mortar fire while the work was going on but it was not effective as they could not observe their fire. After pumping over 2,000 gallons of fuel into the interlocking caves, it was ignited by an incendiary grenade. The resultant explosion undoubtedly killed many Japs and incidentally showered the LCM with debris from the cliff. However, it took two more days of pumping and firing in other cave areas to complete the job. In all, the lone LCM pumped over 10,000 gallons of fuel into the Jap caves on Caballo Island.

Fort Drum

The next job in Manila Bay was Fort Drum (El Fraile Island). This fort was one of the most unusual in the world. Before the war, American Army engineers cut the top off this small rock jutting out of Manila Bay and expanded it into a concrete "battleship," mounting naval gun turrets on it. The only break in the rock and concrete walls of the battleship was a fixed concrete ramp used as an unloading point. This point was always heavily mined and covered by cross fire, making the fort impregnable to waterborne attack. It had surrendered to the Japs when General Wainwright so ordered after Corregidor had been forced to surrender.

To board this concrete battleship it was decided first to plaster it with air and naval bombardment for several days and then run an LSM alongside. A special swinging bridge or gang plank was erected on top of the LSM's bridge to serve as a ramp from the LSM to the top of the fort. As the seas were always rough and currents strong and as there were no mooring posts on the fort, four Army LCVPs were detailed to hold the LSM against the vertical wall. The plan worked well. Agile engineers crept across the swinging gangplank and boarded the fort like pirates of old. The Japs were held below by covering fire of other naval craft.

The mission of these engineers of the 113th Engineer Battalion was to lay a hose from our flamethrower LCM so the fuel could be pumped into the fort. Work went forward rapidly despite sniper fire from occasional Japs. It took very skillful handling of both the LSM and the flamethrower LCM to keep from smashing them against the walls of the battleship.

The fuel line from the LCM broke once due to the bouncing seas but the engineers soon repaired it and the full load of 3,000 gallons was pumped inside the fort. Then a 500-pound TNT charge was lowered into an opening with a time fuze of thirty minutes to give the engineers and craft time to get away. The LSM left the fort but the LCM kept pumping until its tanks were dry. It withdrew only a few minutes before the explosion.

An observer a mile away watching the explosion through his binoculars said that the first blast, presumably the 500-pound TNT charge, was disappointing. Most of that explosion seemed internal. A second later though, a much stronger blast occurred. The battleship really erupted. A column of gray smoke mushroomed 1,000 feet into the air. Pieces of steel and chunks of concrete showered the seas around the fort, some falling dangerously close to the LCM, 1,000 yards away. Smoke poured out of the turrets and vents for hours. Any Japs not killed in the explosions were burned or suffocated. Fort Drum was no longer a Jap fort.

CARABAO ISLAND

The final island mop-up job in Manila Bay was Carabao Island. Here it was necessary for the Navy and Air Forces to breach a concrete seawall ten feet high and six feet thick before our landing craft could land. The bombs of the Air Forces and the guns of the cruiser Phoenix did this effectively and the landing went off at 9:20 A.M. with light opposition. A tremendous underground explosion an hour later, possibly by Japs destroying themselves, unfortunately resulted in numerous American casualties.

LEGASPI

While the island operations were under way in Manila Bay another 592d task group worked with the 158th Regimental Combat Team in a series of amphibious hops around the south shore of Luzon culminating in the landing at Legaspi on the southeastern tip of Luzon on April 1. The Japs pulled out for the mountains.

The 592d Shore Engineers duplicated the 532d's railroad job earlier in Mindoro by repairing and putting into operation what was left of the old Legaspi–Manila narrow-gauge railway. In a couple of weeks the Amphibians had demonstrated their versatility by putting over forty miles of railroad on regular schedule despite occasional skirmishes with the Japs.

For over a month the boats were busy pushing up the east coast of Luzon and mopping up the many adjacent islands. The rocket LCMs were in frequent use. A Jap lieutenant captured on May 7 stated that the day before a whole platoon of Japs in a pocket were killed by rockets which landed in their midst. It was the first time they knew we even had rockets.

The amphibious advance of the Americans up the east coast of Luzon went beyond Infanta, 400 miles up from the Legaspi Peninsula. Two innovations occurred on this advance. The first was the 2d Brigade's entry into psychological warfare when a high-powered loudspeaker was installed on an LCM which cruised up the coast a few hundred yards offshore. A Nisei squad aboard the LCM bombarded the shore with appeals to the Japs to surrender but their efforts were fruitless. The second innovation was the capture of five Jap nurses. All the way from Lae to Leyte there had been tales of the Japs having Geisha girls and nurses with them but no one ran into any until one day a short burst of rocket fire, thrown at a suspicious settlement on the shore of Dingalan Bay, brought out strange quarry. The five emaciated Jap nurses said they had left Manila when the Japs withdrew and that they had undergone all the hardships they could endure hiding in the mountains.

BATANGAS

With Manila Bay in American hands and having encountered little opposition in the Legaspi campaign, the 592d was ordered to move to Batangas with small detachments to continue work at Mariveles and north of Legaspi. In the meantime a boat company of the 542d had been moved from Mindoro to Batangas to perform lighterage for the base. For the first time in more than two years, the 592d under Colonel A. L. Keyes, Jr., entered a spell of relative inactivity and had a chance for what relaxation it could get in the war-damaged Batangas area. All suspected that this was only the lull before the storm, that the Amphibians were getting a rest only because supplies had to be built up and units brought in for the landing on Japan.

APARRI

On June 24 the 4th Brigade received orders to provide a boat company–shore company team for the operation of the Army supply point at Aparri on the extreme north coast of Luzon, in support of combat elements in that sector. Companies C and F, 544th Engineer Boat and Shore Regiment, were assigned this mission.

Company C made the long trip north in their own LCMs. Company F travelled overland. This group of Army Amphibians was, however, not the group closest to Japan at that time as they thought. On April 1, the 1st Brigade Headquarters and Headquarters Company had gained that honor by landing on Okinawa with the Tenth Army. (See Chapter 14.)

Summary

Thus closed the Luzon campaign. Elements of all three of the Engineer Special Brigades had contributed their support in this extensive and difficult campaign. The Amphibians had again shown their worth in the many combat landings and their versatility after the combat phase had been completed. The 4th Brigade had done a remarkable job in getting the ruined port of Manila back to work and to handling more cargo than it had ever handled. The 2d Brigade had won another Distinguished Unit Citation (its eighth) while helping to capture Corregidor. The two regiments of the 3d Brigade had done fine work in Lingayen and were being primed for the invasion of Mindanao, the last Japanese stronghold in the Philippines.

Notes

[1] Landing Ship, Dock.

[2] This was the only occasion on the long drive from Nassau Bay to Corregidor on which Jap naval fire fell near Allied troops. This speaks well for our naval and air forces who kept off the Jap fleet.

[3] LCS = Landing Craft, Support, 36-foot heavily armed and armored.

[4] Petroleum, oils, and lubricants.

13
Mopping up the Visayans, Mindanao and Borneo

As soon as the Sixth Army was well established in Luzon, the Eighth Army under General Eichelberger, with headquarters on Leyte, was launched on the so-called Victor series of operations, the aim of which was to mop up the major islands bordering the Visayan Sea in the heart of the Philippines. Some of these islands were known to have been held very strongly by the Japs. We had been able to obtain considerable information as to the Jap troop disposition and installations from Filipino guerrillas, but of course there were certain areas in which no Filipinos were allowed. These areas might be heavily mined and, in fact, some were.

These Victor operations were to consist of major landings on Palawan, Panay, Mindanao, and Cebu, but with many lesser landings on neighboring islands. These were exactly the type of operations for which the Engineer Special Brigade had been designed. If the Amphibian Engineers had not already justified their existence in the New Guinea operations, they certainly justified it in accomplishing all of the Philippine operations so successfully.

The first one of the Victor operations was assigned to the 532d Regiment, then under Colonel A. M. Neilson. The objective was the liberation of Palawan, an island of the Philippine group in the Sulu Sea, less than one hundred miles north of British North Borneo. Palawan is no small island. It is narrow but it stretches out over two hundred miles. It is fringed by coral reefs like New Guinea, rather than with open beaches like Leyte, and the interior is very mountainous.

In the mid-morning of February 28, 1945, the landing was made without enemy opposition on three beaches near Puerto Princesa, Palawan. Members of the shore party actually reached and entered the town of Puerto Princesa before the combat troops arrived. When the infantry arrived, a welcoming committee of Amphibs was on hand to greet them. Soon the port was in operation and supplies were moving in fast. Japs fought only in small, disorganized groups.

In spite of the poor, stormy weather often prevailing and frequent rough seas, various minor boat missions were run to different places on the island. Due to heavy seas on a 200-mile round trip to Sir John Brooke's Point on March 14, one LCM being towed by an LSM was lost. Seven days later another LCM was lost in the same way while en route to Ulugan Bay. Luckily no men were lost on either occasion. The mission to Ulugan Bay was a 500-mile round trip, all of it being made in the open and stormy waters of the Sulu and South China seas.

The 532d group at Palawan was called upon to support a landing of the 186th Infantry on Busuanga, a small island northeast of Palawan. The 532d group was somewhat different from the usual, in that it used no landing craft but only DUKWs carried to the far shore in LSTs. The loaded DUKWs were launched at sea down the LST ramps. The landing was made without any unusual incident on April 9. The DUKWs were used on patrol both in the waters along the shore and inland. On April 17 our forces left the island after destroying all Jap resistance.

The Palawan operation was neither difficult nor dangerous, but it was vital to control of the South China Sea. The regimental task force furnished the same supervision, functions, and operations that it had executed on Mindoro. In addition to supervision of all port activity, the 532d shore unit erected beach installations, cleared dump sites, constructed or improved roads, and made certain necessary clearances in the town proper. In due course, Puerto Princesa became quite an airbase for local, tactical, patrol, and observation missions. From there Allied planes bombed Borneo and Jap-held sections of China.

THE 542D GOES INTO ACTION

The rest of the Visayan campaign was handled by the 542d Engineer Boat and Shore Regiment. This regiment, under Colonel B. C. Fowlkes, Jr., had made the hot landings at Wakde and Biak in mid-1944. There it underwent many enemy strafing and bombing attacks.

Company A of the 542d moved to the Philippines, with its fifty LCMs carried in Navy LSDs from Hollandia to Leyte. Beginning in December 1944 the balance of the regiment moved unit by unit, by water and by air, to assemble at Leyte. Some entire boat crews were flown from Biak to Leyte to man new LCMs delivered at Leyte direct from the United States. Others made the long trip from Milne Bay at the tip of British New Guinea to Hollandia in LCMs assembled at the boat plant. There they were deck-loaded on Liberty ships or embarked in Navy LSDs for the 1,200-mile trip on to Leyte.

Ahead of the regiment lay the Visayan campaign, the recapture of the central islands of the Philippines—Cebu, with the second largest city of the Commonwealth, Negros, Panay, Bohol, and a flanking assault on the northern coast of Mindanao. But before even the planning phases of the Visayan campaign began, the 542d plunged into the task of operating the Red and White landing beaches near Taclobán, on Leyte, where thousands of tons of supplies and thousands of men kept pouring over the beaches to support the fighting against the Japs making their last stand in the Ormoc corridor on the western side of Leyte.

Taking over gradually from elements of the 532d and 592d, the 542d's shore battalion operated discharge and loading facilities on the two beaches. The boat battalion discharged ships in the stream and also ran resupply, patrol, and reconnaissance missions for the infantry and guerrillas on Samar and smaller islands in the approaches to Leyte.

In January 1945 came the regiment's first combat action against the Japanese in the Philippines when three LCMs of Company A were assigned to the 381st Infantry for patrol and reconnaissance on the southern coast of Samar Island. These LCMs, on the morning of January 27, stood off Santa Margarita village and shelled concentrations of Japanese troops there with 37mm cannon and mortars mounted in the landing craft. Later reports from guerrillas and air observers stated the bombardment accounted for approximately 240 of the enemy—180 killed and 60 wounded. The Amphibians had no casualties.

Company A boatmen swung into the tactical picture in greater strength when, on February 18, fifteen LCMs took aboard a reinforced battalion of the Americal Division, veterans of the Solomons, for a combat assault mission against Japanese installations on the northwest coast of Samar and the islands of Capul and Bin, which controlled a part of the vital San Bernardino Strait, the main shipping route leading north to Luzon. On February 19 the mission to land on Capul Island left the LCM convoy and hit the shore at Capul village after an air attack by four Corsairs. A very bad beach, filled with coral heads, awaited the landing craft, but enemy opposition was light with some knee-mortar and small-arms fire coming from Japanese on the right flank of the beach. Meanwhile, the rest of the convoy proceeded to the town of Allen, on the Samar coast above Capul, and landed there without opposition to find a ghost town in which no one had lived since 1942 when its inhabitants had fled the threat of Japanese occupation.

THE BIRI LANDING

From Allen five LCMs were loaded with Company C, 182d Infantry, for the landing on small Biri Island, an assault which proved to be as bitterly contested in its few brief minutes as the bloody landing at Wakde Island, which won Company A of the 542d the Distinguished Unit Citation.

At 7:45 A.M. four Navy Corsairs swept in over the Biri beachhead to strafe and bomb, and four PT boats slid into position through the quiet morning waters spouting fire from their 40mm and 20mm cannons. Between the flanking PTs two LCMs of the first wave ploughed toward the shore, both heavily loaded with infantrymen. Suddenly when the two craft were about 700 yards from the beach a blast of machine-gun and 20mm fire came from hidden Japanese positions on the beach. Mortar shells began dropping around the two landing barges. It was obvious that the air and naval preparation had been inadequate and that the two LCMs could not effect a landing; so, although damaged, both withdrew out of fire to await orders. Six of the eight crewmen on the two craft were hit and over twenty passengers were casualties. The bottoms of both boats ran red with blood.

The mission, after transferring casualties and re-forming, decided to outflank the enemy positions, and shortly afterward landed the infantry on the other side of Biri Island without opposition. They crossed the island and surprised and killed all of the hundred Japs defending the original beach, capturing eight machine guns and mortars.

PANAY–NEGROS

Meanwhile, to the regimental headquarters on Leyte came the order to prepare for participation in the V-1 operation with the occupation and liberation of Panay and Negros Islands as the major objective. The task for the 542d's Combat Team 3, which had last functioned as a separate task force unit in the early days at Tambu Bay and Morobe in British New Guinea, was to land regiments of the 40th Division and support them in resupply and flanking operations. Making up the 542d's Combat Team 3 were C and D Companies with attached medical and boat maintenance personnel from the 262d Medical Battalion and the 562d Boat Maintenance Battalion, respectively.

Early on March 18 the forty-ship convoy lay off the beach at Tigbaun, some 15 miles below the Panay capital city of Iloilo. A brief naval bombardment and accompanying cruisers and destroyers paved the way for the landing on Red Beach at 10:00 A.M., a landing which encountered no opposition at the beach. As the infantry advanced, Japs were contacted and a small outpost was quickly reduced inland on the road to Iloilo. As the infantry moved toward the capital, 542d reconnaissance showed that Red Beach was unsuitable for the beaching of larger landing craft such as LSTs, so shore party headquarters and facilities were moved within a few hours to Blue Beach. Working under good conditions with favorable terrain, hindered only by a shallow beach from which jetties had to be dozed out for the LSTs, all landing craft were completely unloaded by the next morning. The following day all beach organization was functioning smoothly, the infantry had entered the city of Iloilo, which had been abandoned by the enemy, and the schedule was cleared for planning and staging the next phase of the V-1 operation, the seizure of the neighboring island of Negros. The entire shore party organization moved off the initial beachhead and set up operations in Iloilo itself as soon as it had been captured. Preliminary reconnaissance of the Negros landing beaches was started.

Escorted by two PT boats, control and support craft of Company C made the three-hour run across Guimaras Strait to Pulupandan, projected site for the Negros landing. Soundings were made off the beach, and as no enemy activity was noted ashore, a Navy scout party was landed in a rubber boat. After completing their beach check, the scout party learned from civilian sources that a small Jap garrison nearby had been alerted. The party then quit the beach area, its mission accomplished without incident.

March 29 was D-day for the Negros landing, with all the LCMs of Company C making the journey to the far shore under their own power. At H minus 3½ hours, a detachment of a picket boat, flak and rocket LCMs, and two LCMs landed a reinforced platoon of the 185th Infantry on the right flank of the Negros beachhead to secure the bridge over the Bago River. The beach itself proved to be narrow and so soft that vehicles bogged down, but within a few hours dumps were established between the streets of Pulupandan, which was immediately behind the beachhead, an evacuation station was operating in the town plaza, and shore party headquarters was settled in the local theater. The 542d had chalked up another successful landing to its growing record, a versatile regiment if ever there was one.

CEBU LANDING

Meanwhile at Leyte, the remainder of the regiment was alerted for the V-2 operation which was to encompass the taking of Cebu and surrounding small islands, and landings on the island of Bohol and on the south tip of Negros. Selected as the site for the Cebu landing was Talisay beach, some six miles south of Cebu City and connected with it by an excellent highway. Early intelligence showed that the beach was pillboxed and tank-trapped. The possibility of a rough show was anticipated. March 25 found the Cebu naval convoy sliding through the Mindanao Sea with the 542d LCMs in tow. Aboard the LSTs were the Amphibian Engineers and two regiments of the Americal Division, scheduled to liberate the second largest port of the Philippines, Cebu City, often referred to as "Little Manila." A small American garrison there had surrendered to the Japs after Wainwright surrendered at Corregidor back in the dark days of 1942.

A few lights shone from the coastal villages of Cebu as the darkened convoy steadily headed through the early hours for the beachhead. Soon after daylight revealed the invasion fleet, the Air Forces began heavy bombing of Cebu where enemy naval guns had been reported emplaced. At 7:00 A.M. cruisers and destroyers opened up with blasting salvos. Close inshore, destroyers and smaller craft cruised to shatter pin-point targets at point-blank range while the first waves of amphibian tractors splashed off the ramps of the LSTs and wallowed to the beach. Everyone wondered what lay ahead.

Sudden spouts of sand and flame as the first Buffaloes crawled into shore warned of a mined beachhead, and the following waves of LCMs and LCVs grounded on the beach to find 17 of the swimming tractors knocked out by land mines, the wounded already left behind by the infantry advancing inland. The medical Amphibs immediately went to their rescue and soon had the wounded on the way to hospital LSTs. The hospital LCMs did yeoman service in evacuating them quickly to medical aid aboard the big LSTs.

Warily at first and then with growing speed as they discovered the Japanese mine pattern, demolition crews from Companies E and F of the 542d began sweeping the dune line left behind by the withdrawing Japs. Even regimental clerks turned to uprooting mines. Occasional mortar and sniper fire kept coming over the beach but casualties for the Amphibian Engineers were light in spite of the ticklish business in which they were engaged. Road-blocks and mines were cleared from the lateral road behind the beach as the mechanized equipment of the Americal Division began coming ashore across a badly shallowed beach. By afternoon the beach was well organized, and the infantry was pressing on the outskirts of Cebu City after brief fire fights along the way. The beach was so shallow it was necessary to install ponton causeways. LSTs were being nosed into the ponton ramps when suddenly the submarine alert sounded. Torpedoes had been fired at the vessels standing off the beach. The beached vessels immediately began to retract with the exception of two which could not pull loose, and the convoy stood out to sea to spend the night.

Shortly after sunset a plane was heard overhead, the noise growing to a roar as a lone Nip dived on the LSTs left on the beach. With a nearly perfect target the enemy plane loosed a single bomb which hit the water just between the two LSTs, spraying several of our LCMs cruising about, but causing no casualties or damage. No more planes appeared; the total effort of the Japanese Air Force in the central Philippines had been expended. Our Air Forces had really crippled the Jap Air Force in the Philippines. What a difference from the reaction of Jap air power in the early days of Lae and Finschhafen and even as late as Biak and Leyte! Newcomers to the Western Pacific seemed incredulous when they were told Jap bombers attacked the airstrip at Leyte over fifty times in one night.

Two days later, after unopposed landings on Cauit and Mactan Islands guarding the Cebu harbor and approaches, the 542d moved into the city and set up headquarters in the badly shelled Customs House. It was the first time the unit had occupied a real building since leaving Fort Ord in February 1943. The city was deserted, a mass of shattered buildings, bomb-pocked streets, snarled road-blocks, and naval demolitions which the Japs had left behind in their retreat to the heights overlooking the city where a bitter holding action was being fought.

The next day two Liberty ships nosed alongside the city's sea-wall, the first American vessels to enter the harbor since 1942. Only a few blocks from the Liberties, which were working at night with lights blazing, the Division artillery thundered in its continual pounding of the Jap positions less than a mile away. Jap shells passed our Liberties, but always too high. Machine-gun fire echoed down from the hills, and tracers streaked through the night. During the day, heavy and medium bombers and Army and Navy fighters droned through the air in concentrated attacks on the Japs in caves in the high hills back of the city. Jap air power was just nonexistent.

Minor flanking and landing missions were carried out in April, a small group from Boat Battalion reconnoitering the beaches at Tagbilaran, the main port of Bohol Island, where elements of the Americal were landed April 11. Starting on April 17 the Japanese behind Cebu City began a withdrawal from their heavily defended positions to the northern mountainous portion of the island. Immediately, plans were made to land Americal troops at Danao, some 20 miles to the north of the city, to intercept and cut off the disorganized and retreating enemy. Twenty LCMs of the 2d ESB accomplished this mission without an unfortunate incident.

Ten LCMs accompanied the Americal Division landing at Dumaguete, on the southern tip of Negros Island. Here again the Japs ran from the beach and took to the caves in the mountains. This now accounted for all of the Philippines except Mindanao.

THE 3D BRIGADE HITS MINDANAO

Even before their lighterage work at Lingayen had been completed, the 533d and 543d Regiments of the 3d Brigade had to start planning for the invasion of Mindanao. It may be recalled that General MacArthur's original plan for the invasion of the Philippines called for an initial landing on the southern coast of Mindanao where the Cotobato area would be pinched off and developed before he struck his second big blow at Leyte. Instead, when Admiral Halsey's first big naval strike in the Philippines (in late August 1944) disclosed less Jap opposition in the air than had been expected, the invasion plan was altered to skip Mindanao and strike Leyte. The revised plan worked out beautifully, but the Japs

still held all the important port areas on Mindanao. They had to
be mopped up.

Mindanao is not only the second largest island in the Philippines but also one of the most productive. If the Japs were left
there, the guerrillas could restrict them to limited areas, but they
were totally unable to defeat and capture the 100,000 Japs garri-
soning Zamboanga, Parang, Cotobato, Davao and the other important points.

Accordingly the Eighth Army under Lieutenant General Eichelberger was given the mission of freeing Mindanao. The 3d Brigade
was made available to him for engineer amphibian support. The
Japs had expected the initial landing in the Philippines to be attempted at Davao on the eastern coast. The Americans knew this
area was strongly fortified. Accordingly they avoided that and decided to make their first landing on the peninsula of Zamboanga
where, according to song and legend, the monkeys have no tails.

THE ZAMBOANGA LANDING

The 543d Engineer Boat and Shore Regiment was the one selected to provide amphibian support to the 41st Infantry Division
which was the unit designated by Eighth Army to capture Zamboanga. The 41st were old hands at amphibious attacks, being the
same unit which landed with elements of the 2d Brigade in the first
amphibious assault at Nassau Bay on June 30, 1943. Now they were
to be the first force to invade Mindanao.

The 543d Regiment had no easy job to prepare for its part in
the coming amphibious strike. The headquarters and the Shore
Battalion were at Lingayen where they had landed on January 9,
1945, but the Boat Battalion was far back at Noemfoor off New
Guinea. As soon as alerted this battalion moved under its own
power to Biak. From here one company was lifted by naval shipping to Mindoro where the 41st Division would stage. Another company had to go to Lingayen to reinforce the Amphibian boatmen
there. There was not sufficient shipping to lift the rest of the Boat
Battalion so it moved under its own power first to Morotai in the

Moluccas and, after southern Mindanao had been secured, rejoined
its regiment on Mindanao.

The task force assembled at Mindoro by the first of March, the
543d contributing the entire regiment less the Boat Company held
in Lingayen and the boat units left at Biak. One boat company with
about forty LCMs was with the task force which jumped off from
Mindoro in early March for the landing on Mindanao.

Zamboanga is at the tip of a long peninsula at the southwestern tip of Mindanao. Down the peninsula runs a lofty range of
mountains. At the southern end of the peninsula is a sloping fore-
shore about four miles wide which had been cleared and cultivated
with coconuts and other crops. There was a fair airport there which
the Americans wanted to use as a base for further operations on
Mindanao and to Borneo. Ten miles to the west was a strongly fortified Jap seaplane base. It was estimated that the Jap strength on
the peninsula was over 10,000 and other troops were not far away.

The landing was preceded by the usual heavy bombardment
which had become typical of General MacArthur's landings, culminating in a terrific rocket barrage just before the craft hit the
beach. The beach was excellent although somewhat narrow. Resistance on the beach was light and LSTs soon came in for a dry
landing, no ponton causeways being necessary at all.

It did not take long to find out what became of the defending
Japs. Because of fear of the heavy naval bombardment and the
rocket barrage, they had withdrawn to a strong position in the foothills four miles back from the beaches. From there they had perfect observation for their camouflaged artillery which soon opened
up. Naval vessels on the beach and the shore engineers had heavy
casualties from this well directed fire.

Artillery and mortar fire hampered operations on the beach for
several days. However the infantry pushed in rapidly from the
beach and soon took the city of Zamboanga three miles away and
pushed on to the airfield. Operations were promptly shifted from
the beach which was still under occasional artillery fire to the city
dock which had been repaired and made serviceable by the shore
engineers. Two Liberty ships could be discharged simultaneously

at this fine dock. Filipinos soon returned from the hills to the city and made willing stevedores.

Zamboanga remained the base of operations of the 41st Division for several weeks as they pressed inland to kill or drive the Japs out of their strongholds entrenched in the foothills. As far as the Amphibian Engineers were concerned, the Zamboanga landing was much easier technically than the Lingayen landing in early January but Jap artillery and mortar fire at Zamboanga was considerably heavier and much more accurate than at Lingayen. After experiencing this Jap fire at Zamboanga, the shore engineers wondered more than ever why the Japs' resistance was so light at Lingayen. As a matter of fact, it is still a mystery as to why the Japs in the Western Pacific were so quick to abandon the beaches to the Americans and so slow to counterattack. Word undoubtedly had gotten around among them as to the ferocity of our naval and rocket fire. This may have accounted for their eagerness in abandoning the beaches at first signs of an attack. It is fortunate for the Americans that word of the havoc their defenders wreaked on our LCMs at Wakde Island did not get to their other troops for there the Japs survived a terrific bombardment in enough numbers to pour very heavy fire on the 2d Brigade's small boats as they neared the beach of that tiny island.

In early April 1945 the 543d Regiment moved elements of the 41st Division in its LCMs from Zamboanga to Sanga Sanga Island in the Tawitawi group. This island group had been a Jap naval stronghold in the days of the New Guinea campaign and, at that time, was thought to be heavily fortified. A few rounds of enemy 20mm and mortar fire were encountered but no casualties occurred. Five days later the 543d landed other elements of the 41st Division on Jolo Island in the Sulu Archipelago, encountering no opposition. During April boat elements of the 543d continued their lighterage back in Lingayen as well as at Zamboanga. Boat battalion headquarters and part of Company A was still at Morotai on April 30 waiting for tows to take their craft to Cotobato in southern Mindanao.

PARANG—MALABANG

It was on March 15 that the 533d Regiment, under Colonel Wayne S. Moore, sent officers from Lingayen to Headquarters X Corps on Leyte to attend the first planning for Mindanao. Although harassed for months by Filipino guerrillas, the Japs were known to hold sections of Mindanao. On March 19 the essential points were passed on to the company commanders at San Fabian by Colonel Moore, the regimental commander. Mindoro was designated as the staging area for this operation of the 24th Division. On April 1 the entire Boat Battalion (533d) with over 140 craft left Lingayen and proceeded in its own craft to Mindoro, where it set up next to the 532d (2d ESB) which had been there since the initial landing on Mindoro in December, 1944. The shore engineers with all their heavy equipment followed.

The plan of attack on Parang called for separate landings on Red, White and Blue beaches and on two neighboring islands. To reinforce the amphibian craft of the Navy, the 543d ran a convoy of a hundred LCMs 350 miles from Mindoro under their own power. This convoy stopped over at Zamboanga to refuel from the fuel barges of the 543d Regiment, which regiment was still operating in that area.

The large naval convoy made the trip from Mindoro to Cotobato Bay without untoward incident. When small craft were launched, however, they experienced strong offshore currents which made them a few minutes late at the line of departure. This made no difference though for on none of the beaches was contact made with the enemy. Coastal reconnaissance was immediately initiated in LVTs supported by LCM gun boats and LCSs of the 3d Brigade but again no contact was made. The Japs apparently still feared all naval and rocket bombardment and ran for the interior. LSTs had difficulty reaching shore; they grounded as far as 500 feet offshore. On D-day there were only four ponton causeways with the task force. The shore engineers, realizing the situation, immediately started a sand jetty from shore and the few causeway sections available were used to extend it. Thus three LSTs could unload simultaneously by the next morning. Additional ponton

causeways arrived the next day and a second jetty extending 470
feet from shore was started. About a thousand ponton cubes were
used. When this jetty was completed, all unloading schedules were
easily met.

After securing the Malabang–Parang area, the 24th Division
ordered the simultaneous forcing of both mouths of the Mindanao
River. After bombardment of the shore installation by the cruiser
Cleveland, the two water-borne assault groups in LCMs of the 3d
ESB headed upstream and reached their initial objectives without
opposition. The LCM gun boats provided the only fire power as
the group proceeded farther up stream. On the south branch a few
Japs opposed the advance but all were quickly killed by the accurate machine-gun and 20mm fire from the LCMs. Upon approaching the town of Cotobato, the LCMs let go a hundred rockets. Jap
machine-gun fire was quickly silenced and, for good measure, two
Jap launches and a landing barge were sunk.

The operations of the next day were reported as follows by the
3d ESB boat commander:

The night proved uneventful and much valuable intelligence of enemy movements and disposition further upstream was obtained. Orders were received for the infantry
to hold Lomopog and reconnoiter the road north to Serenaya, and for the gunboats to reconnoiter the river to
Ulandang. No mention was made of reinforcements or any
indication given that those in authority were aware of the
possibility of exploiting the penetration. The reconnaissance to Serenaya had been completed the previous evening,
and, in accordance with the message, was ordered repeated,
and one platoon of infantry embarked to accompany the
gunboats upstream. This party arrived at Ulandang at 10:30
to find that the Japs had left ninety minutes previously,
abandoning a large store of arms and supplies. A quick reconnaissance was made three kilometers north along the
road and a somewhat more limited probe made in the
Dalauan area on the opposite bank. As this road was found

to be in poor condition, thus reducing the value of Ulandang as a jumping off point for further operations, and in view of the obvious continued demoralization of the Japs, decision was made to push on to Paidu Pulangi to secure same as a beachhead for a drive on Fort Pikit. As the force was being re-assembled and re-embarked, a message was received from Commanding General, 24th Division, directing that Ulandang be held and that the force proceed no further upstream. The task unit commander now realized that the division commander was not fully informed as to the extent to which the Japs were disorganized in the valley, and on his own initiative proceeded to Paidu Pulangi where, after a brief bombardment, a landing was effected at 1:00 P.M. Here again, evidence was found of a precipitate withdrawal on the part of the enemy, who left file baskets full of operational papers and arms with shells in the chamber. A perimeter was organized and a strong radio message dispatched to the division commanding general, explaining the desirability of holding this beachhead and attacking Fort Pikit with a minimum delay. When no answer was received to this message for four hours, the task unit commander decided to proceed downstream to Lomopog and guide the balance of the 2d Battalion, 21st Infantry, which had been ordered upstream, directly to Paidu Pulangi. Arriving at Lomopog at 6:15, we found that the assistant division commander had that morning countermanded the order for the battalion to move upstream and had directed that the infantry be withdrawn to Lomopog. The task unit commander directed that a perimeter be established at Paidu Pulangi, consisting of such personnel as could be scraped up from gunboat crews, and decided to proceed to division headquarters himself to present in person the clear picture of complete Jap disorganization which practically dictated that the advance up the river be pressed until real contact was made.

That night another battalion of the 34th Infantry, and the regimental headquarters, arrived at Fort Pikit in LCMs and plans were made for reconnaissance in the direction of Kabacan for R plus 5, to be followed on R plus 6 by a joint land and amphibious attack on the town. The tactical command of the river campaign passed from the 533d to Commanding Officer, 34th Infantry, at that time.

At daylight of R plus 5, Major Lawton, Executive Officer, Boat Battalion, with three gunboats proceeded upstream with considerable difficulty as the boats dragged bottom almost continuously. By noon, the infantry had advanced rapidly along the road and was directed to proceed to the town of Kabacan prior to dark. Radio orders were sent Major Lawton to make all possible speed in order to join the infantry at the town. Late in the afternoon, the infantry battalion ran into approximately 120 Japs in the vicinity of the road junction Route 1–Route 3 and, after a brief skirmish, dug in for the night. Major Lawton and his boats encountered a party of Japs below the ferry, killed three and scattered the balance, and arrived at the ferry expecting to find the infantry either there or shortly to arrive. Contact with them over SCR-300 disclosed the fact that the infantry would not resume its advance until the following day, and that the gunboats would have to hold the ferry during the night, so once more a perimeter, consisting of cooks, radio operators, enginemen and official observers from higher headquarters, was established across the line of retreat of the estimated Jap company which had halted the infantry battalion. Though no concerted attack was made on this position, several infiltration attempts were successfully repulsed, and a total of three Japs killed. The commendable coolness of this detachment is proved by the fact that, despite the exposed conditions, only 18 shots were fired during the entire night, and 17 bullet holes were found in the three Japs.

Early the next morning the infantry occupied the town of Kabacan. As this was the head of navigation of landing craft, the tactical phase of the river operation was concluded.

No account of the river operations would be complete without mention of the magnificent performance of the communications personnel who in addition to handling organic traffic efficiently provided the only reliable communications between infantry units in the river valley during the first days of the operation.

The planners in Eighth Army had predicted it would take at least thirty days to dislodge the Japs from the Mindanao River valley and secure the critical Kabacan area. It was done in six days, due in no small measure to the aggressive action by the Amphibians.

While the 533d and 543d Regiments were invading Mindanao, the 593d continued the evacuation of troops and supplies from Noemfoor Island which was to be abandoned. On May 6, 1945, the advance echelon of the Shore Battalion left Noemfoor by Liberty ship for Batangas in southern Luzon.

The 3d Brigade's Medical Battalion (263d) which had landed at Lingayen continued the evacuation in southern Luzon of XIV Corps troops, handling over 6,000 patients during April. The brigade headquarters was at Biak controlling the 369th Infantry (Negro troops) which maintained the perimeter defense. Biak had never been mopped up and clashes with stray Japs occurred at infrequent intervals, 40 Japs being killed during April.

The 3d Brigade had many administrative and supply difficulties during this period. With only one of its regiments still in New Guinea, brigade headquarters at Biak had a difficult time with the other two regiments first moving to Luzon and then to Mindanao and other nearby islands. The 3d Brigade thus operated over more extensive areas than either the 2d or 4th, especially when the 3d sent its boat group to Borneo to work with the Australians. Fuel supply and distribution of the very limited stock of spare parts, etc., were problems that had to be and were well solved despite the long distances and infrequent shipping. The Brigade's excellent radio net was a major factor in meeting these problems.

THE 3D BRIGADE ATTACKS BORNEO

Before describing the Borneo operation, it is well to summarize where the units of the 3d Engineer Special Brigade were working in May 1945. The 533d Engineer Boat and Shore Regiment continued in support of X Corps on Mindanao. One boat company and

one shore company of the 543d Regiment had moved from
Zamboanga to help the 533d in the Parang and Davao areas. An
unopposed landing was made at Santa Cruz (18 miles below Davao)
on May 3, 1945. At the end of May the 533d Regiment was in the
process of establishing its main base at Bugo on the northern coast
of Mindanao, moving over 350 miles by organic landing craft and
by vehicles.

The 543d Regiment was stationed at many scattered points in
the Western Pacific. Companies A and B were still performing lighterage at Lingayen Gulf, working with the 4th Engineer Special Brigade. The Shore Battalion less Company D was busy at Zamboanga
in Mindanao. Company D operated the beach at Parang under control of the 533d Regiment. Boat elements were working for the 41st
Infantry Division at Tawitawi and Jolo islands in the Sulu Archipelago. Boat Battalion Headquarters and Headquarters Company
and most of Company A with 31 LCMs were performing lighterage
for the Australians at Morotai.

The Boat Battalion of 593d Regiment had been assigned to the
Borneo operation but the rest of the regiment was in the process
of moving from Noemfoor and Biak to Batangas in Southern Luzon.
The 263d Medical Battalion (3d ESB) was continuing its mission
of evacuation by air and by ambulance in the XIV Corps sector in
southern Luzon. Brigade headquarters and service elements were
awaiting shipping at Biak to move to Batangas. The 3d Brigade was
responsible for the defense of Biak. There over 300 Japs had been
killed or taken prisoner during this period. Most of these were
killed by the colored soldiers of the 369th Infantry which was
under operational control of the 3d Brigade from January 20, 1945,
to May 31, 1945.

Borneo is a much larger island than Mindanao and lies southwest of it. Borneo's great value to the Japs lay in its oil. While the
bombers of the Allied air forces could destroy some of the oil tanks,
it was known that the Japs had hidden many of their tanks and
others were underground. Tarakan on the east coast and Balikpapan on the west coast were the major areas under Jap control.

Company B of the 593d Regiment with a boat maintenance platoon attached furnished the Amphibian Engineer support for the May 1 landing by the 9th Australian Division on Tarakan, off the northeastern coast of Borneo. A total of 39 LCMs was taken in on D-day, 17 in a Navy LSD and the remainder either deck-loaded on merchant shipping or towed behind LSTs. Staging was from Morotai.

The sea off Tarakan on D-day was calm with a light rain. The naval bombardment opened up at 7:15 A.M. followed by air bombing. Oil and ammunition dumps were quickly hit, the smoke from the resulting fires hiding the beach under a pall. The first wave of landing boats hit the beach at 8:20 without receiving any enemy fire. In one section beach obstacles were encountered about fifty yards off shore but the Royal Australian Engineers promptly breached them, allowing LSTs to proceed to the beach.

An unusually high tide allowed the first boats to discharge on fairly hard soil but a rapid drop of tide of over nine feet caused untold trouble as succeeding craft grounded farther and farther from the beach in muddy soil. Dozers and tanks bogged down hopelessly. The few tanks that did get to the beach were stopped by a serious tank trap. Ponton cube causeways were immediately launched but the total lack of experienced shore engineers was only too obvious in the slow way they were installed and connected up with the shore.

Due to the difficult unloading, the Amphibian Engineers did not set up ashore at all on D-day. Jap resistance too was greater than anticipated and on D-day the beachhead held by the Australian infantry was very narrow. By D plus 1 the Australian infantry pushed forward and their advance was deep enough to allow the company to set up ashore. A small-boat maintenance area was soon cleared. Despite occasional Jap 75mm and sniper fire, the unloading progressed well after the delay on D-day. One officer of Company B was killed in action on May 5.

On June 10 the Amphibian boatmen with Australian engineers as shore party supported the 9th Australian Division in a landing in Brunei Bay on the west coast of Borneo. This landing was more or less a duplicate of the Tarakan landing on the eastern coast. The soil was soft and the unloading very difficult.

Three weeks later the boatmen of the 593d Boat Battalion were in again, this time in support of the 7th Australian Division at Balikpapan. This was the major Jap oil base in Borneo. Its fall sealed the fate of the Japs in Borneo who took to the hills in disorganized small parties. The 593d Boat Battalion then initiated the usual small-boat lighterage work, occasionally carrying the Aussies on small end runs and reconnaissances down the coast. Then it became the Lost Battalion of the Amphibians. The 3d Brigade wanted the battalion back to get ready for the invasion of Japan but the Aussie high command said their two divisions in Borneo could not exist without the LCMs of the Amphibians to run rations to their isolated detachments. After many weeks' delay, the LCMs were finally transferred to the Australians and the boat units were free to proceed to Manila. But even then there was no shipping going to Manila and a long wait followed. By October 1945 the 3d Brigade had gone to Japan. It was late in November before the "lost battalion" finally got to the Philippines and eventually home. Thus ended the mopping up of the Philippines and Borneo.

14

1st Brigade to Okinawa

After the 1st Brigade had been shifted from the European Theater to the Pacific, the War Department released the following press dispatch:

> The War Department announced today the participation in the Okinawa campaign of one of the first Army units to see combat action in both the European and the Pacific theaters. The unit is the 1st Engineer Special Brigade, a shore engineer command organization which began its career of D-days on the beaches near Oran, North Africa, November 8, 1942.
>
> The 1st Brigade headquarters took over command responsibility for beach supply operations on Okinawa on April 1, having been shipped from Europe through the United States in February of this year.
>
> Activated under the former Engineer Amphibian Command at Camp Edwards, Massachusetts, June 27, 1942, the Brigade was headed overseas within one month of its activation date. After the landings at Oran, the 1st was converted from an amphibian to a shore engineer organization; they helped move the Seventh Army across the beaches at Gela, Sicily, where it had been said that the American Army "first demonstrated to the world that it could conduct a major invasion without the aid of captured port facilities." In September 1943, the Brigade was attached to the Fifth Army for the Gulf of Salerno landings.

A simple stone monument on Utah Beach built by the surviving Engineers honors the men of the 1st Brigade who died to help make the Normandy landings succeed. For two days their section of the beach was swept by direct enfilading fire from German gun positions which were protected against our offshore naval shelling. In the face of this fire, the Engineers never faltered in their responsibility for getting supplies across the beaches to the assault teams moving inland, although some of the engineer battalions sustained thirty per cent casualties.

With the redeployment of the 1st Brigade to the Pacific, Army Engineers now have three amphibian brigades in that theater. [Note: Actually there were four, including the 4th Brigade.] The 2d and 3d Special Brigades have been carrying out the numerous "shore-to-shore" combat landings by means of which General MacArthur has been splitting up and isolating Japanese garrisons in the Philippines. The organization of the 1st Engineer Brigade, however, is considerably different from that of the 2d and 3d. The 2d and 3d are made up of Engineer Boat and Shore Regiments, three to each Brigade, plus a Boat Maintenance Battalion, Brigade Headquarters, and attached Ordnance, Quartermaster, Medical, and Signal units, with a total strength per brigade of between 7000 and 7500 officers and men. The only permanent part of the 1st Brigade, however, is the Headquarters Company. The necessary Engineer combat battalions, Quartermaster, Signal, Medical, Transportation, and Ordnance units are attached to this Brigade Headquarters to constitute a balanced shore party force for a particular operation.

The 5th and 6th Brigades participated with the 1st in the Normandy landings, but no announcement has been made of their subsequent operations. The 6th Brigade was last announced as supervising coal mining operations for the Army in Germany.

The 1st Engineer Special Brigade was still engaged in port operations in Normandy when orders came on December 7, 1944, for it to proceed to the Pacific Theater. Unfortunately though, due to shortage of shipping and to the continued need for engineer troops in the European Theater, only the Headquarters and Headquarters Company were included in the order. After staging in England, the brigade embarked December 23, and made a quick crossing, arriving at Fort Dix, New Jersey, on December 30. After twenty-seven days' leave, the brigade reassembled at Ft. Lewis, Washington, to stage for the Western Pacific. Colonel B. B. Talley commanded this brigade.

Because of the nearness of the Okinawa target date, an advance detachment of the brigade headquarters was flown to Leyte to study the coming operations. The brigade's vehicles were waterproofed, loaded with unit equipment, and then taken aboard the USS *Achenar* (AKA-53) which proceeded direct to Okinawa, arriving on D-day, April 1, 1945. The very next morning an enemy plane crash-dived the AKA-53, inflicting considerable damage. Luckily, no brigade equipment was seriously damaged and a few days later it was all safely unloaded.

The invasion of Okinawa was like pushing a fist down a lion's mouth. At that time few realized that the Jap lion was definitely weakening in his homeland under the combined effects of naval blockade and devastating air attack. Most thought that on his home ground the Japs would fight even harder than in the outlying islands. So the Okinawa landing was looked on as a very difficult job, one to be expensive to both the Navy and the Army.

Only forty days after the initial landing on Iwo Jima, the Tenth Army under General Buckner was to crack the hard nut of Okinawa. The wide dispersion of both troops and shipping made the planning most difficult. Units embarked from the West Coast, Hawaii, Leyte, and the South Pacific. The assembly of the many varied units was finally completed and rehearsals were held in Leyte and in Hawaii. After the seizure of an outlying island on March 26, the Army operation plan called for an assault on April 1 with two corps abreast, each corps with two divisions in the assault, one Marine division afloat in Army reserve and one infantry division on Ulithi in Area reserve. The XXIV Corps with the 7th and 96th Infantry Divisions was to land on the right, the III Amphibious Corps with the 1st and 6th Marine Division on the left.

The plan for shore operations of the Okinawa campaign was based on a progressive development from Division shore party to Corps and then to Army. The transition from Division to Corps was to take place shortly after the respective corps commanders assumed command ashore. The transition from Corps to Army was to occur near the completion of the unloading of the assault shipping. It was not until the last phase, the Army phase, that the 1st Engineer Special Brigade was to assume responsibility for shore operations.

The XXIV Corps shore party was organized at Leyte under the command of Colonel James A. Cunningham, with Lieutenant Colonel Earl Houston (originally the commander of the 561st Engineer Boat Maintenance Company in England and North Africa) as deputy.

This shore party with headquarters at Dulag, Philippine Islands, began planning for the operation at Okinawa during the latter part of February 1945, and continued until embarking aboard the LSV6[1] (*Ozark*) on March 20, 1945, in Leyte Gulf. The XXIV Corps shore party had no active part in the planning of the personnel, equipment and materials required in the initial landings at Okinawa. The infantry divisions were assigned the engineer shore party troops prior to embarking and the responsibility for the initial landings and the supplying of the divisions were the responsibility of each division commander. The Corps shore party was to take over shore operations on orders from the Commanding General, XXIV Corps. This actually took place on D plus 2. The commanding officer of the XXIV Corps shore party thus had many problems of reorganization, policy, etc., to iron out during the most critical period of a beach operation.

It should be mentioned that heretofore, in the Central Pacific operations, engineer shore troops had served as their respective division shore parties, and had continued inland with their divisions, as division troops. New units usually came in to take over the shore operations. This plan differed from that used by General MacArthur who recognized the necessity for continuous shore operations by the same engineer unit which had landed on D-day.

It appears that more definite planning on the shore party organization prior to the operation would have been valuable in order that all personnel at Okinawa would have a clear conception of their mission. Actually what happened was that a group of strangers met on the beaches of Okinawa on D plus 2 and attempted to work out a plan of shore party organization during this critical period. This led to some confusion on the beaches and in the dumps where supplies were sorely needed. During the assault phase numerous landing craft on the beach were not unloaded in the best manner. Some craft, only partly unloaded, were ordered to retract and await further orders from the Navy before beaching again. The majority of these craft were combat-loaded with critical materials and supplies for the various infantry divisions ashore. These supplies were vital to the fighting troops and were scheduled to be in the division dumps by D plus 3. The main reason these supplies were not unloaded on schedule was the lack of DUKWs and LVTs available to shore party units to transfer the supplies from the craft over the reefs to the dumps. It appears there were sufficient DUKWs and LVTs on the island but the divisions took many of the loaded DUKWs and LVTs inland with the combat teams as mobile dumps and did not allow these vehicles to unload in organized dumps and return to the beach for use as ferry craft over the reef. Had they been used to the best advantage, the shortage of supplies would not have been so acute.

The reefs at Okinawa generally extend about 600 feet seaward from the shore and are very rugged. Landing craft that were allowed to beach on the reef at high tide and stay there during a low tide were subject to severe damage to their hulls, due to coral pinnacles punching holes in their bottom skins. The only vehicles that could be used satisfactorily to unload the initial landing craft were DUKWs and LVTs.

Another factor that played an important part in the operation of the Corps Shore Party in the initial phase of this campaign was the lack of proper equipment for the Engineer Shore Party troops, port crews, truck companies, etc. As has been previously stated, the divisions were responsible for the space allotted the Combat Engineers who were used on the initial Shore Party operations. Naturally, a division commander had the main objective of fighting the Japs and not the build-up of supplies for the Corps and Army phase. Consequently, the engineer troops who landed the assault divisions and who were to be diverted to corps shore party troops in the Corps phase were not allowed to bring in the first convoy much of the heavy equipment necessary for beach operation. The majority of the heavy equipment of the shore party, such as crawler cranes, truck cranes and tractors arrived in the build-up convoy, no part of which reached Okinawa before D plus 12 and some not until D plus 30. The well-planned scheme for road nets and for dumps and for jetties over the reefs had to be greatly curtailed or delayed due to this critical lack of heavy equipment. One engineer combat group arrived with only one crawler crane and one 6x6 truck in the assault convoy of the 27th Division.

The 1165th Engineer Combat Group was the shore party for the 27th Infantry Division and had as its mission the landing of this division on Orange Beach. A complete breakdown in the movement of this division over the beach was reported to have followed due to the lack of equipment needed by this engineer group to execute its mission. All the units assigned to the XXIV Corps shore party were considerably under strength in personnel, especially the 504th Port Battalion and the 34th Engineer Combat Battalion of the 1165th Engineer Combat Group.

The above discussion of the difficulties reported to have been encountered by the XXIV Corps shore party at Okinawa has been included in this book to show what will happen if improvised and more or less amateurish shore parties are employed instead of the trained professional shore parties as developed by the Engineer Special Brigade in World War II. No operation requires more careful engineer planning than unloading an army on an enemy-held open beach.

It was not until D plus 8 (April 9) that shore operations on both beaches and the depot operations on South Beach passed to the control of the 1st Engineer Special Brigade under Colonel B. B. Talley. Improvement in the shore situation soon began to appear. The XXIV Corps shore party was inactivated and redesignated the South Beach Shore Party. The 1st Brigade, it should be recalled, consisted only of the Headquarters and Headquarters Company of the original 1st Engineer Special Brigade, all its regimental troops having been left in Europe. Transition from Corps to Army control was completed by April 20. After that date the 1st Brigade controlled all unloading at Okinawa, both Marine and Army.

During the period D plus 1 to D plus 7 activities of the brigade were confined to organized reconnaissance of the beach areas to verify the suitability of locations selected for dump and shore installations, road-nets, communication lines and command post. The development of the beaches during the Division and Corps phases was observed and plans for consolidation under Army control worked out in detail. The transition from Corps to Army was made much smoother than from Divisions to Corps.

Enemy infantry operations against the areas under the control of the 1st Brigade were limited to individual or small groups of soldiers attempting to disrupt operations in the various dumps. By reason of the difficult terrain and the numerous caves throughout the area, our patrols would periodically and thoroughly comb a dump and its surrounding area, only to have sniper fire recommence the next evening. Because of their size the ammunition dumps were particularly vulnerable to these attacks, and on several occasions work was halted when truck drivers and crane operators were fired upon by snipers. As soon as armed personnel in the dump would start in the direction of the firing it would cease and the snipers would disappear. There appeared to be no organized groups nor tactics in these skirmishes but merely the usual fanatical resistance of one or two Japs. On several occasions enemy infiltrators captured by the front-line troops reported that they had been sent to disrupt operations in the rear areas, and then to join other scattered forces in the northern section of the island.

Occasionally infiltration by enemy landing parties caused a cessation of shore operations until these landing parties were disposed of. The continuous enemy air attacks greatly curtailed beach operations, as it was frequently necessary to "smoke" the fleet for as long as six to eight hours at a time. Smoke pots and generators were located on the beach with the wind blowing smoke over the fleet. The smoking of the anchorage area was so thorough that it shut down all DUKW and ferrycraft operation during this period. The continual night bombing and falling flak caused a great deal of damage to shore party personnel and installations. The daylight suicide attacks on ships lying in the harbor adjacent to the beach hampered beach operations, on several occasions the aircraft overrunning the ships and diving into the beach area. Naval gunfire firing at low-flying enemy planes opposite the beach area was another nuisance but did not occur often enough to do excessive damage. The rainy weather during the latter part of April and the first of May mired the roads and made the movement of supplies from the beach area to the front line almost impossible. Supplies then had to be landed by ferrycraft at Noshomota, just north of Naha. These landings were made under direct enemy fire and some casualties to shore party personnel and damaged equipment were sustained.

On one occasion the use by the enemy of artillery fire against the ships anchored offshore was reported. One evening twelve rounds of 150mm artillery were fired from the direction of Naha at two ammunition ships anchored at inshore berths. Both ships moved quickly to a different anchorage and avoided damage. The enemy on several occasions shelled the Katena Airfield with a 150mm gun. While no damage was sustained by the nearby Amphibians, the Marine air group suffered casualties, and a number of planes were destroyed and damaged.

Enemy air activity fell into two classes: first the suicide attacks on ships, and second the aerial bombing of beaches and other installations. Suicide attacks involved diving a plane directly onto the superstructure of a ship. Several of these attacks caused serious damage. The aerial bombardment was aimed most frequently at the Yontan and Katena Airfields; however, the proximity of the 1st Brigade's installations made them vulnerable to hits due to bombing inaccuracies. The military police battalion of the III Amphibious Corps service group received casualties from bomb fragments on several occasions. The bivouac area of this unit was but a short distance from the Yontan field. Several fires were started among the civilian buildings in the town of Sobe and several civilians were killed. No military damage was sustained. Shore installations in rear of Purple and Orange Beaches received four to six bombs at 4:00 A.M. on May 16, resulting in 15 casualties, and damage to several trucks and other pieces of engineer equipment.

While not bearing directly upon installations of the 1st Brigade the use by the enemy of suicide rafts and swimmers should also be mentioned. These personnel, mainly single individuals, would swim considerable distances with explosive charges strapped to their backs, or push a crude raft with the charges placed thereon. The use of flares and a perimeter guard of small craft with alert machine gunners were able to frustrate most of these attempts to damage ships. One ship while being discharged received serious damage to propeller and shaft from one of these sorties. Apparently the suicide craft followed the DUKWs to the ship, placed a charge or charges near the rudder or propeller and withdrew in darkness.

The number of units attached to the brigade varied from 149 during the first week to a maximum of 185 on May 7. Practically all these units had been inoperative (in staging areas or afloat) for over two months. The administration of this heterogeneous task group was therefore no easy matter. The strength of the brigade reached a maximum of 27,353.

It had become obvious, early in the landing of the assault waves, that the fringing coral reefs would be a serious detriment to landing operations. It was necessary, due to the very hard and unpredictable beaching surface of the reef, to prohibit beaching LCVPs and LCMs as soon as sufficient LVTs were ashore to ferry from landing craft to the beach. DUKWs initially could negotiate the reef only at a maximum hazard to hulls and tires. Attempts by the underwater demolition teams to blow channels for landing craft through the reef had proven ineffective and were thenceforth confined to blowing small channels for one-way DUKW traffic. Nonamphibious vehicles could not travel from beach to reef during most stages of the tide. Gapping of the seawall, initial road construction, mine clearance, and obstacle clearance were carried out expeditiously.

Construction of sand causeways from beach to reef was begun on D-day although little was accomplished until more heavy engineer equipment arrived. Causeway construction, improvement, and maintenance continued throughout the operation. Causeways of cubicle ponton and sand construction, adequate for two-way vehicle traffic with pierheads parallel to shore at the reef were eventually constructed in the following locations:

Green 1. An earthen causeway constructed for LSTs exclusively, operational from May 1 to May 20. Capacity: 3 LSTs.

Red 1. A U-shaped floating pier made up of 556 9' x 9' ponton cubicles. This causeway was installed during the first week of operations and was moved about May 1 to Green 1½ Beach. Causeway was moved from Green 1½ Beach to permanent installations at East Machinato starting on May 28. Capacity: 3 LSTs or 4 LSMs, plus 4 to 6 LCTs, barges, or LCMs.

Yellow 3. A floating ponton pier installed about May 1 on the north bank of the Bisha Gawa for unloading LCMs and barges. Capacity: 1 to 14 barges, LCMs, or 4 LCTs.

Orange 1. Two sand-and-cubicle ponton causeways; begun D-day, completed D plus 4. Capacity: 1 LSM or LST.

Orange 2. Same as Orange 1.

Purple 1. One sand causeway; begun D-day, completed D plus 4. Continuously widened and improved, pontons added May 25. Capacity: 6 LCTs.

Purple 2. Two sand-and-cubicle ponton causeways, one
sand causeway; all begun on D-day, completed D plus
4. Capacity: 1 LSM or LST.
White 1. One sand causeway for LSTs only; begun D-day,
completed D plus 5. Capacity: 2 LSTs.

None of the causeways on Hagushi beaches was inoperative for
a period exceeding twenty-four hours throughout the entire period. Channels for one-way DUKW traffic were blown through the
reef on six of the beaches.

An artificial sheltered basin for simultaneous unloading of 12
LCTs was constructed on White 1 Beach. Work on this project
started on April 20 but progressed very slowly due to lack of equipment until May 10 at which time 1 rooter, 4 D-8 dozers, and 3
carryalls were allocated to the task. The project was completed May
27 and consisted of an earthen-diked basin cut in the coral beach
deep enough during neap high tides to permit entry of fully laden
LCTs. LCTs were able to beach in this basin and to continue to
discharge during heavy weather.

Transfer barges, each equipped with a three-ton gasoline-
powered crane, were beached or anchored at the reef and proved
effective, particularly in the early phases, for the transfer of cargo
from landing craft and lighter barges to trucks at low tide and to
DUKWs and LVTs at high tide. Transfer barges diminished in importance as good beaching areas were developed for direct unloading from craft to truck during all tidal stages.

Transfer points, for the transfer of cargo from DUKWs to
trucks, were established behind certain beaches in order to decrease the turnaround time on the DUKW trips and thereby increase their daily unloading capacity. When established, these
transfer points approximately doubled the daily discharge rate of
a DUKW company.

During the period April 9 to May 31, when the 1st Brigade was
in charge of unloading, a total of 1,200,000 measurement tons
was discharged and well over 12,000 casualties were evacuated
over the beaches. More than 16,000 vehicles were unloaded. Battle

casualties in the 1st Brigade and attached troops were 12 killed and 72 wounded; in addition 28 officers and men were drowned during the hazardous unloading.

The 1st Brigade was commended by Major General Fred C. Wallace for its outstanding performance of duty and achievement in the execution of the Shore Party operations from April 9 to May 31. The most noteworthy lesson of the shore party operations at Okinawa was the value of trained and organized shore engineers as exemplified by the work of the 1st Engineer Special Brigade after it took over on April 9.

When relieved by the Island Command, thoughts of the brigade ran to the invasion of Japan but VJ-day changed all that. Instead, the 1st Brigade found itself assigned to the occupation of Korea. Its major attached element was the 532d Engineer Boat and Shore Regiment of the 2d Brigade. The occupation landing went off well on September 12, 1945. Here the 1st Brigade continued in charge of shore operations until it was inactivated in January 1946. Its last commanding officer was Colonel Robert J. Kasper, formerly of the 2d Brigade.

The 1st Engineer Special Brigade had the most extended field of operations of any of the Special Brigades—Cape Cod to England to North Africa to Sicily to Italy to Normandy to Leyte to Okinawa to Korea. While it did not have as many landings to its credit as the 2d Brigade, the volume of its shore operations in Normandy and Okinawa exceeded those of any other brigade. No one can say the 1st Brigade did not pay its way manyfold in World War II.

NOTES

[1] Landing Ship, Vehicle, the latest type of naval landing craft.

15
Victory, Occupation and Home

In June 1945 plans for the invasion of Japan began to take form.

It has since been announced to the public that the invasion was to be in two main pushes, one by the Sixth Army on the southern island of Kyushu, with a later push by the Eighth Army against the very doors of Tokyo. When GHQ figured up the number of Engineer Amphibian brigades which would be needed for the two operations, the total came to nine brigades. Actually only three and the headquarters of a fourth were available so other plans had to be made. There was neither time nor shipping to bring the 5th and 6th Brigades from Europe and anyhow these brigades had had no amphibian work since the invasion of Normandy. They had been converted to engineer construction troops rather than maintained as amphibian specialists. Moreover, most of the original Amphibs had left the units either by transfer or by return to the United States because of high points.

At the end of June 1945 the Amphibian brigades in the western Pacific were widely dispersed. The 2d Brigade was operating on every major island of the Philippines, supplying outlying islands but mainly getting reequipped and rehabilitated for the invasion of Japan. The brigade headquarters was near the headquarters of Eighth Army on Leyte but was slated to move to Luzon to be near Headquarters XI Corps with which it was scheduled to participate in the Kyushu landing.

The 3d Brigade was even more widely dispersed than the 2d. Its headquarters was way to the rear on Biak but was slated to move to Batangas in southern Luzon. The Boat Battalion of the 593d was with the Aussies in Borneo; the 593d Shore Battalion was still at Zamboanga on Mindanao. The 543d had its regimental headquarters at Zamboanga but two boat companies were still at Dagupan on Luzon, and other detachments were at Biak and at Morotai. The 533d was at Davao and Cotabato on Mindanao but with a detachment also on Biak. To assemble these scattered forces to stage for the invasion of Japan was no easy matter.

The 4th Brigade was better off for it had finally gotten its long-lost boat battalion back from Australia and was well concentrated in the Manila area. There it had been kept busy on port work but was moved back to Lingayen in August to get ready for the invasion of Japan. The 534th Engineer Boat and Shore Regiment was finally assigned to support the 25th Infantry Division; the 544th to support the 33d Infantry Division; and the 594th to support the 43d Division.

The 1st Brigade, which really consisted only of the Headquarters and Headquarters Company, was still on Okinawa engaged in running the port with numerous attached DUKW and port companies. It was decided that it could not be released from Okinawa, at least not for the initial landing on Japan.

The 692d and the 411th Engineer Base Shop Battalions were setting up a new barge and LCM assembly plant at Batangas, having moved up from Milne Bay and Finschhafen. High pressure was being used to get craft assembled in time for the projected invasion.

At a conference at GHQ at Manila on June 25, 1945, attended by all three brigade commanders, Generals Heavey, Hutchings and Ogden, a plan was worked out by which the 2d and 4th were to support the Sixth Army in the first landing and then be released as soon as practicable to return to the Philippines and stage with the Eighth Army for its Tokyo invasion. Sixth Army objected to this plan, saying that in view of the unknown quality of the Jap resistance in his homeland, it would not be able to release the two brigades on time. The 3d Brigade was scheduled to join the 2d and 4th and all three brigades would support the second major landing,

the Tokyo landing. It appeared some divisions would have to impro-
vise shore parties in the absence of Amphibian Engineers. If the
landings had come off, the Amphibian Engineers would have had
the busiest times of their careers. It was indeed gratifying to them
to know that they were badly needed for this final big show, but all
realized it would probably be the toughest job of their long careers.

By July 4 some inkling began to trickle through that the invasion of Japan scheduled for November 1 might never occur. B-29
aviators from Guam sent thousands of dollars to Manila betting
that the war would be over by September 1. Yet not many really
believed this. Few knew how really effective had been the submarine blockade of Japan and how devastating the B-29 bombings
and fires which swept Tokyo, Yokohama and other cities. So the
Amphibians continued preparation at full speed for the landings
on Kyushu. Every craft, every dozer, every crane and every weapon
must be in perfect order for this critical job.

When peace did come, everyone was thankful. No one wanted
to make that combat landing on Japan. There was no longer any
novelty or excitement in an amphibious assault on an enemy shore.
The men were tired and longing for home. Yet it was gratifying to
know that the Amphibian Engineers had proved themselves so well
in New Guinea and the Philippines that nine brigades were wanted
for the invasion of Japan when only three were available, and that
General MacArthur had recommended that the Engineer Special
Brigade organization be continued in the Regular Army after the
war because of "their outstanding contribution to the success of
amphibious operations in the Western Pacific."

Peace brought no rest to the Amphibians. The 2d Brigade soon
found itself assigned to the initial task forces to land in Japan and
Korea for the occupation. The 2d Brigade less the 532d Regiment,
but with the 594th of the 4th Engineer Special Brigade attached,
landed at Yokohama with Eighth Army. The 592d Engineer Boat
and Shore Regiment landed the first seaborne troops, the 1st Cavalry Division, on September 4, 1945, exactly two years after the
532d's landing with the Australians at distant Lae in New Guinea.
A few days later the 532d Regiment of the 2d Brigade landed in

Korea in support of XXIV Corps. This regiment there came under
the 1st Engineer Special Brigade which had moved from Okinawa
to Korea.

It was not long before the 3d Brigade and the rest of the 4th
Brigade staged from the Philippines to various parts of Japan. The
Amphibians really covered the Japanese homeland, all the way
from Hokkaido on the north to Kyushu on the south. In addition
to the sight-seeing all the GIs engaged in, the Amphibs were particularly anxious to see the beaches on which they had been slated
to land in the invasion of Japan. What they saw made them all the
happier that the invasion did not come off. Hollow as the internal
strength of Japan might have become, there was no question but
that their beaches were well defended. Would the Japs have stuck
to their defenses or would the naval bombardment and the terrific
rocket barrages have made them abandon the beaches as they had
done so frequently before? The Kyushu beaches were difficult from
another angle, surf. The Sagami beaches off Yokohama were not
particularly difficult but the immediate shore was either a bluff
with many obstacles or a river valley cut by many tributaries and
fringed with swamps. The famous Buddhist shrine island of
Enoshima in Sagami Bay had been turned into a veritable Gibralter.
Yes, the Amphibs were mighty glad they did not have to assault
those beaches!

The Japs were so docile and the damage to their docks so little
(our bombers purposely spared them) that the Amphibs soon ran
out of work in Japan. High-point men were shipped home as
quickly as ships were available. On October 15 the 2d Brigade
turned its Port of Yokohama job over to the newly formed Port
Command and prepared to move home as a unit, as it had been
selected in accordance with General MacArthur's recommendation,
to be a unit of the post-war Army. Actually though, it was December 3 before the shipping situation allowed its departure for home.
During this interim, the 2d Brigade dropped from its normal
strength of 7,800 to only 300 but then expanded back to 4,600 as
men rushed to enlist in the Regular Army to join the Brigade and
go back to the States. The 3d Brigade followed the 2d in only a few

days and was inactivated in January 1946 in California. The 4th Brigade spread out in the Tokyo, Nagoya and Kobe areas, had to remain in Japan to carry on the occupation just as the 532d Engineer Boat and Shore Regiment of the 2d Brigade had to remain in Korea. At this writing all of these units are either inactivated or at home. The home station of the 2d Engineer Special Brigade appropriately is Fort Ord, California, from which the 2d, 3d, and 4th Brigades all staged for the Western Pacific.

In the meantime the 1st Brigade was inactivated in Korea in January 1946, by Colonel Kasper (formerly of the 2d Brigade) who was the last of the many commanders of the 1st Engineer Special Brigade. The 5th and 6th Brigades had returned from Europe in October 1945. It had been decided that they would not go to the Pacific as the 1st Brigade had done. These two brigades, both activated in England and with the Normandy beaches as their crowning amphibious accomplishment, came "home" to Carrabelle (Camp Gordon Johnston, Florida), old training ground of the 2d and 3d and 4th Brigades, to be inactivated. The 5th Brigade, then under Colonel W. D. Bridges, closed out its career on October 20, 1945, a year to the day after the 2d Brigade had landed at Leyte. The 6th Brigade, under Colonel Howard Ker, was inactivated a few days later.

The men with the famous blue-and-gold Amphibian shoulder patch spread out in every direction headed for home, their job over and mighty well done. Starting out in a new field of warfare they had shown versatility, courage, efficiency, and heroism. Many of them had made the supreme sacrifice—in North Africa, in Sicily and Italy, in Normandy, in New Guinea and New Britain, in the Admiralties and Morotai, in the Philippines and Borneo, and even in Japan and Korea.

UP RAMP, you Amphibian Engineers! Your job is done. You have lived up to and even exceeded the high traditions of the Corps of Engineers, of the Army and of your Country.

APPENDIX A
CHRONOLOGY

1942

MAY

6   Corregidor surrenders.

7   Joint Chiefs of Staff issue orders directing creation of Amphibian Engineer units.

      Jap invasion of Australia turned back in battle of Coral Sea.

JUNE

5   Engineer Amphibian Command activated at Camp Edwards.

7   Jap thrust at Hawaiian Islands decisively beaten in battle of Midway.

10   Japs occupy Attu and Kiska in the Aleutian Islands.

15   1st Engineer Amphibian Brigade activated at Camp Edwards.

20   2d Engineer Amphibian Brigade activated at Camp Edwards.

21   Tobruk falls to Rommel's Army.

28   Germans launch huge offensive in Russia.

JULY

5   Rommel is halted at El Alamein

240

AUGUST

7   1st Brigade leaves New York for Scotland, on short notice.

1st Marine Division lands on Guadalcanal.

8   3d Engineer Amphibian Brigade activated at Camp Edwards.

19   Costly raid on Dieppe by Canadians

25   Battle of Stalingrad begins.

25-31 Allies drive off Jap attempt to seize Milne Bay.

SEPTEMBER

15   First big landing exercise at Cape Cod. 2d ESB lands 36th Division on Martha's Vineyard in large-scale maneuver.

Japs repulsed in attempt to take Port Moresby by drive over Owen Stanley Mountains.

OCTOBER

1-31   2d Brigade moves to Carrabelle.

Battles rage at Stalingrad, in Europe and Guadalcanal in Western Pacific.

24-27 Alert reaches Carrabelle for 2d Brigade to go to Fort Ord, Calif.

Rommel decisively defeated at El Alamein by British Eighth Army which included the 9th Australian Division.

25   3d Brigade alerted at Cape Cod for move to Carrabelle.

Task force loads in Scotland for the North Africa invasion.

NOVEMBER

8   1st Brigade at Oran.

American and British forces invade French North Africa.

21   1st Brigade and 411th Base Shop Battalion are established at Fort Ord.

Beginning of struggle to oust Japs from Buna-Gona area of New Guinea.

24 Siege of Stalingrad broken.

DECEMBER

25 Allies bogged down in Tunisia.

1943

JANUARY

19 Buna-Gona costly fight ends with fall of Sananaoada in New Guinea.

23 Cadre for 4th Brigade leaves Carrabelle for Fort Devens, causing considerable shuffling of assignments.

British Eighth Army takes Tripoli.

31 2d Brigade embarks at San Francisco for Australia.

Stalingrad battle ends with surrender of German Sixth Army.

FEBRUARY

9 Jap resistance on Guadalcanal ceases.

14 Americans defeated by Rommel at Kasserine Pass in Tunisia.

APRIL

7 First LCVP launched by 411th at Cairns, Australia.

MAY

11 First amphibian engineers (592d) land in New Guinea—at Port Moresby to operate boats to Lakekamu River.

7th Infantry Division lands on Attu.

12   Decisive Allied victory in Tunisia.

JUNE

30   Stranded boatmen of 532d EBSR at Nassau Bay save day for MacKechnie Task Force by repelling Jap night attack. Lieutenants Ely and Keeley and seven amphibians killed in desperate fight.

Landings on Woodlark, Kiriwina, Nassau Bay and New Georgia start major Allied offensive in SWPA. 2d Brigade loses 30 craft in towering surf at Nassau Bay but safely lands every passenger from 43d Division.

JULY

5   Craft and engineers of both 532d and 542d are kept busy supplying the advance on Salamaua.

Germans launch great offensive in Russia directed at Kursk.

10   Allies invade Sicily.

AUGUST

7   German thrust in Russia halted and thrown back.

SEPTEMBER

3   Italy surrenders.

4   532d EBSR lands its own Shore Party from Morobe and supports Australians from Milne Bay.

9th Australian Division participates in first large amphibian attack in SWPA, a few miles east of Lae.

9   Part of 1st Brigade is in the action.

Allies land at Salerno on Italian mainland.

11   542d Boat is first to land on Salamaua Peninsula.

Salamaua, New Guinea falls.

16   Lae, New Guinea, captured by Aussies after 532d
       EBSR takes battalion around mouth of
       flooded Busu River in their LCVPs.

22   532d Boats go back to Lae to bring up another
       Australian brigade of infantry.

       532d EBSR assists 9th Australian Division in a
       surprise landing north of Finschhafen.

OCTOBER

1   Fifth Army occupies Naples.

2   532d boats support the operation

       Aussies capture Finschhafen.

NOVEMBER

1   1119th Engineer Group arrives in South Wales
       and is redesignated 5th Engineer Special Bri-
       gade.

       3d Marine Division lands on Bougainville. (No
       Army Amphibians.)

6   Russians capture Kiev.

21-23 Tarawa and Makin, Gilbert Islands, captured.

DECEMBER

15   592d EBSR helps 112th Cavalry Regiment land
       at Arawe, New Britain.

26   2d ESB task force occupies Long Island.

       592d EBSR and 2d ESB Support Battery partici-
       pates with 1st Marine Division in landing at
       Cape Cloucester.

1944

JANUARY

2   542d EBSR goes in at Saidor.

126th RCT lands at Saidor.

Shore Battalion, 533d EBSR takes over operation of Sixth Army base beach at Cape Cretin from 2d ESB.

Sixth Army Headquarters completes set-up at Cape Cretin.

9   Russia reenters Poland.

22   Anglo-American VI Corps lands at Anzio near Rome.

31   Central Pacific forces invade Kwajalein in the Marshall Islands.

FEBRUARY

1   First Army issues Operation Plan "Neptune" for invasion of Normandy.

15   Headquarters, Engineer Special Brigade Group activated in England.

New Zealanders occupy Green Island southeast of Rabaul.

18-21   533d Boat Battalion moves via Oro Bay to Finschhafen.

19-22   Eniwetok in Marshall Islands captured.

28   Company A, 563d EBM Battalion arrives at Borgen Bay, New Britain.

29   Shore and boat elements of 592d EBSR and 2d Brigade Support Battery assist.

1st Cavalry Division reconnaissance force lands at Los Negros, Admiralty Islands.

MARCH

10   2d Engineer Brigade Support Battery in several small landings in Admiralties.

Japs from Burma invade northeast India.

11   Company A, 533d EBSR boats land 1st Marines at Linga-Linga Plantation, Eleonora Bay, New Britain.

15   5th ESB completes Exercise Fox with 1st Infantry Division in Cornwall.

Fifth Army stopped cold in Italy by German defense of Cassino.

21   Russians reenter Rumania.

26   Marines land at Emirau completing encirclement of Rabaul area.

APRIL

19   General MacArthur brought ashore in Company A, 533d LCVP at Borgen Bay.

20   4th ESB closes out at Carrabelle.

22   542d EBSR supports 24th Division at Tanahmerah Bay.

24th, 32d, and 41st Divisions land at Aitape and Hollandia on New Guinea. MacArthur's largest operation to date goes off perfectly.

532d EBSR supports 41st Division at Humboldt Bay.

543d EBSR supports 32d Division at Aitape.

MAY

1   594th Boat Battalion arrives at Milne Bay.

3-7   1st ESB, 5th ESB, 6th ESB all busy on rehearsals and getting equipment ready for invasion.

Dress rehearsal for invasion of Normandy.

11   Allies resume offensive in Italy.

19   Company A, 542d and 593d support landing.

163d Combat Team invades Wakde Island and nearby shore of New Guinea.

20   4th ESB opens Brigade CP at Oro Bay.

27   542d EBSR supports landing.

Remainder of 41st Division lands on Biak Island.

28   534th Boat Battalion in full operation at Balimba barge assembly plant at Brisbane, Australia.

JUNE

1   108th RCT moved from Borgen Bay to Arawe in A and Company boats, 533d EBSR.

Embarkation for invasion of Normandy begins.

6   1st Brigade on Utah Beach; 5th and 6th Brigades on Omaha Beach.

Allies invade Normandy.

15   V Amphibious Corps lands on Saipan. First B-29 raids on Japan.

19   All three brigades intensify their efforts on Normandy beaches.

Three-day storm hits Normandy beaches.

27   Cherbourg captured by American VII Corps.

JULY

2   2d ESB Support Battery and 3d ESB participate in Noemfoor landing.

158 RCT seizes Noemfoor Island,

13   Scheduled shore-to-shore attack of 124th RCT (31st Division) from Aitape to Naparake canceled because of Jap breakthrough on the Driniumor River.

20   III Amphibious Corps assaults Guam.

25   Americans break out of Normandy beachhead.

30   543d EBSR lends support. Amphibians operating 1,400 miles from their base at Milne Bay.

6th Division lands at Sansapor near Northern tip of New Guinea.

AUGUST

15   4th ESB relieves 3d ESB in New Britain.

Southern France invaded by American Seventh Army.

25   4th ESB trains at Oro Bay with the 11th Airborne Division.

Paris liberated.

SEPTEMBER

10   Americans cross German border.

15   4th Brigade in action.
      Morotai, Dutch East Indies, and Peleliu, West-
      ern Carolines, invaded.

OCTOBER

20   2d Brigade supports landing.
      Sixth Army invades Leyte.

21   First Army captures Aachen.

NOVEMBER

19   ESBs close out Omaha Beach.

DECEMBER

1   6th ESB takes over defense of Cotentin Penin-
      sula.

7   2d Engineer Brigade Support Battery and detach-
      ment of 592d EBSR help 77th Division.
      77th Division lands at Ormoc on western Leyte.

15   532d EBSR in Mindoro invasion.

25   592d ESB assists at Palompon.
      Landing at Palompon closes last Jap exit from
      Leyte.

1945

JANUARY

9   4th ESB, two regiments of 3d ESB, and small boat
      detachment of 2d ESB. 592d EBSR supports
      both Nasugbu and Subic Bay landings.
      Sixth Army lands at Lingayen Gulf on 6 beaches.
      11th Airborne Division lands at Nasugbu. XI
      Corps lands at Subic Bay.

FEBRUARY

1   Sixth Army enters Manila.

19 Marines land on Iwo Jima.

25 3d ESB Convoy service to guerrilla-held points and PT refueling station on northern Luzon inaugurated.

26 542d boats badly shot up on this landing. Biri Island, north of Samar, is taken.

28 532d EBSR from Mindoro supports 186th. 186th RCT lands on Palawan Island.

MARCH

7   4th ESB moves from Dagupan to Manila. Remagen bridgehead across Rhine seized by 9th Armored Division.

10 543d EBSR in this landing. 41st Division lands at Zamboanga.

18 542d EBSR furnishes amphibian support. 40th Division invades Panay.

23 Main crossing of the lower Rhine.

27 542d EBSR supports landing. Americal Division lands on Cebu.

29 542d EBSR in action. 6th ESB takes over the Ruhr coal mines. 40th Division invades Negros.

APRIL

1   5th Brigade from Paris to LeHavre. 2d Brigade supports landing at Legaspi in southern Luzon.
    Tenth Army invades Okinawa; 158th RCT lands at Lingayen; Ruhr encircled by First and Ninth Armies.

5   Caballo Island in Manila Bay falls to 592d EBSR and Fort Drum is next.
    Joint MacArthur–Nimitz command of all Pacific forces announced for invasion of Japan.

12   President Roosevelt dies.

13   1st Brigade takes over shore party at Okinawa.
        Russians capture Vienna.

22   Russians in Berlin.

25   Russians and Americans meet on the Elbe River.

MAY

1   593d Boat Bn. goes in with Australians.
        Australians land at Tarakan, Borneo.

7   Germans surrender.

8   5th ESB at LeHavre.
        V-E Day.

10   542d EBSR supports landing
        108th RCT lands at Macajalar Bay, Mindanao.

12   Headquarters, 3d ESB at Biak.
        Australians finally capture Wewak.

13   Capture of Balete Pass after bitter struggle seals
        fate of Japs on Luzon.

JUNE

10   5th ESB leaves France for Carrabelle.
        Australians land at Brunei Bay, Borneo.

21   Jap resistance ceases on Okinawa.

25-30   Using A and B Company, 533d boats, 155th RT is
        moved 100 miles up Agusan River to trap last
        Japs in northern Mindanao.

JULY

1   3d ESB furnishes boats but not shore engineers
        for Borneo invasion.
        Australians land at Balikpapan, Borneo.

4   MacArthur announces Philippines campaign
        completed.

12   B Company, 533d boats with 21st RCT make
        final amphibious assault of the War at head
        of Sarangani Bay.

Last combat landing of the war occurs in Mindanao.

AUGUST

6 533d Shore Battalion sails for Oahu from Leyte to stage for invasion of Japan.

First atomic bomb dropped on Hiroshima.

8 2d ESB Headquarters moves from Leyte to Manila to plan for invasion of Japan.

Russians enter War against Japan.

10 3d ESB Headquarters at Batangas in Southern Luzon.

Japs sue for peace, but announce certain reservations to Potsdam terms.

14 4th ESB Headquarters back at Lingayen (from Manila).

Japs accept President Truman's terms; War over.

28 First American troops land by air in Japan at Atsugi.

SEPTEMBER

1 Japs sign surrender in Tokyo Bay.

2 V-J Day.

12 2d ESB supports 1st Cavalry Division in first amphibious landing in Japan. Both 3d ESB and 4th ESB follow.

Appendix B
Troop List

TROOPS OF THE ENGINEER AMPHIBIAN COMMAND

Engineer Special Brigades sent to the Pacific had the standard boat-shore type or organization of the initial brigade sent to that theater (2d Engineer Special Brigade). The 3d and 4th were similar to the 2d Engineer Special Brigade as follows:

Brigade Hq. and Hq. Company	2d ESB	3d ESB	4th ESB
Engineer Boat & Shore Regiment	532	533	534
Engineer Boat & Shore Regiment	542	543	544
Engineer Boat & Shore Regiment	592	593	594
Engineer Boat Maintenance Bn.	562	563	564
Medical Amphibian Battalion	262	263	264
Ordnance Company	162	163	164
Ordnance Medical Maint. Co.	3498	3499	3492

Quartermaster Hq. and Hq. Company (originally QM Battalions)			
Truck Company (QM)	695	693	694
Gasoline Supply Company (QM)	189	198	199
Signal Company Amphibian	287	288	289
Amphibian Truck Company	5204		

The 1st Engineer Special Brigade was sent from Cape Cod to England as a two-regiment brigade, one a boat regiment (591st) and the other a shore regiment (531st). Other organic units were a medical battalion (261st), a boat maintenance company (561st), an ordnance platoon (161st) and a quartermaster battalion (361st). When the 1st Engineer Special Brigade redeployed from the Atlantic

252

to the Pacific, only the Brigade Headquarters and Headquarters Company were involved as the old boat and shore regiments had been reorganized into other engineer units after the Normandy invasion and remained on engineer work in the European Theater.

The 5th and 6th Engineer Special Brigades were formed in England especially to serve as shore parties for the Normandy invasion. They had no boat elements to man landing craft. Their organization was neither of the type of the 1st Engineer Special Brigade nor of the 2d, 3d or 4th Engineer Special Brigades. In both brigades the framework was a group of three engineer combat battalions. The list of the organic and attached engineer amphibian units for the Normandy invasion is listed at the end of this Appendix.

On VJ-day the Chief of Engineers, in Washington, was busily engaged preparing plans for the activation of the 7th Engineer Special Brigade for use against Japan, but when peace came these plans were cancelled. The 7th Brigade never got beyond the authorization stage.

In addition to the six brigades, special Amphibian engineer troops were organized as follows:

540th Engineer Shore Regiment (96 officers, 4 warrant officers, 1,980 enlisted men) was formed at Camp Edwards, Massachusetts, under Colonel George A. Marvin from personnel of the 2d Engineer Special Brigade on September 11, 1942, and shipped (less the 3d Battalion which was inactivated on October 2, 1942) to Fort Bragg, N.C., to form with the 36th Engineer Combat Regiment, additional shore parties for the projected 1943 invasion across the English Channel. Instead it participated as shore party in the North African landing and went on to Sicily, Salerno, Anzio and southern France, making a very creditable record.

411th Engineer Base Shop Battalion was activated at Camp Edwards, Massachusetts, in the summer of 1942. A composite platoon of this battalion moved to England with the 1st Brigade. Company A moved to Carrabelle, Florida, with the 2d Brigade in October 1942. In late November the battalion staged at Fort Ord, California, and moved on to Australia in December 1942. The battalion was organized and taken overseas by Major (later Colonel) James A. Bender.

692d Engineer Special Shop Battalion was activated at Camp Edwards, Massachusetts, in May 1943. In addition to the usual Headquarters and Headquarters Company, it consisted of a power plant repair company, a hull repair company, a salvage and dockage company and a depot company. In early December 1943 the battalion staged at New Orleans and was subsequently moved to New Guinea. This battalion later served in the Philippines and returned to the U.S. for inactivation in January 1946. The commander of this battalion was Lieutenant Colonel Paul E. Gieselmann who organized it and took it overseas.

Amphibian Truck Companies: In the spring of 1943 at Townsville, Australia, the 2d Engineer Special Brigade formed the first amphibian truck company in the Southwest Pacific. This company was later designated the 5411th Amphibian Truck Company and had the best record of any DUKW company in General MacArthur's command. In June 1943 the 4th Engineer Special Brigade formed the 464th, 465th and 466th Amphibian Truck Companies and moved them to Charleston, S.C., for movement overseas.

No list of Amphibian Engineer troops would be complete without mention of the *36th* and *40th Engineer Combat Regiments*. Both of these regiments were used so frequently as shore parties in the European Theater that they came to be regarded as Amphibian Engineers. A battalion of the 540th Engineer Shore Regiment was absorbed in the 36th Engineers just prior to the Morocco show.

ENGINEER SPECIAL BRIGADE GROUP
INVASION OF NORMANDY

1. *Group Headquarters: Omaha Beach*
    Commanding General   Brigadier General William M. Hoge
    Deputy Colonel   Timothy L. Mulligan
    Chief of Staff   Colonel Leland B. Kuhre

2. *Units Assigned or Attached: Omaha Beach*
    (Total T/O strength—21,928)
    5th Engineer Special Brigade (T/O strength—6,756)
        Colonel Doswell Gullatt, Commanding
            Deputy: Colonel William C. D. Bridges
        37th Engineer Battalion (Lieutenant Colonel Rice, Major Smith)
        336th Engineer Battalion
        348th Engineer Battalion
        61st Medical Battalion
        210th MP Company
        30th Chemical Decontamination Co.
        294th Signal Company (Joint Assault)
        251st Ordnance Battalion
            616th Ordnance Am. Co.
            3466th Ordnance MAM Co.
        533d Quartermaster Service Battalion
            4141st Quartermaster Sv. Co.
            4142d Quartermaster Sv. Co.
            4143d Quartermaster Sv. Co.
        131st Quartermaster Battalion (Mobile)
            453d TC Amphibious Tk. Co.
            458th TC Amphibious Tk. Co.
            459th TC Amphibious Tk. Co.
        619th Quartermaster Battalion
            97th Quartermaster Rhd Co.
            559th Quartermaster Rhd Co.
            Company A, 203d Gas Sup. Co.
        Attached:
        440th Engineer Depot Co. (1 platoon)
        467th Engineer Maintenance Co. (1 platoon)
        1219th Engineer F. F. Platoon
        26th Bomb Disp. Squadron

1st Medical Depot Sec.

3d Auxiliary Surg. Gp (8 Tms)

    VHF Sig. Unit (Br)

175th Signal Rep. Det.

215th Signal S&I Sec.

980th Signal Co. Radio Link

162d Signal Photo Co. Det. 4

6th Naval Beach Battalion

607th Graves Registration Co. (2 Platoons)

4042d Quartermaster Tk. Co.

487th Port Battalion

    184th Port Company

    185th Port Company

    186th Port Company

    187th Port Company

    282d Port Company

    283d Port Company

502d Port Battalion

    270th Port Company

    271st Port Company

    272d Port Company

    273d Port Company

6th Engineer Special Brigade (T/O strength—6,630)

    Colonel Paul W. Thompson, Commanding

      (wounded June 6, 1944 and succeeded by Colonel Timothy L. Mulligan)

    147th Engineer Battalion (Lt. Col. Neill)

    149th Engineer Battalion (Lt. Col. Taylor)

    203d Engineer Battalion (Lt. Col. Thorley)

    60th Medical Battalion

        453d Col. Company

        499th Col. Company

        500th Col. Company

        634th Clearing Company

    214th MP Company (Capt. Sheerer)

    31st Chemical Decontamination Company

    293d Joint Assault Signal Company

    74th Ordnance Battalion

        618th Ordnance Ammunition Company

        3565th Ordnance MAM Company

538th Quartermaster Battalion
    967th Quartermaster Service Company
    3204th Quartermaster Service Company
    3205th Quartermaster Service Company
280th Quartermaster Battalion (Lt. Col. 'Wolf)
    460th TC Amphibious Tk. Company
    461st TC Amphibious Tk. Company
    463d TC Amphibious Tk. Company
95th Quartermaster Battalion (Mobile)
    88th Quartermaster Rhd Company
    555th Quartermaster Rhd Company
    3820th Gas Supply Company
Attached:
1602d Engineer Map Depot Detachment
440th Engineer Depot Company (1 platoon) & Company Hq.
467th Engineer Maintenance Company (1 platoon)
27th Bomb Disposal Squadron
—Medical Dep. Section
3d Auxiliary Surgical Group (4 Tms)
—VHF Signal Unit (Br)
175th Signal Rep. (Det)
218th Signal S&I (Det)
9th A.F. Beach Party
162d Signal Photo Company (Det. 5)
7th Naval Beach Battalion (Commander Leaver)
607th Graves Registration Company (3 platoons)
3704th Quartermaster Truck Company
494th TC Port Battalion
    238th Port Company
    239th Port Company
    240th Port Company
    241st Port Company
517th TC Port Battalion
    797th Port Company
    798th Port Company
    799th Port Company
    800th Port Company
    284th Port Company
    285th Port Company
11th Port Headquarters (T/O strength—8,542)

Colonel Whitcomb, Commanding
334th Harbor Craft Company
990th Port Signal Service Company
509th Port Battalion
514th Port Battalion
    306th Port Company
    307th Port Company
    308th Port Company
    309th Port Company
    526th Port Company
    527th Port Company
    528th Port Company
    529th Port Company
1st Battalion 358th Engineer GS Regiment
688th Quartermaster Battalion
    4058th Quartermaster Service Company
    145th Quartermaster Service Company
    91st Quartermaster Service Company
512th Quartermaster Battalion (Mobile)
    4009th Tk. Company
    3582d Tk. Company
    3583d Tk. Company
512th Quartermaster Group (Mobile)
    467th Amphibious Tk. Company
    468th Amphibious Tk. Company
    469th Amphibious Tk. Company
174th Quartermaster Battalion (Mobile)
    470th Amphibious Tk. Company
    819th Amphibious Tk. Company
    821st Amphibious Tk. Company
763d MP Battalion (ZI)—Company C
302d MP Escort Gd. Company
3531st Ordnance MAM Company
40th Signal Construction Company—Det. A
501st Port Battalion
    434th Port Company
    435th Port Company
    436th Port Company
    437th Port Company
556th Quartermaster Battalion (Serv.)

3263d Service Company
4093d Service Company
4182d Service Company
4183d Service Company
554th Quartermaster Battalion (Serv.)
3104th Service Company
3219th Service Company
4146th Service Company
440th Engineer Depot Company (less 3 platoons)

3. *Units Assigned or Attached. Utah Beach*
1st Engineer Special Brigade—(T/O strength—16,252)
Colonel Eugene M. Caffey, Commanding
Brigadier General James P. Wharton, commanded during period May-June 1944
531st Engineer Shore Regiment (Colonel Underwood)
24th Amphibious Truck Battalion
462d Amphibious Truck Company
478th Amphibious Truck Company
479th Amphibious Truck Company
306th Quartermaster Battalion
556th Quartermaster Rhd Company
557th Quartermaster Rhd Company
3939th Quartermaster Gas Supply Company
191st Ordnance Battalion
3497th Ordnance MAM Company
625th Ordnance Am. Company
161st Ordnance Platoon
449th MP Company
Quartermaster Hq. 1st Engr. Special Brigade
3206th Quartermaster Service Company (1 section)
577th Quartermaster Battalion
3206th (1 section) Quartermaster Service Company
3207th Quartermaster Service Company
4144th Quartermaster Service Company
286th Joint Assault Signal Company
261st Medical Battalion, Companies A, B, & C
33d QM Decontaminating Company
Units Attached to 1st Brigade:
23d Ordnance Bomb Disposal Squadron

165th Signal Photo Team (Det. E)
490th Port Battalion
    226th Port Company
    227th Port Company
    228th Port Company
    229th Port Company
518th Port Battalion
    298th Port Company
    299th Port Company
    300th Port Company
    301st Port Company
    278th Port Company
    279th Port Company
519th Port Battalion
    302d Port Company
    303d Port Company
    304th Port Company
    305th Port Company
    280th Port Company
    281st Port Company
38th Engineer (US) Regiment (2 battalions)
1605th Engineer Map Section
440th Engineer Dep. Company (1 platoon)
1217th Engineer F. F. Platoon
1218th Engineer F. F. Platoon
1st Medical Dep. Company (2 Sect. Sup Platoon)
6th Surgical Group (12 teams)
175th Signal Rep. Company (Det.)
218th Signal Dep. Company (Det.)
980th Signal Service Company (Det.)
999th Signal Service Company (Sp Det.)
3111st Signal Service Battalion (Sp Det.)
165th Signal Photo Team (Det. E)
607th Quartermaster Graves Registration Company (1 platoon)
262d Quartermaster Battalion
    4061st Service Company
    4088th Service Company
    4090th Service Company
    4190th Service Company
244th Quartermaster Service Battalion

3877th Gas Supply Company
3878th Gas Supply Company
522d Rhd Company
4041st Quartermaster Truck Company
3683d Quartermaster Truck Company
3684th Quartermaster Truck Company
3692d Quartermaster Truck Company
4002d Quartermaster Truck Company
308th Quartermaster Rhd Company
537th Quartermaster Battalion
    4083d Quartermaster Service Company
    4092d Quartermaster Service Company
    4132d Quartermaster Service Company
23d Ordnance Bomb Disposal Squadron
3516th Ordnance MAM Company
783d Military Police Battalion, Company D
301st Military Police, PW Esc. Guard Company
595th Military Police, PW Esc. Guard Company
815th T. C. Amphibious Truck Company
816th T. C. Amphibious Truck Company
817th T. C. Amphibious Truck Company
818th T. C. Amphibious Truck Company
2d Naval Beach Battalion
Det. VIII AF Intransit Dep. Group
Det. A, 11th Port

APPENDIX C
AWARDS AND DECORATIONS

Unfortunately all the Engineer Special Brigades did not keep tabulations of their awards and decorations. However, it is interesting to publish what records are available.

The Distinguished Unit Citation is awarded to an entire unit only for extraordinary heroism in combat. All members of the command who were present when the action occurred are entitled to wear the Distinguished Unit badge.

The Meritorious Service Unit Plaque is awarded a unit for superior performance of duty not in combat. All members of the unit during the period for which awarded are entitled to wear the Meritorious Service Unit emblem on the right sleeve of the uniform.

Individual awards range from the Medal of Honor to the Purple Heart.

I

DISTINGUISHED UNIT CITATION

The Distinguished Unit Citation is the highest award a unit can receive. The entire 2d Engineer Special Brigade was twice recommended to General MacArthur for this highest award; but in view of the War Department general policy against awarding it to units as large as a brigade, it was decided by General Headquarters that it could be given only to subordinate elements of the brigade. The following is a list of brigade units which have been awarded the Distinguished Unit Citation. They are listed in the order the awards were made:

General Orders   War Department
No. 75   Washington 25, D.C., 18 September 1944

IX. Battle Honors. 2. As authorized by Executive Order No. 9396 (sec. I, Bull. 22, WD, 1943), superseding Executive Order No. 9075 (sec. III, Bull. 11, WD, 1942), citation of the following unit in General Orders, No. 123, Headquarters Sixth Army, 2 August 1944, as approved by the Commanding General, United States Army Forces in the Far East, is confirmed under the provisions of section IV, Circular No. 333, War Department, 1943, in the name of the President of the United States as public evidence of deserved honor and distinction. The citation reads as follows:

Company A, 542d Engineer Boat and Shore Regiment, is cited for outstanding performance of duty in action against the enemy, 18 May 1944, at Wakde Island, Dutch New Guinea. Charged with landing initial assault troops and subsequent reinforcements on Wakde Island, the men of this unit carried out their mission with heroic success. Though the island had been heavily bombarded, the first craft approaching through difficult coral reefs were subjected to intense crossfire of automatic weapons and snipers. To manipulate their craft the coxswains and crews had to expose themselves fully to this fire. As coxswains and crews were killed or wounded, other members of the crew took their places to land the infantry and return for reinforcements. Despite continued heavy losses, these men carried out their missions with unflinching determination and bravery, and made a vital contribution to the ultimate success of the entire operation.

General Orders   War Department
No. X 76   Washington 25, D.C., 22 September 1944

XII. Battle Honors. 1. As authorized by Executive Order No. 9396 (sec. I, Bull. 22, WD, 1943), superseding Executive Order No. 9075 (sec. III, Bull. 11, WD, 1942), citation of the following unit in General Orders, No. 47,

Headquarters 41st Infantry Division, 27 July 1944, as approved by the Commanding General, United States Army Forces in the Far East, is confirmed under the provisions of section IV, Circular No. 333, War Department, 1943, in the name of the President of the United States as public evidence of deserved honor and distinction. The citation reads as follows:

Collecting Platoon, Company B, 262d Medical Battalion, is cited for outstanding performance of duty in action against the enemy. Following the landing in the vicinity of Humboldt Bay, Dutch New Guinea, circumstances forced the establishment of large supply dumps for the Task Force among numerous dumps of enemy ammunition, bombs, and food, found in the beachhead. For two days all supplies of the Task Force were landed in this area, resulting in gasoline, ammunition, rations and bombs extending along a narrow beachhead for a distance of approximately 1½ miles. The Collecting Platoon, Company B, 262d Medical Battalion, had set up an aid station upon arrival at the beach in the center of the dump area. At about 2030 hours, 23 April 1944, an enemy bomber made a direct hit on one of the ammunition dumps. The explosion which followed set off fires which rapidly spread. Throughout the night and until about 1700 hours, 24 April 1944, continuous and terrific explosions and fires alternately shook and illuminated the beach. All supplies for a distance of approximately 1 mile were destroyed. Throughout the night of 23 April 1944 and until 1200 hours the following day the 2 officers and 44 men of this unit maintained their aid station. They moved continuously through the holocaust of the burning dumps and tremendous explosions emitting great danger from fire, flying shrapnel, and concussion. Despite these conditions, litter squads returned again and again into the burning area to rescue their comrades while the remainder of the personnel applied first aid. More than two hundred men were treated and evacuated by the platoon. Many lives were saved by the effective aid they so efficiently provided. It was only after all casualties and personnel had been evacuated from the danger area that the platoon retired to a place of security. The heroism and determination of every man in this platoon, operating under the most hazardous and adverse conditions, exemplify the highest traditions of the military service.

General Orders   War Department
No. 53   Washington 25, D.C., July 1945

X. Battle Honors. As authorized by Executive Order 9396 (sec. I. WD Bul. 22, 1943), superseding Executive Order 9075 (sec. III, WD Bul. 11, 1942), the following unit is cited by the War Department under the provisions of section IV, WD, Circular 333 1943, in the name of the President of the United States as public evidence of deserved honor and distinction. The citation reads as follows:

The 503d Parachute Infantry Regiment with the following attached units:

Detachment, 592d Engineer Boat and Shore Regiment, Companies A and F

These units, organized as a task force, distinguished themselves by extraordinary heroism and outstanding performance of duty in action against the enemy during the period 16 to 28 February 1945. This force was directed to seize the enemy-held island fortress of Corregidor, one of the most difficult missions of the Pacific war. A long prepared and fanatical enemy, strongly intrenched in numerous tunnels, caves, dugouts, and crevices, awaited the assault in commanding and extensively fortified positions. The small dropping area for parachutists was bordered extensively by sheer cliffs, with resultant variable air currents and eddies; and previous bombings and naval gunfire had cut trees and shrubs close above ground, creating hazardous stakes which threatened to impale descending troops. The approach by sea, through shallow water known to be mined, led to a beach protected by land mines. At 0830 on 16 February, the initial assault was made by parachute drop on terrain littered with debris and rubble. Heavy casualties were sustained. Two hours later the amphibious elements advanced by sea through the minefield to the beach and, though many lives were lost and much equipment destroyed by exploding mines, this element moved rapidly inland and under heavy enemy fire seized Malinta Hill. Meanwhile, the airborne elements, though subjected to intense enemy fire and suffering increasing casualties, were organized into an aggressive fighting force as a result of the initiative of commanders of small units. Advancing doggedly against fanatical resistance, they had, by nightfall, secured "The Top of the Rock," their initial objective. On the following morning the entire task force began a systematic reduction of enemy positions and the annihilation of defending forces. Innumerable enemy tunnels and caves were sealed by demolitions after hand-to-hand fighting, only to have the enemy emerge elsewhere through an intricate system of interconnecting passageways. Direct fire of our supporting weapons, employed to seal tunnels and caves, often resulted in the explosion of enemy-emplaced demolitions and ammunition dumps, causing heavy casualties to our troops. Under increasing pressure the enemy, cut off from reinforcements, exploded demolitions in tunnels, destroying themselves as well as elements of our task force. At the completion of this desperate and violent struggle, 4,509 enemy dead were counted. Prisoners taken totaled 19. Throughout the operation all elements of the task force, combat and service troops alike, displayed heroism in the highest degree. Parachuting to earth or landing on the mined beaches, they attacked savagely against a numerically superior enemy, defeated him completely, and seized the fortress. Their magnificent courage, tenacity, and gallantry avenged the victims of Corregidor of 1942 and achieved a significant victory for the United States Army.

GENERAL ORDERS   WAR DEPARTMENT

No. 66   WASHINGTON 25, D.C., 10 AUGUST 1945

BATTLE HONORS. As authorized by Executive Order 9396 (sec. I, WD Bul. 22, 1943), superseding Executive Order 9075 (sec. III, WD Bul. 11, 1942), citations of the following units in the general orders indicated are confirmed under the provisions of section IV, WD Circular 333, 1943, in the name of the President of the United States as public evidence of deserved honor and distinction:

The 2d Engineer Special Brigade Support Battery (Provisional) is cited for outstanding performance of duty in action against the enemy at Biak Island, Netherlands East Indies, from 27 May to 14 June 1944. This unit rendered outstanding support to the task force which captured Biak Island. During the advance toward Mokmer Airdrome the overland route of supply was cut on several occasions by enemy activity. Landing vehicles, tracked, of this battery provided the only means of supplying organizations with food, ammunition, and medical supplies, and made many landings under fire to accomplish their mission. On return trips casualties were evacuated from the beach to landing craft standing off shore. When enemy fire became so intense as to prevent supply of the forces by daylight, landing vehicles, tracked, ran throughout the nights despite the danger of uncharted coral reefs. The rigor of their services is demonstrated by the fact that by 12 June only 7 landing vehicles, tracked, remained out of 54 which had begun the operation, because of enemy action and navigational difficulties. The tireless and gallant efforts of all members of this unit made possible the capture of Mokmer Airdrome. The lives of many casualties were saved because of prompt evacuation by landing vehicles, tracked. Acts of gallantry and heroism were numerous but difficult to single out of the uniformly high standard of achievement set by all personnel of the 2d Engineer Special Brigade Support Battery

(Provisional). (General Orders 80, Headquarters 41st Infantry Division, 31 October 1944, as approved by the Commander-in-Chief, United States Army Forces, Pacific.)

Shore Battalion, 592d Engineer Boat & Shore Regiment
For outstanding performance of duty in action against
the enemy in the Admiralty Islands, from 2 March to 6
March 1944. On 2 March 1944 this battalion landed on
White Beach, Los Negros Island, as an element of the Task
Force. Its mission was entirely an engineering project which
consisted of clearing the beach, building ramps out to amphibious craft, constructing a beach road net, developing
beach dumps and, with attached units, unloading troops,
equipment and supplies. Within thirty minutes after landing and while still in the process of organizing the beachhead, the beach was subjected to enemy mortar and sniper
fire which continued spasmodically throughout the day.
Despite numerous casualties, due to little or no cover, this
unit carried on with courageous determination and complete disregard of danger to accomplish its mission. Only
after all craft had retracted and darkness caused work to
stop on the beach did this unit retire, and then not to rest
but to take up defensive positions on the west flank of the
Task Force perimeter. The positions had hardly been taken
when the enemy began a series of infiltration and "Banzai"
attacks, directed against the west flank of the perimeter,
which lasted throughout the night. Amid considerable confusion, due to the lack of infantry training, with many troops
seeing action for the first time, the officers and men of the
Shore Battalion met every advance of the enemy with such
determination, tenacity and courage that the enemy was
driven off on every occasion with heavy casualties. Enemy
infiltration was particularly prevalent and hand-to-hand
combat, with knives and bayonets, was evident everywhere.
When the enemy action ceased at dawn, the battalion returned to its task on the beach where it worked till night,

returning then to the perimeter positions. During the night the attacks were renewed, but with the same intrepidity and valor the attacks were repulsed. The following day, when the infantry was held up by impassable terrain, the unit went out beyond the front lines to build roads in the face of sniper fire so that infantry and artillery force could be brought to bear on the enemy. Although working every day on the beach bringing in vital supplies and equipment, this unit returned every night to positions on the perimeter to fight the enemy. The unusual devotion to duty, grim determination, battle discipline and conspicuous gallantry of the officers and men of the Shore Battalion, 592d Engineer Boat and Shore Regiment had a stimulating effect on all troops of the Task Force and reflects the highest credit upon the United States Army.

Boat Battalion, 592d Engineer Boat & Shore Regiment

For conspicuous and heroic action against the enemy at Leyte, Philippine Islands, from 5 November until 10 December 1944. The battalion, then operating 170 small craft unloading ships at White Beach, Leyte, Philippine Islands, and landing combat patrols at various points on Leyte and Samar Islands was called upon to supply front line troops by landing supplies at Pinamopoan Point. For four days, the officers and men of this unit determinedly landed on the rocky beach, in the face of the direct fire of a machine gun which the infantry could not locate. Each day, as the ramps of the LCMs were lowered onto the beach the machine gun would open fire directly into the well deck of the craft. Despite the fact that the boat crews were not responsible for unloading their craft, they voluntarily and with complete disregard of their own safety, unloaded the boats while the coxswains remained at the helm to keep the boats on the beach. Later the unit participated in the assault landing at Ipil, carrying troops and supplies for the final attack on Ormoc. Although the landing was made against only moderate enemy shore resistance, a fierce enemy air attack developed, later in the day, which forced all craft off the beach. The LCMs of the battalion remained close inshore despite the desperate attempts of the enemy pilots and furnished supporting fire which destroyed two enemy planes and helped discourage any sustained attack on the beach. The enemy planes then attacked the shipping offshore scoring a direct hit on one ship and setting it afire. Two naval craft attempted to aid the ship but were driven off by the planes. Without hesitation the boats of this unit got under way to assist. The enemy planes then made two desperate attacks on the craft in an attempt to drive them off. In addition, shore batteries opened up and it was only due to the superb handling of the boats and their machine guns that no direct hits were suffered and at least one enemy plane was destroyed. As a result of this heroic action, the LCMs affected the rescue of 16 survivors. On the following day, while returning to the near shore with battle casualties and other personnel and without naval escort, the LCM convoy was spotted by enemy planes and attacked constantly for over an hour. Again the skillful handling of the boats and deadly fire from their guns accounted for four enemy planes and prevented serious damage. In all this unit accounted for 11 planes destroyed and several probably destroyed which in itself is an enviable record. The determination, conspicuous heroism and high esprit de corps of the Boat Battalion, 592d Engineer Boat and Shore Regiment are in keeping with the highest traditions of the military service.

GENERAL ORDERS   WAR DEPARTMENT
No. 2   WASHINGTON 25, D.C., 5 JANUARY 1946

BATTLE HONORS. 5. *Company A, 532d Engineer Boat and Shore Regiment*, is cited for extraordinary heroism at Nassau Bay, New Guinea, from 29 June to 2 July 1943. After a hazardous midnight landing in tremendous surf, the boat crews of Company A, who had been charged with placing a combat team ashore in enemy territory, left their wrecked craft and prepared themselves for the inevitable fight for the beachhead. With rifles and with machine guns torn from their landing craft, they joined in a desperate 12-hour battle and, suffering heavy casualties, held the portion of the perimeter which bore the brunt of the enemy attack. In the grim fight which at times involved hand-to-hand combat, the amphibian engineers, as individuals and as a group, displayed extraordinary resolution and courage. As a unit comprising one-fifth of the American forces on Nassau Beach, their courageous action was the factor which saved the entire force from destruction by a superior enemy force. In the adaptability, determination, and willingness to sacrifice, which they displayed, *Company A, 532d Engineer Boat and Shore Regiment* lived up to the highest combat traditions of their corps and of the Army of the United States. (General Orders 272, Headquarters Sixth Army, 2 December 1945, as approved by the Commander in Chief, United States Army Forces, Pacific.)

GENERAL ORDERS   WAR DEPARTMENT
No. 36   WASHINGTON 25, D.C., 19 APRIL 1946

BATTLE HONORS. 1. *The Boat Battalion, 532d Engineer Boat and Shore Regiment*, is cited for extraordinary heroism on New Guinea from 4 September to 15 December 1943. The *Boat Battalion, 532d Engineer Boat and Shore Regiment*, supporting an Australian division in operations against Lae and Finschhafen, made a major contribution to the rapid and conclusive defeat of the enemy in the Huon Peninsula area. With their small landing craft, they solved the problem of supplying advancing troops where swampy, river-rutted terrain precluded the building of supply roads, which enabled a maximum strategic advantage to be gained. After the assault on Red Beach 14 miles east of Lae, the battalion fought off attack after attack of strafing enemy airplanes, which attempted to destroy the LCM's and LCV's exposed in the open roadstead. In over 40 attacks directed at them, the battalion definitely destroyed 3 enemy airplanes and possibly were responsible for destroying 10 others. In some instances, boatmen were killed at their guns while fighting off head-on attacks. Despite the nerve-wracking daylight hours of fighting and of constant alert, the boat crews were always prepared for the nightly missions to the forward areas, where they were to engage in resupply, movement of reinforcements and artillery, and evacuation of casualties. Even though daylight missions would have been exceptionally hazardous with coast defense guns, artillery, and mortars prepared to take their toll, the night missions were almost as dangerous. Japanese search airplanes were constantly sweeping the coast to attack convoys, which they could track down from the phosphorescent wakes of the boats. On the forward beach, always well within enemy rifle range, the boat battalion could generally expect a greeting of mortar and machine-gun fire when the noise of their motors could be detected. Members of the battalion willingly worked periods of 48 to 56 hours at a time, subordinating their comfort and safety to the accomplishment of the task at hand. At no time did they turn back when under fire or fail to complete a mission. At the final defense line before Lae, the battalion played its most heroic role. The Japanese were strongly entrenched behind the Busu River and a detachment of Australians had been cut off by sudden rising water on the enemy side near the mouth of the stream. Boats of the battalion were rushed to this point and in 63 continuous hours moved over 1,500 reinforcements to the precarious beachhead on the enemy side. During this time, they were in full view of the enemy and under a constant hail of fire. Eighteen days after the initial assault near Lae, the second large scale assault by the boat battalion was made at Scarlet Beach, 5 miles north of Finschhafen, with an Australian brigade. Here again under even heavier air attack from as many as 40 to 50 enemy airplanes, the boat crew performed similar coastwise missions in the advance toward the town. Then, after Finschhafen fell on 29 October, the threat of enemy counterattack from the north with large forces necessitated the immediate reinforcement of the brigade with the balance of the Australian division which was still at Lae. Large naval craft could not be used to transport these troops with their equipment and supplies, so the boat battalion, with their tiny boats, willingly accepted the responsibilities and risk involved. Each complete trip between Lae and Finschhafen required about 22 hours of running time for the small craft. Day after day, the boat crews made consecutive runs without rest or hot food, nearly always soaked by the heavy rains or baked by the sun. During the hours of darkness, the route could be marked by strings of tracer bullets as well as bomb splashes from enemy search airplanes intent on breaking or disrupting this frail channel of communication. Every available boat was used every day during the 5 weeks that it took to move the balance of the division with their equipment and supplies over the 70 hazardous miles between Lae and Finschhafen. Not a passenger nor a boatload of supplies was lost, even though on some trips boats were cut by shrapnel and men were blown overboard by concussion from bombs. Through the heroism, grim determination, conspicuous gallantry, and excellent battle discipline of its members, the *Boat Battalion, 532d Boat and Shore Regiment*, enabled Allied forces to achieve remarkable gains with minimum loss. (General Orders 249, Headquarters Sixth Army, 11 November, 1945, as approved by the Commander in Chief, United States Army Forces, Pacific.)

SUMMARY

To 20 April 1946 (In order of award):
1. Company A, 542d Engineer Boat and Shore Regiment.
2. Collecting Platoon, Company B, 262d Medical Battalion.

3. Companies A and F, 592d Engineer Boat and Shore Regiment.[1]

4. Support Battery, 2d Engineer Special Brigade.

5. Shore Battalion, 532d Engineer Boat and Shore Regiment.

6. Shore Battalion, 592d Engineer Boat and Shore Regiment.

7. Boat Battalion, 592d Engineer Boat and Shore Regiment.

8. Company A, 532d Engineer Boat and Shore Regiment.

9. Boat Battalion, 532d Engineer Boat and Shore Regiment.

II

MERITORIOUS SERVICE UNIT PLAQUE

Headquarters and Headquarters Company, 2d Engineer Special Brigade

From 1 October 1944 to 31 March 1945, the Headquarters and Headquarters Company, 2d Engineer Special Brigade performed its function in the service, direction and administration of the Brigade in an exceptionally superior manner. During the period from 1 October to 12 October on which date the first echelon embarked at Hollandia to participate in the initial assault on the island of Leyte, the personnel worked day and night in the preparation and loading of equipment. An entire Liberty Ship had to be completely unloaded and the Brigade equipment reloaded aboard two LSTs and the same Liberty Ship in a period of four days. On A-day, 9 officers and 32 enlisted men debarked on Red Beach, Leyte. Twelve direct hits were scored on these 2 LSTs and the casualties suffered by this company were 2 officers and 2 enlisted men wounded in action. Members of the company assisted in caring for other casualties and in extinguishing fires. Immediately upon debarkation the CP and a perimeter defense were established on the beach; every man worked with feverish zeal and energy to unload the LSTs in as short a time as possible. Despite heavy mortar and sniper fire and numerous air raids, the job was accomplished in record time. The mess personnel operating with planned efficiency, served hot food to the personnel of the company and many neighboring units throughout the day. On A plus 2, the second echelon of 5 officers and 43 enlisted men debarked on White Beach, Leyte. A brief reconnaissance of the area located a temporary camp area on Monument Beach near Tacloban. On A plus 4, the remainder of the company debarked from the Liberty ship. From 1 October 1944 to 31 March 1945 this company moved and reestablished the entire Brigade Headquarters in six different locations, at Hollandia, Dutch New Guinea; Red Beach, Tacloban, Telegrapho, Tanauan and San Roque, Leyte, Philippine Islands. These moves were made in order to cooperate with the Air Corps and a General Hospital in the establishment of their installations. On every one of the 16 major amphibious landings in the Philippine Campaign in which a unit of the Brigade participated, at least 1 officer and 2 enlisted men of this organization accompanied the task force for liaison and other purposes. The officers and men of this company have demonstrated remarkable efficiency, initiative, and outstanding devotion to duty and by their long hours of hard work, ingenuity, and professional skill have been largely responsible for the successful execution of the Brigade activities throughout the entire Philippine Campaign.

Quartermaster Headquarters and Headquarters Company, 2d Engineer Special Brigade

For superior performance and devotion to duty from 25 September 1944 to 31 May 1945. During this period, the Quartermaster Headquarters and Headquarters Company, 2d Engineer Special Brigade has, under very difficult conditions, performed its function of supplying the units of the Brigade for combat operations in an exceptionally superior manner. From 25 September 1944 to 12 October 1944, this company had to supply the entire Brigade with Quartermaster supplies for participation in the Leyte Operation. This task was rendered most difficult as the company had to move their installations from Finschhafen to Hollandia at the same time they were delivering supplies to our task groups at Biak, Maffin Ban, Hollandia and Manus. At Leyte, Philippine Islands, on A plus 4, the Liberty ship bringing in the bulk of the company's personnel and supplies was bombed and strafed by enemy planes. From then on this company was subjected to almost constant enemy air attacks. On 25 October a bomb was dropped in their bivouac area, killing three of their men and wounding seven. Despite this tragedy the remaining personnel continued their duties of supplying the Brigade, preparing their warehouses, unloading their supplies from the Liberty ship and manning a perimeter defense. Immediately after the initial phase of the Leyte Operation this company started supplying the Brigade for subsequent combat landings in the Philippine Islands. From 1 October 1944 to 31 May 1945 this company moved and partially reestablished their installations in six different locations without allowing any serious interference in supply of the Brigade units. A shortage of supplies has been another of the numerous handicaps faced by this company, but through the initiative and untiring efforts of its officers and men, they have met every situation. The combined efforts of all men in the Quartermaster Headquarters and Headquarters Company, 2d Engineer Special Brigade, to supply the Brigade for its 51 combat landings from 20 October 1944 to 31 May 1945 in the liberation of the Philippine Islands have been an inspiration to this command and a contributing factor in the success attained.

287th Signal Company, 2d Engineer Special Brigade
    Under the provisions of Section I, Circular No. 345, War Department, 23 August 1944, as amended, in addition to the Meritorious Service Unit Plaque awarded to the 287th Signal Company, as announced in General Orders No. 4, Headquarters, Sixth Army, 9 January 1945, a Star to the

Meritorious Service Unit Plaque is awarded to this unit by the Commanding General, Eighth Army. For superior performance and devotion to duty from 15 December 1944 to 15 June 1945. During military operations in the Philippine Islands, this unit was assigned to an Engineer Special Brigade. Its function was to provide signal supply, and to maintain wire and radio communications and radar installations in all echelons of command. Operating with a highly mobile headquarters, the company successfully maintained unbroken wire and radio networks with Brigade units throughout the Philippine Islands. Numerous radio installations were completed, and seriously damaged telephone equipment was rapidly repaired. At Cebu the company, in the face of enemy shelling, effectively made radar installations. In accomplishing its mission in a superlative manner, the 287th Signal Company displayed unusual initiative and great devotion to duty, and consistently maintained high standards of morale, military courtesy and discipline.

The above award is the second one for the 287th Signal Company, this company having won its first award for the six months period, June 15, 1944 to December 15, 1944, when it was so active in New Guinea and at Leyte. The members of this company therefore, are entitled to a Star on their Meritorious Service Emblem.

162d Ordnance Maintenance Company

For superior performance and outstanding devotion to duty from 1 January 1944 to 30 June 1944. As a part of an Engineer Special Brigade, this company displayed untiring energy, cheerfulness and great efficiency in carrying out their assigned duties. As a result of the extended efforts of the officers and men, many new ingenious devices were developed out of salvage materials to meet urgent operational needs. Among these accomplishments were improved gun mounts and special installations of barrage rocket launchers for landing craft. These special developments proved their worth in combat operations throughout the Southwest Pacific Area. On one occasion, in order to meet an operational deadline, this company performed, in three days, the enormous task of uncrating, assembling, checking, greasing and road testing sixteen 2½-ton trucks. The company not only worked on Brigade vehicles, instruments and armament, but also performed numerous jobs for the Air Corps and other army agencies. The officers and men displayed fine discipline and morale. This unit, at all times, maintained a high standard of appearance of personnel, installations and equipment.

262d Medical Battalion

This unit served with an Engineer Special Brigade, operating First Aid Stations in New Guinea, Biak Island, and the Philippine Islands from 1 October 1944 to 1 February 1945. Company A was attached to a Cavalry Division, Company C to an Infantry Division and Headquarters Detachment to a Medical Group for the operations of Leyte Island. The unit set up clearing stations on the invasion beaches handling casualties efficiently and with a minimum delay, working long hours through frequent air raids and extremely adverse weather conditions. Evacuation stations were set up and functioning within one-half hour after the clearing stations were established. For many hours these were the only medical facilities available. During this period the battalion handled 2549 admissions, 11067 evacuations (by air and water) and 19490 treatments. In addition to this, treatment was rendered to numerous Filipino civilians. The initiative, ability, determination, and devotion to duty displayed by the battalion was exemplary, and was responsible in a great measure for the superior medical services rendered in these operations.

562d Engineer Boat Maintenance Battalion

The entire 562d Engineer Boat Maintenance Battalion was also awarded the Meritorious Service Unit Plaque for its excellent work in maintaining craft of the Brigade during the critical Leyte operations. Their preliminary work in New Guinea was so thoroughly done that not a single landing craft broke down due to mechanical deficiency although the companies of this battalion were frequently moved throughout the various islands of the Philippines. They always set up promptly in their new areas and worked day and night in keeping up the maintenance standards of the Brigade. During most of this period the Battalion was commanded by Lieutenant Colonel Ralph T. Simpson of Knoxville, Tennessee.

III

INDIVIDUAL DECORATIONS

MEDAL OF HONOR

Private Junior N. Van Noy, 532d Engineer Boat and Shore Regiment. For conspicuous gallantry and intrepidity above and beyond the call of duty in action with the enemy near Finschhafen, New Guinea, on 17 October 1943 he was gunner in charge of a machine-gun post only five yards from the water's edge when the alarm was given that three enemy barges loaded with troops were approaching the beach in the early morning darkness. One landing barge was sunk by Allied fire, but the other two beached ten yards from Private Van Noy's emplacement. Despite his exposed position, he poured a withering hail of fire into the debarking enemy troops. His loader was wounded by a grenade and evacuated. Private Van Noy, also grievously wounded, remained at his post, ignoring calls of nearby soldiers urging him to withdraw, and continued alone to fire with deadly accuracy. He expended every round and was found covered with wounds, dead beside his gun. In this action, Private Van Noy killed at least half of the thirty-nine enemy taking part in the landing. His heroic tenacity at the price of his life not only saved the lives of many of his comrades but enabled them to annihilate the attacking detachment.

[*Note.* Private Van Noy was the first Engineer soldier and the first member of the Army Service Forces to win the Medal of Honor in the War.]

MEDAL OF THE DISTINGUISHED SERVICE ORDER
OF THE COMMONWEALTH OF AUSTRALIA

Lieutenant Colonel (later Colonel) Ernest D. Brockett, Jr., 532d Engineer Boat and Shore Regiment, for heroism at Lae and Finschhafen.

DISTINGUISHED SERVICE CROSS

2d Lt, Charles C. Keele, 532d Engineer Boat and Shore Regiment. For extraordinary heroism in action near Nassau Bay, New Guinea, on 2 July 1943. After the initial landing of American forces on Nassau Bay, medical supplies were urgently needed. Despite the probability of enemy attack, Second Lieutenant Keele, in command of a small craft, proceeded in broad daylight to effect the delivery. Before the trip was half completed, enemy aircraft attacked the boat. Although wounded five times, Second Lieutenant Keele refused to allow the crew to turn back to the nearest hospital, and insisted that the vessel continue. The supplies were delivered, in spite of the rough seas. More than ten hours elapsed before he could reach a hospital, and he died of his wounds five days later. In placing the completion of his mission ahead of his own welfare, Second Lieutenant Keele showed the true quality of a soldier.

1st Lt. Henderson E. McPherson, 532d Engineer Boat and Shore Regiment. For extraordinary heroism in action near Lae, New Guinea, on 13, 14 and 15 September 1943. During the advance on Lae, units of Australian infantry were held up by the flooded Busu River. On 13 September, one battalion, making the crossing by rubber boats and by swimming, had lost a large part of its weapons and ammunition. They were left in a precarious position facing strong enemy positions about three hundred yards from the river. During the night, the landing craft commanded by First Lieutenant McPherson ferried urgently needed equipment to this battalion. He then voluntarily continued to ferry reinforcements around the mouth of the river, under fire from machine guns, mortars and seventy-five millimeter guns. When the steering gear was damaged by enemy fire, he rigged an emergency tiller and steered from an exposed position in the stern. Although about forty trips were necessary, occupying forty-eight hours, First Lieutenant McPherson declined relief and finished the undertaking. His efforts were an important factor in breaking the resistance of the enemy at this point and hastening the capture of Lae. He displayed admirable courage, skill and determination in this engagement.

T/4 Robert F. Winter, 592d Engineer Boat and Shore Regiment. For extraordinary heroism in action near Arawe, New Britain, on 18 December 1943. During a reconnaissance patrol, the landing craft on which Technician Winter was gunner and signalman was attacked by several enemy barges. Although seriously wounded in both legs, he propped himself up and continued firing. His accurate fire held off the enemy barges long enough for his patrol to beach the craft, destroy equipment, and remove supplies to the shore. When the patrol started back through dense mangrove swamps toward Arawe, carrying Technician Winter on a stretcher, the progress was very slow. With a keen

realization of the importance of the information about enemy dispositions which the quick return of the patrol would
make available to our forces, and with great courage and
unselfishness, Technician Winter insisted that the patrol
leave him behind for rescue at a later time. With a limited
quantity of water, rations, and medical supplies, he was
concealed in a grove from which he was not rescued until
after a period of thirteen days had passed. The display of
bravery, fortitude, and high devotion to duty of Technician
Winter contributed significantly to the early return of the
patrol with important information.

SILVER STAR

Alvarez, Candido, Pvt., 542d EBSR, Nassau Bay, N.G., 20 July 43
Angerer, Joe, T/5, 542d EBSR, Salamaua, N.G., 20 Aug. 43
Babcock, Merle L., Pfc., 532d EBSR, Sulu Sea, PI, 21 Dec. 44
Benner, Clarence J., T/4, 592d EBSR, Arawe, N.B., 17 Dec. 43
Bowen, Jack N., T/5, 542d EBSR, Wakde Island, DNG, 18 May 44
Brim, Byron A., 1stLt., 542d EBSR, Biak Island, DNG, 27 May 44
Briney, Clifford, T/5, 592d EBSR, Admiralty Island, 15 Mar. 44
*Brockett, Ernest D., Jr., Lt.Col., 532d EBSR, Lae, N.G., 18 Sept. 43
    Humboldt Bay, N.G., 24 Sept. 44
Brush, Douglas C., T/5, 542d EBSR, Wakde Island, DNG, 18 May 44
Burritt, Harry, Jr., T/4, 542d EBSR, Nassau Bay, N.G., 20 July 43
*Chambers, Ralph F., S/Sgt., 542d EBSR, Tambu Bay, N.G., 20 July 43
    Biri Island, PI, 20 Feb. 45
Claypool, Charles B., Lt.Col., 532d EBSR, Humboldt Bay, N.G., 22 Apr. 44
Cunningham, Vincent S., Capt., 262d Med. Bn., Humboldt Bay, N.G., 23
    Apr. 44
Dalton, Robert F., 2dLt., 532d EBSR, Humboldt Bay, N.G., 23 Apr. 44
DeFord, Don D., Capt., 542d EBSR, Biak Island, DNG, 27 May 44
Enders, Edward E., T/5, 532d EBSR, Humboldt Bay, N.G., 23 Apr. 44
Finnegan, Michial J., T/4, 542d EBSR, Wakde Island, DNG, 18 May 44
Gunning, Thomas E., Jr., Pvt., 542d EBSR, Biri Island, PI, 20 Feb. 45
Hammond, Ernest R., T/4, 532d EBSR, Lae, N.G., 14 Sept. 43

* Also awarded Oak Leaf Cluster.

Heath, Robert S., 1stLt., 532d EBSR, Humboldt Bay, N.G., 23 Apr. 44

Helleskov, Erik, T/Sgt., 542d EBSR, Salamaua, N.G., 20 Aug. 43

Holstlaw, Albert W., T/4, 532d EBSR, Lae, N.G., 14 Sept. 43

Kump, Richard A., Pvt., 532d EBSR, Lae, N.G., 6 Sept. 43

Lane, Charles K., Major, S/Btry., Biak Island, DNG, 11 June 44

Loiselle, Francis M., S/Sgt., 532d EBSR, Nassau Bay, N.G., 30 July 43

Long, Philip W., Lt.Col., 542d EBSR, Biak Island, DNG, 29 May 44

Mackie, Franklin N., T/4, 542d EBSR, Biri Island, PI, 20 Feb. 45

Makart, Carl D., Major, 532d EBSR, Humboldt Bay, N.G., 23 Apr. 44

McAdams, Francis T., S/Sgt., 532d EBSR, Lae, N.G., 14 Sept. 43

Mulliken, Wallace M., Capt., 542d EBSR, Tambu Bay, N.G., 20 July 43

Neilson, Alexander M., Col., 532d EBSR, Mindoro Island, PI, 18 Dec. 44

Pearson, Bowater, T/Sgt., 532d EBSR, Nassau Bay, N.G., 30 June 43

Peters, Anthony T., Pfc., 592d EBSR, Ipil, Leyte, PI, 8 Dec. 44

Pierce, John Q., T/Sgt., 532d EBSR, Sulu Sea, PI, 21 Dec. 44

Plante, John J., T/4, 542d EBSR, Tambu Bay, N.G., 20 July 43

Poffenbanger, John O., 1stLt., 532d EBSR, Finschhafen, N.G., 25 Sept. 43

Pomeroy, Harry, Pvt., 542d EBSR, Biri Island, PI, 20 Feb. 45

Popa, Stephen, Cpl., 532d EBSR, Finschhafen, N.G., 17 Oct. 43

Radetski, Paul P., T/5, 532d EBSR, Lae, N.G., 14 Sept. 43

*Rising, Harry N., Major, 532d EBSR, Finschbafen, N.G., 10 Oct. 43
    Humboldt Bay, N.G., 23 Apr. 44

Roughton, Miles U., T/4, 532d EBSR, Nassau Bay, N.G., 9 July 43

Stevenson, Edwin T., Capt., S/Btry, Ormoc, Leyte, PI, 7 Dec. 44

Sweatte, Felix G., T/Sgt., 532d EBSR, Nassau Bay, N.G., 30 June 43

Swenson, George W. P., 1stLt., S/Btry, Dempta Bay, N.G., 23 Apr. 44

Swisher, Stephen A., III, 1stLt., 262d Med. Bn., Humboldt Bay, N.G., 23
    Apr. 44

Waldum, Harold P., T/4, 592d EBSR, Admiralty Is., 17 Mar. 44

Welch, Arthur R., T/4, 592d EBSR, Arawe, N.B., 26 Feb. 44

Welch, William H., Pfc., 542d EBSR, Tambu Bay, N.G., 20 July 43

Wells, Robert E., Major, 542d EBSR, Biak Island, 7 June 44

Winger, George W., Pfc., 532d EBSR, Lae, N.G., 14 Sept. 43

Wodrsch, Lester H., T/5, 542d EBSR, Wakde Island, DNG, 18 May 44

Zeman, George J., T/5, 542d EBSR, Wakde Island, DNG, 18 May 44

Legion of Merit

Cerrina, Joseph, T/Sgt., 162d Ordnance Maintenance Company

Claypool, Charles B., Lt.Col., 532d Engineer Boat and Shore Regiment

Conley, Orvel, T/4, 592d Engineer Boat and Shore Regiment
Fokianos, John, S/Sgt., 542d Engineer Boat and Shore Regiment
Goldsworthy, Ronald A., S/Sgt., 542d Engineer Boat and Shore Regiment
Heavey, William F., Brig.Gen., Hq., 2d Engineer Special Brigade
Ivey, Ellis M. Jr., 1stLt., 562d Engineer Boat Maintenance Battalion
Jones, Ralph W., Jr., Capt., 542d Engineer Boat and Shore Regiment
Kaplan, Leonard, Lt.Col., 592d Engineer Boat and Shore Regiment
Keyes, Allen L., Col., 592d Engineer Boat and Shore Regiment
Long, Philip W., Lt.Col., 542d Engineer Boat and Shore Regiment
Magnuson, Harry J., S/Sgt., 542d Engineer Boat and Shore Regiment
Neff, John K., Lt.Col., 592d Engineer Boat and Shore Regiment
O'Halloran, Thomas G., S/Sgt., 542d Engineer Boat and Shore Regiment
Shaul, Rex K., Major, 592d Engineer Boat and Shore Regiment
Steiner, John J. F., Col., 532d Engineer Boat and Shore Regiment
Rising, Harry N., Major, 532d Engineer Boat and Shore Regiment
Volgenau, Elmer P., Lt.Col., Headquarters, 2d Engineer Special Brigade
Walker, Howard D., T/4, 542d Engineer Boat and Shore Regiment
Wells, Robert E., Capt., 542d Engineer Boat and Shore Regiment

SOLDIER'S MEDAL

Bray, Biron G., Pvt., 592d EBSR, Arawe, N.B., 26 Feb. 44
Cathers, Earle R., Pvt., 287th Sig. Co., Yeppon, Aust., 28 Apr, 43
Cerrina, Joseph, T/Sgt., 162d Ord. Co., Finschhafen, N.G., 8 Sept. 44
DeHaut, William P., T/5, 532d EBSR, San Pedro Bay, PI, 11 Apr. 45
Gilbert, Ellis C., T/5, 592d EBSR, Cape Sudest, N.G., 2 Feb. 44
Goldberg, Edward H., Pvt., 592d EBSR, Dixon, Illinois, 27 Dec. 42
Hampton, George T., Pfc., 592d EBSR, Cairns, Aust., 13 Sept. 43
Hueter, Ernest B., 1stLt., 592d EBSR, Cape Cod, Mass., 2 Oct. 42
Manieri, Tyrell D., 1stSgt., 532d EBSR, Nassau Bay, N.G., 30 July 43
McGuire, William B., 1stLt., 532d EBSR, Manila, PI, 11 May 45
Mould, Herbert J., Pvt., 532d EBSR, Palawan, PI, 6 June 45
Nordle, Louis F., T/4, 532d EBSR, Lae, N.G., 15 Nov. 43
Shelton, Leo A., T/5, 532d EBSR, Humboldt Bay, N.G., I May 44
Springer, Odey L., T/5, 592d EBSR, Leyte, PI, 18 Nov. 44
Surratt, Virgil R., T/4, 562d EBM Bn., San Pedro Bay, PI, 17 Nov. 44

BRONZE STAR MEDAL

Abell, Leslie H., 1stLt., 592d EBSR, MA† Admiralty Is., 9 Mar.–30 Apr. 44

Addis, Laverne C., T/5, 532d EBSR, HA‡ Mindoro Is., PI, 15 Dec. 44

*Aguiar, Arthur J., T/4, 532d EBSR, MA New Guinea, 4 Sept. 43–1 June 44

    HA Sulu Sea near PI, 21 Dec. 44

Ambler, Arthur E., T/5, 532d EBSR, MA New Guinea, 30 July 43–15 Feb. 44

Anderson, George F., T/Sgt., 532d EBSR, MA New Guinea, 4 Sept.–8 Oct. 43

Anderson, Glen H., T/5, 532d EBSR, MA New Guinea, 30 June 43–7 Mar. 44

Anderson, John R., T/Sgt., 532d EBSR, MA Humboldt Bay, N.G., 22 Apr–1 May 44

Anderson, Ray E., S/Sgt., 562d EBM Bn., MA Leyte, PI, 1 Sept.–9 Oct. 44

Antioco, Fred P., T/5, 532d EBSR, MA Lae, N.G., 13 Sept.–15 Sept. 43

Antonucci, Angelo A., S/Sgt., 542d EBSR, MA Hollandia, DNG, 22 Apr.–17 July 44

Archacki, Stanley R., Pfc., 542d EBSR, HA Biak Island, NEI, 27 May 44

Aring, Forrest, T/4, 532d EBSR, MA New Guinea, 30 June 43–7 Mar. 44

Armstrong, Franklin J., T/4, 592d EBSR, HA Admiralty Is., 11 Mar. 44

Arthur, Charles S., T/4, 532d EBSR, HA Nassau Bay, N.G., 9 July 44

Axtell, Chandler A., S/Sgt., S/Btry, HA Leyte, PI, 7 Dec. 44

Bagozzi, Julie G., M/Sgt., 562d EBM Bn., MA New Guinea and Leyte, PI, 1 Nov. 43–10 May 45

Baker, Joseph H., Capt., 592d EBSR, MA Admiralty Is., 15 Mar.–25 Apr. 44

Balint, Louis, S/Sgt., 542d EBSR, MA New Guinea, 15 Nov. 43–22 June 44

Ball, Martin O., 1stSgt., 532d EBSR, MA Lae, N.G., 4 Sept.–1 Oct. 43

Ball, Virgil G., T/5, 532d EBSR, MA New Guinea, 4 Sept. 43–1 June 44

Balthrop, John E., Jr., T/4, 542d EBSR, HA Cebu, PI, 26 Mar. 45

Baratti, Vincent J., S/Sgt., 532d EBSR, HA Lae, N.G., 4 Sept. 43

Barlow, Willard J., T/4, 532d EBSR, MA New Guinea, 30 June 43–7 Mar. 44

Barnard, Buelen, S/Sgt., 542d EBSR, HA Biak Island, NEI, 7 June 44

Barnett, Burton E., S/Sgt., 532d EBSR, HA Mindoro Island, PI, 18 Dec. 44

Barrett, Arthur H., Major, Hq., 2d ESB, MA New Guinea and PI, 23 Sept. 44–30 Mar. 45

Bass, George N., Jr., Capt., Hq., 2d ESB, MA Leyte, PI, 27 Dec. 44–14 Mar. 45

Beal, Asa J., T/4, 532d EBSR, MA New Guinea, 30 June 43–7 Mar. 44

Beals, Daniel W., Sgt., S/Btry, HA Leyte, PI, 7 Dec. 44

Beaver, Walter D., Capt., S/Btry, HA Biak Island, NEI, 8 June 44

    * Also awarded Oak Leaf Cluster.

    † Indicates award was made for meritorious achievement.

    ‡ Indicates award was made for heroic action.

Benda, Wilbur L., Sgt., 532d EBSR, MA New Guinea, 22 Sept.–15 Oct. 43

Beyers, Robert W., T/4, 532d EBSR, HA Lae, N.G., 12 Sept. 43

Bickness, Laverne M., S/Sgt., 532d EBSR, MA New Guinea, 30 June 43–7 Mar. 44

Bidwell, Charles E., S/Sgt., 532d EBSR, MA New Guinea, 4 Sept.-8 Oct. 43

Blanchard, Karl W., Lt.Col., Hq., 2d ESB, MA Leyte, PI, 26 Dec. 44–21 Mar. 45

Bludworth, Richard W., Jr., T/Sgt., 562d EBM Bn., HA Oro Bay, N.G., 7 July 43

Bober, Edward J., T/5, 532d EBSR, HA Mindoro Island, PI, 18 Dec. 44

Boles, Ernest E., T/5, 592d EBSR, HA Leyte, PI, 7 Dec. 44

Bostrom, Carl G., T/5, 532d EBSR, MA Finschhafen, N.G., 22 Sept.–10 Oct. 43

Branistedt, Walter E., T/5, 532d EBSR, HA Lae, N.G., 4-8 Sept. 43

Breeding, Dalton, T/4, 592d EBSR, HA Cape Gloucester, N.B., 25 Jan. 44

Brewer, Orville G., T/5, 532d EBSR, HA Mindoro Island, PI, 15 Dec. 44

Brockett, Ernest D., Jr., Lt.Col.. 532d EBSR, MA Palo, Leyte, PI, 20-28 Oct. 44

Brown, Louis J., T/4, 532d EBSR, HA Nassau Bay, N.G., 2 July 43

Brunello, Paul, S/Sgt., 532d EBSR, HA Finschhafen, N.G., 21 Oct. 43

Buchanan, Harold J., T/Sgt., 562d EBM Bn., MA Leyte, PI, 22 Oct. 44–30 Mar. 45

Budde, Walter H., T/5, 532d EBSR, MA Finschhaferi, N.G., 22 Sept.–15 Oct. 43

Bugdumus, Anthony, T/5, 532d EBSR, HA Lae, N.G., 11-12 Sept. 43

Buffoni, Harry J., T/4, 532d EBSR, MA New Guinea, 4 Sept.–10 Oct. 43 & 22 Apr.–10 May 44

Burke, Lou, T/Sgt., 532d EBSR, HA Lae, N.G., 13 Sept. 43

Burnside, Frank E., S/Sgt., Hq. 2d ESB, MA SWPA, 2 July 44–10 May 45

Burns, Allen R., T/4, 532d EBSR, MA Lae & Finschhafen, N.G., 4 Sept. 43–15 Feb. 44

Butler, Wilfred J., T/4, 542d EBSR, HA Biak Island, NEI, 7 June 44

Byock, Seymour, T/4, 592d EBSR, MA Cape Gloucester, N.B., 26 Dec. 43–8 May 44

*Byrnes, William H., T/5, 532d EBSR, HA Lae, N.G., 8 Sept. 43 HA Leyte, PI, 20 Oct. 44

Campbell, Bruce B., 1stLt., 532d EBSR, MA New Guinea, 4 Sept. 43–10 May 44

Canning, John V., T/5, 542d EBSR, MA New Guinea, 7 Aug. 43–25 Jan. 44

Cantanzarita, Salvatore J., Pfc., 262d Med. Bn., HA Biak Island, NEI, 7-16 June 44

Carrerio, Joseph J., 2dLt., 562d EBM Bn., MA Leyte, PI, 22 Oct. 44–1 Feb. 45

Cartwright, Harry A., Jr., T/5, 542d EBS, HA Biak Island, NEI, 7 June 44

Castelluzzj, Frank, T/5, 532d EBSR, MA Finschhafen, N.G., 22 Sept. 43–1 Feb. 44

Caudill, Woodrow, T/5, 532d EBSR, HA Finschhafen, N.G., 16-17 Oct. 43

Chambers, Ralph F., S/Sgt., 542d EBSR, HA Biak Island, NEI, 7 June 44

Chatterton, Harley M., Jr., Capt., 542d EBSR, MA Biak Island, NEI, 20 July–27 Aug. 44

Cheek, Horace L., 1stLt., 542d EBSR, MA Cebu, PI, 26-28 Mar. 45

Christie, Roy 5., T/4, 532d EBSR, MA Lae & Finschhafen, N.G., Sept. 43–Feb. 44

Clapso, Joseph E., Pvt., 562d EBM Bn.. MA New Britain, 26 Dec. 43–8 May 44

Clark, Benjamin H., Jr., S/Sgt., 592d EBSR, MA New Britain, 22-24 Feb. 44

Claypool, Charles B., Lt.Col., 532d EBSR, MA Mindoro Island, PI, 22 Nov-31 Dec. 44

Clift, Mortimer A., Capt., Hq. 2d ESB, HA Lae, N.G., 11-12 Sept. 43

Coates, Frank K., S/Sgt., 532d EBSR, HA Leyte, PI, 20 Oct. 44

Cobb, Grover G., T/5, 542d EBSR, MA New Guinea, 7 Aug. 43–25 Jan. 44

Coleman, Edward C., 1stLt., 592d EBSR, MA Legaspi, Luzon, PI, 1 Apr.–25 June 45

Collier, Barron, Jr., Capt., Hq 2d ESB, MA Lae, N.G., 4 Sept.–3 Oct. 43

Commandella, Emil H., T/4, 532d EBSR, MA New Guinea, 4 Sept., 43–1 June 44

Conway, Thomas R., Pfc., 542d EBSR, HA Biak Island, NEI, 7 June 44

Cormier, John W., T/4, 532d EBSR, HA Hollandia DNG, 23 Apr. 44

Crampton, Joseph H., T/5, 532d EBSR, HA Hollandia DNG, 23 Apr. 44

Crouch, Onie, T/4, 532d EBSR, MA New Guinea, 30 June 43–7 Mar. 44

Crowther, Russell L., T/5, 592d EBSR, MA Admiralty Is., 9 Mar.–30 Apr. 44

Davidson, Lester W., Sgt., 532d EBSR, HA Nassau Bay, N.G., 3 July 43

Davis, Carthon W., T/5, 542d EBSR, MA Biak Island, NEI, 27 May–15 Aug. 44

Davis, Donald B., 1stLt., S/Btry, HA Biak Island, NEI, 7 June 44

Davis, Melvin A., T/Sgt., 542d EBSR, MA New Guinea, 17 May–5 July 44

DeCook, Alphonse J., T/5, 532d EBSR, HA Lae, N.G., 4-8 Sept. 43

DeFord, Don D., Major, 542d EBSR, MA Cebu, PI, 26-28 Mar. 45

Denk, Lawrence L., T/4, 532d EBSR, MA Hollandia, DNG, 22-28 Apr. 44

Depoy, Darold L., T/5, 592d EBSR, HA Cape Gloucester, N.B., 25 Jan. 44

Dibble, Wortham W., 1stLt., 532d EBSR, HA Hollandia, DNG, 23 Apr. 44

Dicks, John A., T/4, 532d EBSR, MA New Guinea, 30 June 43–7 Mar. 44

Dobron, John F., T/5, 532d EBSR, MA New Guinea, 23 Sept. 43–1 Feb. 44

Dodge, Cecil E., T/5, 532d EBSR, HA Lae, N.G., 8 Sept. 43

Dodgen, Leonard L., T/4, 542d EBSR, HA New Guinea, 17 May 44

Domer, William G., WO/JG, 592d EBSR, MA Admiralty Is., 2 Mar. 44

Donahue, Philip T., Pvt., 532d EBSR, HA Hollandia, DNG, 23 Apr. 44

D'Onofrio, Francis A., 2dLt., 542d EBSR, HA Biak Island, NEI, 7 June 44

Doran, James J., 1stLt., 592d EBSR, MA Corregidor, PI, 16 Feb-1 Mar. 45

Drinkwater, Leslie M., T/4, 532d EBSR, MA New Guinea, 4 Sept. 43–15 Feb. 44

Duhrkipp, Walter, S/Sgt., 562d EBM Bn., MA Cape Gloucester, N.B., 26 Dec. 43–

8 May 44

Duffy, John E., 1stLt., 562d EBM Bn., MA Admiralty Is., 9 Mar.-30 Apr. 44

Duin, Fred H. F., T/4, 532d EBSR, MA New Guinea, 3 Sept. 43–1 May 44

Duncan, Joe L., T/3, 563d EBM Bn., MA New Guinea, 27 Sept. 43

Durr, Ray E., T/4, 532d EBSR, MA Lae, N.G., 4 Sept.-1 Oct. 43

Durstine, Raymond L., T/4, S/Btry, HA Leyte, PI, 7 Dec. 44

Dyer, Robert R., T/4, 287th Sig., MA SWPA, 14 Mar. 43–31 May 45

Earle, William P. S., Jr., 1stLt., 532d EBSR, HA Lae, N.G., 6 Sept. 43

Edmondson, Ralph D., S/Sgt., 532d EBSR, MA Romblon Is., PI, 11-12 Mar. 45

Edwards, E. L., Lt.Col., 542d EBSR, MA Leyte & Cebu, PI, 15-31 Mar. 45

Egan, Robert, T/Sgt., 532d EBSR, MA Nassau Bay, N.G., 30 June-15 Aug. 43

Eitman, Reinhardt A., T/4, 532d EBSR, HA Lae, N.G., 13-15 Sept. 43

*Elder, Russell F., T/4, 532d EBSR, MA Lae, N.G., 13-15 Sept. 43
    HA Leyte, PI, 20 Oct. 44

Ely, Kermit S., T/S, 532d EBSR, MA Lae, N.G., 13 Sept. 43

Erie, Thomas E., Sgt., 562d EBM Bn., MA Cape Gloucester, N.B., 26 Dec. 43–8 May 44

Essig, Edward J., T/4, 532d EBSR, MA Admiralty Is., 1 May-21 July 44

Etsitty, Dick, Pfc., 532d EBSR, MA Lae & Finschhafen, 4 Sept.-30 Oct. 43

Etter, Ivan C., T/5, 532d EBSR, MA Hollandia, DNG, 22-24 Apr. 44

Eulosiewicz, Frank T., S/Sgt., 532d EBSR, MA New Guinea, 3 Sept. 43–1 May 44

*Fanfara, Walter S., Pvt., 532d EBSR, MA Lae, N.G., 13 Sept. 43
    HA Leyte, PI, 20 Oct. 44

Farrahar, George L., T/5, 532d EBSR, MA Lae, N.G., 13-15 Sept. 43

Ferall, Charles C., Capt., 592d EBSR, MA Admiralty Is., 1 May-21 July 44

Fiejdaz, Stanley A., T/Sgt., Hg Co., 2d ESB, MA Leyte, PI, 20-21 Oct. 44

Fitzgerald, Ronald N., 2dLt., 532d EBSR, MA Lubang, PI, 20-23 Feb. 45

Fleming, Frank J., Pfc., 532d EBSR, HA Hollandia, DNG, 23 Apr. 44

Fleming, Leslie H., Sgt., 532d EBSR, HA Nassau Bay, N.G., 3 July 43

Fletcher, John T., T/5, 532d EBSR, HA Nassau Bay, N.G., 30 June-1 July 43

Flowers, Don M., Pvt., 532d EBSR, HA Hollandia, DNG, 23 Apr. 44

Flynn, George B. J., S/Sgt., 542d EBSR, MA SWPA, 1 Oct. 42–1 Feb. 45

Fortnum, Horace W., T/4, 532d EBSR, MA New Guinea, 4 Sept. 43–1 June 44

Forton, Vincent R., 1stLt., 562d EBM Bn., MA Leyte & Mindoro, 22 Oct. 44–1 Feb. 45

Foster, Edwin T., 1stLt., 532d EBSR, MA Lae, N.G., 4-12 Sept. 43

Foster, Howard E., T/5, 532d EBSR, MA New Guinea, 4 Sept. 43–1 June 44

Fowikels, Benjamin C., Col., 542d EBSR, MA Biak Island, NEI, 27 May-16 June 44

Franklin, Arthur E., T/5, 532d EBSR, HA Hollandia, DNG, 23 Apr. 44

Franzeen, Arnold C., Pvt., 532d EBSR, MA Palawan Is., PI, 28 Feb.-4 Mar. 45

Frey, Lawrence R., T/4, 532d EBSR, MA New Guinea, 4 Sept. 43–1 June 44

Friese, George F., Capt., 562d EBM Bn., MA Leyte, PI & New Guinea, 25 July-6 Dec. 44

Fuson, Jack C., Major, 532d EBSR, MA Lubang, PI, 16-18 Feb. 45

Gade, Harold G., T/4, 532d EBSR, MA Lae & Finschhafen, N.G., Sept. 3-Feb. 44

Gagliardo, Louis J., T/4, 542d EBSR, HA Biak Island, NEI, 7 June 44

Ganguzza, Anthony A., T/4, 562d EBM Bn., MA Leyte, PI, 22 Oct.-12 Nov. 44

Garber, Harry F., Lt.Col., 542d EBSR, MA Capul & Biri Is., PI, 19-22 Feb. 45

Garrison, Sherman F., Pfc., 532d EBSR, HA Mindoro Is., PI, 15 Dec. 44

Gaskill, Linewood G., T/4, 532d EBSR, MA New Guinea, 30 June 43–7 Mar. 44

*Gasper, Albert W., Major, 532d EBSR, MA Hollandia, DNG & Leyte, PI, 1-28 Oct. 44
    HA Mindoro Is., PI, 18 Dec. 44

Gatipon, Ernest G., T/4, 532d EBSR, MA New Guinea, 4 Sept.-30 Oct. 43

Gaulding, Aubrey E., Sgt., 287th Sig., MA Lae & Finschhafen, N.G., 4 Sept.-25 Oct. 43

Gentessee, George E., T/5, 532d EBSR, MA Nassau Bay, N.G., 3 July 44

Gessert, Arnold W., Pfc., 532d EBSR, MA Lae, N.G., 4 Sept.-1 Oct. 43

Glogowski, Stanley J., T/5, 532d EBSR, HA Solo Sea (near PI), 21 Dec. 44

Godbout, Joseph O., T/5, 542d EBSR, HA Biak Island, NEI, 7 June 44

Gold, Everett E., T/4, 532d EBSR, MA New Guinea, 4 Sept.–30 Oct. 43

Graham, Wesley J., 2dLt., 592d EBSR, MA Leyte, PI, 25 Nov. 44–15 Jan. 45

Green, James L., Pfc., 592d EBSR, HA Hollandia, DNG, 18 May 44

Greene, Sam A., Pfc., 532d EBSR, HA Leyte, PI, 20 Oct. 44

George, Constantine M., T/4, 592d EBSR, Corregidor

Gubitz, Nathan, T/5, 532d EBSR, MA New Guinea, 4 Sept. 43–1 June 44

Gutknecht, John W., Capt., 592d EBSR, MA Maffin Bay, DNG, 9 Aug.–9
   Oct. 44

Haldorson, Ole J., T/4, 532d EBSR, MA New Guinea, 4 Sept. 43–1 June 44

Hammill, William J., Sgt., 532d EBSR, MA Leyte, PI, 20 Oct. 44

Hammond, Ernest R., T/4, 532d EBSR, HA Philippine Islands, 21 Dec. 44

Hanchulak, Nicholas, Cpl., 532d EBSR, HA Finschhafen, N.G., 17 Oct. 43

Harper, Samuel D., 1stLt., 592d EBSR, HA Leyte, PI, 7 Dec. 44

Harris, Rutherford, Capt., 532d EBSR, HA Mindoro Is., PI, 18 Dec. 44

Hartnett, Paul, T/4, 532d EBSR, HA Nassau Bay, N.G., 9 July 43

Hatcher, Robert C., 1stLt., 532d EBSR, HA Finschhafen, N.G., 16-17 Oct. 43

Heavey, William F., Brig.Gen., Hq. 2d ESB, MA Leyte, PI, 20 Oct. 44

Henneke, Roy E., T/4, 532d EBSR, MA Lae & Finschhafen, N.G., Sept.
   43–Feb. 44

Hennessey, Kieran W., Capt., 262d Med. Bu., MA Leyte, PI, 20 Oct.–31
   Dec. 44

Henry, Robert E., T/4, 532d EBSR, MA Lae & Finschhafen, N.G., Sept.
   43–Feb. 44

Henick, Edward R., T/5, 532d EBSR, HA Lae, N.G., 6 Sept. 43

Herr, Lawrence R., Pfc., 532d EBSR, MA Leyte, PI, 25 Oct. 45

Higdon, James, Jr., T/4, 532d EBSR, MA New Guinea, 30 June 43–7 Mar.
   44

High, Lacy E., S/Sgt., 542d EBSR, MA Leyte, PI, 31 Jan.-25 Feb. 45

Holland, Archie L., Jr., Capt., 542d EBSR, MA Saidor, N.G., 1 Jan.-28
   Mar. 44

Holmquist, Earl W., Pfc., 542d EBSR, MA Cebu, PI, 26-28 Mar. 45

Holmes, Kenneth T., T/5, 532d EBSR, HA Hollandia, DNG, 23 Apr. 44

Holtsberry, Thomas J., T/4, 532d EBSR, HA Finschhafen, N.G., 16-17 Oct.
   43

Hopkins, John E., T/4, 532d EBSR, MA New Guinea, 30 June 43–7 Mar. 44

Houghtaling, Edward L., T/Sgt., Hq. Co. 2 ESB, MA New Guinea & Leyte,
   PI, 15 Sept. 44–1 June 45

Hovey, Daryl G., T/4, 542d EBSR, HA Wakde Island, DNG, 18 May 44

Huber, George W., Hg. Co. 2 ESB, MA New Guinea & Leyte, PI, 15 Sept. 44–26 Dec. 44

Huetter, Bernard R., Jr., Capt., 532d EBSR, MA Leyte, PI, 20-28 Oct. 44

Huffman, Thomas B., 1stLt., 532d EBSR, HA Lae, N.G., 11-12 Sept. 43

Hughes, Ernest, T/4, 592d EBSR, HA Cape Gloucester, N.B., 25 Jan. 44

Hummel, Raymond L., Pfc., 542d EBSR, HA Biak Island, NEI, 7 June 44

Hund, Charles M., T/4, 532d EBSR, HA Lae, N.G., 11-12 Sept. 43

Huss, Otis P., T/4, 532d EBSR, MA New Guinea, 30 June 43–7 Mar. 44

Jacobs, Paul H., Major, Hq. 2d ESB, MA Leyte, PI, 1 Jan.–19 June 45

Jager, Kenneth W., 1stSgt., 532d EBSR, MA Hollandia, DNG, 23 Apr. 44

Jarboe, William H., T/4, 532d EBSR, MA New Guinea, 30 June 43–7 Mar. 44

Jellison, Louis R., S/Sgt., 532d EBSR, HA Nassau Bay, N.G., 9 July 43

Jenkins, Carl L., T/5, 532d EBSR, MA Hollandia, DNG, 28 Apr. 44

Jenkins, John M., Major, 542d EBSR, MA Leyte, PI, 10 Dec. 44–15 Mar. 45

Jepeal, Peter H., Cpl., 532d EBSR, HA Lae, N.G., 4-8 Sept. 43

Jerger, Lorenz, T/4, 542d EBSR, MA Biri Is., PI, 20 Feb. 45

Jobe, Harmon, T/4, 542d EBSR, HA Wakde Island, DNG, 18 May 44

Johniken, Wayne E., S/Sgt., 532d EBSR, MA Lae, N.G., 4-14 Sept. 43

Johnson, Wallace E., T/5, 532d EBSR, HA Finschhafen, N.G., 16-17 Oct. 43

Jones, Charles C., Sgt., 262d Med Bn., MA Lae, N.G., 4-12 Sept. 43

Jones, Edwin L., Pfc., 532d EBSR, HA Lae, N.G., 4-8 Sept. 43

Jones, Ralph W., Jr., Major, 542d EBSR, MA Capul & Biri Is., PI, 19-22 Feb. 45

Julius, Ben J., Cpl., 532d EBSR, HA Philippine Is., 21 Dec. 44

Kaplan, Leonard, Lt.Col., 592d EBSR, MA Admiralty Is., 29 Feb.–18 May 44

Karnatz, Edward G., Pvt., 542d EBSR, HA Biak Island, NEI, 27 May 44

Karpinski, Raymond L., T/4, 532d EBSR, HA Hollandia, DNG, 23 Apr. 44

*Kasper, Robert J., Col., 532d EBSR, MA Biak Island, NEI, 10 June–30 July 44

    MA Leyte, PI, 6 Oct. 44–24 Mar. 45

Keefe, John J., S/Sgt., 542d EBSR, MA New Guinea, 15 Nov. 43–22 June 44

Kejonen, Otto A., T/5, 532d EBSR, MA Lae, N.G., 6 Sept. 43

Kelch, James R., T/5, 532d EBSR, MA New Guinea, 4 Sept. 43–1 June 44

Kendall, Leonard B., T/4, 532d EBSR, MA New Guinea, 4 Sept. 43–1 June 44

Kenney, Clarence J., T/4, 532d EBSR, HA Hollandia, DNG, 23-24 Apr. 44

Kightlinger, Edward S., T/5, 532d EBSR, MA New Guinea, 30 June 43–7 Mar. 44

Kimble, Essel E., T/5, 592d EBSR, HA Cape Gloucester, N.B., 25 Jan. 44

King, Robert P., S/Sgt., 592d EBSR, HA Corregidor

Kirk, Elden L., T/5, 542d EBSR, MA Biak Island, NEI, 27 May–8 Aug. 44

Knecht, Robert L., Pfc., 542d EBSR, HA Biak Island, NEI, 7 June 44

Knetter, Charles, T/5, 532d EBSR, HA Hollandia, DNG, 23 Apr. 44

Koeln, Herman A., Capt., 592d EBSR, HA Corregidor

Kowalczyk, Charles J., T/5, 532d EBSR, HA Hollandia, DNG, 23 Apr. 44

Krist, Edmund J., T/4, 532d EBSR, HA Mindoro Is., PI, 18 Dec. 44

Kurik, Joseph J., T/Sgt., 542d EBSR, HA Cebu, PI, 26 Mar. 45

Lapidus, Earl A., 1stLt., 562d EBM Bn., MA Leyte, PI, 23 Nov. 44–7 Apr. 45

Lawrence, John M., T/4, 532d EBSR, HA Mindoro Is., PI, 30 Dec. 44

Lawson, Albert F., T/4, 532d EBSR, HA Finschhafen, N.G., 16-17 Oct. 43

Lazarowitz, Herman, T/4, 532d EBSR, MA Lae & Finschhafen, N.G., 4 Sept.–30 Oct. 43

Lebak, Donald K., Pfc., 532d EBSR, HA Lae, N.G., 6 Sept. 43

Leclair, Leonard A., Major, Hq. 2 ESB, MA New Guinea & Leyte, PI, 28 July 43–14 Feb. 45

Leder, Emanuel S., T/5, 532d EBSR, HA Nassau Bay, N.G., 2 July 43

Lee, Jack A., 2dLt., 532d EBSR, MA Lae & Finschhafen, N.G., 4 Sept.–8 Oct. 43

Lee, Robert C., Capt., 532d EBSR, MA Leyte & Mindoro Is., PI, 20 Oct. 44–1 Feb. 45

Leibner, Snydey, S/Sgt., 532d EBSR, HA Lae, N.G., 6 Sept. 43

Leonard, Charles W., T/Sgt., 592d EBSR, MA Leyte, PI, 20 Dec. 44–1 Jan. 44

Levy, Ira W., 1stLt., 592d EBSR, HA Cape Gloucester, N.B., 25 Jan. 44

Lewman, Joseph A., T/4, 532d EBSR, MA New Guinea, 30 June 43–7 Mar. 44

Lillegard, Elmer L., T/5, 542d EBSR, HA Biak Island, NEI, 27 May 44

Linscott, Cecil H., T/4, 532d EBSR, MA New Guinea, 30 June 43–7 Mar. 44

Long, Philip W., Lt.Col., 542d EBSR, MA Luzon, Panay & Negros Is., PI, 10 Mar.–15 Apr. 45

Lorek, Joseph W., Pvt., 542d EBSR, HA Biak Island, NEI, 27 May 44

Lowell, Ross S., S/Sgt., 592d EBSR, MA Cape Gloucester, N.B., 26 Dec. 43–8 May 44

Lucchi, Lucius B., S/Sgt., 532d EBSR, HA Nassau Bay, N.G., 3 July 43

Luther, Clyde S., T/4, 592d EBSR, HA Arawe, N.B., 17 Dec. 43

Lynn, William R., T/4, 532d EBSR, MA New Guinea, 30 June 43–7 Mar. 44

Maciuska, Philip J., Cpl., 532d EBSR, HA Lae, N.G., 4-12 Sept. 43

Madden, George E., T/4, 532d EBSR, MA New Guinea, 30 June 43–7 Mar. 44

Majernik, Joseph, Pfc., 542d EBSR, MA Cebu, PI, 26-28 Mar. 45

Manchester, Madison J., 2dLt., 592d EBSR, HA Admiralty Is., 2-4 Mar. 44

Manieri, Tyrell T., 1stSgt., 532d EBSR, MA Nassau Bay, N.G., 29 June–4 July 43

Mann, Thomas K., Pfc., 542d EBSR, HA Cebu, PI, 14 Apr. 45

Marshall, Tony, T/5, 542d EBSR, HA Biak Island, NEI, 7 June 44

Martin, John P., Cpl., 542d BBSR, HA Biak Island, NEI, 27 May 44

McCampbell, Elmo H., T/5, 532d EBSR, MA Lae & Finschhafen, N.G., 4 Sept.–30 Oct. 43

McGinty, Thomas J., T/5, 532d EBSR, MA Lae & Finschhafen, N.G., Sept. 43–Feb. 44

McGovern, John T., T/5, 542d EBSR, MA Biri Island, PI, 20 Feb. 45

McGrath, James G., T/4, 532d EBSR, MA Lae & Finschhafen, N.G., 4 Sept. 43–15 Feb. 44

McGraw, Lowell S., Capt., 262d Med Bn., MA Leyte, PI, 20 Oct.–31 Dec. 44

McGregor, Melvin L., T/4, 532d EBSR, MA New Guinea, 4 Sept.–20 Oct. 43

McLane, Miles P., T/4, 532d EBSR, HA Lae, N.G., 6 Sept. 43

McLaurin, Edward E., T/5, 532d EBSR, HA Hollandia, DNG, 23 Apr. 44

McPherson, Henderson E., Capt., 532d EBSR, MA Mindoro Is., PI, 21 Dec. 44

*Meier, Raymond O., Capt., 532d EBSR, MA Leyte, PI, 20 Oct. 44
HA Hollandia, DNG, 23 Apr. 44

Meyer, Fred B., 1stLt., 532d EBSR, HA Lae, N.G., 13-14 Sept. 43

Michalkiewicz, Leo A., Pvt., 532d EBSR, HA Mindoro Island, PI, 28 Dec. 44

Midthassel, Reidar, T/4, 532d EBSR, MA New Guinea, 30 June 43–7 Mar. 44

Miller, Frederick W., Jr., Pvt., 592d EBSR, HA Admiralty Is., 2 Mar. 44

Mills, Elijah, T/5, 542d EBSR, MA Cebu, PI, 26-28 Mar. 45

Mills, Willie C., T/Sgt., 532d EBSR, MA Lae, N.G., 4-14 Sept. 43

Mitchell, Bert M., Major, Hq., 2 ESB, MA New Guinea & Leyte, PI, 16 Aug. 43–11 May 45

Molenda, Joseph A., Pfc., 542d EBSR, MA Cebu, PI, 26-28 Mar. 45

Molloy, John J., Capt., 592d EBSR, MA Leyte, PI, 26 Dec. 44–10 Jan. 45

Molosso, Robert P., 1stLt., 532d EBSR, MA Nassau Bay, N.G., 29 June–15 Aug. 43

Mooney, Francis M., T/5, 532d EBSR, HA Hollandia, DNG, 23 Apr. 44

Moore, Joseph G., Pvt., 542d EBSR, HA Biak Island, NEI, 7 June 44

Moskowitz, Victor, S/Sgt., 532d EBSR, MA Nassau Bay, N.G., 9 July 43

Motto, Charles P., Lt.Col., 542d EBSR, MA Visayan Group, PI, 1 Mar.–10 May 45

Mulliken, Wallace M., Capt., 542d EBSR, MA Biak Island, NEI, 27 May–
16 June 44

Nagy, Frank J., Pfc., 532d EBSR, HA Nassau Bay, N.G., 9 July 43

Navarra, Michael A., Pfc., 532d EBSR, MA Lae, N.G., 13-15 Sept. 43

*Neilson, Alexander M., Col., 532d EBSR, MA Hollandia, DNG, 30 Apr.–
6 May 44
MA Leyte, PI, 1-28 Oct. 44

Nelson, L. J., S/Sgt., 592d EBSR, MA Leyte, PI, 5 Nov. 44–5 Jan. 45

Neuhaus, Richard, 1stLt., 532d EBSR, MA Nassau Bay, N.G., 29 June-15
Aug. 43

Neva, Oscar H., T/5, 532d EBSR, MA Lae & Finschhafen, N.G., 4 Sept.–
30 Oct. 43

Newton, Cecil J., Capt., 532d EBSR, MA Nassau Bay, N.G., 29 June–15
Aug. 43

Nizzi, Joseph, M/Sgt., 562d EBM Bn., MA Leyte, PI, 16 Nov. 44–1 Feb. 45

Nolan, John, T/4, 542d EBSR, HA Biak Island, NEI, 7 June 44

Norris, J. Jonathan, 1stLt., 542d EBSR, HA Biak Island, NEI, 7 June 44

Numinen, Tauno, T/5, 532d EBSR, MA Lae & Finschhafen, N.G., 4 Sept.
43–15 Feb. 44

Oakley, Clyde C., 1stLt., 532d EBSR, MA Nassau Bay, N.G., 29 June–14
Aug. 43

Oliver, Ernest, Cpl., 532d EBSR, MA Finschhafen, N.G., 22 Sept.–15 Oct.
43

Oliver, Willie L., T/Sgt., 592d EBSR, MA Admiralty Is., 9 Mar.–30 Apr. 44

Olsen, Ole K., T/4, 532d EBSR, HA Mindoro Is., PI, 18 Dec. 44

Oppido, Albert A., 1stLt., 532d EBSR, HA Lae, N.G., 6 Sept. 43

Pahre, John A., T/5, S/Btry, HA Leyte, PI, 7 Dec. 44

Pappas, Steve N., T/5, 542d EBSR, HA Wakde Island, DNG, 9 July 44

Parks, Winfred L., T/4, 532d EBSR, HA Mindoro Is., PI, 28 Dec. 44

Parrot, Amos D., 2dLt., 532d EBSR, MA Lae & Finschhafen, N.G., 4 Sept.
43–10 Sept. 44

Payne, Alonzo W., T/3, 562d EBM Bn., MA Philippine Islands, 22 Oct.
44–25 Jan. 45

Peakler, Michael J., T/Sgt., 562d EBM Bn., MA Leyte, PI, 24 Oct. 44–1
Feb. 45

Penaluna, William S., S/Sgt., 532d EBSR, MA Lae, N.G., 4 Sept.–1 Oct. 43

Perez, Henry L., Pfc., 532d EBSR, MA Lae & Finschhafen, N.G., 4 Sept.–
30 Oct. 43

Perkins, Clifford E., T/4, 532d EBSR, MA Lae & Finschhafen, N.G., 4
Sept.–1 Oct. 43

Riggins, James W., T/4, 532d EBSR, MA Hollandia, DNG, 23 Apr. 44

Rigney, Edward T., Lt.Col., 287th Sig., MA New Guinea, 11 Aug. 43–13 Oct. 44

Rising, Harry N., Lt.Col., 532d EBSR, MA Leyte, PI, 20-28 Oct. 44

*Ritchie, Balis, T/5, 532d EBSR, HA Lae, N.G., 13-15 Sept. 43
    HA Leyte, PI, 20 Oct. 44

Robb, John A., T/4, S/Btry, HA Leyte, PI, 7 Dec. 44

Robertson, Hurman O., T/5, 532d EBSR, HA Hollandia, DNG, 23 Apr. 44

Rodeman, Wayne A., 1stLt., 532d EBSR, MA Nassau Bay, N.G., 29 June–15 Aug. 43

Rodgers, Robert W., T/4, 542d EBSR, HA Biak Island, NEI, 7 June 44

Rosen, Abraham E., Lt.Col., 262d Med Bn., MA Leyte, PI, 20 Oct. 44

Rosenbauer, Leonard J., T/4, 532d EBSR, MA Lae, N.G., 6-22 Sept. 43

Rotkovitz, Henry M., S/Sgt., 532d EBSR, HA Leyte, PI, 20 Oct. 44

Ruel, Emery W., Cpl., 532d EBSR, HA Hollandia, DNG, 23 Apr. 44

Ruger, Arlington, S/Sgt., 532d EBSR, MA Lae, N.G., 4 Sept.-15 Oct. 43

Rury, Franklin, T/5, 592d EBSR, MA Lae & Finschhafen, N.G., Sept. 43–Feb. 44

Rutherford, John H., Pfc., 542d EBSR, MA Cebu, PI, 26-28 Mar. 45

Rutt, William H., Sgt., 542d EBSR, MA Cebu, PI, 26-28 Mar. 45

Sagan, Chester T., T/5, 542d EBSR, MA Cebu, PI, 26-28 Mar. 45

Savage, Donald, T/5, 542d EBSR, HA Biak Is., NEI, 7 June 44

Scalzo, Felix N., T/3, 562d EBM Bn., MA Cape Gloucester, N.B., 26 Dec. 43–8 May 44

Schenk, Edward S., Capt., 562d EBM Bn., MA Biak Island, NEI, 27 May–1 Oct. 44

Schlede, Karl G., T/Sgt., 532d EBSR, MA New Guinea, 30 June 43–10 Mar. 44

Schmidt, Andres, Sgt., 532d EBSR, MA Finschhafen, N.G., 22 Sept.–15 Oct. 43

Schroth, Edward J., S/Sgt., Hq. Co. 2 ESB, MA New Guinea & Leyte, PI, 18 Aug. 43–31 Mar. 45

Scott, George B., T/4, 532d EBSR, MA Lae & Finschhafen, N.G., 4 Sept.-30 Oct. 44

*Scott, William C., Capt., 262d Med En., MA Arawe, N.B., 15 Dec. 43–9 Mar. 44
    MA Leyte & Luzon Is., PI, 20 Oct. 44–20 Mar. 45

Seay, Earl V., Pfc., 592d EBSR, HA Admiralty Is., 18 Mar. 44

*Seipt, Henry M., Jr., Major 592d EBSR, MA Admiralty Is., 2-31 May 44
    MA Philippine Is., 2-27 Feb. 45

Shimel, Albert C., Sr., T/5, 542d EBSR, HA Biak Island, NEI, 7 June 44

Sickert, Walter, T/4, 562d EBM Bn., MA Cape Gloucester, N.B., 26 Dec. 43–8 May 44

Silverstein, Israel, T/5, 532d EBSR, HA Mindoro Island, PI, 30 Dec. 44

Simpon, Ralph T., Lt.Col., 562d EBM Bn., BN MA Leyte, PI, 26 Dec. 44–31 Mar. 45

Simpson, Arthur A., S/Sgt., 592d EBSR, MA Admiralty Is., 9 Mar.–28 Apr. 44

Sims, James D., T/4, 532d EBSR, HA Hollandia, DNG, 23 Apr. 44

Skewes, Charles C., Sgt., 532d EBSR, MA Hollandia, DNG, 22 Apr.–1 May 44

Skidmore, James K., T/4, 532d EBSR, MA New Guinea, 30 June 43–7 Mar. 44

Smith, Charlie, Cpl., 542d EBSR, HA Biak Island, NEI, 7 June 44

Smith, Donald W., Sgt., 532d EBSR, HA Lae, N.G., 4-8 Sept. 43

Smith, William J., T/4, 532d EBSR, HA Hollandia, DNG, 23 Apr. 44

Spelts, Milton O., Capt., Hq. 2d ESB, MA Leyte, PI, 1 Feb.-15 June 45

Snell, George V., 1stLt., 542d EBSR, HA Biak Is., NEI, 7 June 44

Spicer, John G., T/5, 592d EBSR, MA Cape Gloucester, N.B., 26 Dec. 43–8 May 44

Spiriti, Joseph A., T/5, 532d EBSR, HA Leyte, PI, 20 Oct. 44

Spofford, Warren H., T/4, 532d EBSR, MA New Guinea, 4 Sept.–10 May 44

Stachowicz, Walter J., Pvt., 592d EBSR, HA Leyte, PI, 7 Dec. 44

Stafford, Thomas I., 1stLt., 592d EBSR, MA New Guinea & Leyte, PI, 29 Sept.–23 Oct. 44

Stejskal, Ludwig, Cpl., 532d EBSR, MA Finschhafen, N.G., 22 Sept.–15 Oct. 43

Stephens, Charles E., 1stLt., 592d EBSR, HA Leyte, PI, 7 Dec. 44

Stevenson, Edwin T., Capt., S/Btry, HA Biak Island, NEI, 7 June 44

Stewart, Martin L., Pvt., 542d EBSR, HA Biak Island, NEI, 7 June 44

Stewart, Robley H., 1stLt., 542d EBSR, HA Biak Island, NEI, 7 June 44

Stewart, Thomas H., 1stLt., 542d EBSR, MA Cebu, PI, 15-30 Mar. 45

Stickney, Frederick R., T/5, 542d EBSR, HA Biak Island, NEI, 7 June 44

Stiker, Milton P., 1stLt., 532d EBSR, HA Leyte, PI, 20 Oct. 44

Stiles, William, 1stLt., 542d EBSR, MA New Guinea, 2 Jan.-17 May 44

Strahm, Elgin A., S/Sgt., 532d EBSR, HA Nassau Bay, N.G., 30 June–1 July 43

Stringer, Omer B., T/4, 532d EBSR, MA New Guinea, 30 June 43–7 Mar. 44

Strominger, Kermit H., Pfc., 542d EBSR, MA Biak Island, NEI, 27 May–26 Sept. 44

Suda, Leo J., Pvt., 592d EBSR, HA Leyte, PI, 7 Dec. 45

Sulier, Donald W., 1stLt., 562d EBM Bn., MA New Guinea, 12 Oct. 43–15 Jan. 44

Sullivan, Joseph, Pfc., 542d EBSR, MA Cebu, PI, 26-28 Mar. 45

Sullivan, Joseph F., T/4, 262d Med Bn., MA Lae, N.G., 4-6 Sept. 43

Svagerko, John, T/5, 542d EBSR, HA Biak Island, NEI, 7 June 44

Terry, Milo E., T/5, 532d EBSR, HA Nassau Bay, N.G., 30 June–1 July 43

Thompson, Francis D., T/4, 532d EBSR, MA New Guinea, 30 June 43–7 Mar. 44

Tiberi, Daniel J., T/4, 532d EBSR, HA Nassau Bay, N.G., 30 June–1 July 43

Tidd, Carl L., T/Sgt., 532d EBSR, MA Lae & Finschhafen, N.G., 6-29 Sept. 43

Tomkins, Ralph L., T/4, 532d EBSR, MA Hollandia, DNG, 23 Apr. 44

Tonda, Antonio J., Pfc., 532d EBSR, MA Finschhafen, N.G., 22 Sept.–12 Oct. 43

Tornensis, Paul M., T/5, 532d EBSR, MA New Guinea, 4 Sept.–10 Oct. 43 & 22 Apr.-10 May 44

Townsend, Arthur E., 1stLt., 542d EBSR, MA Philippine Is., 31 Jan.–25 Feb. 45

Trojan, Joseph, Pfc., 532d EBSR, HA Mindoro island, PI, 30 Dec. 44

Tubolino, Angelo M., T/5, 532d EBSR, HA Lae, N.G., 11-12 Sept. 43

Tucker, Milfred R., S/Sgt., 532d EBSR, HA Finschhafen, N.G., 16-17 Oct. 43

Tucker, William R., Lt.Col., 592d EBSR, MA Leyte, PI, 20 Oct. 44

Turner, Robert L., T/5, 592d EBSR, HA Leyte, PI, 7 Dec. 44

Tuttle, Charles L., Major, 262d Med Bn., MA Cebu, PI, 26 Mar. 45

Ullery, James J., T/5, 532d EBSR, HA Mindoro Is., PI, 30 Dec. 44

Unde, Leo W., T/4, 592d EBSR, MA Cape Gloucester, N.B., 26 Dec. 43–8 May 44

Van Hoy, Joe M., Major, 542d EBSR, MA Cebu, PI, 26-28 Mar. 45

Vermette, Armand P., T/4, 532d EBSR, MA Guinea, 4 Sept.–1 June 44

Visnaw, Thomas D., T/4, 532d EBSR, MA New Guinea, 4 Sept. 43–1 June 44

Viti, Peter, T/4, 542d EBSR, HA Wakde Island, DNG, 18 May 44

Wagers, Cyril M., T/4, 532d EBSR, MA Lae & Finschhafen, N.G., Sept. 43–Feb. 44

Waisler, Norman, T/4, 532d EBSR, HA Hollandia, DNG, 23 Apr. 44

Walker, Howard D., T/4, 542d EBSR, HA Biak Island, NEI, 7 June 44

*Walker, James T., Capt., 532d EBSR, MA Lae & Finschhafen, N.G., 22 Apr.-30 May 44
MA Leyte, PI, 20-28 Oct. 44
MA Mindoro Island, PI, 22 Nov.–31 Dec. 44

*Waters, Michael K., 1stSgt., 532d EBSR, MA Hollandia, DNG, 23 Apr. 44
HA Mindoro Island, PI, 18 Dec. 44

Weaver, Ralph R., T/4, 532d EBSR, HA Mindoro Island, PI, 18 Dec. 44

Webber, Milton W., T/4, 532d EBSR, HA Lae, N.G., 4-8 Sept. 43

Weil, Robert L., 1stLt., 542d EBSR, MA Wakde Island, DNG, 17 May–8 June 44

Weinstein, Max, T/5, 532d EBSR, HA Hollandia, DNG, 23 Apr. 44

Wells, John A., Major, 562d EBM Bn., MA Leyte, PI, 22 Oct.–15 Nov. 44

Westcott, Austin T., T/4, 542d EBSR, HA Biak Island, NEI, 7 June 44

Whealton, Carlton D., Pvt., 542d EBSR, HA Biak Island, NEI, 7 June 44

White, George F., Pvt., 542d EBSR, HA Biak Island, NEI, 7 June 44

Wiley, William H., Capt., 542d EBSR, MA Biak Island, NEI, 10 June–27 Aug. 44

Wilkas, Edward C., T/5, 532d EBSR, MA New Guinea, 4 Sept. 43–1 Mar. 44

Williams, David D., 1stLt., Hq. 2d ESB, HA Arawe, N.B., 17-24 Dec. 44

Williams, Doremous L., T/Sgt., 532d EBSR, MA Lae & Finschhafen, N.G., 4 Sept.-30 Oct. 43

Winchester, Ray D., T/4, 532d EBSR, MA New Guinea, 30 June 43–7 Mar. 44

Wing, James K., T/4, 532d EBSR, MA New Guinea, 4 Sept. 43–1 June 44

Winkel, Kenneth R., T/5, 542d EBSR, HA Biak Island, DNG, 7 June 44

Wolfe, Jeremiah J., 1stLt., 532d EBSR, MA Lae & Finschhafen, N.G., 4 Sept. 43–10 Dec. 44

Wolfe, Lawrence A., T/5, 542d EBSR, HA Biak Island, NEI, 7 June 44

Wolz, A. Richard, 1stLt., 532d EBSR, MA New Guinea & PI, 1 July 43–15 Feb. 45

Woods, Charles, S/Sgt., 532d EBSR, MA New Guinea, 20 July 43–15 Feb. 44

Woodworth, William H., Capt., 592d EBSR, MA Admiralty Is., 2-31 Mar. 44

Yurkovich, Henry, S/Sgt., 532d EBSR, MA Hollandia, DNG, 23 Apr. 44

Zarndt, Lloyd H., S/Sgt., 532d EBSR, MA Lae, N.G., 4 Sept.–3 Oct. 43

Zaudke, Paul A., T/5, 542d EBSR, MA Hollandia, DNG, 22 Apr.–11 May 44

Military Order of the Purple Heart

Adams, Lamar O., T/4, 562d EBM Bn., WIA[†] San Jose, Leyte, PI, 2 Nov. 44

Adams, Lewis A., Pvt., 592d EBSR, WIA White Beach, Leyte, PI, 25 Oct. 44

Adams, Walter D., Pvt., 532d EBSR, WIA Tacloban, Leyte, PI, 24 Nov. 44

Agard, Charles H., Pvt., 592d EBSR, WIA White Beach, Leyte, PI, 24 Oct. 44

Allen, William D., Pvt., S/Btry, WIA Palisade, Leyte, PI, 8 Dec. 44

Allison, Clarence, T/5, 592d EBSR, WIA Corregidor Is., PI, 16 Feb. 45

Alvarez, Candide, Pvt., 542d EBSR, WIA Biak Island, NEI, 30 May 44

Anastas, William T., Pvt., 592d EBSR, WIA White Beach, Leyte, PI, 25 Oct. 44

Anderson, Clair E., Pfc., 542d EBSR, WIA Saidor, N.G., 3 Jan. 44

Anderson, Vernal L., Pvt., 532d EBSR, WIA Red Beach, Leyte, PI, 20 Oct. 44

Anglin, Joseph M., Pvt., 532d EBSR, WIA Lae, N.G., 5 Sept. 43

Anson, Glen A., T/4, 542d EBSR, WIA Wakde Island, DNG, 18 May 44

Armstrong, Franklin J., T/4, 592d EBSR, WIA Admiralty Is., 11 Mar. 44

Arnold, Charles E., T/5, 532d EBSR, WIA Liloan, Leyte, PI, 25 Oct. 44

Asbury, Edmon C., Sgt., 562cl EBM Bn., WIA Tacloban, Leyte, PI, 12 Nov. 44

Asman, Charles B., T/4, 562d EBM Bn., WIA Biak Island, NEI, 1 June 44

Atakai, Kirkije P., Pfc., 592d EBSR, WIA Tacloban, Leyte, PI, 25 Oct. 44

Bachofner, Laurie C., Pvt., 532d EBSR, WIA Palo, Leyte, PI, 12 Nov. 44

Bailey, Franklin T., T/5, 562d EBM Bn., WIA Biak Island, NEI, 1 June 44

Baker, Harry S., Pvt., 592d EBSR, WIA White Beach, Leyte, PI, 26 Oct. 44

Baker, Howard G., Pfc., 542d EBSR, KIA‡ Biak Island, NEI, 12 June 44

Baker, Joseph H., Capt., 592d EBSR, WIA San Jose, Leyte, PI, 4 Nov. 44

Baran, Walter J., Pfc., 532d EBSR, WIA Red Beach, Leyte, PI, 20 Oct. 44

Barnaby, William V., Sgt., 532d EBSR, WIA Hollandia, DNG, 23 Apr. 44

Barnett, Burton E., S/Sgt., 532d EBSR, WIA Lae, N.G., 5 Sept. 43

Barrett, Arthur H., Major, Hq. 2d ESB, WIA Palo, Leyte, PI, 20 Oct. 44

Barry, Murray M., Pvt., 592d EBSR, WIA Admiralty Is., 2 Mar. 44

Bartelson, Loren E., T/5, 592d EBSR, KIA Cape Gloucester, N.B., 16 Feb. 44

Bartosh, John J., Pvt., 532d EBSR, WIA Finschhafen, N.G., 22 Sept. 43

Bass, Emuel W., Pvt., 189th GS Co., WIA Tacloban, Leyte, PI, 25 Oct. 44

Basso, Frank M., Pvt., 542d EBSR, WIA Wakde Island, DNG, 2 June 44

Baumea, Ignacio M., Pvt., 592d EBSR, WIA Admiralty Is., 4 Mar. 44

Baumgardner, Ralph C., Pfc., 532d EBSR, WIA Surigao Str., Bohol, PI, 28 Dec. 44

Beach, James F., Pvt., 532d EBSR, WIA Red Beach, Leyte, PI, 20 Oct. 44

Beach, William P., Pvt., 542d EBSR, WIA Biak Island, NEI, 30 June 44

Becker, John M., T/4, 592d EBSR, WIA Tacloban, Leyte, PI, 25 Oct. 44

Begy, Willard J., Pvt., 532d EBSR, WIA Nassau Bay, N.G., 12 Sept. 43

Benjamin, Clifford L., T/5, 592d EBSR, WIA White Beach, Leyte, PI, 29 Oct. 44

Bernett, Joseph W., Pvt., 532d EBSR, WIA Hollandia, DNG, 24 Apr. 44

Berquist, Arthur R., T/5, 287th Sig. Co., WIA Palo, Leyte, PI, 20 Oct. 44

* Also awarded Oak Leaf Cluster.
† Wounded in action.
‡ Killed in action.

Berry, Chester W., Pvt., 532d EBSR, WIA Finschhafen, N.G., 25 Sept. 43

Betz, George W., Pfc., 532d EBSR, WIA Tambu Bay, N.G., 22 Aug. 43

Bilak, John, T/5, S/Btry, WIA Biak Island, NEI, 27 May 44

Binney, Myron T., T/4, 592d EBSR, WIA Cape Gloucester, N.B., 28 Dec. 43

Bird, Merlin B., Pfc., 532d EBSR, WIA Red Beach, Leyte, PI, 25 Oct. 44

Bivona, Gus A., Pfc., 562d EBM Bn., WIA San Pedro Bay, Leyte, PI, 2 Nov. 44

Blair, Robert E., Pfc., 592d EBSR, KIA White Beach, Leyte, PI, 20 Oct. 44

Blanchette, George, T/4, 532d EBSR, WIA Lae, N.G., 6 Sept. 43

Blanton, John W., Pfc., 562d EBM Bn., WIA San Pedro Bay, Leyte, PI, 26 Oct. 44

Blom, Edwin R., T/5, 532d EBSR, WIA Tacloban, Leyte, PI, 25 Oct. 44

Boccio, Joseph O., Capt., 532d EBSR, WIA Lae, N.G., 5 Sept. 43

Boles, Ernest E., T/4, 592d EBSR, WIA Palisade, Leyte, PI, 8 Dec. 44

Bologna, Lorenzo G., Pfc., 532d EBSR, WIA Nassau Bay, N.G., 1 July 43

Bowden, John W., Pvt., 532d EBSR, WIA Hollandia, DNG, 23 Apr. 44

Bowen, Jack N., T/5, 542d EBSR, WIA Wakde Island, DNG, 18 May 44

Boyle, James R., Cpl., 592d EBSR, KIA Admiralty Is., 2 Mar. 44

Bradica, Emil Jr., T/5, 562d EBM Bn., WIA San Jose, Leyte, PI, 18 Jan. 45

Brand, Cecil O., T/4, 532d EBSR, WIA Tacloban, Leyte, PI, 1 Nov. 44

Bray, William T., Pvt., 592d EBSR, WIA White Beach, Leyte, PI, 25 Oct. 44

Breslin, James B., T/4, 592d EBSR, WIA Admiralty Is., 11 Mar. 44

Brewer, Orville, Pvt., 532d EBSR, WIA Finschhafen, N.G., 23 Jan. 44

Brewer, Stanley G., Pvt., 592d EBSR, KIA Arawe, N.B., 13 Feb. 44

*Brjney, Clifford, T/5, 592d EBSR, WIA Admiralty Is., 15 Mar. 44
    WIA White Beach, Leyte, PI, 28 Oct. 44

Brockett, Ernest D., Jr., Lt.Col., 532d EBSR, WIA Red Beach, Leyte, PI, 20 Oct. 44

Brockmeyer, Donald, T/5, 542d EBSR, WIA Wakde Island, DNG, 18 May 44

Brown, Harry I., 1stLt., 532d EBSR, WIA Lae, N.G., 28 Sept. 43

Brown, Paul W., Pvt., 532d EBSR, WIA Red Beach, Leyte, PI, 20 Oct. 44

Brucher, Henry C., Pfc., 542d EBSR, KIA Saidor, N.G., 3 Jan. 44

Brush, Douglas C., T/5, 542d EBSR, WIA Wakde Island, DNG, 18 May 44

Buran, Stanley, T/4, 532d EBSR, WIA Red Beach, Leyte, PI, 26 Oct. 44

Buckley, Arthur R., Sgt., 532d EBSR, WIA Hollandia, DNG, 24 Apr. 44

Buckley, John F., S/Sgt., 592d EBSR, KIA Admiralty Is., 3 Mar. 44

Bull, Byron B., T/5, 542d EBSR, KIA Wakde Island, DNG, 18 May 44

Bumby, Andrew L., T/5, 592d EBSR, WIA White Beach, Leyte, PI, 26 Oct. 44

Burch, Johnnie M., Pfc., 532d EBSR, KIA Red Beach, Leyte, PI, 20 Oct. 44

Burgoyne, John W., Pvt., 532d EBSR, WIA Lae, N.G., 6 Sept. 43

Burgquist, Stanley, Pvt., 532d EBSR, WIA Lae, N.G., 6 Sept. 43

Burke, George F., T/5, 532d EBSR, WIA Lae, N.G., 6 Sept. 43

Burks, Robert C., Pvt., 592d EBSR, WIA Cape Gloucester, N.B., 8 Jan. 44

Butch, Joseph J., T/4, 562d EBM Bn., WIA San Jose, Leyte, PI, 5 Nov. 44

Byard, Lyman G., T/5, 532d EBSR, WIA Surigao Str., Bohol, PI, 28 Dec. 44

Byrnes, William H., T/5, 532d EBSR, WIA Liloan, Leyte, PI, 20 Oct. 44

Campbell, Bruce B., 1stLt., 532d EBSR, WIA Mindoro Island, PI, 21 Dec. 44

Canese, Harry F., Cpl., 592d EBSR, WIA White Beach, Leyte, PI, 26 Oct. 44

Capristo, Frank, T/5, 532d EBSR, WIA Red Beach, Leyte, PI, 25 Oct. 44

Carlberg, Allen A., T/5, 542d EBSR, WIA San Pedro Bay, Leyte, PI, 24
    Nov. 44

Carnes, Robert W., T/4, 592d EBSR, WIA White Beach, Leyte, PI, 25 Oct. 44

Casey, Obie, Pfc., 542d EBSR, KIA Wakde Island, DNG, 18 May 44

Cassel, James R., T/4, 532d EBSR, WIA Red Beach, Leyte, PI, 6 Dec. 44

Castigliego, Gaetano, T/4, 532d EBSR, WIA Tacloban, Leyte, PI, 26 Oct. 44

Cave, Benjamin E., 1stLt., 592d EBSR, WIA Cancobato Bay, Leyte, PI, 25
    Oct. 44

Cawi, Victor A., T/5, 532d EBSR, KIA Lae, N.G., 6 Sept. 43

Chambers, Ralph F., S/Sgt., 542d EBSR, WIA Biri Island, PI, 20 Feb. 45

Chandler, John L., Pvt., 532d EBSR, WIA Red Beach, Leyte, PI, 25 Oct. 44

Charboneau, George W., Pvt., QM Hq. Hq. Co., KIA Tacloban, Leyte, PI,
    25 Oct. 44

Charles, Norman H., Pvt., Hq Co 2 ESB, WIA Tacloban, Leyte, PI, 25 Oct. 44

Chavez, Francisco A., T/5, 542d EBSR, WIA Biak Island, NEI, 30 May 44

Chriswell, David E., Pfc., 189th GS Co., KIA Tacloban, Leyte, PI, 25 Oct. 44

Cicora, Samuel A., T/5, 542d EBSR, WIA Biak Island, NEI, 30 May 44

Clark, Emray F., Pvt., 542d EBSR, KIA Wakde Island, DNG, 18 May 44

Clark, Merman K., Pvt., 542d EBSR, WIA Cebu, PI, 21 Apr. 45

Cobey, John E., Pvt., 592d EBSR, WIA Tacloban, Leyte, PI, 25 Oct. 45

Cohen, Herbert I., Pvt., 592d EBSR, WIA Cape Gloucester, N.B., 29 Jan. 44

Cohen, Hyman, T/4, 532d EBSR, KIA Red Beach, Leyte, PI, 20 Oct. 44

Cohen, Stephen, Pfc., 592d EBSR, WIA Corregidor Is., PI, 19 Feb. 45

Coleman, Frank B., Pfc., 262d Med Bn., KIA Finschhafen, N.G., 25 Sept. 43

Collier, Barron, Jr., Capt., Hq. 2d ESB, WIA Biak Island, NEI, 27 May 44

Collins, Francis W., S/Sgt., 532d EBSR, WIA Mindoro Island, PI, 21 Dec. 44

Conklin, Roscoe R., 1stLt., 562d EBM Bn., WIA San Jose, Leyte, PI, 18 Jan. 4

Contrillo, Joseph J., Pvt., 592d EBSR, WIA White Beach, Leyte, PI, 25 Oct. 4

Cooper, Richard U., 1stLt., 287th Sig. Co., WIA Palo, Leyte, PI, 20 Oct. 44

Corrigan, George W., Jr., Pvt., 542d EBSR, WIA Biak Island, NEI, 30 May 44

Corrigan, James H., T/5, 562d EBM Bn., WIA San Jose, Leyte, PI, 18 Jan. 45

Criscuolo, Salvatore, Jr., Pfc., 287th Sig. Co., WIA Palo, Leyte, PI, 20 Oct. 44

Crow, Olin E., T/5, 532d EBSR, WIA Finschhafen, N.G., 25 Sept. 43

Cunningham, Joe A., T/4, 562d EBM Bn., WIA San Jose, Leyte, PI, 18 Jan. 4

Cunningham, Robert J., T/5, 532d EBSR, WIA Lae N.G., 6 Sept. 43

Curlee, Roy M., Pvt., 542d EBSR, WIA Wakde Island, DNG, 18 May 44

Dailey, George A., Pfc., 532d EBSR, KIA Lae, N.G., 6 Sept. 43

Danberry, Lloyd A., T/5, 532d EBSR, WIA Lae, N.G., 6 Sept. 43

Dancy, George P., S/Sgt., 532d EBSR, WIA Hollandia, DNG, 4 July 44

Daubert, Vernon O., T/4, 592d EBSR, WIA Cape Gloucester, N.B., 16 Feb. 4

Davis, Edward F., Cpl., 532d EBSR, WIA Lae, N.G., 6 Sept. 43

Davis, James H., Pvt., 532d EBSR, WIA Tacloban, Leyte, PI, 31 Oct. 44

Davis, Melvin A., Sgt., 542d EBSR, WIA Biak Island, NEI, 17 Aug. 44

Dawson, Lloyd B., T/5, 542d EBSR, WIA Wakde Island, DNG, 18 May 44

Deans, Robert R., Capt., 532d EBSR, WIA Lae, N.G., 25 Sept. 43

DeBellis, Salvatore, T/4, 532d EBSR, WIA Lae, N.G., 4 Sept. 43

DeCesare, Frank J., 1stLt., 532d EBSR, WIA Finschhafen, N.G., 25 Sept. 43

DeLance, Lyle, Pvt., 532d EBSR, WIA Lae, N.G., 4 Sept. 43

Deschenes, Edgar A., T/4, 532d EBSR, WIA Palo, Leyte, PI, 3 Nov. 44

Dewar, Norman L., T/5, 592d EBSR, WIA White Beach, Leyte, PI, 25 Oct. 4

Dickensheets, Richard F., T/4, 287th Sig. Co., WIA Palo, Leyte, PI, 20 Oct. 4

Dickey, Murray L., Pfc., 532d EBSR, WIA Red Beach, Leyte, PI, 26 Oct. 44

Dickinson, Arthur, Pvt., 189th QM GS Co., WIA Tacloban, Leyte, PI, 25 Oct. 4

Dippolito, Louis, Pfc., 542d EBSR, WIA Cebu, PI, 3 Apr. 45

Ditmars, Milton E., Pfc., 532d EBSR, WIA Finschhafen, N.G., 27 Sept. 43

Dobosz, William J., Pvt., 532d EBSR, WIA Finschhafen, N.G., 25 Sept. 43

Dodge, Cecil E., T/5, 532d EBSR, WIA Surigao Str., Bohol, PI, 28 Dec. 44

Dodson, Charles S., T/4, 532d EBSR, WIA Finschhafen, N.G., 25 Sept. 43

*Domer, William G., WO/JG, 592d EBSR, WIA White Beach, Leyte, PI, 25 Oct. 44

WIA White Beach, Leyte, PI, 29 Oct. 44

Donahue, William J., Pfc., 532d EBSR, KIA Surigao Str., Bohol, PI, 28 Dec. 4

Donohue, Thomas M., Pvt., 592d EBSR, WIA Palisade, Leyte, PI, 8 Dec. 44

Doro, John, Pfc., 592d EBSR, KIA White Beach, Leyte, PI, 25 Oct. 44

Drozel, John J., Pvt., 562d EBM Bn., WIA San Jose, Leyte, PI, 18 Jan. 45

Duncan, Homer D., Pvt., 532d EBSR, WIA Red Beach, Leyte, PI, 20 Oct. 44

Duncan, Melvin L., T/5, 532d EBSR, WIA Finschhafen, N.G., 23 Jan. 44

*Eads, John W., T/4, 532d EBSR, WIA Finschhafen, N.G., 25 Sept. 43
    Hq. Co. 2d ESB
    WIA Palo, Leyte, PI, 21 Oct. 44

Earle, William P. S., 1stLt., 532d EBSR, WIA Lae, N.G., 6 Sept. 43

Edminister, Jack E., T/4, 592d EBSR, WIA Corregidor Is., PI, 7 Mar. 45

Edwards, Alfred N., T/5, 592d EBSR, KIA Arawe, N.B., 16 Dec. 43

Eidson, Clyde W., T/4, 592d EBSR, KIA Arawe, N.B., 26 Dec. 43

Elendt, Walter G., T/4, 587th Sig. Co., WIA Palo, Leyte, PI, 20 Oct. 44

Elliott, Donald R., Pvt., 592d EBSR, WIA Admiralty Is., 4 Mar. 44

Ely, Arthur C., 2dLt., 532d EBSR, KIA Nassau Bay, N.G., 1 July 43

Emery, Leonard E., Sgt., 592d EBSR, KIA White Beach, Leyte, PI, 25 Oct. 44

Englebrecht, James W., Pvt., 532d EBSR, WIA Hollandia, DNG, 21 Apr. 44

Enos, Raymond E., T/4, 592d EBSR, WIA White Beach, Leyte, PI, 25 Oct. 44

Eppinger, Clarence J., Pfc., 542d EBSR, WIA Saidor, N.G., 2 Jan. 44

Eschenauer, Herman, S/Sgt., 542d EBSR, WIA Wakde Island, DNG, 18
    May 44

Eshpeter, Albert M., Pvt., 532d EBSR, WIA Oro Bay, N.G., 18 June 43

Estabrook, Paul F., T/4, 287th Sig. Co., WIA Palo, Leyte, PI, 20 Oct. 44

Estes, Joseph H., T/5, 532d EBSR, Finschhafen, N.G., 25 Sept. 43

Estorge, Leonard, 1stLt., QM Hq. Hq. Co., WIA Tacloban, Leyte, PI, 25
    Oct. 44

Etter, Ivan, T/5, 532d EBSR, WIA Hollandia, DNG, 23 Apr. 44

Evans, Wilton M., Pvt., S/Btry, WIA Biak Island, NEI, 2 June 44

Farina, Louis P., Pvt., 592d EBSR, WIA White Beach, Leyte, PI, 25 Oct. 44

Farmer, Joseph L., Jr., Pvt., 592d EBSR, WIA White Beach, Leyte, PI, 25
    Oct. 44

Fay, Thomas M., T/4, 542d EBSR, WIA San Pedro Bay, Leyte, PI, 24 Nov. 44

Feldman, Seymour, Pvt., 532d EBSR, WIA Oro Bay, N.G., 18 June 43

Fenley, Vincent J., Pfc., 542d EBSR, KIA Biri Island, PI, 20 Feb. 45

Fennell, Frank, Jr., 1stSgt., 532d EBSR, WIA Palo, Leyte, PI, 20 Oct. 44

Ferguson, Allen B., T/Sgt., 592d EBSR, WIA White Beach, Leyte, PI, 24
    Oct. 44

*Finnegan, Michial J., T/4, 542d EBSR, WIA Wakde Island, DNG, 18 May 44
    WIA San Pedro Bay, Leyte, PI, 24 Nov. 44

Firehock, Harry E., T/4, 532d EBSR, WIA Hollandia, DNG, 2 May 44

Fishole, Bernard J., T/4, 592d EBSR, WIA White Beach, Leyte, PI, 25
    Oct. 44

Fleenor, Fred L., Pvt., 592d EBSR, WIA Tacloban, Leyte, PI, 4 Nov. 44

Fletcher, John T., T/5, 532d EBSR, KIA Nassau Bay, N.G., 1 July 43

Flowers, Don M., Pvt., 532d EBSR, WIA Hollandia, DNG, 24 Apr. 44

Fortney, Carl M., Pvt., 592d EBSR, KIA White Beach, Leyte, PI, 27 Oct. 44

Foster, Edwin T., 1stLt., 532d EBSR, WIA Lae, N.G., 6 Sept. 43

Fowler, Clyde C., T/Sgt., 542d EBSR, WIA Wakde Island, DNG, 18 May 44

Fowler, John, Pvt., 542d EBSR, WIA Wakde Island, DNG, 18 May 44

Fowlkes, William H., Capt., 542d EBSR, WIA Toem, DNG, 17 May 44

Fryar, Earl, T/5, 532d EBSR, WIA Lae, N.G., 6 Sept. 43

Frye, Paul F., 1stLt., 532d EBSR, WIA Lae, N.G., 28 Sept. 43

Fuson, Jack C., Major, 532d EBSR, WIA Red Beach, Leyte, PI, 20 Oct. 44

Gaffney, Francis X., T/5, 592d EBSR, KIA Cape Gloucester, N.B., 16 Feb. 44

Garcia, Jesus V., T/5, 532d EBSR, KIA Surigao Str., Bohol, PI, 28 Dec. 44

Gasper, Albert W., Major, 532d EBSR, WIA Hollandia, DNG, 21 Apr. 44

Gaaton, Samuel E., T/5, 542d EBSR, WIA Wakde Island, DNG, 18 May 44

Gatton, George W., T/5, 592d EBSR, WIA Cape Gloucester, N.B., 26 Jan. 44

Gaul, Benjamin F., T/5, 542d EBSR, WIA San Pedro Bay, Leyte, PI, 24 Nov. 44

Gaulding, Aubrey E., Sgt., 287th Sig. Co., WIA Finschhafen, N.G., 25 Sept. 43

George, Grover C., Sgt., 532d EBSR, WIA Lar., N.G., 6 Sept. 43

Geretine, Ossie J., T/5, 592d EBSR, WIA Corregidor Is., PI, 16 Feb. 45

Giberson, James R., Pvt., 532d EBSR, WIA Finschhafen, N.G., 23 Jan. 44

Gill, Clarence L., T/5, 592d EBSR, WIA White Beach, Leyte, PI, 24 Oct. 44

Gillett, Carl W., T/4, 532d EBSR, KIA Sunigao Str., Bohol, PI, 28 Dec. 44

Gilliam, Carl I., Pfc., 592d EBSR, WIA Lae, N.G., 5 Sept. 43

Gleespan, Dale C., Pvt., 542d EBSR, KIA Biak Island, NEI, 27 May 44

Glicker, Benny, Pvt., 532d EBSR, WIA Finschhafen, N.G., 22 Sept. 43

Glover, Gordon W., T/5, 532d EBSR, WIA Finschhafen, N.G., 22 Oct. 43

Goings, James L., T/4, 287th Sig. Co., WIA Palo, Leyte, PI, 20 Oct. 44

Golden, Gilbert, 1stLt., 592d EBSR, WIA White Beach, Leyte, PI, 25 Oct. 44

Goldman, Asbury A., Pfc., 592d EBSR, WIA Admiralty Is., 2 Mar. 44

Goodpaster, Walter, Pvt., 542d EBSR, WIA Biak Island, NEI, 5 July 44

Gordy, Eugene M., 2dLt., 542d EBSR, WIA Wakde Island, DNG, 14 June 44

Graham, Charles T., T/5, 542d EBSR, WIA Schneider Harbor, N.G., 14 Feb. 44

Grant, Wilson I., T/4, 592d EBSR, WIA Arawe, N.B., 15 Dec. 43

Gray, Clarence E., Jr., T/4, 592d EBSR, WIA White Beach, Leyte, PI, 29 Oct. 44

Gray, Robert B., Pfc., 542d EBSR, KIA Wakde Island, DNG, 18 May 44

Greene, Dayne L., Pvt., 592d EBSR, WIA White Beach, Leyte, PI, 25 Oct. 44

Greene, Kenneth W., Pfc., 542d EBSR, WIA Finschhafen, N.G., 1 Sept. 43

Gross, Thomas, Pvt., 592d EBSR, WIA Cape Gloucester, N.B., 16 Feb. 44

Gunning, Thomas E., Jr., Pvt., 542d EBSR, WIA Biri Island, PI, 20 Feb. 45

Hale, John F., T/5, 592d EBSR, WIA White Beach, Leyte, PI, 25 Oct. 44

Hallett, Daniel L., Pfc., 532d EBSR, WIA Finschhafen, N.G., 25 Sept. 43

Halligan, Albert H., Pvt., 532d EBSR, WIA Red Beach, Leyte, PI, 20 Oct. 44

Halinan, Paul J., Capt., 542d EBSR, WIA Biak Island, NEI, 8 June 44

Hamblin, Owen G., Sgt., 592d EBSR, WIA San Jose, Leyte, PI, 24 Nov. 44

Hamilton, Carlos E., T/5, 592d EBSR, WIA Pinamopoan, Leyte, PI, 19 Nov. 44

Hamilton, G. T., 2dLt., 542d EBSR, WIA Augusan, Mindanao, PI, 15 May 45

Hammer, Edward K., 1stLt., 592d EBSR, WIA Finschhafen, N.G., 25 Sept. 43

Hampton, George T., T/5, 592d EBSR, WIA Admiralty Is., 3 Mar. 44

Hannon, Vernon E., T/5, 532d EBSR, WIA Finschhafen, N.G., 27 Oct. 43

Hanson, Francis O., Pfc., 532d EBSR, WIA, Lae, N.G., 6 Sept. 43

Hardy, Gilbert N., T/4, 562d EBM Bn., WIA San Jose, Leyte, PI, 18 Jan. 45

Harkins, John M., Pfc., 532d EBSR, WIA Finschhafen, N.G., 25 Sept. 43

Harmel, Robert E., Cpl., 532d EBSR, WIA Hollandia, DNG, 19 May 44

Harper, Samuel D., 1stLt., 592d EBSR, WIA Palisade, Leyte, PI, 8 Dec. 44

Harris, Lee, S/Sgt., 592d EBSR, WIA White Beach, Leyte, PI, 25 Oct. 44

Hartman, George W., 1stLt., 542d EBSR, WIA Cebu, PI, 26 Mar. 45

Hartnett, Earl A., Pfc., 542d EBSR, WIA Wakde Island, DNG, 18 May 44

Hartnett, Paul E., T/4, 532d EBSR, WIA Nassau Bay, N.G., 9 July 43

Hayward, Lee, Pfc., 532d EBSR, WIA Hollandia, DNG, 23 Apr. 44

Hayward, Peter H., Pvt., 592d EBSR, WIA White Beach, Leyte, PI, 25 Oct. 44

Heath, Robert S., 1stLt., 532d EBSR, WIA Hollandia, DNG, 23 Apr. 44

*Heavey, William F., BrigGen., Hq. 2d ESB, WIA Tacloban, Leyte, PI, 5 Nov. 44

Heffernan, Harold Q., Pfc., 262d Med Bn., WIA Finschhafen, N.G., 25 Sept. 43

Herr, Lawrence R., Pfc., 532d EBSR, WIA Finschhafen, N.G., 25 Sept. 43

Herrick, Edward R., T/4, 532d EBSR, WIA Lae, N.G., 6 Sept. 43

Hibbens, Sylvester C., Pfc., 592d EBSR, WIA Lae, N.G., 5 Sept. 43

Hibstenberg, John M., Sgt., 532d EBSR, WIA Lae, N.G., 6 Sept. 43

Hindin, Nathan A., Pvt., 532d EBSR, WIA Red Beach, Leyte, PI, 20 Oct. 44

Hoffman, Miles A., Pvt., 532d EBSR, WIA Tambu Bay, N.G., 2 Aug. 43

Hoffmire, George H., T/5, 592d EBSR, WIA White Beach, Leyte, PI, 24 Oct. 44

Holmes, Alfred, T/5, 532d EBSR, WIA Lae, N.G., 6 Sept. 43

Holton, Franklin C., M/Sgt., 162d Ord. Co., WIA Red Beach, Leyte, PI, 25 Sept. 44

Holtsberry, Thomas J., T/4, 532d EBSR, WIA Hollandia, DNG, 18 May 44

Holz, Richard M., Pvt., 542d EBSR, WIA Wakde Island, DNG, 18 May 44

Holzmacher, Edward G., Pvt., 592d EBSR, WIA Palisade, Leyte, PI, 8 Dec. 44

Hornar, Lawrence N., T/4, 532d EBSR, WIA Lae, N.G., 5 Sept. 43

Howe, Irwin C., Pfc., QM Hq. Hq. Co., WIA Tacloban, Leyte, PI, 25 Oct. 44

Hubschman, John, Pvt., Med Det., 2 ESB, WIA Red Beach, Leyte, PI, 20 Oct. 44

Huckleberry, Dan J., Pvt., 532d EBSR, KIA Finschhafen, N.G., 24 Jan. 44

Hunt, Roger R., T/4, 532d EBSR, KIA Hollandia, DNG, 24 Apr. 44

Hutchison, Raymond L., Pvt., 592d EBSR, WIA White Beach, Leyte, PI, 24 Oct. 44

Incorvaia, Nicholas, 562d EBM Bn., WIA San Jose, Leyte, PI, 24 Oct. 44

Isbach, Martin G., Jr., Pvt., 592d EBSR, WIA White Beach, Leyte, PI, 25 Oct. 44

Jackson, Estill, Pvt., 592d EBSR, WIA Admiralty Is., 2 Mar. 44

Jackson, Norris J., Pfc., 542d EBSR, WIA Biak Island, NEI, 15 June 44

Jacobs, Lloyd C., T/5, 532d EBSR, WIA Lae, N.G., 5 Sept. 43

Janowski, Theodore J., Pfc., 592d EBSR, WIA San Jose, Leyte, PI, 24 Nov. 44

Jenkins, William K., T/4, 542d EBSR, WIA Wakde Island, DNG, 18 May 44

Jobes, Philip E., T/5, 532d EBSR, WIA Red Beach, Leyte, PI, 20 Oct. 44

Johnson, Marvin H., Sgt., 532d EBSR, KIA Finschhafen, N.G., 3 Oct. 44

Johnson, Neil B., T/5, 592d EBSR, WIA Red Beach, Leyte, PI, 10 Dec. 44

Jones, Robert E., T/5, 592d EBSR, WIA Cape Gloucester, N.G., 8 Jan. 44

Juul, Vern W., T/5, 532d EBSR, WIA Lae, N.G., 6 Sept. 43

Kaderabek, Joseph T., T/5, 532d EBSR, WIA Lae, N.G., 4 Sept. 43

Kallio, Jaimer E., T/4, 592d EBSR, WIA Arawe, N.B., 13 Feb. 44

*Kaplan, Joseph, T/4, 592d EBSR, WIA Tacloban, Leyte, PI, 24 Oct. 44 KIA Corregidor Is., PI, 16 Feb. 45

Kaplan, Leonard, Lt.Col., 592d EBSR, WIA Admiralty Is., 2 Mar. 44

Kapustka, Stanley J., T/5, 532d EBSR, WIA Lae, N.G., 6 Sept. 43

Kavanaugh, Charles V., T/5, 532d EBSR, WIA Red Beach, Leyte, PI, 20 Oct. 44

Kazee, William A., Pvt., 592d EBSR, WIA Admiralty Is., 4 Mar. 44

Keaney, John L., Pvt., 532d EBSR, KIA Surigao Str., Bohol, PI, 28 Dec. 44

Keele, Charles C., 2dLt., 532d EBSR, KM Nassau Bay, N.G., 7 July 43

Kejonen, Otto A., Pvt., 532d EBSR, WIA Lae, N.G., 6 Sept. 43

Kelly, John J., T/4, 532d EBSR, WIA Nassau Bay, N.G., 1 July 43

Kelly, Michael F., T/4, 532d EBSR, WIA Lae, N.G., 6 Sept. 43

Kenny, Joseph T., T/4, 532d EBSR, WIA Red Beach, Leyte, PI, 20 Oct. 44

Kerr, George E., T/5, 542d EBSR, WIA Hollandia, DNG, 23 Apr. 44

Kinder, Robert R., Pvt., 592d EBSR, WIA Admiralty Is., 3 Mar. 44

Kinnett, Orval R., T/5, 592d EBSR, WIA Corregidor Is., 16 Feb. 45

Kirk, Elders L., T/5, 542d EBSR, WIA Cebu, PI, 12 Apr. 45

Klaiman, Milton H., Pvt., 532d EBSR, WIA Lae, N.G., 5 Sept. 43

Klingensmith, Marshall V., Pfc., 542d EBSR, WIA Cebu, PI, 26 Mar. 45

Koenig, Jack J., Pvt., 532d EBSR, WIA Finschhafen, N.G., 25 Sept. 43

Kolodziej, Joseph C., T/5, 532d EBSR, WIA Finschhafen, N.G., 13 Oct. 43

Kordick, Leo C., T/4, 542d EBSR, WIA Tambu Bay, N.G., 20 Aug. 43

Kowal, Stanley A., Pvt., 532d EBSR, WIA Hollandia, DNG, 23 Apr. 44

Krasicki, Thomas J., T/4, 542d EBSR, WIA Red Beach, Leyte, PI, 20 Oct. 44

Kreig, Robert D., T/5, 592d EBSR, WIA Lae, N.G., 6 Sept. 43

Kridler, Dale R., S/Sgt., 189th GS Co., WIA Tacloban, Leyte, PI, 25 Oct. 44

Krumm, Francis H., T/5, 532d EBSR, WIA Hollandia, DNG, 23 Apr. 44

Kubis, Michael B., Major, Hq. 2d ESB, WIA Palo, Leyte, PI, 20 Oct. 44

Kump, Richard A., Pvt., 532d EBSR, KIA Lae, N.G., 6 Sept. 43

Kwiatkowski, Walter, T/5, 542d EBSR, WIA San Pedro Bay, Leyte, PI, 24 Nov. 44

Lamphear, Edgar M., T/5, 592d EBSR, WIA Cape Gloucester, N.B., 16 Feb. 44

Lang, Rolland F., 2dLt., 532d EBSR, KIA Finschhafen, N.G., 7 Oct. 43

Lankford, Hiram P., T/5, S/Btry, KIA Biak Island, NEI, 9 June 44

LaRock, Neil J., Pfc., 532d EBSR, WIA Finschhafen, N.G., 23 Jan. 44

LaRusso, Richard C., T/4, 542d EBSR, WIA Wakde Island, DNG, 18 May 44

Latham, Ector B., Major, 532d EBSR, WIA Saidor, N.G., 6 Mar. 44

Leard, Edwin L., T/4, 532d EBSR, KIA Lae, N.G., 6 Sept. 43

*Lederer, Seymour G., Capt., 592d EBSR, WIA Hollandia, DNG, 22 Apr. 44 WIA White Beach, Leyte, PI, 24 Oct. 44

Lemmons, Emette E., Sgt., 592d EBSR, WIA Admiralty Is., 12 Mar. 44

*Leoiness, Joseph W., Pvt., 592d EBSR, WIA Arawe, N.B., 21 Dec. 43 WIA Arawe, N.B., 26 Dec. 43

Levy, Ira W., 2dLt., 592d EBSR, WIA Cape Gloucester, N.B., 25 Jan. 44

Lewis, Lester N., Pvt., 562d EBM Bn., WIA San Jose, Leyte, PI, 18 Nov. 44

Linder, Arthur S., Pvt., 532d EBSR, WIA Red Beach, Leyte, PI, 20 Oct. 44

Lindsey, William C., Pfc., QM Hg. Hg. Co., WIA Tacloban, Leyte, PI, 25 Oct. 44

Lish, Newton E., Pfc., 562d EBM Bn., WIA San Jose, Leyte, PI, 18 Jan. 45

Liston, Edwin R., T/4, 592d EBSR, WIA White Beach, Leyte, PI, 25 Oct. 44

Livingston, George R., T/5, 532d EBSR, WIA Nassau Bay, N.G., 1 July 43

Ljunggren, Walter E., S/Sgt., 262d Med Bn., WIA Lae, N.G., 4 Sept. 43

Loder, Richard A., Jr., T/5, 532d EBSR, WIA Mindoro Is., PI, 21 Dec. 44

LoForte, John F., Pfc., 542d EBSR, WIA Biak Island, NEI, 11 June 44

Logsdon, Olen, T/5, 592d EBSR, WIA White Beach, Leyte, PI, 25 Oct. 44

Loiselle, Francis M., S/Sgt., 532d EBSR, Nassau Bay, N.G., 1 July 43

Lombard, Bernard W., T/5, 542d EBSR, WIA Wakde Island, DNG, 18 May 44

Long, Lowell K., 1stLt., 562d EBSR, WIA San Jose, Leyte, PI, 18 Jan. 45

Lorek, Joseph W., Pvt., 542d EBSR, WIA Biak Island, DNG, 27 May 44

Loring, Terence E., Pvt., 592d EBSR, KIA Admiralty Is., 3 Mar. 44

Love, James, T/4, 592d EBSR, WIA Cape Gloucester, N.B., 16 Feb. 44

Luchetta, Thomas L., Pfc., 592d EBSR, WIA White Beach, Leyte, PI, 25 Oct. 41

Lyskooka, Julius, Pfc., 542d EBSR, WIA Biak Island, NEI, 28 May 44

Maas, Louis E., T/4, S/Btry, WIA Biak Island, NEI, 27 May 44

MacCormick, George A., 532d EBSR, WIA Red Beach, Leyte, PI, 20 Oct. 44

Mackie, Franklin N., T/4, 542d EBSR, WIA Biri Island, PI, 20 Feb. 45

Major, Harry R., Pfc., 542d EBSR, WIA Biak Island, NEI, 12 Aug. 44

Manchester, Tyrell T., 1stSgt., 532d EBSR, WIA N.G., 28 Sept. 43

Manieri, Tyrell T., 1stSgt., 532d EBSR, WIA Lae, N.G., 28 Sept. 43

Maniscalco, Frank A., S/Sgt., 532d EBSR, WIA Lae, N.G., 6 Sept. 43

Manley, Russell, O., Pvt., 542d EBSR, WIA Biak Island, NEI, 12 June 44

Marinel, Karl H,, T/5, 532d EBSR, WIA Mindoro Island, PI, 15 Dec. 44

Marks, Eugene H., T/4, 592d EBSR, WIA Tacloban, Leyte, PI, 27 Oct. 44

Marotta, Ralph J., Pvt., 532d EBSR, WIA Nassau Bay, N.G., 1 July 43

Martin, Franklin J., T/5, 592d EBSR, WIA White Beach, Leyte, PI, 29 Oct. 44

Martin, Lorenza C., T/4, 532d EBSR, WIA Lae, N.G., 5 Sept. 43

Marvin, Melvin E., T/4, 592d EBSR, WIA Tacloban, Leyte, PI, 4 Nov. 44

Matalon, Emanuel, Pfc., 542d EBSR, WIA Biak Island, NEI, 5 July 44

Matson, Kenneth E., T/4, 532d EBSR, WIA Nassau Bay, N.G., 1 July 43

Mauritho, Russell R., Jr., Pvt., 532d EBSR, WIA Surigao Str., Bohol, PI, 28 Dec. 44

Maxwell, Kurt F., Pfc., 262d Med. Bn., KIA White Beach, Leyte, PI, 12 Nov. 44

Mayhew, Ralph A., T/4, 592d EBSR, WIA Tacloban, Leyte, PI, 18 Jan. 45

McAdam, Francis T., S/Sgt., 532d EBSR, WIA Red Beach, Leyte, PI, 24 Oct. 44

McAnally, Thomas J., M/Sgt., 532d EBSR, WIA Nassau Bay, N.G., 5 July 43

McAuley, Daniel A., T/5, 532d EBSR, WIA Nassau Bay, N.G., 30 Jun 43

McBride, Melvin O., Pfc., 542d EBSR, WIA Wakde Island, DNG, 18 May 44

McCarthy, John R., T/4, 542d EBSR, WIA Wakde Island, DNG, 18 May 44

McCaskill, Thomas E., Pfc., 532d EBSR, WIA Mindoro Island, PI, 18 Dec. 44

McCauley, Ralph R., Pvt., 532d EBSR, WIA Oro Bay, N.G., 18 June 43

McConnell, Roland P., T/4, 532d EBSR, KIA Hollandia, DNG, 25 Apr. 44

McDonald, Robert F., Jr., S/Sgt., 592d EBSR, WIA White Beach, Leyte, PI, 24 Oct. 44

McDonough, John R., Pfc., 592d EBSR, WIA Admiralty Is., 9 Apr. 44

McGovern, John T., T/5, 542d EBSR, WIA Biri Island, PI, Feb. 45

McKeogh, Philip M., Pfc., 592d EBSR, WIA Corregidor Is., PI, 19 Feb. 45

McLane, Miles P., T/4, 532d EBSR, WIA Lae, N.G., 6 Sept. 43

McLaughlin, Loren D., T/5, 532d EBSR, WIA Hollandia, DNG, 28 July 44

McNeal, Raburn G., T/5, 562d EBM Bn., WIA San Jose, Leyte, PI, 18 Jan. 45

Medley, Bernard W., Cpl., 592d EBSR, KIA White Beach, Leyte, PI, 25 Oct. 44

Meheran, Robert J., Pvt., 592d EBSR, WIA Corregidor Is., PI, 16 Feb. 45

Merkt, Cornell R., Pvt., 592d EBSR, WIA White Beach, Leyte, PI, 25 Oct. 44

Messmer, Harry A., Jr., T/5, 592d EBSR, WIA Admiralty Is., 2 Mar. 44

Michalek, Edmond S., Pfc., 562d EBM Bn., WIA San Jose, Leyte, PI, 18 Jan. 45

Michele, Leopold J., T/5, 592d EBSR, WIA Arawe, N.B., 26 Jan. 44

Mickey, Glenn H., T/5, 532d EBSR, WIA Mindoro Island, PI, 15 Dec. 14

Mihoch, Andrew, Pvt, 542d EBSR, WIA Red Beach, Leyte, PI, 26 Oct. 44

Miles, Robert C., T/5, 592d EBSR, KIA Cape Gloucester, N.B., 16 Feb. 44

Miller, Frederick W., Jr., Pvt., 592d EBSR, WIA Admiralty Is., 4 Mar. 44

Miller, Leon A., T/5, 532d EBSR, WIA Finschhafen, N.G., 23 Jan. 44

Miller, Willard H., Pvt., 532d EBSR, WIA Lae, N.G., 6 Sept. 43

Miraglia, Victor E., T/5, QM Hq. Hq. Co., WIA Tacloban, Leyte, PI, 25 Oct. 44

Mooney, Francis M., T/5, 532d EBSR, KIA San Pedro Bay, Leyte, PI, 26 Oct. 44

Moore, Joseph H., Pvt., S/Btry, WIA Noemfoor Is., NEI, 2 July 44

Moore, Ola E., Sgt., 532d EBSR, WIA Red Beach, Leyte, PI, 20 Oct. 44

Moreau, Dallas N., Pfc., 532d EBSR, WIA Nassau Bay, N.G., 1 July 43

Moss, Charlie F., Pfc., 262d EBM Bn., WIA Lae, N.G., 4 Sept. 43

Moyer, William J., T/5, 592d EBSR, WIA Corregidor Is., PI, 16 Feb. 45

Murphy, Charles M., T/Sgt., 532d EBSR, WIA Lae, N.G., 6 Sept. 43

Murphy, John J., T/4, 532d EBSR, WIA Liloan, Leyte, PI, 21 Oct. 44

Nabors, Jack J., Pvt., 532d EBSR, WIA Finschhafen, N.G., 19 Oct. 43

Nachreiner, Walter J., T/4, 592d EBSR, WIA Admiralty Is., 3 Mar. 44

Nagy, Frank J., Pfc., 532d EBSR, WIA Nassau Bay, N.G., 9 July 43

Nasher, John, T/5, 592d EBSR, WIA White Beach, Leyte, PI, 20 Oct. 44

Naumea, Ignacio M., Pvt., 592d EBSR, WIA Admiralty Islands, 4 Mar. 44

Needs, Everett L., Pfc., 532d EBSR, WIA Finschhafen, N.G., 22 Sept. 43

Nelson, Harold L., T/5, 532d EBSR, KIA Oro Bay, N.G., 18 June 43

Nissenbaum, Robert, Pvt., 542d EBSR, WIA Hollandia, DNG, 8 June 44

Norton, David W., Pfc., 592d EBSR, WIA Arawe, N.B., 12 June 44

Norton, Robert F., Pvt., 532d EBSR, WIA Lae, N.G., 4 Sept. 43

Nutter, Nial H., T/4, 592d EBSR, WIA Pinamopoan, Leyte, PI, 23 Nov. 44

Nyfield, Arthur, Pfc., 542d EBSR, WIA Agusan, Mindanao, PI, 15 May 45

Oakley, Clyde C., 1stLt., 532d EBSR, WIA Tambu Bay, N.G., 12 Aug. 43

O'Brien, Willie H., Pvt., 592d EBSR, WIA San Jose, Leyte, PI, 25 Oct. 44

Odegard, Adolph H., Pvt., S/Btry, WIA Biak Island, NEI, 28 May 44

Olson, Arthur A., T/4, 592d EBSR, WIA, Cape Gloucester, N.B., 8 Jan. 44

Olson, Melvin W., Cpl., 532d EBSR, WIA Lae, N.G., 4 Sept. 43

O'Neal, Paul J., Cpl., 532d EBSR, WIA Finschhafen, N.G., 22 Oct. 43

O'Neil, Frederick H., 592d EBSR, KIA Corregidor Is., PI, 17 Feb. 45

Orrick, Virgil J., T/5, 532d EBSR, WIA Lae, N.G., 6 Sept. 43

Orser, Gillbet I., T/5, 592d EBSR, WIA Lae, N.G., 5 Sept. 43

Osborne, William C., T/5, 592d EBSR, WIA Arawe, N.B., 21 Dec. 43

O'Toole, Patrick H., T/5, 592d EBSR, WIA Lae, N.G., 5 Sept. 43

Ott, Carl, Pvt., 592d EBSR, WIA Admiralty Islands, 4 Mar. 44

Padgett, John W., Pvt., 532d EBSR, WIA Balacan Is., PI, 26 Nov. 44

Pahoskik, Isadore, Pvt., 592d EBSR, KIA Arawe, N.B., 26 Dec. 43

Palmer, William H., S/Sgt., 592d EBSR, WIA White Beach, Leyte, PI, 25 Oct. 44

Paper, Charles, 1stLt., 562d EBM Bn., WIA Tacloban, Leyte, PI, 24 Dec. 44

Pappas, Ernest G., Cpl., 532d EBSR, WIA Nassau Bay, N.G., 1 July 43

Parker, Leo R., Pfc., 532d EBSR, WIA Lae, N.G., 6 Sept. 43

Parks, Winfred L., T/4, 532d EBSR, WIA Surigao Str., Bohol, PI, 28 Dec. 44

Parquette, Archer, Pvt., 532d EBSR, WIA Finschhafen, N.G., 23 Jan. 44

Parr, Chester I., T/4, 542d EBSR, WIA San Pedro Bay, Leyte, PI, 24 Nov. 44

Pasiut, Stanley J., Jr., Pvt., 542d EBSR, WIA Schneider Harbor, N.G., 17 Feb. 44

Pecoraro, Charles F., Capt., 532d EBSR, KIA Finschhafen, N.G., 25 Sept. 43

Peery, Harold O., T/4, 542d EBSR, WIA Admiralty Islands, 7 Mar. 44

Pena, John L., T/4, 542d EBSR, WIA Nassau Bay, N.G., 30 June 43

Penaluna, William S., S/Sgt., 532d EBSR, WIA Lae, N.G., 6 Sept. 43

Pensabene, Thomas J., T/5, 592d EBSR, WIA Pinamopoan, Leyte, PI, 22 Nov. 44

Perez, Clifton J., Pvt., 592d EBSR, WIA White Beach, Leyte, PI, 25 Oct. 44

Perkins, Clifford, T/4, 532d EBSR, WIA Finschhafen, N.G., 25 Sept. 43

Perkins, Kenneth W., Pfc., 542d EBSR, WIA Cebu, PI, 12 Apr. 45

Perrone, Frank T., T/Sgt., 592d EBSR, KIA Arawe, N.B., 15 Dec. 43

Perrone, Michael J., Pvt., S/Btry, WIA Noemfoor Is., NEI, 2 July 44

Persing, Leon R., T/5, 592d EBSR, WIA Cape Gloucester, N.B., 26 Feb. 44

*Peters, Anthony T., Pfc., 592d EBSR, WIA Palisade, Leyte, PI, 7 Dec. 44
    WIA Palisade, Leyte, PI, 8 Dec. 44

Petersen, James L., S/Sgt., 532d EBSR, WIA Red Beach, Leyte, PI, 20
    Oct. 44

Peterson, Gerald E., Capt., 532d EBSR, WIA Lae, N.G., 28 Sept. 43

Peterson, Paul, T/5, 532d EBSR, WIA Hollandia, DNG, 23 Apr. 44

Phelps, Eugene L., T/5, 542d EBSR, WIA Hollandia, DNG, 22 Apr. 44

Philbert, Romuald L., Jr., S/Sgt., 532d EBSR, WIA Lae, N.G., 6 Sept. 43

Phillips, Kenneth E., T/4, 542d EBSR, WIA Wakde Island, DNG, 18 May 44

Pinkston, Ester C., S/Sgt., 592d EBSR, WIA White Beach, Leyte, PI, 25
    Oct. 44

Pino, Matthew, T/5, 532d EBSR, WIA Tacloban, Leyte, PI, 26 Oct. 44

Poffenbarger, John O., 1stLt., 532d EBSR, WIA Finschhafen, N.G., 25
    Sept. 43

Polite, Andrew W., T/5, 592d EBSR, WIA Red Beach, Leyte, PI, 10 Dec. 44

Pomeroy, Harry, Pfc., 542d EBSR, KIA Biri Island, PI, 20 Feb. 45

Popa, Stephen, Cpl., 532d EBSR, WIA Finschhafen, N.G., 17 Oct. 43

Pospichal, Alfred T., 1stLt., 532d EBSR, WIA Mindoro Is., PI, 4 Jan. 45

Pouquette, Emile J., Pfc., 542d EBSR, KIA Biak Island, NEI, 2 June 44

Powderly, Vernon A., T/5, 592d EBSR, KIA Lae, N.G., 6 Sept. 43

Powers, Eugene A., 2dLt., 592d EBSR, WIA Arawe, N.B., 27 Jan. 44

Price, George V., S/Sgt., 592d EBSR, WIA White Beach, Leyte, PI, 25 Oct. 44

Price, Snowden L., T/4, 532d EBSR, KIA Nassau Bay, N.G., 1 July 43

Prindeville, Thomas J., Pvt., 532d EBSR, WIA Red Beach, Leyte, PI, 20
    Oct. 44

Priore, Joseph A., Pvt., 542d EBSR, WIA Biak Island, NEI, 29 May 44

Provitero, Ciro J., Pfc., 532d EBSR, WIA Finschhafen, N.G., 23 Jan. 44

Pruitt, George B., Pvt., 592d EBSR, WIA Arawe, N.B., 16 Dec. 43

Pruitt, Noah L., Jr., Pvt., 592d EBSR, WIA Arawe, N.B., 16 Dec. 43

Puzar, Julius, Pfc., 542d EBSR, WIA Biak Island, NEI, 11 June 44

Pyles, Carl, T/4, 592d EBSR, WIA Arawe, N.B., 16 Dec. 43

Quintana, Samuel S., T/5, 532d EBSR, WIA Lae, N.G., 5 Sept. 43

Rainey, Clifford B., T/4, 592d EBSR, WIA Arawe, N.B., 12 Jan. 44

Ramage, James, Pvt., 542d EBSR, WIA Wakde Island, DNG, 18 May 44

Randall, James A., Pfc., 542d EBSR, WIA Cebu, PI, 12 Apr. 45

Ratzlaff, Bernard M., T/5, 532d EBSR, WIA Lae, N.G., 4 Sept. 43

Rector, Clifford F., T/5, 532d EBSR, KIA Hollandia, DNG, 27 Apr. 44

Reece, George W., Pvt., 542d EBSR, WIA Biak Island, NEI, 2 June 44

Reed, Marvin A., T/4, 532d EBSR, KIA Nassau Bay, N.G., 1 July 43

Reed, Robert, T/5, 542d EBSR, WIA Agusan, Mindanao, PI, 15 May 45

Reidy, Neil F., T/4, 532d EBSR, WIA Lae, N.G., 6 Sept. 43

Repole, Nicholas, T/5, 592d EBSR, WIA Admiralty Island, 9 Apr. 44

Reynolds, Henry E., Pvt., 592d EBSR, WIA Admiralty Island, 9 Apr. 44

Reynolds, Ulric H., 1stLt., 542d EBSR, WIA Biak Island, NEI, 3 Aug. 44

*Rich, William O., Pvt., 542d EBSR, WIA Saidor, N.G., 2 Jan. 44
    WIA Biak Island, NEI, 5 July 44

Richards, Fred C., Capt., 592d EBSR, WIA Pinamopoan, Leyte, PI, 23 Nov.
    44

Ridgeway, Donald F., 2dLt., 542d EBSR, WIA Wakde Island, DNG, 18
    May 44

Rising, Harry N., Jr., Lt.Col., 532d EBSR, WIA Finschhafen, N.G., 25 Sept.
    43

Rivera, Joseph P., Jr., Pfc., 592d EBSR, WIA Cape Gloucester, N.B., 8
    Jan. 44

Roberts, James H., Pvt., 592d EBSR, WIA Dulag, Leyte, PI, 22 Nov. 44

Roberts, Lloyd B., Pvt., 532d EBSR, WIA Nassau Bay, N.G., 1 July 43

Rogers, Thomas J., 1stLt., 532d EBSR, WIA Lae, N.G., 5 Sept. 43

Rolen, James F., 1stLt., 532d EBSR, WIA Hollandia, DNG, 23 Apr. 44

Rossman, Robert E., Pvt., 542d EBSR, WIA Biak Island, NEI, 17 Aug. 44

Rothrock, L. D. C., T/4, 542d EBSR, WIA Tacloban, Leyte, PI, 24 Oct. 44

Rotkovitz, Henry M., Sgt., 532d EBSR, WIA Lae, N.G., 4 Sept. 43

Rouzer, Robert J., T/Sgt., 532d EBSR, KIA Red Beach, Leyte, PI, 20 Oct. 44

Rowlett, Thomas S., Jr., Pvt., 592d EBSR, WIA San Jose, Leyte, PI, 24
    Nov. 44

Ruel, Emery W., Cpl., 532d EBSR, WIA Hollandia, DNG, 23 Apr. 44

Ruffner, Grant, T/4, 592d EBSR, KIA White Beach, Leyte, PI, 29 Oct. 44

Russell, Robert W., T/4, 542d EBSR, WIA Wakde Island, DNG, 18 May 44

Sabin, Harlan J., T/4, 532d EBSR, WIA Finschhafen, N.G., 25 Sept. 43

Sacci, Joseph V., T/5, 532d EBSR, WIA Mindoro Island, PI, 15 Dec. 44

Sacks, Isidore B., Pvt., 592d EBSR, WIA Bay Bay, Leyte, PI, 13 Dec. 44

Sakmer, Joseph, Pfc., 562d EBM Bn., WIA San Jose, Leyte, PI, 18 Jan. 45

Salata, Frank E., T/4, S/Btry, WIA Cancobato Bay, Leyte, PI, 18 Nov. 44

Sams, Elmer M., Cpl., 592d EBSR, WIA Admiralty Islands, 9 Apr. 44

Sandberg, Morris J., Pfc., 542d EBSR, WIA Island, DNG, 18 May 44

314 WILLIAM F. HEAVEY

Sargent, Lawrence V., Pvt., 592d EBSR, WIA White Beach, Leyte, PI, 27 Oct. 44

Saunders, James E., Pvt., 592d EBSR, WIA Admiralty Islands, 2 Mar. 44

Savage, Donald K., T/5, 542d EBSR, WIA Biak Island, NEI, 15 June 44

Schafer, Charles J., Pfc., 532d EBSR, WIA Hollandia, DNG, 23 Apr. 44

Scott, Frank H., T/4, 532d EBSR, WIA Liloan, Leyte, PI, 20 Oct. 44

Seidel, Arthur C., T/5, 592d EBSR, WIA Arawe, N.B., 16 Dec. 43

Self, Finis J., T/4, 287th Sig. Co., WIA Tacloban, Leyte, PI, 25 Oct. 44

Selle, Robert P., T/4, 532d EBSR, WIA Lae, N.G., 6 Sept. 43

Shapiro, Benjamin, Pvt., 532d EBSR, WIA Lae, N.G., 6 Sept. 43

Shatraw, Napoleon L., Pfc., 542d EBSR, WIA Saidor, N.G., 9 Mar. 44

Shaw, George C., III, Pvt., 532d EBSR, WIA Red Beach, Leyte, PI, 20 Oct. 44

Shearer, Earl D., T/4, 592d EBSR, WIA Corregidor Is., PI, 16 Feb. 45

Sheleva, John, Jr., Pvt., 592d EBSR, WIA White Beach, Leyte, PI, 25 Oct. 44

Shelly, Clarence J., T/3, 562d EBM Bn., WIA San Pedro Bay, Leyte, PI, 26 Oct. 44

Shoemaker, Harlan A., T/4, 532d EBSR, WIA Hollandia, DNG, 25 Apr. 44

Shong, Lyle S., Pfc., 542d EBSR, WIA Wakde Island, DNG, 18 May 44

Simmons, John P., T/4, 532d EBSR, WIA Red Beach, Leyte, PI, 20 Oct. 44

Smith, John R., S/Sgt., 562d EBM Bn., WIA San Jose, Leyte, PI, 18 Jan. 45

Smith, Rodney J., T/5, 592d EBSR, WIA Admiralty Islands, 18 Mar. 44

Smith, Stacy E., T/5, 542d EBSR, WIA Biak Island, NEI, 12 June 44

Snell, Lathan E., Pvt., 592d EBSR, WIA White Beach, Leyte, PI, 25 Oct. 44

*Sokol, Jack, T/5, 532d EBSR, WIA Balacan Island, PI, 28 Nov. 44
    WIA Mindoro Island, PI, 15 Dec. 44

Spadoni, Gildo J., T/4, 532d EBSR, WIA Red Beach, Leyte, PI, 26 Oct. 44

Speer, James H., Pfc., 542d EBSR, WIA Biak Island, NEI, 29 May 44

Sroczynski, Harold A., Pvt., 532d EBSR, WIA Tacloban, Leyte, PI, 22 Oct. 44

*Staszak, Frank S., Pfc., 592d EBSR, WIA Admiralty Islands, 4 Mar. 44
    WIA Admiralty Islands, 4 Mar. 44

Steele, Otis B., Pvt., 592d EBSR, WIA White Beach, Leyte, PI, 25 Oct. 44

Stejskal, Ludwig, Cpl., 532d EBSR, WIA Red Beach, Leyte, PI, 20 Oct. 44

Stender, Harold G., T/5, 532d EBSR, WIA Hollandia, DNG, 23 Apr. 44

Stephens, Emmit L., T/5 592d EBSR, WIA Pinamopoan, Leyte, PI, 19 Nov. 44

Stevens, Charles B., 1stSgt., 562d EBM Bn., WIA San Jose, Leyte, PI, 3 Nov. 44

Stewart, Martin L., Pvt., 542d EBSR, KIA Iloilo, Panay, PI, 25 Mar. 45

Stienhaus, Paul H., Pvt., 532d EBSR, WIA Red Beach, Leyte, PI, 24 Oct. 44

Stiles, William, 1stLt., 542d EBSR, KIA Toem, DNG, 17 May 44

Stimart, Clarence F., Pvt., 592d EBSR, WIA Arawe, N.B., 16 Dec. 43

Stone, William P., Pvt., 532d EBSR, WIA Finschhafen, N. G., 20 Oct. 43

Strahm, Elgin A., S/Sgt., 532d EBSR, KIA Nassau Bay, N.G., 1 July 43

Streb, John P., Pvt., 532d EBSR, WIA Hollandia, DNG., 23 Apr. 44

Sutherland, James R., T/5, 532d EBSR, KIA Lae, N.G., 4 Sept. 43

Sweeney, Hubert P., 2dLt., 592d EBSR, KIA Cape Gloucester, N.B., 16 Feb. 44

Swink, Theodore W., Pvt., 592d EBSR, WIA Admiralty Islands, 2 Mar. 44

Tanner, Charles D., Pvt., 542d EBSR, WIA Saidor, N.G., 4 Jan. 44

Taylor, Ralph W., Pvt., 532d EBSR, WIA Red Beach, Leyte, PI, 20 Oct. 44

Tepley, Joseph L., T/5, 592d EBSR, WIA Arawe, N.B., 16 Dec. 43

Terry, Milo E., T/5, 532d EBSR, KIA Nassau Bay, N.G., 1 July 43

Therriault, Octave, Pfc., QM Hq. Hq. Co., WIA Tacloban, Leyte, PI, 25 Oct. 44

Thompson, Durward A., T/5, 592d EBSR, KIA Arawe, N.B., 26 Jan. 44

Thomson, Ronald F., 2dLt., 592d EBSR, KIA Cape Gloucester, N. B., 26 Feb. 44

Tiberi, Daniel J., T/4, 532d EBSR, KIA Nassau Bay, N.G., 1 July 43

Timmen, Keith D., Pvt., 532d EBSR, WIA Finschhafen, N.G., 25 Sept. 43

Tolway, Lew A., T/3, 592d EBSR, WIA San Jose, Leyte, PI, 3 Nov. 44

Tomaski, Andrew L., T/5, 542d EBSR, KIA Cebu, PI, 2 Apr. 45

Tomblinson, Billy C., Pfc., 542d EBSR, WIA Cebu, PI, 12 Apr. 45

Tonge, William K., Pvt., 287th Sig Co., WIA Tacloban, Leyte, PI, 25 Oct. 44

Toolan, Francis J., T/4, 592d EBSR, WIA Admiralty Islands, 16 Mar. 44

Torres, Fred L., T/5, 592d EBSR, KIA Arawe, N.B., 26 Dec. 44

Tozzi, Charles P., Pfc., QM Hq. Hq. Co., KIA Tacloban, Leyte, PI, 25 Oct. 44

Triano, Pietro, Pvt., 542d EBSR, KIA Wakde Island, DNG, 18 May 44

Trocha, Paul, T/5, 542d EBSR, WIA Lae, N.G., 6 Oct. 43

Troxell, James D., Pk., 592d EBSR, WIA Admiralty Islands, 17 Mar. 44

Tubolino, Angelo M., T/4, 532d EBSR, WIA Finschhafen, N.G., 23 Jan. 44

Turner, Robert L., T/5, 592d EBSR, WIA Palisade, Leyte, PI, 8 Dec. 44

Umpleby, Robert A., Pvt., 542d EBSR, WIA San Pedro Bay, Leyte, PI, 24 Nov. 44

Valek, Joseph J., Pfc., 542d EBSR, WIA Agusan, Mindanao, PI, 15 May 45

*Van Noy, Junior N., Pvt., 532d EBSR, WIA Finschhafen, N.G., 20 Sept. 43 KIA Finschhafen, N.G., 17 Oct. 43

Vella, Carlo C., Pvt., 262d Med Bn., WIA Lae, N.G., 5 Sept. 43

Veneski, Michael, Pvt., 592d EBSR, WIA Admiralty Islands, 4 Mar. 44

Villa, Walter B., Pfc., 532d EBSR, KIA Finschhafen, N.G., 25 Sept. 43

Visingard, George, T/4, 592d EBSR, WIA White Beach, Leyte, PI, 25 Oct. 43

Volo, Louis J., Jr., T/4, 592d EBSR, WIA Admiralty Islands, 2 Mar. 44

Voytek, John J., T/5, 532d EBSR, WIA Lae, N.G., 2 Oct. 44

Wagner, John W., T/5, 542d EBSR, WIA Wakde Island, DNG, 18 May 44

Walkney, Joseph E., Cpl., 592d EBSR, KIA Admiralty Islands, 4 Mar. 44

Walsh, Charles D., T/5, 542d EBSR, WIA Wakde Island, DNG, 18 May 44

Waltz, Dwaine R., Pvt., 562d EBM Bn., KIA Surigao Str., Bohol, PI, 28 Dec. 44

Ward, Junior W., Pvt., 532d EBSR, WIA Oro Bay, N.G., 18 June 43

Watson, Clell L., Pvt., 532d EBSR, WIA Mindoro Island, PI, 15 Dec. 44

Watson, Harry T., Jr., 1stLt., 542d EBSR, WIA Tambu Bay, N.G., 11 Sept. 43

Weiss, Charles C., T/4, 542d EBSR, WIA San Pedro Bay, Leyte, PI, 24 Nov. 44

Weitzel, Leonard R., 1stSgt., 542d EBSR, WIA Cebu, PI, 28 Mar. 45

Welch, Arthur R., T/4, 592d EBSR, WIA Cape Gloucester, N.B., 26 Feb. 44

Wells, Robert F., Pfc., 562d EBM Bn. WIA San Jose, Leyte, PI, 18 Jan. 45

West, Alton J., T/4, 532d EBSR, KIA Lae, N.G., 12 Sept. 43

Westwood, Walter W., T/5, 532d EBSR, WIA Lae, N.G., 6 Sept. 43

Whealton, Canton D., Pvt., 542d EBSR, WIA Biak Island, NEI, 15 June 44

Whetstone, Leon, T/4, 592d EBSR, WIA San Jose, Leyte, PI, 4 Nov. 44

White, Clyde B., Pvt., 532d EBSR, WIA Lae, N.G., 6 Sept. 43 White, William A., Lt.Col., 592d EBSR, WIA Arawe, N.B., 16 Dec. 43

Wilbanks, Grover C., T/5, 592d EBSR, WIA Red Beach, Leyte, PI, 10 Dec. 44

Wildung, William H., Pvt., 592d EBSR, WIA Admiralty Islands, 4 Mar. 44

Wilkins, John F., T/4, 592d EBSR, WIA Concabato Bay, Leyte, PI, 25 Oct. 44

Williams, Charles F., T/4, 532d EBSR, WIA Cancobato Bay, Leyte, PI, 4 Nov. 44

Wilson, Manuel F., Sgt., 532d EBSR, WIA Red Beach, Leyte, PI, 24 Oct. 44

Wilson, Walter L., T/5, 592d EBSR, WIA Admiralty Islands, 11 Mar. 44

Wince, Roger R., S/Sgt., S/Btry, WIA Hollandia, DNG, 22 Apr. 44

Wing, James K., T/4, 532d EBSR, WIA Red Beach, Leyte, PI, 20 Oct. 44

Winter, Robert F., T/4, 592d EBSR, WIA Arawe, N.B., 18 Dec. 43

Wodrich, Lester H., T/5, 542d EBSR, WIA Wakde Island, DNG, 18 May 44

Wolf, Lawrence J., T/5, 592d EBSR, WIA Tacloban, Leyte, PI, 4 Nov. 44

Wolff, John J., Pfc., 532d EBSR, WIA Lae, N.G., 6 Sept. 43

Wolz, Richard A., 2dLt., 532d EBSR, WIA Lae, N.G., 6 Sept. 43

Wondra, Frank J., Pfc., 262d Med Bn., WIA Red Beach, Leyte, PI, 21 Oct. 44

Wood, John L., Pfc., 592d EBSR, WIA Lae, N.G., 5 Sept. 43

Wright, David L., Pvt., 592d EBSR, WIA White Beach, Leyte, PI, 25 Oct. 44

Yanoski, Joseph J., Pvt., 532d EBSR, KIA Lae, N.G., 6 Sept. 43

Yeatts, Clarence J., T/5, 592d EBSR, WIA Cape Gloucester, N.B., 29 Jan. 44

Yodice, Michael J., Pfc., 542d EBSR, WIA Red Beach, Leyte, PI, 10 Dec. 44

Zapadka, Henry, Pfc., 592d EBSR, WIA White Beach, Leyte, PI, 25 Oct. 44

Zehna, Lee, Pvt., 532d EBSR, KIA Mindoro Island, PI, 21 Dec. 44

Znoj, Stanley A., T/5, 592d EBSR, WIA Cape Gloucester, N.B., 8 Jan. 44

Zubieta, Pete, Jr., Pfc., 542d EBSR, KIA Tambu Bay, N.G., 20 Aug. 43

2D ENGINEER SPECIAL BRIGADE
OFFICERS DECORATIONS

	Brig. Hqs. Co.	Med. Det. 2d ESB	287th Sig. Co.	Quartermaster	262d Med. Bn.	562d Engr. Bt. Maint. Bn.	532d Engr. BT & SH Regt.	542d Engr. BT & SH Regt.	592d Engr. BT & SH Regt.	Support Battery	Total
Distinguished Service Order							1				1
Distinguished Service Cross							2				2
Legion of Merit	2					1	3	3	5		14
Silver Star					2		10	5		3	20
Oak Leaf Cluster							2				2
Bronze Star	15		1		13	12	53	25	27	3	149
Oak Leaf Cluster					1	1	10		2		14
Soldier's Medal							1		1		2
Purple Heart	4		1	1		3	26	8	18		61
Oak Leaf Cluster	1								2		3
Total	22¹		2	1	16	17	108	41	55	6	268

¹Also one Distinguished Service Medal.

2D ENGINEER SPECIAL BRIGADE

DECORATIONS—ENLISTED MEN

	Brig. Hqs. Co.	Med. Det., 2d ESB	287th Sig. Co.	162d Ord. Co.	Quartermaster	262d Med. Bn.	562d Engr. Bt., Maint. Bn.	532d Engr. BT & SH Regt.	542d Engr. BT & SH Regt.	592d Engr. BT & SH Regt.	189th Gas Co.	3498th Ord. MM Co.	Support Battery	Total
Medal of Honor								1						1
Distinguished Service Cross										1				1
Legion of Merit				1					5	1				7
Silver Star								14	6	6				26
Oak Leaf Cluster									1					1
Bronze Star	9		2			4	18	229	66	39		0	5	372
Oak Leaf Cluster								7	1	1				9
Soldier's Medal			1	1			1	5		5				13
Purple Heart	2	1	9	1	6	7	23	247	107	180	4	0	10	597
Oak Leaf Cluster	1							3	2	5				11
Total	12	1	12	3	6	11	42	506	188	238	4	0	15	1038

4TH ENGINEER SPECIAL BRIGADE
1 December 1945
AWARDS

	MANILA	MOROTAI	NEW GUINEA	LINGAYEN	TOTAL
Purple Heart		5		11	16
Legion of Merit	3		1	2	6
Silver Star	7			2	9
Soldiers Medal	2	5	3	10	20
Bronze Star	76	2	4	34	116

The Meritorious Service Unit Plaque was awarded to the following units of the 4th Brigade:
  164th Ordnance Company
  564th Engineer Boat Maintenance Battalion
  534th Engineer Boat and Shore Regiment

5TH ENGINEER SPECIAL BRIGADE

TO 1 SEPTEMBER 1944

ROSTER OF INDIVIDUAL AWARDS

37th Engineer Combat Battalion

Capt. Louis J. Drnovich	Silver Star
Capt. Elbert E. Scudero	Bronze Star
1stLt. Merle D. Kirstein	Bronze Star
1stLt. Robert P. Ross	DSC
1stLt. Charles L. Peckham	Bronze Star
Sgt. Joe Cuiksa	Bronze Star
Sgt. Zolton Simon	Bronze Star
Sgt. Frank A. Chesney	Bronze Star
T/4 Charles I. Moon	Bronze Star
Cpl. Wilbert L. Crane	Bronze Star
Cpl. Ennis H. Nestle	Bronze Star
T/5 Paul J. Vallarella	Bronze Star
Pfc. Kenneth S. Weston	Silver Star
Pfc. Lee Presley	Bronze Star
Pvt. John P. McDonald	Bronze Star
Pvt. Joseph H. Peznanski	Bronze Star
Pvt. Leonard M. Campos	Bronze Star
Pvt. Vinton W. Dove	DSC
Pvt. William J. Shoemaker	DSC

3361h Engineer Combat Battalion
    Lt.Col. Paul D. Bennett   Bronze Star
    T/5 Byron C. Ruyle   Bronze Star
    Pvt. Delbert M. Hattrup   Bronze Star

348th Engineer Combat Battalion
    Lt.Col. Earl P. Houston   Bronze Star
    1stLt. Morris W. Selfe   Bronze Star
    2dLt. Walter Sidlowski   Bronze Star

61st Medical Battalion (Separate)
    Pvt. Ruben V. Avaios   Bronze Star

131st Quartermaster Battalion
    S/Sgt. B. D. Wallingsford   Bronze Star

251st Ordnance Battalion
    S/Sgt. Saul Kanowsky   Soldiers Medal
    Pfc. James L. Keeley   Soldiers Medal
    Pvt. Joseph A. Gardner   Soldiers Medal
    Pvt. Matthew Rendulich   Soldiers Medal

210th Military Police Company
    Pfc. John Massucco   Bronze Star

487th Port Battalion
    T/5 Lawrence E. Hubbard   Bronze Star

502d Port Battalion
    Lt.Col. James T. Pierce   Bronze Star
    1stLt. W. B. Morris   Soldiers Medal
    S/Sgt. Herbert R. Brooks   Soldiers Medal
    Sgt. Scott Clay   Soldiers Medal
    Cpl. Robert D. Bond   Soldiers Medal
    Pvt. William H. Beach   Soldiers Medal

Headquarters & Headquarters Company, 5th Engineer Special Brigade
    Col. Doswell Gullatt   Bronze Star
    Col. William D. Bridges   Bronze Star
    Lt.Col. Irvin M. Rice   Bronze Star

Lt.Col. Allan G. Pixton	Bronze Star
Major Lucien D. Adams	Bronze Star
Major Clarence C. Cook	Bronze Star
Capt. Charles R. DeArman	Bronze Star
M/Sgt. Alvin A. Nielsen	Bronze Star
T/4 Roger W. Nekola	Bronze Star

NOTES

[1] Companies A and F, 592d Engineer Boat and Shore Regiment, are included twice in the above awards. The 26 officers and 543 men of these two companies who earned their first Distinguished Unit Citation at Corregidor are therefore entitled to the Oak Leaf Cluster for their second Citation.

Several units of the 1st ESB (especially the 147th and 149th Engineer Combat Battalions) and of 5th and 6th ESB won the Distinguished Unit Citation on the beaches of Normandy.

Appendix D
Killed in Action and Died of Wounds

1st Engineer Special Brigade
Not listed because complete list is not available.

2d Engineer Special Brigade
Ely, Arthur C., 2dLt., 532d EBSR, KIA Nassau Bay, N.G., 1 July 43
Keele, Charles C., 2dLt., 532d EBSR, KIA Nassau Bay, N.G., 7 July 43
Lang, Rolland F., 2dLt., 532d EBSR, KIA Finschhafen, N.G., 7 Oct. 43
Manchester, Madison J., 2dLt., 592d EBSR, KIA Admiralty Is., 3 Mar. 44
Pecoraro, Charles F., Capt., 532d EBSR, KIA Finschhafen, N.G., 25 Sept. 43
Stiles, William, 1stLt., 542d EBSR, KIA, Toem, DNG, 17 May 44
Sweeney, Hubert P., 2dLt., 592d EBSR, KIA Cape Gloucester, N.B., 16 Feb. 44
Thomson, Ronald F., 2dLt., 592d EBSR, KIA Cape Gloucester, N.B., 26 Feb. 44
Baker, Howard G., Pfc., 542d EBSR, KIA Biak Island, NEI, 12 June 44
Bartelson, Loren E., T/5, 592d EBSR, KIA Cape Gloucester, N.B., 16 Feb. 44
Blair, Robert E., Pfc., 592d EBSR, KIA White Beach, Leyte, PI, 20 Oct. 44
Boyle, James R., Cpl., 592d EBSR, KIA Admiralty Is., 2 Mar. 44
Brewer, Stanley G., Pvt., 592d EBSR, KIA Arawe, N.B., 13 Feb. 44
Brucher, Henry C., Pfc., 542d EBSR, KIA Saidor, N.G., 3 Jan. 44
Buckley, John F., S/Sgt., 592d EBSR, KIA Admiralty Is., 3 Mar. 44
Bull, Byron B., T/5, 542d EBSR, KIA Wakde Island, DNG, 18 May 44
Burgh, Johnnie M., Pfc., 532d EBSR, KIA Red Beach, Leyte, PI, 20 Oct. 44
Casey, Obie, Pfc., 542d EBSR, KIA Wakde Island, DNG, 18 May 44
Cawi, Victor A., T/5, 532d EBSR, KIA Lae, N.G., 6 Sept. 43
Charboneau, George W., Pvt., QM, Hg. Hq. Co., KIA Tacloban, Leyte, PI, 25 Oct. 44

Chavez, Francisco A., T/4, 592d EBSR, KIA Cape Gloucester, N.B., 16 Feb. 44

Chriswell, David E., Pfc., 189th GS Co., KIA Tacloban, Leyte, PI, 25 Oct. 44

Clark, Emray F., Pvt., 542d EBSR, Wakde Island, DNG, 18 May 44

Cohen, Hyman, T/4, 532d EBSR, KIA Red Beach, Leyte, PI, 20 Oct. 44

Coleman, Frank B., Pfc., 262d Med Bn., KIA Finschhafen, N.G., 25 Sept. 43

Dailey, George A., Pfc., 532d EBSR, KIA Lae, N.G., 6 Sept. 43

Donahue, William J., Pfc., 532d EBSR, KIA Surigao Str., Bohol, PI, 28 Dec. 44

Doro, John, Pfc., 592d EBSR, KIA White Beach, Leyte, PI, 25 Oct. 44

Edwards, Alfred N., T/5, 592d EBSR, KIA Arawe, N.B., 16 Dec. 43

Eidson, Clyde W., T/4, 492d EBSR, KIA Arawe, N.B., 26 Dec. 43

Emery, Leonard E., Sgt., 529th EBSR, KIA White Beach, Leyte, PI, 25 Oct. 44

Estes, Joseph H., T/5, 532d EBSR, KIA Finschhafen, N.G., 25 Sept. 43

Fenley, Vincent J., Pfc., 542d EBSR, KIA Biri Island, PI, 20 Feb. 45

Fletcher, John T., T/5, 532d EBSR, KIA Nassau Bay, N.G., 1 July 43

Fortney, Carl M., Pvt., 592d EBSR, KIA White Beach, Leyte, PI, 27 Oct. 44

Gaffney, Francis X., T/5, 592d EBSR, KIA Cape Gloucester, N. B., 16 Feb. 44

Garcia, Jesus V., T/5, 532d EBSR, KIA Surigao Str., Bohol, PI, 28 Dec. 44

Gillett, Carl W., T/4, 532d EBSR, KIA Surigao Str., Bohol, PI, 28 Dec. 44

Gleespan, Dale C., Pvt., 542d EBSR, KIA Biak Island, NEI, 27 May 44

Gray, Robert B., Pfc., 542d EBSR, KIA Wakde Island, DNG, 18 May 44

Huckleberry, Dan J., 532d EBSR, KIA Finschhafen, N.G., 24 Jan. 44

Hunt, Roger R., T/4, 532d EBSR, KIA Hollandia, DNG, 24 Apr. 44

Johnson, Marvin H., Sgt., 532d EBSR, KIA Finschhafen, N.G., 3 Oct. 43

Kaplan, Joseph, T/4, 592d EBSR, KIA Corregidor Is., PI, 16 Feb. 45

Keaney, John L., Pvt., 532d EBSR, KIA Surigao Str., Bohol, PI, 28 Dec. 44

Kump, Richard A., Pvt., 532d EBSR, KIA Lae, N.G., 6 Sept. 43

Lankford, Hiram P., T/5, S/Btry, KIA Biak Island, NEI, 9 June 44

Leard, Edwin L., T/4, 532d EBSR, KIA Lae, N.G., 6 Sept. 43

Loring, Terence E., Pvt., 592d EBSR, KIA Admiralty Is., 3 Mar. 44

Maxwell, Kurt F., Pfc., 262d Med Bn., KIA White Beach, Leyte, PI, 12 Nov. 44

McConnell, Roland P., T/4, 532d EBSR, KIA Hollandia, DNG, 25 Apr. 44

Medley, Bernard W., Cpl., 592d EBSR, KIA White Beach, Leyte, PI, 25 Oct. 44

Miles, Robert C., T/5, 592d EBSR, KIA Cape Gloucester, N.B., 16 Feb. 44

Mooney, Francis M., T/5, 532d EBSR, KIA San Pedro Bay, Leyte, PI, 26 Oct. 44

Nelson, Harold L., T/5, 532d EBSR, KIA Oro Bay, N.G., 18 June 43

O'Neil, Frederick H., T/5, 592d EBSR, KIA Corregidor Is., PI, 17 Feb. 45

Pahoski, Isadore, Pvt., 592d EBSR, KIA Arawe, N.B., 26 Dec. 43

Perrone, Frank T., T/Sgt., 492d EBSR, KIA Arawe, N.B., 15 Dec. 43

Pomeroy, Harry, Pfc., 542d EBSR, KIA Biri Island, PI, 20 Feb. 45

Pouquette, Emile J., Pfc., 542d EBSR, KIA Biak Island, NEI, 2 June 44

Powderly, Vernon A., T/5, 592d EBSR, KIA Lae, N.G., 6 Sept. 43

Price, Snowden L., T/4, 532d EBSR, KIA Nassau Bay, N.G., 1 July 43

Rector, Clifford F., T/5, 532d EBSR, KIA Hollandia, DNG, 27 Apr. 44

Reed, Marvin A., T/4, 532d EBSR, KIA Nassau Bay, N.G., 1 July 43

Rouzer, Robert J., T/Sgt., 532d EBSR, KIA Red Beach, Leyte, PI, 20 Oct. 44

Ruffner, Grant, T/4, 592d EBSR, KIA White Beach, Leyte, PI, 29 Oct. 44

Stewart, Martin L., Pvt., 542d EBSR, KIA Iloilo, Panay, PI, 25 Mar. 45

Strahm, Elgin A., S/Sgt., 532d EBSR, KIA Nassau Bay, N.G., 1 July 43

Sutherland, James R., T/5, 532d EBSR, KIA Lae, N.G., 4 Sept. 43

Terry, Milo E., T/5, 532d EBSR, KIA Nassau Bay, N.G., 1 July 43

Thompson, Durward A., T/5, 592d EBSR, KIA Arawe, N.B., 26 Jan. 44

Tiberi, Daniel J., T/4, 532d EBSR, KIA Nassau Bay, N.G., 1 July 43

Tomaski, Andrew L., T/5, 542d EBSR, KIA Cebu, PI, 2 Apr. 45

Torres, Fred L., T/5, 592d EBSR, KIA Arawe, N.B., 26 Dec. 44

Tozzi, Charles P., Pfc., QM Hq. Hq. Co., Tacloban, Leyte, PI, 25 Oct. 44

Triano, Pietro, Pvt., 542d EBSR, KIA Wakde Island, DNG, 18 May 44

Van Noy, Junior N., Pvt., 532d EBSR, KIA Finschhafen, N.G., 17 Oct. 43

Villa, Walter B., Pfc., 532d EBSR, KIA Finschhafen, N.G., 25 Sept. 43

Walkney, Joseph E., Cpl., 592d BBSR, KIA Admiralty Islands, 4 Mar. 44

Waltz, Dwaine R., Pvt., 562d EBM Bn., KIA Surigao Str., Bohol, PI, 28 Dec. 44

West, Alton J., T/4, 532d EBSR, KIA Lae, N.G., 12 Sept. 43

Yanoski, Joseph J., Pvt., 532d EBSR, KIA Lae, N.G., 6 Sept. 43

Zehna, Lee, Pvt., 532d EBSR, KIA Mindoro Island, PI, 21 Dec. 44

Zubieta, Pete, Jr., Pfc., 542d EBSR, KIA Tambu Bay, N.G., 20 Aug. 43

Note: Lack of space prohibits listing many other Amphibians.

2D ENGINEER SPECIAL BRIGADE
OFFICER CASUALTIES

	Brig Hqs Co	Med Det 2 ESB	287th Sig Co	Quartermaster	262d Med Bn	562d EBM Bn	532d EBSR	542d EBSR	592d EBSR	Support Btry	TOTAL
KIA							4	1	3		8
WIA	5		1	1		3	22	7	15		54
NON-BATTLE DEATHS					1	1	1				3
TOTAL	5		1	1	1	4	27	8	18		65

2D ENGINEER SPECIAL BRIGADE
ENLISTED CASUALTIES

	Brig Hqs Co	Med Det 2d ESB	287th Sig Co	162d Ord Co	Quartermaster	262d Med Bn	562d EBM Bn	532d EBSR	542d EBSR	592d EBSR	189th Gas Co	3498th Ord MMCo	Support Battery	TOTAL
KIA					2	2	1	31	14	24		1	1	76
WIA	2	1	9	1	4	5	22	219	95	161	3		9	532
NON-BATTLE DEATHS						1	1	14	11	10	1			38
TOTAL	2	1	9	1	6	8	24	264	120	195	4	1	10	646

5th Engineer Special Brigade
    (6 June 44 through 26 June 44)
  Headquarters, 5th Engineer Special Brigade
    Lt.Col. Vivien G. Clark
    2dLt. John B. Carter
  Headquarters Company, 5th Engineer Special Brigade
    M/Sgt George M. Maresca
  30th Chemical Decontamination Company
    Pfc. Ben Shelton
    Pvt. Hoyt M. Walker
  37th Engineer Combat Battalion
    Lt.Col. Lionel F. Smith
    Capt. Allen H. Cox, Jr.
    Capt. Louis J. Drnovich
    Capt. Paul F. Harkleroad
    T/Sgt. William Grande
    S/Sgt. David R. Greekmore
    Sgt. Michael Di Benedette
    Sgt. Lester E. Rust
    T/4 Hugh M. Ingram
    T/4 John L. McMurray
    T/4 Charles I. Moon
    Cpl. William H. Bowker
    Cpl. William D. Franko
    T/5 Harin I. Bakica
    T/5 Robert J. Krueger
    Pfc. James Smith
    Pfc. John P. Zelvis
    Pvt. Rodger D. Andrews
    Pvt. Oscar E. Cleaveland
    Pvt. James A. Cochran
    Pvt. Frank R. Joniak
    Pvt. Willard J. Werner
    Pvt. John E. Williams
    Pvt. Ralph E. Wise
  459th Amphibian Truck Company
    Cpl. Myron J. Komstadius
    T/5 Thomas L. Nurtney
    T/5 Albert J. Roberts
    Pfc. Daniel E. Kepler

Pvt. Earnest J. Holbrooks
Pvt. Jamie E. McComb
203d Quartermaster Gas Supply Company (Company A)
(Now 3833d QM Gas Supply Co.)
Sgt. William T. Stover
210th Military Police Company
Sgt. Steve J. Tepovich
Pvt. Robert L. Barker
251st Ordnance Battalion
616th Ordnance Ammunition Company
Pvt. James S. Isbell
3466th Ordnance MAM Company
T/5 Leslie L. Speirs
294th Joint Assault Signal Company
Pvt. Louis A. Moore
336th Engineer Combat Battalion
2dLt. Hyman J. Barash
S/Sgt. Edwin J. Nenadal
Cpl. Teddy J. Wojtczak
Pfc. Jack W. Wheeler
Pvt. Herbert J. Sanbron
348th Engineer Combat Battalion
Pvt. Jerome J. Bernstein
Pvt. Albert E. Soto
467th Engineer Maintenance Company
Cpl. Thomas J. Lane, Jr.
Pvt. Harry A. McDonough
61st Medical Battalion
393d Medical Collecting Company
Sgt. Shirley J. Phillips
Pfc. Darius W. Crites
Pvt. Charles H. Manning
643d Medical Clearing Company
Pvt. William A. Francis
131st Quartermaster Battalion (Mobile)
453d Amphibian Truck Company
S/Sgt. Frank G. Kisasonak
Cpl. Joseph J. Sterbank
T/5 Richard H. Connell
Pfc. George Kashula

Pvt. William E. Mensch

Pvt. James R. Reed

458th Amphibian Truck Company

1stLt. Howard T. Kearney

Pvt. Raymond E. Shock

487th Port Battalion

282d Port Company

Pfc. Donald E. Avon

Pfc. Guy L. Tillis

Pvt. James M. Hare

502d Port Battalion

270th Port Company

T/5 Isaiah Foreman

Pfc. Oscar G. Bailey

Pfc. James E. Bowler

Pvt. John S. Brannon, Jr.

271st Port Company

Pfc. Sandy Butler

533d Quartermaster Battalion

4142d Quartermaster Service Company

Pfc. Joseph M. Fisk

Pvt. Richard J. Haburchak

Pvt. Jessie F. A. Tidwell

Pvt. Lupe Villarreal

4143d Quartermaster Service Company

Pvt. Donald E. Simmons

4042d Quartermaster Truck Company

T/Sgt. Abner L. Adams

APPENDIX E
WAR DEPARTMENT PRESS RELEASES ON AMPHIBIANS

AMPHIBIAN ENGINEERS PLAY BIG PART
IN SUCCESS OF MACARTHUR'S OPERATIONS

When the hard-bitten veterans of General Douglas MacArthur's Engineer Special Brigades rammed the bows of their landing craft onto the beaches at Leyte, they reached the halfway mark on their own road to Tokyo.

The identification of the 2d Engineer Brigade as a part of the Leyte task force marks the latest milestone in a road which was begun more than fifteen months ago and 2000 miles from the Philippines, when a handful of 36-foot LCVPs, reinforced with three captured Jap barges and a lone LCM, bucked a blinding storm and heavy seas to land a task force of the 41st Infantry Division behind the Jap lines at Nassau Bay, New Guinea. The engineer boat crews fought as infantry in that operation and they fought as infantry again and again in the many campaigns which followed.

One brigade, Brigadier General William F. Heavey's 2d, has been in almost all of the leapfrog landings which have carried General MacArthur on his road back to Bataan. Out of action only 15 days in a twelve-month stretch, its record of battle participation in the Southwest Pacific, recalls the bitter drive up the coast of New Guinea and through the Bismarcks, through the mangrove swamps and the coral reefs and across the bodies of dead Japs. Nassau Bay, Salamaua, Lae, Finschhafen, Sio, Saidor, Hollandia, Tanahmerah Bay, Aitape, Sarmi, Wakde and Biak in New Guinea, Lorengau in the Admiralties, Los Negros, Tami, and Long Island in Vitiaz Strait, bloody Arawe and Cape Gloucester in New Britain are a part of their record. The Biak assault was the twentieth successful combat landing for this particular brigade. Engineer Amphibians were at Sansapor and Noemfoor also, and at Morotai in the action which cleared the way for the smash into Leyte.

Engineers scout, map, and chart the beaches and offshore waters ahead of each new landing. They man the small landing and amphibious craft which put the initial assault waves ashore, clear the beaches of mines and barbed wire or other obstacles, improve beach landing facilities, and later build ship berths. Engineers build roads across the beaches to airstrips which they construct as the heart of a new base protected by wire, minefields and tank traps. These bases, with their troops, planes and supplies, can hold the Japs pinned tight in the jungle and are used to open the way for new blows. Not one of these bases has been lost to the enemy.

In the 7,000 islands of the Philippines, base-to-base strategy is made to order for the Engineer-Air Force team which will be MacArthur's striking weapon against the Japanese garrison. The narrow straits and the many bays separating the islands can be operating roads for the Army Engineer Amphibs, who have come to look upon water as a highway, rather than an obstacle.

With air superiority around each forward base virtually assured, the little boats of the Amphibs will give the American forces a mobility which the same air superiority will deny to the Japanese. Under friendly air cover, the engineer brigades consider themselves capable of dealing with anything they run up against on the sea or ground. They are prepared to—and will—strike anywhere; and when they strike, they stick. What heavy cargo trucks have been to the campaign in France, the Army's LCMs and DUKWs will be to the campaign in the Islands. Water transport will take the place of roads.

The success of the Amphibian Engineers in the Pacific, as well as in the European and Mediterranean theaters, is no accident. Their development began in 1942, when the Army was seeking an answer to the amphibious technique the Japanese were using with such high success in Malaya.

Since the Engineers were already skilled in river-crossing operations, a few Engineer officers were assigned to establish the Engineer Amphibian Command at Camp Edwards, Massachusetts, where "shore-to-shore" amphibious tactics were improvised, improved, and perfected.

Men with small-craft experience were rounded up from the Army and from civilian life, and their ranks filled with landlubbers who were taught small-boat operation in the waters off Cape Cod, and later in the Gulf of Mexico off Camp Gordon Johnston, Florida. Brigades were organized into boat and shore teams—the boat teams to make the landing with assault infantry and combat engineers aboard, the shore teams to establish the beachhead supply system for the advancing troops. The doctrine was sound. The brigades proved it the hard way—in battle.

As tough as it was on the beaches of North Africa in November, 1942, when the first brigade went in, or at Salerno and Anzio, where one shore engineer regiment fought in the front line as infantry for forty-seven days before they were relieved, it still was tougher in the Pacific. There nature, as well as man, fought back. No long-inhabited sandy beaches met the brigades in New Guinea—rather, forests, sago swamps, hidden coral heads, black muck, and sudden storms. There were no towns for furlough relaxation; and there weren't many furloughs. There were no roads, no already-built airfields, no known water supply sources. If you wanted those things you built them. Engineers with bulldozers and air compressors built them.

The Amphibian Engineers manned not only their boats and their beach bulldozers, they manned machine guns and antitank guns and rocket-launchers. At Nassau Bay, 68 Engineer boatmen stood off between 400 and 700 Japs in one night ashore, fighting back with knives and small arms alone. On Red Beach at Lae, a shore battalion took twelve days of almost uninterrupted bombing and strafing; and as the Australian task force from Lae pushed toward Finschhafen, a shore battalion of engineers provided part of the perimeter defense. At Sio, boatmen of the 2d Brigade fired rocket barrages for the first time in the Southwest Pacific. At Arawe, engineer rocket fire knocked out Jap pillboxes holding up the cavalry's advance. On Scarlet Beach at Finschhafen, Engineer Private Junior N. Van Noy almost single-handedly broke up a Japanese amphibious counterattack. He was awarded the Medal of Honor posthumously.

On Wakde Island, May 1944, a boat company of an Engineer Boat and Shore Regiment (542d) was awarded the Distinguished Unit Citation for heroic success in landing initial assault troops and subsequent reinforcements against particularly bloody opposition. Ten days later at Biak, using rocket LCVPs and rocket DUKWs in addition to Combat Buffaloes and Cargo LCMs, a brigade task element shot down at least seven Jap planes, poured rocket fire on enemy strong- points in caves along the shore, evacuated one infantry battalion under fire, served as floating observation posts for our artillery; and ashore cleaned out with borrowed bazookas and their own dynamite and grenades several Jap dugouts and mortar positions, in addition to their usual shore engineer duties.

Another ten days later, and more than 16,000 miles away, three Engineer Special Brigades set up on the beaches of Normandy and supply operations which were to make possible the decisive defeat of the German Seventh and Fifteenth Armies.

The brigades, with their scarlet seahorse insignia and golden anchor shoulder patch, have but one motto for the Philippines, and for what may lie beyond. The motto is: "Put 'Em Across."

SPECIAL!

ARMY ENGINEER SPECIAL BRIGADES TURNED INVASION BEACHES
INTO GIANT PORT, 6TH ENGINEER SPECIAL BRIGADE,
NORMANDY BASE SECTION, FRANCE—

For five months after the Allied invasion of Europe, the Germans took a daily licking on the same beaches where the Reichswehr first reeled and broke on June 6, 1944.

Back on those stretches of sand and shale along the Channel coast the 1st, 5th, and 6th Engineer Special Brigades, functioning as a part of the tremendous contribution of the Normandy Base

Section to the supply effort of the Communications Zone, created a vast supply funnel to provision our Armies for their great advances of the summer and fall.

While the Germans were succeeding in their strategy of maintaining a desperate stranglehold on every major port except Cherbourg, a steady flow of arms, food and equipment poured up from the beaches over a constantly extending supply line to the racing Armies.

The amount of tonnage that moved across the open stretches of coast line was staggering.

This imposing feat was accomplished by Engineer Special Brigades specially designed and long trained for just this function, which followed in close support of the assault wave in the invasion.

Typical of these units is the Sixth Engineer Special Brigade which funneled through a two-mile strip of beach a monthly flow of supplies.

The Brigade function reduced itself in simple terms to a matter of moving cargo on shore and then in a "double play" shift from transfer points to dumps where it was set for rapid transport to the front.

This impression of simplicity was heightened by a glance at the operations on the beaches. Just back from the high water mark stood control towers (not unlike those at an airfield) from which officers directed a steady movement from the water inland.

This was a deceptive impression. Actually the Brigade operation involved precise planning with integration of varied units. The core of the organization comprised Engineer Combat Battalions, Quartermaster Battalions, and Amphibious Truck or "duck" Battalion, Port Battalions, and a Naval Beach Battalion. In addition there were Truck and Ordnance units along with Signalmen, Medics, Military Police and similar subsidiary units.

Almost without exception these units and practically every man in the command had received intensive amphibious training, specially pointing to the crucial first few hours on the beach.

The 6th Brigade hit a particularly hot sector of the beach. Just to the rear rose 100-foot hills from which Jerry was raining a hail of artillery and small-arms fire. The beach itself was cluttered with mines and obstacles.

Under these conditions the preliminary work in getting operations underway proved costly. Before the invasion was hours old casualties included the brigade commander and three battalion commanding officers.

Col. Paul W. Thompson of Alexandria, Virginia, the brigade commander, was seriously wounded when he advanced with two Ranger lieutenants on a sniper nest. He was evacuated because of his wounds and the command was subsequently assumed by Colonel T. L. Mulligan, of Tarrytown, New York, who had been one of the pioneers in training engineers for amphibious operations.

Other key personnel hit the shore badly burned and half drowned after swimming from LCIs which had been hit by rocket-type oil shells.

The first responsibility for fitting the beach rested with the engineer battalions. It was their job to clear the mines and obstacles as well as provide security.

In one instance equipment unloaded from landing craft had started to pile up in a sector where an exit had not yet been cleared, through the sea wall. Standing there in a growing snarl, the trucks and jeeps made an inviting target for the Jerry gunners zeroed in from their emplacements in the hills.

Tanks had blasted away at the 10-foot reinforced concrete wall without succeeding in forcing an opening.

Then Master Sergeant Meredith Atwood of the 147th Battalion and Atlanta, Georgia, took over. A seasoned demolitions expert, he selected a group of men and distributed a large amount of high-powered fancy stuff among them. They rushed through the heavy fire in short spurts across the beach. As rapidly as possible they set their charges and then made for whatever cover they could find in the lead-chewed sands.

A similar situation on a point further down the beach was cleared up by Cat operators who sat high in their flak nests bulling their way through the tangle of obstacles the Germans had strewn over the beaches.

Gradually the volume of incoming supplies mounted as the Engineers cleared the beach mines and the gate-like Element C and tetrahedron obstacles and the plague of sniper fire diminished.

Volunteer sniper-hunting parties handled this last difficulty. Lieutenant General John C. H. Lee presented the Silver Star Medal to Staff Sergeant George W. Bercaw, Jr., of Union City, New Jersey, and Private First Class Robert A. Gamble of Blanket, Texas, both of Headquarters Company, for their activities in cleaning out nests of snipers who were hampering operations.

Under the direction of beachmasters from the naval beach battalion landing craft nudged their way on to the beach and swung down their ramps to disgorge their payloads of equipment and personnel.

Coasters and Liberty ships transferred some part of their cargoes to huge tugborne barges or self-propelled Rhinos.

But the major share of the ship-to-shore burden was borne in those early days by the "ducks." The lumbering, seafaring 6x6s brought in sixty per cent of all the tonnage that moved over the beaches.

The two-man crews of many of those amphibian trucks probably had one of the loneliest assignments of anybody involved in the invasion.

Loaded to the gunwales (DUKW men favor a nautical turn of speech) with ammunition, they were turned loose ten miles out in the darkened Channel waters to make their own way in.

Some of them didn't make it. The large majority that reached shore with their precious cargo kept right on going, up to the fighting men ahead who needed the stuff in their business. And while they were at it some of the "duck" drivers took a hand in the business themselves.

On one of his ammo runs Corporal Malcom Brain was bothered by snipers while moving up to the front. He was bothered again on the way back, so he pulled his land-boat to a halt on the narrow French road and went poling into the hedgerows. He and his assistant driver returned with six prisoners.

Under more normal circumstances the "ducks" heave to alongside the ships and take on cargo swung over the side in nets pre-loaded by troops of the port battalions who plugged away at their unspectacular but vital job for 12-hour stretches, come storm or air raids.

They have been entitled to moments of uneasiness, too, as they literally sat on loads of TNT while terrific barrages of flak sought out some raiding representative of the Luftwaffe.

On shore the "ducks" made their way to the transfer point where the loaded nets swung out by cranes and the hardy little vehicles returned to the water for still another load.

At the transfer point the quartermaster troops quickly sort the loads into various classifications to be dispatched by truck to dumps handling specific types of supplies.

With everybody involved working on a schedule of at least twelve hours, and operations generally falling into a smooth pattern, the flow of supplies increased until a backlog was built up.

This proved doubly fortunate a couple of weeks after D-day, when a roaring gale thundered in from the Channel whipping a mountainous surf on to the beach. Ships of all types pitched violently about in the outer waters, and smaller craft were tossed violently onto the beach.

For almost three days operations had to be suspended. While they waited for the storm to subside, the Engineers improved the roads they had cut through the hills and continued the clearing of the beach. Meanwhile, they were given very convincing testimony of the part they were playing in the battle for France when word came back from the front that ammunition was being rationed.

When the storm lessened in force to a point where it was feasibly safe to resume operations, the brigade applied new pressure. Steadily the figures mounted, with tonnage records created and broken until it became apparent that the combined efforts of the brigades were approaching the capacity of the world's greatest ports.

New problems developed as the tempo of our armies' advance heightened, and the number of troops increased. Each time a solution was found with no small amount of improvisation.

The vastly extended supply lines provided one nettling problem which was solved with the inauguration of the now famed "Red Ball" express to transport supplies from the beaches to the front lines.

The beaches were still a major supply lifeline to our armies after they had battled their way into Germany itself.

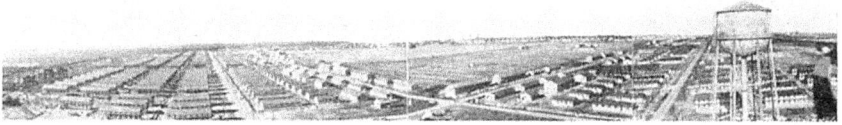

Camp Edwards, Falmouth, Massachusetts, birthplace of the Amphibian Engineers. (Signal Corps photo)

Shore engineers install markers and prepare a roadway at Cape Cod in 1942. (Signal Corps photo)

Amphibian Engineers land 45th Division troops in one of the first landings at Cape Cod. Note the old type LCPRs. (Signal Corps photo)

The first DUKW on the Pacific coast. An instruction group in the operation of an amphibian truck at Monterey, California. (2d ESB PRO photo)

U.S. troops boarding assault boats prior to the landings in North Africa, 1942. (Signal Corps photo)

A general view taken on D-day on the beach at Gela, Sicily, July 10, 1943. (Signal Corps photo)

This photograph, made at low tide on the invasion coast at Grandcamp-les-Bains, France, shows German Teller mines affixed to posts and planted several hundred feet from the beach at high tide. (Signal Corps photo)

Troops and materiel pour ashore on Normandy, June 12, 1944. (Signal Corps photo)

In the foreground, infantry troops are assembling under the shelter of the cliffs at the extreme eastern end of the beach beyond Exit F-1, while in the background a jeep rolls off the ramp of an LCT. The beach at this point was not very suitable for landing, but was defiladed from the enemy guns which were shelling the main sections of the beach.

Amphibian Engineers' command post in captured German emplacements on Omaha Beach. (Signal Corps photo)

The artificial harbor from Omaha Beach before the storm. (Signal Corps photo)

Van Noy and Poppa of the 532d fight the Japs at Scarlet Beach. (Reproduced through
courtesy of Look)

Noemfoor, Dutch New Guinea, on July 2, 1944. Coral reef exposed at low tide over which Alligators of the 2d ESB support battery carried the first assault troops. LCMs of the 3d ESB are in the background. (Signal Corps photo)

LCVs of Company A, 542d EB&SR, moving into the shore at Wakde Island under fire with their important cargo of equipment and supplies. (American Red Cross photo by Dick Day)

Saidor, New Guinea, January 2, 1944. LCVPs of Company B, 542d EB&SR, carry assault troops to the beach through the surf. (Signal Corps photo)

Arawe, New Britain, December 15, 1943. Hitting the beach in coral-studded waters. Despite many reefs, LCVPs of Company B, 592d EB&SR, get infantry to the beach in time to accompany Alligators inland. (Signal Corps photo)

This bulldozer of the 4th ESB mired in the muck along the shore of Morotai Island in the Halmahera group. Many vehicles met a similar fate as they attempted to land.

Huge fires spring up on the beach at Leyte after terrific bombardment by American artillery prior to the invasion of the island. The first wave of landing craft manned by the 2d ESB and by the Seventh Amphibious Fleet approach Red Beach on D-day. (Signal Corps photo)

Shore engineers of the 2d Brigade prepare jetties to reach beached LST ramps on the beach at Leyte.

Yellow Beach, Leyte, October 22, 1944. An aerial view of LSTs on the beach on D plus 2. (Signal Corps photo)

LCMs of the 2d ESB and LCVPs are unloaded on the beach at Leyte on D plus 1. (Signal Corps photo)

Lt.Gen. Richard K. Sutherland, former President Sergio Osmena of the Philippines, General Douglas MacArthur, and Brig.Gen. Carlos Romulo head for shore in an LCVP of the 2d ESB to inspect the Leyte beachhead on D-day. (Signal Corps photo)

Company A, 592d EB&SR, lands infantry from an LCM on the rock-bound beach of Jap-held Caballo Island near Luzon, March 28, 1945. (Signal Corps photo)

An aerial photo showing landing craft proceeding to Corregidor. Covered by naval craft, 2d ESB LCMs (592d EB&SR) are en route to landing on Corregidor from Bataan. (Signal Corps photo)

Landing craft of the 2d ESB en route from Mariveles to attack on Corregidor. The first wave has just hit the beach. The third wave is in the background. (Signal Corps photo)

Engineers landing on Fort Drum (El Fraile Island) in Manila Harbor by special ramp from the bridge of an LSM to the top of the fort wall. The LSM is from the Seventh Amphibious Fleet; LCVPs and the LCM are from the 2d ESB. (Signal Corps photo)

LCMs of the 2d ESB stand off Fort Drum to observe the explosion after pumping fuel oil into the concrete battleship. (Signal Corps photo)

Painting the shipment number on a 2d ESB LCM to go back to the States from Yokohama, November 28, 1945.

Final review of the 2d Brigade at Yokohama, October 2, 1945.

Brig.Gen. William F. Heavey (top left) commander of the 2d Brigade throughout all its operations. (Bachrach photo) Maj.Gen. William M. Hoge (top right) commander of the Engineer
Special Brigade Group in the Normandy landing. Maj.Gen. Daniel Noce (center) founder of
the Engineer Amphibian Command. Brig.Gen. Henry Wolfe (lower left), Commanding
General, 1st Engineer Special Brigade in Operation Torch. Brig.Gen. Henry Hutchings, Jr.,
(lower right), Commanding General, 4th Engineer Special Brigade (Portillo Studio photo).

COACHWHIP PUBLICATIONS

COACHWHIPBOOKS.COM

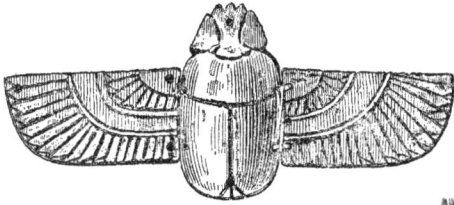

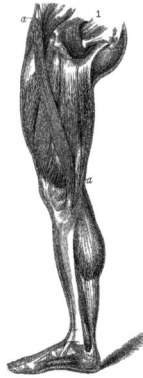

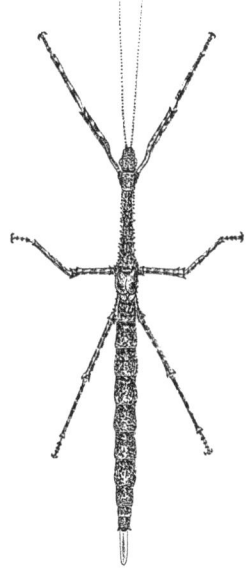

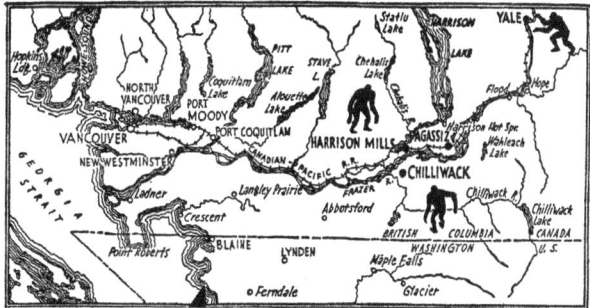

BOMBARDMENT AVIATION

ISBN 1-61646-054-7

BASTOGNE

The Story of the First Eight Days
In Which the 101st Airborne Division Was
Closed Within the Ring of German Forces

COLONEL S. L. A. MARSHALL

BASTOGNE

ISBN 1-61646-062-8

TANK-FIGHTER TEAM

LIEUTENANT ROBERT M. GERARD

(FORMERLY OF THE FRENCH ARMORED FORCE)

TANK-FIGHTER TEAM

ISBN 1-61646-023-7

PSYCHOLOGICAL WARFARE

ISBN 1-61646-055-5

www.ingramcontent.com/pod-product-compliance
Lightning Source LLC
Chambersburg PA
CBHW031232090426
42742CB00007B/172